The Arts and Human Development

"Bear Village," by a 6-year-old girl. Reprinted from *Art and Visual Perception* by Rudolf Arnheim by permission of Professor Rudolf Arnheim, Faber & Faber Ltd., and the University of California Press. Originally published by the University of California Press; reprinted by permission of The Regents of the University of California.

The Arts and Human Development

A PSYCHOLOGICAL STUDY OF THE ARTISTIC PROCESS

With a New Introduction by the Author

HOWARD GARDNER

BasicBooks
A Division of HarperCollins*Publishers*

FOR MY PARENTS

AND

FOR ILE

Paperback edition copyright © 1994 by Howard Gardner.
Published by BasicBooks, A Division of HarperCollins Publishers, Inc.

First published in 1973 by John Wiley & Sons, Inc.

Library of Congress Cataloging-in-Publication Data

Gardner, Howard.
  The arts and human development.

  "A Wiley-Interscience publication".
  Bibliography: p:
    1. The arts — Psychology.   2.   Aesthetics.
I.   Title.

NX165.G-37   701'.15   72–13404
ISBN 0–471–29145–5 (cloth)
ISBN 0–465–00440–7 (paper)

94 95 96 97 ♦/HC 9 8 7 6 5 4 3 2 1

Contents

v

Figures, Tables, and Works of Art

Preface and Overview

Ever since I first became interested in psychology, I have been especially intrigued by two questions: What is the most suggestive way to speak about the nature and course of human development? What factors enable individuals to create and to appreciate works in the various art forms? I had considered these questions for some time before realizing that they were closely related, that one had a better prospect of answering each to the extent that the other was also considered. And so making a case for the interrelations between two fields has become my major undertaking for the past few years; I would hope to convince developmental psychologists to consider the arts, and aestheticians to ponder the nature of human development. I would encourage artists and nonartists to appreciate the common links (rather than the alleged gulf) between them.

As my training is in developmental psychology, this book is drafted from the perspective of that field. I have done considerable reading in aesthetics and in the literature of various art forms. I have consulted artists and aestheticians, and have lingered over paintings, poems, and musical compositions of child and master; I hope these experiences have been as educational as they have been enjoyable. But the canons for evidence and value are scarcely uniform for artist, aesthetician, and psychologist; accordingly I have had to evolve a language and a form of argument which, if all goes well, will be acceptable to all groups, but which risks being inadequate all the way around. It will perhaps be of help to this diverse readership to mention the major questions and issues treated in the following chapters.

Psychologists have for the most part assumed that individual development leads to the "end states" of the scientific thinker or the normal personality. As a result their approaches have been one-sided; they have neglected aspects of knowing and action that they do not view as central to the scientist or the healthy individual. It has seemed to me that, by positing a different end-state, it should be possible to provide a more comprehensive view of the full range of developmental processes. As the terminus for development I propose "participation in the artistic process" —the capacity to be a creator, performer, critic, or audience member in an art form. The purpose of this book is to suggest how the child develops toward one or more of these artistic roles, and, in the process, to illuminate certain developmental processes and consider certain perennial questions in aesthetics.

Evidence from different sources is required to support the claims that the artistic process can shed new light on developmental questions, and that aesthetic issues can be illuminated by the data of developmental psychology. First it is necessary to specify basic systems of development in organisms and to show that these are essential for and found widely in artistic and protoartistic activities. Next, the processes whereby these developing systems unfold and interact during childhood must be specified. Finally, the activities of mature artists, critics, performers, and audience members, as well as the characteristics of the functioning artistic process, must be examined in the light of developmental considerations.

Perhaps the chief mystery confronting the student of artistic development is the relationship between the mature adult practitioner—the skilled poet, the painting master, the virtuoso instrumentalist or composer —and the young child playing with words, humming and inventing melodies, effortlessly producing sketches and paintings while engaging in many other activities that have only a tenuous relationship to the arts. Clearly there are important differences in skill, acquaintance with the artistic tradition, sensitivity to nuance between the child and the adult participants in the artistic process. But a more fundamental question for the psychologist is whether the schoolchild must pass through further, qualitatively different stages in order to become an artist (as it has been argued that he must pass through qualitatively different stages en route to becoming a practicing scientist). On this question I have arrived at an unexpected conclusion: the child of 7 or 8 has, in most respects, become a participant in the artistic process and he need not pass through any further qualitative reorganizations. I provide various lines of evidence for this conclusion, and present several works of art created by children ranging in age from 3 to 8 to document it.

The view of artistic development may be seen as supplementary to the monumental developmental framework proposed by Jean Piaget. Piaget focuses upon intellectual or scientific development and discerns a series of qualitatively different stages, which culminate in the advent of formal operations at adolescence. With formal operations one is able to reason in propositions, capturing experience and perception in verbal statements and performing logical operations such as negation or conjunction upon these statements. The ability is crucial for the scientist engaged in hypotheticodeductive thought and is also necessary, I believe, for the critic who must reason in a logical manner about his experiences with art objects. The range of capacities, operations, and stages which (for Piaget) characterize all of development do not, however, provide an adequate explanation of artistic development. I see the present work as fleshing out the picture of development proposed by Piaget, extending it to the vast majority of people who are not scientists and do not reason in the manner of scientists, but who nonetheless participate in a significant way in complex intellectual activities. And through focusing on the integration of cognitive and affective experience and the range of activities in which different personality types may become engaged, the work also supplements the picture of development put forth by psychoanalysts and others concerned with personality and emotional development.

In outlining this argument in the following pages I touch on a number of related questions and issues. In the first chapter previous works in the psychology of art and in developmental psychology are reviewed, and the principal virtues and difficulties of these efforts are pinpointed. Characteristics of the arts are described, the three developing systems are introduced, and the artistic process is more fully outlined. In the second chapter the operations of the developing systems in animals and human infants are described. This discussion provides a counterpoint to later artistic development, since infants and most animals, whatever their facility with the developing systems, do not utilize symbols to an appreciable extent. Yet certain incipient symbolic capacities possessed by higher animals are considered, and certain animal capacities that prove suggestive in defining the limits of human art—such as bird song and chimpanzee painting—are also examined.

The third and fourth chapters of the book are an exposition of the child's initial use of symbols and his first experiences and achievements in the aesthetic realm. The first stages through which the child passes as he gains facility with symbols, symbol systems, and media of communication are reviewed. Through the concepts of *modes* and *vectors*, the relationship between the child's initial experience in the world and his capacity to deal with the world on the level of symbols is explored. An attempt is also made to apply a new conceptual framework to the study of the young child, and to tie together the disparate contributions of

Piaget, Freud, Erikson, Werner, and the Gestalt and ethological schools. In the fifth chapter previous research on the development of artistic capacities is critically reviewed, proposals for more promising research are considered, and an emerging picture of the broad outlines of general artistic development is described. Throughout the middle portion of the book the relationships among various child activities and their connection to subsequent achievements in the arts are considered.

The final chapters outline the later stages of artistic development and address a number of general questions in the areas of aesthetics, psychology, and education. In Chapter 6 the nature of skill development, training in the arts, and problem-solving in the artistic process are considered. Common threads found in the biographies of artists are described and the training regimens adopted by specific artists are analyzed. In the final chapter a number of themes introduced earlier are confronted: the relationship between Piaget's theory and the present view of development; the commonalities and differences between scientific and artistic development and scientific and artistic "truth"; the relationship between artistic accomplishment and neurosis, psychosis, and developmental history; the tension between achievement in the area of science and comprehension and production in the arts.

Naturally I hope that most readers will follow my argument and the various ancillary discussions from opening to closing page. Since backgrounds and interests will vary greatly, however, I should indicate both that Chapters 2 and 5 contain a fair amount of technical material, which may be of limited interest to nonpsychologists, and that the last two chapters may be of particular interest to artists and educators. Even though the preceding direction of the argument is summarized, and its future course is anticipated throughout, it seems only fair to alert the reader that some of the going may be difficult, for the terrain is unexplored and the evidence often suggestive rather than decisive. When conclusions are based on my informal observations as a parent, teacher, and researcher, I have not provided references; but detailed bibliographical information on quotations, experimental studies, and various theoretical perspectives is provided at the end of the book.

To place the study in perspective I begin with a consideration of earlier investigations in developmental and aesthetic psychology. Those acquainted with traditional perspectives may wish to know how the current study modifies them; others coming to the study afresh may find this brief sketch of earlier work helpful. My aim is not to provide comprehensive summaries or critiques, but rather to convey the flavor of these positions. Since theoretical revisions characteristically occur in reaction to positions taken by previous works, I have indicated where I disagree with, disregard, or build upon the ideas of others. However, the presentation of my own ideas on artistic development does not presuppose familiarity with competing or complementary theoretical stances. Therefore, those interested primarily in the argument of this book may proceed directly to the section of Chapter 1 on "The Artistic Process."

Because the present position dictates a reorientation of attention and method in two fields, I have elected to state my conclusions as directly as possible. Upon review of this work, psychologists and aestheticians may conclude that the proposed convergence has been forced, and that a separation in the interest of both parties is in order. Before any such conclusions are reached, however, I hope that some researchers will be attracted to the kinds of studies and questions I have outlined, for, whatever the final evaluation, research about the development of artistic capacities can provide an important corrective to the one-sided study of "scientific" skills that presently pervades the psychological literature. I hope as well that aestheticians may be convinced that what seems plausible a priori becomes more convincing if it can be empirically demonstrated, and that artists might come to feel that their area can be studied seriously without undue reduction or irreparable loss of innocence.

HOWARD GARDNER

Cambridge, Massachusetts
October 1972

ACKNOWLEDGMENTS

Many individuals have shaped my views on the arts and human development, teaching, demonstrating, questioning, arguing, and sometimes even agreeing with me during a decade spent in the uniquely stimulating intellectual climate of the Boston area. So extensive is my debt that I am not certain where my own ideas begin and those of others—some close friends, other persons I have never met—leave off. I am grateful to Drs. Jeanne Bamberger, Irvin Child, Eugene Green, Diana Korzenik, John Kennedy, Michael Maratsos, David Perkins, Sheldon White, and especially Kurt Fischer, each of whom read large segments of the manuscript and commented critically on it; and to my wife Judy, who provided a productive blend of criticism, suggestion, and encouragement. I also want to thank Dr. Roger Brown, who encouraged me to undertake and then to complete this work; members of Project Zero and its founder Dr. Nelson Goodman, who listened for hours to many of my ideas when they were yet more inchoate; Eric Valentine and Christine Valentine who offered a great many valuable editorial suggestions; Bill Lohman, who assisted throughout with the preparation of the manuscript; and the various institutions and granting agencies who have generously supported my research and given me time to think. It is a privilege to remember the children, including Kerry and Jay, who have shown me so much more than I have been able to capture in these pages.

I also want to thank the following individuals and publishers for permitting me to reprint copyrighted materials:

To Professor Rudolf Arnheim, The University of California Press, and Faber and Faber Limited for permission to reproduce a drawing "Bear Village," from R. Arnheim, *Art and Visual Perception.*

To Blackie and Sons Ltd. for permission to quote poems from S. Lane and M. Kemp, *An Approach to Creative Writing in the Primary School.*

To George Braziller for permission to quote text materials from Jean-Paul Sartre, *The Words*.

To *British Journal of Aesthetics* and Professor Harold Osborne for permission to recapitulate an argument from H. Gardner, "From Mode to Symbol."

To Professor Roger Brown for permission to reproduce a transcription of Adam's speech made in the course of research on "The Child's Acquisition of Grammar," supported by NIMH Grant MH-07088, Roger Brown, Principal Investigator.

To *Daedalus* for permission to quote text materials from W. Kahn, "Uses of Painting Today." Reprinted by permission of *Daedalus*, the Journal of the American Academy of Arts and Science, Boston, Mass., Summer 1969, *The Future of the Humanities*.

To Doubleday and Company, Inc. for permission to quote text materials from C. Lévi-Strauss, "Overture to The Raw and the Cooked," in *Structuralism*.

To Professor N. Frijda and the Academic Press for permission to quote text materials from N. Frijda, "Recognition of Emotion" in L. Berkowitz (ed.) *Advances in Experimental Social Psychology*.

To Ginn and Co., for permission to quote text materials from J. Mursell, *Education for Musical Growth*.

To Harvard University Press for permission to quote text materials from S. Langer, *Philosophy in a New Key;* and to Harvard University Press and Faber and Faber Ltd. for permission to quote text materials from T. S. Eliot, *The Use of Poetry and the Use of Criticism*.

To Hogarth Press Ltd. and to Basic Books Inc. for permission to quote text materials from Chapter IX, "The Relation of the Poet to Day-Dreaming" (first published in *Neue Revue*, I, 1908) in *Collected Papers of Sigmund Freud*, edited by Ernest Jones, M.D. Volume IV, translation supervised by Joan Riviere.

To Holt, Rinehart and Winston for permission to quote a musical composition "The Santa Fe," from A. Pierce, *Teaching Music in the Elementary School*.

To Indiana University Press and Midland Books for permission to quote text materials from L. L. Whyte (ed.), *Aspects of Form*.

To International Universities Press for permission to quote text materials from R. Holt (ed.), *Motives and Thought;* from J. Piaget, *The Origins of Intelligence in Children;* from E. Kris, *Psychoanalytic Explorations in Art;* to International Universities Press and Professor Evelyn Pitcher for permission to quote stories from E. Pitcher and E. Prelinger, *Children Tell Stories;* to International Universities Press and Mrs. Erica Werner for permission to quote a figure from H. Werner, *Comparative Psychology of Mental Development*.

To *The Journal of Aesthetic Education* and Professor Ralph Smith for permission to recapitulate an argument from H. Gardner, "Problem-Solving in the Arts."

To The Journal Press for permission to reproduce a figure from K. Bridges, "A Genetic Theory of the Emotions."

To Mrs. Ray Kaempfer for permission to reproduce a drawing by Gidi Kaempfer.

To Professor Lawrence Kubie and the *Psychoanalytic Quarterly* for permission to quote text materials from "Body Symbolization and the Development of Language."

To Longman, Green, and Co., for permission to quote a poem by June Robinson appearing in M. Langdon, *Let The Children Write.*

To Macmillan Company for permission to reproduce a drawing from V. Lowenfeld and W. L. Brittain, *Creative and Mental Growth,* copyright 1964, and to Macmillan Company and Professor Irving Kaufman for permission to reproduce a drawing from *Art and Education in Contemporary Culture,* copyright 1966.

To Mouton, Publishers for permission to reproduce transcriptions of a child's speech from R. Weir, *Language in the Crib.*

To Dr. Margaret Naumburg and Grune & Stratton for permission to quote text materials from M. Naumburg, *Schizophrenic Art* (1950).

To the *New Yorker* and E. Frascino for permission to reproduce a drawing from the *New Yorker* of May 20, 1972.

To Oxford University Press for permission to quote text materials from D. Cooke, *The Language of Music.*

To Princeton University Press and Routledge and Kegan Paul for permission to quote text materials from *The Collected Works of Paul Valéry* edited by Jackson Mathews, Bollingen Series XLV, *The Art of Poetry,* Vol. 7, translated by Denise Folliot (© 1958) by Bollingen Foundation, reprinted by permission of the Princeton University Press; to Princeton University Press and Professor Ernest Gombrich for permission to quote text material from *Art and Illusion* by E. H. Gombrich, Bollingen Series XXXV, number 5, in the A. W. Mellon Lectures in the Fine Arts (© 1960, 1961, 1969) by the Trustees of the National Gallery of Art, Washington, D.C., reprinted by permission of the Princeton University Press.

To G. P. Putnam for permission to reproduce musical compositions from S. Coleman, *Creative Music for Children.*

To Random House for permission to quote text materials from V. S. Pritchett, *The Cab at the Door;* to Random House and Pantheon Books/ A Division of Random House for permission to reproduce stories from E. Richardson *In The Early World;* from H. Read, *Education Through Art* (third edition); and from N. Podhoretz, *Making It* (1967).

To Routledge and Kegan Paul for permission to reproduce musical compositions from G. Révész, *The Psychology of a Musical Prodigy.*

To Saint Martin's Press, Inc., and Macmillan and Co., Ltd. for permission to quote text materials from E. Stein (ed.), *Arnold Schoenberg's Letters* (1965).

To Schocken Books and The City Council of the West Riding of Yorkshire and Chatto and Windus for permission to reproduce stories and poems from A. B. Clegg, *The Excitement of Writing.*

To Simon and Schuster and Penguin Books Ltd. for permission to quote poems by T. Anthony ("A Little Egg"), S. Forman ("The Grass"), P. Thompson ("My Feelings"), and H. Farley ("I Love") from R. Lewis (ed.) *Miracles,* copyright © 1966 by Simon and Schuster. Reprinted by permission.

To *The Times Literary Supplement* (London) for permission to quote text materials from A. Coleman, "T. S. Eliot and Keith Douglas."

To Mrs. William Travers, Headmistress, and the Parents' Association of The Brooks School of Concord, Mass., for permission to reproduce figures from The Brooks School Calendar.

To UNESCO for permission to quote text materials from E. Ziegfeld (ed.), *Education Through Art.*

To the University of California Press for permission to reproduce poems from K. Chukovsky, *From Two to Five;* and to quote text materials from R. Arnheim, *Visual Thinking.* Originally published by the University of California Press. Reprinted by permission of the Regents of the University of California.

To The University of Chicago Press for permission to quote text materials from E. Wasiolek (ed.), *The Notebooks for The Idiot by Dostoyevsky.*

H. G.

INTRODUCTION TO THE PAPERBACK EDITION

As my first literary offspring, *The Arts and Human Development* occupies a special place in my mind and in my soul. The themes that it introduced more than two decades ago have remained dominant in most of my subsequent research and writing. The republication of this book gives me a welcome opportunity to examine the origins of these artistic, developmental, and educational themes; in addition, I use this prefatory note to reflect on the ways in which my thinking — and that of others — has remained constant, as well as the ways in which conceptualizations have altered during the ensuing period.

As I look back over my scholarly career, I can clearly see its moment of crystallization. As a young student in the mid-1960s, I read the writings of the developmental psychologist Jean Piaget and realized that the work he had so brilliantly launched would become my life's work as well. I was stimulated by Piaget's synoptic vision of the development of children's thinking; I was intrigued by his explorations of the parallels between the thinking of children and the maturation of various scholarly disciplines. Even more, I was fascinated by his demonstrations of the strange and exotic ideas held by children; I found myself convinced by his assertion that the child's view of the world is qualitatively different from that of the adult.

At the same time, however, I was uneasy with the overall picture that Piaget (1970) had portrayed. Somehow it failed to connect with a vital part of my own personal experience. As a child, I had been a serious pianist and had briefly considered a career as a performer. As a young adult, I continued my love of music while dabbling in other art forms as well. I considered the arts to be an intellectual, a cognitive, enterprise, one that involves problem solving and problem finding; I knew that the arts assumed great importance the world over. Yet Piaget had virtually nothing to say about the arts — for him, the developed individual *was* the developed scientist. Nor was Piaget alone in this conceit; virtually all other developmentalists paid scant regard to the arts.

Now, with the benefit of hindsight, I am able to parse my ensuing scholarly life into three decade-long quarrels with the Piagetian legacy. In the 1960s, I explored seriously a view of development that placed the arts centrally in human cognition and affect; and I explored the range of "end states" that exist within and across several art forms. This story, which grew out of a clash between the theoretical claims of Piaget and my own life experiences, was related in *The Arts and Human Development*.

In the 1970s, fueled by a myriad of findings in neuropsychology (see Gardner, 1975), I found it increasingly difficult to embrace the standard view of intelligence as a single competence measured by a single IQ test. While Piaget was not a particular devotee of intelligence theory or testing, he had been trained in the original laboratory of Alfred Binet and Théodore Simon, and he always considered intellect to be "of a piece." During that decade, I saw my task as the reconciliation of my view of the arts as a separate domain with the far more differentiated picture of cognition that was emerging from developmental and neurological evidence. My second quarrel with Piaget became the center of my most discussed work, *Frames of Mind: The Theory of Multiple Intelligences* (1983).

During the 1980s, like many other Americans trained in developmental psychology, I became concerned with issues of education. My own research, and that of others, convinced me that much of schooling was ineffective in bringing about an important educational goal: the enhancement of human understanding. This unhappy result came about, I concluded, because school as currently implemented is not able to revise the powerful but typically inadequate theories and concepts that children develop spontaneously in their early years. The encounter between my ideas about intelligence and evidence from schooling led to the writing of a third book, *The Unschooled Mind: How Children Learn and How Schools Should Teach* (1991). Although not usually recognized as such, this book actually represents my most profound quarrel with Piaget. In it I question the central claim of developmental psychology: that most children pass through a set of stages, culminating in the attainment of formal operational thought at the time of early adolescence. Instead, I conclude that most of us remain, with respect to most domains, at the level of the five-year-old thinker.

In rereading *The Arts and Human Development*, a book that I had not examined in many years, I was of course curious to see whether I could discern hints of the latter two quarrels with Piaget. Interestingly, I had virtually nothing to say about intelligence per se in this first book, and there are only scattered hints about differences among various intellectual or artistic domains. In contrast, I had already become very critical of the notion of formal operational thought — a criticism of Piaget that would become almost universal in the ensuing decades. In *The Arts and Human Development*, I focused on the many positive features of the mind of the five year old, indicating the various ways in which the thought of the child anticipated the thinking of the mature artistic practitioner. (The many children's works·that are reproduced attempt to make this point by exemplification as well as through argument.) But like my colleagues at the time, I was not yet sensitive to the powerful limitations of these early conceptions *or* to the surprising endurance of early *mis*conceptions despite many years of school.

I have tried to reconstruct my state of mind as a student, when I began the work that led to *The Arts and Human Development*. In 1967, I was fortunate enough to find an intellectual home at a new research project, Harvard University's Project Zero, where, under the tutelage of the distinguished philosopher Nelson Goodman (1968, 1978), a number of students and young scholars enjoyed the opportunity to discuss and to conduct research on aspects of artistic cognition. Thus began a career-long focus on the similarities and differences between the mind of the child and the mind of the artist. Also, taking a leaf from Piaget, I undertook a series of experimental explorations of the development of artistic thinking and skills (Gardner 1982, 1990). The first fruits of this work, which became a leitmotif of research at Project Zero over the ensuing two decades, appear in *The Arts and Human Development*.

Another trait that emerged during my student days was an impulse toward synthesizing and theorizing. During this doggedly empiricist era, this trait was at best tolerated, save in certain quarters. I felt a keen desire to draw together the disparate philosophical and empirical work on art, development, and cognition, and to confer upon it my own theoretical spin. This preoccupation stimulated the writing of *The Arts and Human Development* as well as a parallel volume, published in the same year, *The Quest for Mind: Piaget, Lévi-Strauss, and the Structuralist Movement* (1973). In this essentially lonely process, I discovered that I liked to write and, with the latter book, that I could address a general as well as a scholarly public. *The Arts and Human Development* turned out to be my only full-length book written chiefly for scholars.

One benefit of its academic style is that it makes it easy now to identify precisely my claims in 1973 and to indicate where I would revise, and where I would retain, the book's findings and conclusions. Beginning with the theoretical material in the first chapter, I find too exclusive a reliance on mainstream developmental writers of the cognitive and psychoanalytic persuasion. Today I would introduce — though not uncritically — a cognitive-scientific perspective (Anderson, 1983; Chomsky, 1980; Fodor, 1983; Gardner, 1985; Marr, 1982; Newell, 1990; Newell and Simon, 1972; Pinker, 1994; Rumelhart and McClelland, 1986), as well as research from neurology, neuropsychology, and sociobiology (Changeux, 1985; Damasio, in press; Edelman, 1987; Gazzaniga, 1992; Geschwind, 1974; Wilson, 1975).

On the topic of developing systems (Chapter 2), I now recognize a far more complex picture. While evidence continues to accumulate in support of the combining of initially disparate systems, there is also considerable evidence for systems initially connected with one another as well as for amodal forms of perception and action (Baillargeon, 1987; Bower, 1982; Carey and Gelman, 1991; Karmiloff-Smith, 1992; Spelke, 1991; Wagner et al., 1981). The concept of "perceiving," "making," and "feeling" systems, while scarcely the last word in theorizing, remains a convenient way to organize findings, particularly when one is attuned to the arts.

I am struck by the relative freshness and continuing interest of the key theoretical ideas in Chapters 3 and 4: the mode-and-vector hypothesis and the centrality of symbols. No one could have anticipated the vast amount of research on metaphor of the last twenty years, nor the explosion of books and papers on symbolizing (Winner, 1988; Ortony, 1993). Yet at the same time, the specific ideas about modal-vectoral representation in infancy, and its recapitulation at the level of symbols, can help make sense of recent research and also to stimulate fresh lines of study (Bamberger, 1991; Bates, 1979; Cohen, 1988; Greenfield, 1991; Karmiloff-Smith, 1992; Savage-Rumbaugh et al., 1986). I also note with pleasure the key distinctions made between perception of persons and perception of objects, and between presymbolic and symbolic thinking. Were I to write a general psychology of human thought today, I would place these ideas at the very center of my treatment.

Not surprisingly, it is Chapter 5, a review of empirical work, that has become most out-of-date. We at Project Zero can claim at least a little credit for that. Fortunately there are a number of competent reviews that can bring the interested reader up-to-date (Applebee, 1977; Astington, 1993; Bamberger, 1991; Cox, 1992; Davidson and Scripp, 1988; Davis and Gardner, 1992; Deutsch, 1982; Eisner, 1992; Freeman, 1980; Gardner, 1980, 1990; Gardner and Perkins, 1989; Golomb, 1992; Hargreaves, 1986; Mandler, 1984; Salomon, 1979; Sloboda, 1987, 1988; Winner, 1982). I feel that the organizing principles that undergird the 1973 review of the literature are still justifiable, but today, in light of multiple intelligences theory, I would pay much more attention to the differences across domains and media. And the list of problems and questions for future research (pages 181–83) could still fuel a few centuries' worth of doctoral dissertations.

The final chapters look ahead to future work. In Chapter 6, I considered questions of artistic training and education. Along with others, we at Project Zero have been pioneers in developing fresh approaches to the training of artistic skills and competences. Our most prominent endeavor, Arts PROPEL (Gardner, 1989; Winner, 1992; Zessoules, Wolf, and Gardner, 1988), is constructed around three artistic roles: Perceiver, Producer, and Reflecter—a trio that recalls the range of roles analyzed in this book. In chapter 6 I also treat a number of perennial and vexing questions about the nature of creativity in the sciences and the arts. Little did I anticipate that two decades later I would carry out precisely the set of intensive case studies for which I then called, in *Creating Minds: An Anatomy of Creativity as Seen Through the Lives of Freud, Einstein, Picasso, Stravinsky, Eliot, Graham, and Gandhi* (1993).

The concluding chapter of *The Arts and Human Development* recapitulates a number of themes, culminating with a decisive break from Piaget on the prevalence and importance of operational thinking. It is sobering to realize that this attack, at the time regarded as daring, would now be considered conventional wisdom or even common sense.

In his pathbreaking study of Picasso's masterpiece *Guernica*, the eminent psychologist of art Rudolf Arnheim (1962) notes how much of the final massive and intricate work is contained in the hastily-executed first sketch. At a far more modest level, I am intrigued — and a bit unsettled — to see how many of the themes of my early and middle career are anticipated in the pages of my first book.

While I am struck by the continuity in work, I am also encouraged by the progress that has been realized. In the historical sliver of only twenty years, our knowledge of both the conceptual issues and the empirical facts about the arts and human development has increased significantly. The above paragraphs may create the impression that researchers at Project Zero have been largely responsible for these advances. I am enough of a student of the *zeitgeist* to realize that many of these changes were already in the air (Csikszentmihalyi, 1988). Still, I would be less than honest if I did not express my excitement at having been present on the scene when these ideas were first beginning to take shape. I trust that some of that excitement comes through in the words that you have just read — and in the pages that follow.

Cambridge, Massachusetts
April 1994

REFERENCES

Anderson, J. 1983. *The architecture of cognition*. Cambridge: Harvard University Press.

Applebee, A. 1977. *The child's concept of a story*. Chicago: University of Chicago Press.

Arnheim, R. 1962. *Picasso's Guernica*. Berkeley: University of California Press.

Astington, J. 1993. *The child's discovery of the mind*. Cambridge: Harvard University Press.

Baillargeon, R. 1987. Young infants' reasoning about the physical and spatial characteristics of a hidden object. *Child Development*, 2, 179–200.

Bamberger, J. 1991. *The mind behind the musical ear*. Cambridge: Harvard University Press.

Bates, E. 1979. *The emergence of symbols*. New York: Academic Press.

Bower, T. G. R. 1982. *Development in infancy*. San Francisco: Freeman.

Carey, S., and R. Gelman. 1991. *The epigenesis of mind*. Hillsdale, N.J.: L. Erlbaum.

Changeux, J-P. 1985. *Neuronal man*. New York: Pantheon Books.

Chomsky, N. 1980. *Rules and representations*. New York: Columbia University Press.

Cohen, L. B. 1988. An information-processing approach to infant cognitive development. In *Thought without language*. Edited by L. Weiskrantz. Oxford, Eng.: Clarendon Press.

Cox, M. 1992. *Children's drawings*. London: Penguin.

Csikszentmihalyi, M. 1988. Society, culture, and person: A systems view of creativity. In *The nature of creativity*. Edited by R. Sternberg. New York: Cambridge University Press.

Damasio, A. In press. *Descartes' error*. New York: Putnam.

Davidson, L., and L. Scripp. 1988. Young children's musical representations: Windows on music cognition. In *Generative processes in music*. Edited by J. Sloboda. Oxford, Eng.: Clarendon Press.

Davis, J., and H. Gardner. 1992. The cognitive revolution: Its consequences for the understanding and education of the young child as artist. In *1992 Yearbook of the National Society for the Study of Education*. Edited by B. Reimer and R. A. Smith. Chicago: University of Chicago Press.

Deutsch, D. 1982. *The psychology of music*. New York: Academic Press.

Edelman, G. 1987. *Neural Darwinism*. New York: Basic Books.

Eisner, E. 1992. *The enlightened eye*. New York: Macmillan.

Fodor, J. A. 1983. *The modularity of mind*. Cambridge: MIT Press.

Freeman, N. 1980. *Strategies of representation in young children*. New York: Academic Press.

Gardner, H. 1973; republished 1981. *The quest for mind*. Chicago: University of Chicago Press.

———. 1975. *The shattered mind: The person after brain-damage*. New York: Vintage Books.

———. 1980. *Artful scribbles: The significance of children's drawings*. New York: Basic Books.

———. 1982. *Art, mind, and brain: A cognitive approach to creativity*. New York: Basic Books.

———. 1983; republished 1993. *Frames of mind: The theory of multiple intelligences*. New York: Basic Books.

———. 1985. *The mind's new science: A history of the cognitive revolution*. New York: Basic Books.

———. 1989. Zero-based arts education: An introduction to Arts PROPEL. *Studies in Art Education*, 30(2), 71–83.

———. 1990. *Art education and human development*. Los Angeles: J. Paul Getty Trust.

———. 1991. *The unschooled mind: How children think and how schools should teach*. New York: Basic Books.

———. 1993. *Creating minds: An anatomy of creativity as seen through the lives of Freud, Einstein, Picasso, Stravinsky, Eliot, Graham, and Gandhi*. New York: Basic Books.

Gardner, H., and D. Perkins. 1989. *Art, mind, and education*. Urbana: University of Illinois Press.

Gazzaniga, M. 1992. *Nature's mind*. New York: Basic Books.

Geschwind, N. 1974. *Selected papers*. Dodrecht, Germany: Reidel Publishers.

Golomb, C. 1992. *The child's conception of a pictorial world*. Berkeley: University of California Press.

Goodman, N. 1968; republished 1976. *Languages of art*. Indianapolis: Hackett.

———. 1978. *Ways to worldmaking*. Indianapolis: Bobbs-Merrill.

Greenfield, P. M. 1991. Language, tools, and brain. *Behavioral and Brain Sciences*, 14(4), 531–95.

Hargreaves, D. 1986. *The developmental psychology of music*. New York: Cambridge University Press.

Karmiloff-Smith, A. 1992. *Beyond modularity*. Cambridge: MIT Press.

Mandler, J. 1984. *Stories, scripts, and scenes*. Hillsdale, N.J.: Erlbaum.

Marr, D. 1982. *Vision*. San Francisco: Freeman.

Newell, A. 1990. *Unified theories of cognition*. Cambridge: Harvard University Press.

Newell, A., and H. Simon. 1972. *Human problem solving*. Englewood Cliffs, N.J.: Prentice-Hall.

Ortony, A. 1993. *Metaphor and thought*. New York: Cambridge University Press.

Piaget, J. 1970; republished 1983. Piaget's theory. In *Handbook of child psychology*. Edited by P. Mussen. New York: Wiley.

Pinker, S. 1994. *The language instinct*. New York: Morrow.

Rumelhart, D., J. McClelland, and the PDP Research Group. 1986. *Parallel distributed processing*. Cambridge: MIT Press.

Salomon, G. 1979; reprinted 1994. *Interaction of media, cognition, and learning*. San Francisco: Jossey-Bass.

Savage-Rumbaugh, S., K. McDonald, R. Sevcik, W. Hopkins, and E. Rupert. 1986. Spontaneous symbolic acquisition and communicative use by pygmy chimpanzees. *Journal of Experimental Psychology: General*, 115, 211–35.

Sloboda, J. 1987. *The musical mind*. Oxford, Eng.: Clarendon Press.

——, ed. 1988. *Generative processes in music*. Oxford, Eng.: Clarendon Press.

Spelke, E. 1991. Physical knowledge in infancy: Reflections on Piaget's theory. In *The epigenesis of mind*. Edited by S. Carey and R. Gelman. Hillsdale, N.J.: Erlbaum.

Wagner, S., E. Winner, D. Cicchetti, and H. Gardner. 1981. Metaphorical mapping in human infants. *Child Development*, 52, 728–31.

Wilson, E. O. 1975. *Sociobiology*. Cambridge: Harvard University Press.

Winner, E. 1982. *Invented worlds*. Cambridge: Harvard University Press.

——. 1988. *The point of words*. Cambridge: Harvard University Press.

——, ed. 1992. *The Arts PROPEL handbooks*. Cambridge: Harvard Project Zero.

Zessoules, R., D. Wolf, and H. Gardner. 1988. A better balance: Arts PROPEL as an alternative to discipline-based art education. In *Beyond DBAE: The case for multiple visions of art education*. Edited by J. Burton, A. Lederman, and P. London. University Council on Art.

The Arts and Human Development

ONE

The Relationship of Art to Human Development

DEVELOPMENTAL RESEARCH

The systematic study of human development began about two centuries ago when a number of natural scientists looked to the young child for clues about the species, the primitive, the sick, and the normal.* During the latter part of the nineteenth century several "baby biographies" or "baby diaries," including one by Charles Darwin, were kept and published. The psychologically oriented parent or relative would record detailed observations of an infant, generally without offering much interpretation or commentary. Such disinterested yet painstaking observation culminated in the comprehensive studies by Gesell and his associates undertaken in the first half of this century, in which timetables for the appearance of a wide range of human capacities were drawn up.

While the neutral accumulation of facts may serve certain purposes, the majority of students of child development now emphasize the value of, and need for, observations and experiments conducted within a more or less explicit theoretical framework. They rightly challenge those who continue to gather innumerable facts without adequately examining the reason for such collecting, or the possibility that a different guiding question might elicit an alternate set of facts. Among the theoretically minded students of children, those of a strict learning theory or behaviorist orientation do not regard infants as qualitatively different from

*References organized by page will be found at the end of the book.

1

adults, except in the sense that the former have had less experience and may therefore be thought of as somewhat less complex. They hold that the child's behavior can be analyzed into discrete, independent units—such as stimuli, responses, drive states. For example, Bijou and Baer indicate that "the potential for virtually every behavior observed in the adult is present in the newborn," and view development as the "chaining of these differentiated discriminated operants into ever longer and more complex chains of greater and greater number and variety." Terrell echoes the same theme: "the likelihood of variables which are known to apply at a simple behavioral level to be relevant also at a more complex level is greater than the probability that variables suggested as relevant in complicated, poorly controlled studies are in fact relevant at that level."

For the followers of Hull, Skinner, and other learning theorists, the child (like the animal) provides the occasion for viewing, in elemental form, the universal principles of learning and behavior, be they conditioning, reinforcement, trial and error learning, or mediation. Such analysts are loathe to state that the child may at any time advance from one "stage" to another, that there may be complete reorganizations of systems within the child, that humans differ in a qualitative way from animals, that symbols are of a different order than signs, or that new forms of learning may come to the fore during the life of the organism. Perhaps because such attributions would create serious theoretical difficulties, these psychologists hesitate to assign significant reorganizing or creative capacities to the child, whose behavior seems explicable in terms of schedules of reinforcement or drive reduction.

Although recognizing the elegance of accounting for all psychological phenomena in terms of the terse vocabulary and mechanisms of these orientations, I have rejected the behaviorist approach because, whatever its original uses and merits within American psychology, it has in recent years rarely led to questions, experiments, or observations relevant to the present topic. Numerous reasons can be cited, which range from the inevitable encrustation surrounding widely accepted theories, and the peculiar appropriateness of these paradigms for studies of animal behavior, to the lack of adequate or even intuitively satisfying definitions for crucial terms. These and other arguments against the behaviorist scheme have been developed at great length in many places and need not be iterated here.

Despite the inadequacies of this theoretical position, investigators who subscribe to it have produced many important findings that I will draw upon. And indeed, the methodological postulates of the behaviorist—particularly his positivism—are the canons by which nearly every experimental psychologist, irrespective of his theoretical stance, conducts his workaday research. My dissatisfaction with behaviorism reflects an assessment of its explanatory power in future years. I feel that, following upon a generation of powerful and magnetic theorists of human development, theory-building will in the coming years be more of a collective effort, drawing together postulates in an eclectic (though not careless) way, using those constructs, laws, and orientations that seem of heuristic value. Some efforts in this direction can already be seen.

Those students of developmental psychology who reject both the atheoretical and the behaviorist approaches have generally found positions outlined by Piaget, Freud, and their followers to yield the richest insight. Prolific writers, Freud and Piaget have commented on nearly every aspect of human behavior and development; in addition, each of their theories has crucial implications for those of other psychologists. Nonetheless, the emphases in their writings have been different, and the task of integrating their perspectives remains for the future.

Although its implications now extend to many areas, the psychoanalytic tradition is deeply linked to the study of human personality and emotional/affective life. The models that Freud developed derived from his earlier neurological work and from his readings in the psychology and biology of his day, but his theorizing grew out of his clinical work with patients suffering from hysteria, nervous disorders, and character difficulties. Nearly all of Freud's most enduring insights can be traced to his therapeutic encounters or to his self-analysis, in which he sought to discover the roots of motivation, the nature of unconscious thought, and the genetic antecedents of the adult personality.

I differ with those who would disqualify Freud's theory of personality and neurosis because it is steeped in the maladies of *fin de siècle* Vienna. Freud's view of the human personality, with its powerful drives, arsenal of defenses, tripartite mental personality, constant interplay of pleasure and reality principles, primary and secondary processes, love and work, Eros and Thanatos, provides perhaps the most vibrant, dynamic, and satisfying portrait of both normal and diseased personality yet proposed.

For all its magnificence and penetration, however, the psychoanalytic perspective has severe limitations for the study of human development. Freud devoted no special attention to the study of children and tended to regard the child as an adult in matters of cognition. He commented, for instance, that "the child perhaps does not behave different from the average uneducated woman in whom the same polymorphous perverse disposition exists." Furthermore, despite his contention that each stage of infantile sexuality had its characteristic erogenous zone and behaviors, Freud appeared unwilling to allow qualitative differences between thoughts or affects realized at different times in the life cycle—for example, before and after the advent of symbol use. Memories perdured in identical form throughout the individual's life; they could be accurately recalled, evoking similar phenomenal experience whenever relived. While Freud quite readily adopted a developmental perspective in explaining the etiology of a specific human ailment, he underemphasized the extent to which subsequent events might color or even totally transfigure the nature of an earlier experience. The development of the human personality represented for Freud, a series of layers deposited one upon another, each stratum retaining its specific character.

Owing to his relative ignorance about children, Freud's statements about the young frequently appear misguided or unsupported. His contentions that children know how to interpret pregnancy correctly, that children view sexual acts as violent, and that they are preoccupied with the nature of marriage and sex are at best unproved; his notion that the newborn hallucinates an image of his mother's breast contradicts all that is now supposed about the development of "representational thought"; his statements concerning infantile narcissism do not even consider the possibility that the child has yet to evolve any sense of self. Freud probably considered the infant more helpless and passive, less exploratory and competent than he is, and supererogatorily attributed aggressive or evil tendencies to the young organism.

Even though others have modified some of the least tenable Freudian dicta about childhood, the analytic tradition still lacks a coherent view of the nature of the child's thought processes. Freud was himself aware of this gap, commenting that "as a psychoanalyst I must of course be more interested in affective than in intellectual phenomena, more in the unconscious than in the conscious life." Thus the psychoanalytic tradition has simply bypassed the entire problem of language development, accepting without protest Freud's associationistic speculations. In addition, concept formation, moral judgment, problem solving, and logical reasoning are either ignored, assumed to be present at an early age, or viewed as defense mechanisms or substitute behaviors. Freud viewed the infant as able to conceptualize complex notions, the young child as lacking not in reasoning ability but simply in information, the amnesia concerning childhood as due simply to repression. It seems reasonable to conclude that Freud, like the behaviorists and associationists, tended to view the child simply as an immature, simpler adult; he did not seriously explore the possibility of reorganizations of mental structures with maturation of the organism. At best, Freud sensed differences between child and adult but made little progress in clarifying them.

The psychoanalytic contribution to developmental psychology seems restricted, then, to the following: a description (often by extrapolation from the abnormal) of an end state—the healthy adult human personality; a model of the child passing through a series of (psycho-) sexual stages with emotional concomitants, any one of which may become the basis for fixation or later regression; and a demonstration that certain experiences, attachments, fears, and desires permeate the lives of all human beings from an early age, and can exert a powerful influence on their subsequent behavior.

Despite numerous lacunae, I feel the psychoanalytic tradition has made significant progress toward elucidating the development of the "affective," "emotional," or "feeling," life of the individual, particularly the relationship between early experience and later character, and the relationship between psychosexual experience and cognitive processes. Freud's contribution to the understanding of human development is substantial but, perhaps owing to the sources of his insight, one-sided, emphasizing the personality and the emotional life of the individual. Freud himself sensed those limitations when he commented

The direct observations of children have the disadvantage of working upon data which are easily misunderstandable; psychoanalysis is made difficult by the fact that it can only reach its data, as well as its conclusions, after long detours. But by cooperation the two methods can attain a satisfactory degree of certainty in their findings.

One major position in developmental psychology stresses those facets of life that are "felt," the other concentrates on the "thinking" or "cognitive processes" of the developing individual. Unlike Freud, who turned to children in search of an explanation for adult difficulties, Piaget is preeminently a developmental psychologist. Accordingly, the study of infants and children has been his principal concern for more than half a century. In that time he has examined and written about children's changing conceptions of a staggering variety of areas, ranging from the epistemologists' concerns—space and causality—to the metaphysicians' preoccupations—morality and dreams.

Despite this range, Piaget's goal is specifiable: he is interested in those mental processes that culminate in scientific thought, an end state that can be expressed in logical terms. And his major contribution can be crisply summarized: Piaget has demonstrated that children conceptualize in a manner qualitatively different from adults. Whereas Kant described space, time, and causality as a priori categories, imminent in all thought, Piaget views the adult forms of these categories as the logical end state toward which child thought is gradually evolving. Landmarks along the way are considered separate stages and are described in terms of incomplete, semilogical forms isomorphic to the child's thought. Piaget defers from those areas where it is not possible to outline the intermediate and end states toward which thought is tending. He indicates, for example: "I have not the slightest desire to generalize from the case of logic to the rest of mental life. Logic is the only field where equilibrium is fully achieved," and admits that "the creative imagination is a magnificent subject which remains to be investigated." Accordingly, Piaget has devoted minimal attention to the child's conception of performances or experiences in the realms of art, fantasy, humor, affect, and other areas that he considers "figurative" rather than "operative."

Where Freud had little to say about logical or scientific thought, Piaget has outlined his position on the relationship between affective and cognitive development. He seems to waver in this formulation between competing stances. First, he postulates that affect is an inseparable concomitant of all behavior, with cognition providing the structure and affect the "energetic aspect." In arguing thus, Piaget depicts affect as a motor for all behavior; it determines the force of action but has no structure. However, Piaget also treats the affective life of the child as if it were a separate realm, associated primarily with social objects, having its unique history, emphases, schemes, reactions, and energy. He even traces the evolution of affect, maintaining that it commences with a hereditary makeup of emotions, then entails movement away from the initial state of egocentrism, a growing sense of "self" and "other," and the construction of affective objects. In his descriptions of the older child, Piaget also isolates the "affective realm," making reference to the values that adolescents adopt and the relations governing family life during the later period.

Piaget's confusion may have resulted from his defining affect as "energetics," while simultaneously attempting to integrate the findings of others who have viewed affect as the realm of experience which involves other people and emotions. He wants to retain his own purely cognitive framework (thought as the structure of all activity), even while allowing for the phenomenon studied by more affect-oriented psychologists: The task sometimes proves too unwieldy. A discussion of Piaget's attempt to reconcile Freud's views on affect with his own and a critique of this effort have been included with the bibliographical notes.

Piaget's interests have directed him toward a cognitive approach to human development as one-sided as Freud's emphasis on personality and affect. For Piaget, development involves a series of qualitatively different cognitive stages; for Freud, the process consists of a sequence of dominant affects, any one of which may recur in unaltered form. Where Piaget posits discrete, structured stages, Freud finds sequences that blend into one another. Consequently, the two most significant contributors to developmental psychology do not speak to the same questions or, when they do, are either misinformed or obscure. These disparate approaches may be a necessary result of emphases on two different groups—neurotics and children engaged in problem-solving activities. Orientations are more likely to be translatable when they can be brought to bear on the same general area of investigation.

Several other psychologists interested in development, sharing this view, have made initial attempts to bring about a reconciliation between the cognitive and affective approaches. Gouin-Décarie has traced the development of the object concept in both the Piagetian sense, the child's comprehension of the permanence of material objects, and the Freudian sense, the child's attachment to his caretaker. Wolff has made similar syntheses of infant cognitive and emotional development and has explored the possibilities of explaining language acquisition through an integration of affective and cognitive approaches. And Carmichael has traced the development of a sense of irony by noting how the adolescent becomes able to appreciate the awkward justaposition of the two affects.

Such attempts suggest that the integration of affect and cognition is most likely to be realized if one focuses on pursuits where feeling and knowing are recognized as being intertwined, such as the arts. In my view, any psychological analysis of the arts and the artist presupposes an integrated view of human development. I suggest that, collectively, the artist, audience member, performer, and critic provide a viable and holistic end state for human development; I propose to examine the child's progression toward these termini. These suggestions will be pursued after a brief survey of previous psychological approaches to the arts.

PREVIOUS PSYCHOLOGICAL STUDIES IN AESTHETICS

Many scholars have examined the arts from a psychological perspective. There is hardly any consistent agreement on the nature of the arts, and few commentators have emphasized precisely the same aspect of the artistic process. A separate work is doubtless needed to sort out these views, but such inquiry is not essential to my purpose. Nevertheless, a sketch of major orientations is revealing when accompanied by some specifications of their inadequacy or incompleteness. My comments will be directed toward several general orientations, specific theorists being cited for illustrative purposes.

As the critic Abrams has perceptively indicated, aestheticians have over the centuries emphasized different facets of the arts—either the work itself, the universe being portrayed, the creating artist, or the audience. Psychologies derived from these disparate approaches have necessarily construed the arts in different ways. Aestheticians who focus upon the artist tend to think of him as an inexhaustible fount from whom masterpieces flow; those concerned with the audience generally focus upon the public's expectations and the procedures whereby such expectancies might be violated, met, or otherwise toyed with; those who consider the work itself to be central often posit universal standards of aesthetic forms observed by creators and honored by the audience; those treating art as a mirror of the universe look to the world for standards of beauty and proportion, regarding the artist as one who sees more clearly or records more faithfully. To be sure, none of these approaches necessarily contradicts any other, though very often those that emphasize one viewpoint neglect other aspects of the aesthetic process.

Among those who have focused upon the work itself, one might include the mathematician Birkhoff, who believed that the merit of any aesthetic work could be ascertained and described by a mathematical formula relating degree of order to degree of complexity. Birkhoff examined a large number of simple geometric forms and sought to order them on his measure of aesthetic merit. Should Birkhoff have proved accurate in his conclusions (using some independent measure), one would still have to explain the basis and the acquisition of universal standards. Are they built into the human mind or drawn from nature? Are they independent products of cultural evolution in disparate parts of the world? More flexible approaches to the constructs of order and complexity would also be needed to account for intricate and novel works.

Indeed Birkhoff's formulae have never been related to forms of art more intricate than polygons, and even there they prove indifferent predictors of the tastes of individuals or the arts of various cultures. Experiments have shown that individuals most knowledgeable about art had the least agreement with the judgments predicted by Birkhoff. Nonetheless, it remains possible that Birkhoff may have described one sort of classical aesthetic ideal. Such an emphasis on the work per se may be of interest for certain modern critics bent upon eliminating historical or psychological explanations for the impact of a work; it proves unsatisfactory for explaining how individuals participate in the aesthetic process. A position that seeks to relate art objects to pre-ordained standards of harmony and beauty cannot adequately account for the diverse experiences of observers or the successive revolutions in artistic practice.

Involved in a related pursuit are those analysts who feel that the arts should mirror the structure and the content of the observable universe. This view, early found in Plato's harsh condemnation of the poet, periodically surfaces in empiricistic psychological writings, where it is assumed that each individual carries about an internal "image" or "copy" of the outside world which he draws upon in his behavior, be it mundane or creative.

A forthright statement appears in the writings of Biedermann, who downgrades the Pompeian painters because "they had not yet achieved the ability of the sculptors contemporaneous with them to record details and individual characteristics, such as warts, wrinkles, and facial expressions." Leonardo conveys the same sentiment when he advises his students:

That painting is most praiseworthy which conforms most to the object portrayed. I put this forward to embarrass those painters who would improve on the works of nature, such as those who represent a child a year old, whose head is a fifth of its height, while they make it an eighth.

And E. H. Gombrich presents a sophisticated version in his insistence that a correct painting will yield no erroneous information about the world:

To say of a drawing that it is a correct view of Tivoli does not mean, of course, that Tivoli is bordered by wave lines. It means that those who understand the notion will derive no false information from the drawing . . . the complete portrayal might be one which gives as much correct information about the spot as we would obtain if we looked at it from the very spot where the artist stood.

Even the structuralist stand, taken by the literary critic Northrup Frye and others, highlights the relationship between works of art and the universe in which they are produced. By positing archetypical forms isomorphic with the seasons of the year, the fruits of nature, or the qualities of the body, such commentators indicate that the design of the world in which men and literature are found will determine the principal forms and genres of art.

While these views are useful in explicating certain forms of representational art and for elucidating the initial responses of children to art works, they prove poor tools for clarifying other, equally crucial aspects of the arts, such as the possibility for nonrepresentational works, or the manner in which artists "play" with their knowledge of the world. Indeed, with the decline of representational arts, it becomes increasingly irrelevant to speak of the arts as imitating nature. Either this position is simply wrong or it widens the concept of nature (or life) to the point of vagueness or tautology. In addition, numerous studies of perception and behavior have demonstrated that individuals do not imitate exactly what they perceive (nor do they perceive what is "there"). Rather, each individual may be thought of as possessing a set of behavioral patterns or schemes that organize his observations and actions. The child who observes an apple with a pin thrust through it may not draw what he perceives; instead, and perhaps for good reason, he allows the viewer to follow the pin even as it passes through the fruit. When the mature Western artist hides the pin, he is subscribing to a drawing convention rather than to some sort of absolute or intuitively obvious standard; whether his portrayal of the apple resembles a photograph depends less on his manual skill or perceptual powers than on the style of his era, the schemes at his disposal, and the representational attitude he has learned. Certainly artists may seek to imitate nature, yet this ideal is only one of many legitimate goals, and indeed a goal characteristic of less sophisticated practitioners.

If the iconic theory is dubious in the visual arts, it is even less relevant in other domains; few musicians claim that they are imitating nature, and those who succeed are scarcely to be envied. Furthermore, the notion that nature is somehow unequivocally *there*, available to be seen by anyone and then imitated in the "correct way," is directly antithetical to the contemporary views of art in which different or even unique representations often are especially to be prized. In all, a view of the arts as somehow mirroring physical properties of Nature or the World emerges as either simple-minded or useless.

Avowed psychologists often seek to relate the arts to fundamental perceptual tendencies of the human mind. In conformity with the approach to criticism that centers on the audience, such analysts conceive of the art work as an attempt by the artist to set up and then toy with various expectations on the part of an audience. Berlyne, who has described a number of variables (change, complexity, conflict) that activate certain psychological states (attention, curiosity, and surprise), is a leading proponent of this position. According to this view, forms of communication such as humor or the arts violate an expectation already present in the organism or created by skilled artistic technique, in order to heighten interest. Works that violate expectancy to a moderate extent, that are neither totally familiar nor wholly alien, are thought to constitute the most effective artistic presentations. It is possible sometimes to measure the complexity or the degree of departure from expectancy.

In the wake of cybernetics and information theory, this orientation has gained much currency, particularly among students of music. More than one monograph has purported to account for aesthetic appeal through a quantification of uncertainty. Moles writes explicitly of bits and information, while Meyer speaks of the inhibition of a tendency to respond; but both argue that the elements of a musical (artistic) work create and resolve expectations, thereby yielding aesthetic meaning. Meyer's analyses, though often insightful, rarely proceed beyond the common sense level. Moles, on the other hand, attempts a mathematical treatment of a number of aesthetic problems, but his firmest results apply to questions of doubtful interest, such as the optimal placement of compositions on a concert program. Although the relationship of information theory to temporal art forms may be suggestive, analyses have failed to treat the arts and mathematics with equal seriousness. Either the mathematics is only brought in metaphorically, or the arts are only brought in tangentially.

The informational approach is intended to apply to all forms of art, but students of the visual arts have had difficulty specifying the discrete units that might contribute to audience expectation and the objective probabilities for the occurrence of such units. Perhaps, as some suggest, such a specification may in principle be impossible. They also question what the *rules* of painting or sculpture might be, particularly in the wake of Moles's facile assertion that "an art is exactly defined by the set of rules it follows." Nonetheless, the general language of tension arousal, expectation, and resolution has sometimes proved useful to analysts of spatial as well as temporal art forms.

An information theory approach may help describe the phenomenal experience of an audience member, but it seems less relevant for elucidating the role of the artistic creator. Except for those showmen who seek chiefly to shock, communication of unexpected messages does not seem a dominant artistic goal. The artist's ignorance of this goal does not, of course, refute the informational analysis; yet one must note that many artists speak of their overwhelming desire to communicate precisely and clearly. Does it seem likely that artists are trying to communicate clearly and that those who happen inadvertently to violate expectancies most effectively are heralded by their audiences? More

likely, perhaps, those artists will be most esteemed who have the most
timely, subtle, or significant messages to convey or who can communicate their message on a variety of levels. And yet, often the simplest and
most direct sort of statements are effective, particularly in the aftermath
of a romantic period. One could invoke "violation of expectancy" to
explain such a countercurrent, but this characterization would by-pass
the question of why certain works continue to interest despite the
passage of time.

Like the approach that focuses on the work itself, such concentration on audience expectations fails to recognize the divergent expectancies audiences may have; analysts account for an ideal perceiver,
rather than for the melange of critics, connoisseurs, and dabblers of
which any audience is actually composed. And, most damagingly, this
approach by-passes the crucial questions of which works are most effective and the reasons for their effectiveness. Two works might contain
the same amount of information, or uncertainty, yet one is a sonata by
Mozart, the other a randomly generated pattern of no apparent interest.
Perhaps one could learn to love the random pattern or disdain Mozart
but, in the meantime, it seems plausible to assume greater significance
inherent in the formal arrangements and the specific themes of the
Mozart work. Information theory offers no way of characterizing differences in structure or quality between two equally complex or "uncertain" works, however. It has avoided the description of aesthetic forms,
components, and their significance, a task logically prior to an account
of informational units and audience expectancy. This orientation may
have provided a useful way of talking about certain kinds of artistic
experiences, particularly in forms having specifiable units, but accounts
neither for the appeal of certain art objects nor for the elements involved
in the artistic process.

Another psychologically oriented group focuses on the artist, emphasizing the great fertility of his imagination. Exponents of this view find
the kernel of artistic creation in the human ability to think divergently,
to generate new uses for objects, to combine or juxtapose two previously
held notions, images, skills. Such analysts generally contend that all
people have this ability, concurring with Guilford that "what the creative geniuses have in the way of traits, they merely have to a much
greater degree." Anyone acquainted with artists will find this difficult to
dispute. Certainly there is such a generative skill, whether it belongs
only to a chosen few as a birthright, is present in many individuals but
needs special cultivation in order to unfold, or inheres in every person
but in varying degrees. Yet because this faculty has typically been

described in general terms—"an ability to provide novel or unusual ideas"—it makes one think of the clever person rather than the artist and suggests, if unwittingly, that success at cocktail parties epitomizes artistic excellence. The fact that these analysts generally lump together artistic and scientific creativity only compounds the confusion; we need to recognize distinctness as well as commonalities between the products of artists and scientists.

The kind of task employed to tap the creative potential is convenient but suspect. The subject is typically asked to list uses of, names for, or qualities associated with an object; the number of responses given in a specified period is usually the measure of divergent thought. Yet it is obviously the *quality* of responses that should be taken into account, and this quality may prove difficult to measure. A single unique response may be more telling than 30 clever ones, and the response of the poet may either be the most banal (an inkblot is an inkblot) or akin to the madman's. Indeed, the creative artist may well be the one who rejects the whole problem or task, or who discovers new tasks, rather than the one who is skillful at solving puzzles conjured up by a psychologist. If one represents the *convergent* thinker as the individual who guides several thoughts or elements toward one solution

```
a
b
c  ———  x
d
e
```

and the *divergent* thinker as one who uses a single thought or element as the point of departure for many new ones

```
      x1
      x2
a  ——— x3
      x4
      x5
```

the creative artist might in some instances be the individual who settles on a single thought and performs one operation on it

```
x  ———  x1
```

or the one who draws on a number of disparate strands and arranges them (through his technical skill with a symbolic medium) into a wholly new configuration:

In each instance, a manipulation of elements occurs, but the skilled artist need conform neither to the convergent nor to the divergent model. Accordingly, empirical investigations that faithfully capture the circumstances surrounding artistic creation have been difficult to realize. Indeed, models of convergent and divergent thought barely suggest the complexity of behavior involved in "Knowledge of a medium." Furthermore, the relative ease with which performance on "divergent thinking tests" can be improved through brief training suggests that this faculty may not adequately model artistic activity.

The philosopher Cassirer and his followers, notably Susanne Langer, offer another variant of "mind" psychology, which emphasizes the uniquely human capacity to employ symbolic forms. According to this view, human knowledge is inseparable from the ability to make abstractions, to capture and convey their content in symbol systems such as music, painting, and formal or natural languages. The arts have their evolutionary origins in the first generalized categories, which the primitive man extracts or, better, constructs from his experience and makes the foundation for his language, myths, and rituals; they represent men's efforts to control elements of these experiences, to give meaning to their private and social lives, to correlate subjective consciousness with material objects.

Scientific knowledge also arises from this fundamental capacity to know and symbolize, but strives toward explanatory models that can be expressed in translatable languages. Langer contrasts such "discursive" symbolism with the "presentational" symbolism characteristic of artistic products. A presentational form is integral, inviolate; it cannot be paraphrased, translated, or defined in terms of other symbols; it must be apprehended whole, in its original form. Art forms tend to be presentational, conveying the artist's knowledge of feeling life, or more precisely, his comprehension of the *forms* of feelings. Bach's music presents the master's comprehension of the contours of feeling life and not, as Schweitzer thought, his sound pictures of specific emotions. Langer resists specifying the range or forms of feeling, declaring instead that feeling is "anything felt," whether the operation of a sense organ or a reaction to a complex situation. Vision is the way the optic apparatus feels; frustration and expectation the way the organism feels. She speaks of "whatever is felt in any way, as sensory stimulus or inward tension, pain, emotion, or interest. Feeling includes the sensitivity of very low animals and the whole realm of human awareness and thought, the sense of justice and the perception of meaning, as well as emotion and sensation."

By and large, Langer elects to convey her conception of the arts presentationally, through numerous examples drawn from diverse aesthetic realms. She contends that the various art forms are "virtual" forms of experience that capture within a symbolic medium intuitions about space, time, memory, and so forth. In *Mind: An Essay on Human Feeling,* she seeks to found a full philosophy of the mind upon the basic tendency of organic matter to pulsate, to assume rhythmic patterns, to achieve a balanced form, and ultimately to feel. All these ways of feeling have characteristic forms, and a closer study of their forms shows a striking resemblance between them and the forms of growth, motion, development, and decline known to the biologist—the typical forms of vital processes. Such pervasive feelings are seen as the root of that form of knowledge identified with the arts.

Langer's contribution to aesthetics, which began as an explication of Cassirer's position, has become a consummate personal statement, worthy of careful study. In an effort to present an integrated and exhaustive account of the nature of Art, her examination of the sources of Mind draws learnedly upon philosophy and biology. Judgment cannot yet be passed on this difficult and still incomplete work. Nonetheless, my impression is that Langer's argument, by consistently alternating between the level of physiological investigations and the plane of philosophical elucidation, seeks to reduce the role of psychological explanation. To be sure, her enterprise has succeeded in clarifying issues at these distant levels and has suggested numerous fascinating affinities. But unless Langer can demonstrate that psychological considerations such as representational skills, individual differences, methods of learning, sensitivity to patterns, information processing capacity, and developmental stages are not relevant to aesthetic study, or unless she inserts between the biological and the philosophical levels some manner of psychological explanation, she will have created an aesthetic that by-passes the role of the individual as perceiver and as creator. Furthermore, her characterization of the artist as an expert in the realm of feeling seems inadequate, for it neglects both the attainment of requisite skills and the insistent influence of the sociological context.

The Cassirer tradition has argued convincingly that man is a symbolic and abstracting creature, alone capable of the arts. Yet without an in-depth examination of individual psychological development, one will be unable to explain why participation in the arts may assume varied forms; why appreciation and understanding differ so markedly across individuals; and how the bundle of reflexes, affects, and percepts associated with the infant can ever culminate in the composition of symphonies and poems.

Langer shares with the Gestalt school of psychology several themes adopted in the present work: the arts as an area in which humans naturally participate; the forms and contents of the arts as important in human life; the realm of knowledge as involving art and science, discourse and presentation. For the most part, however, these observers ignore the genetic approach; they are interested in the end state of the mature creator or perceiver, not in the changing world-view of the growing child. And when they do deal with infant art or perception, they tend to regard it as a simpler, more primitive example of the adult form, rather than as one with its own characteristics. Such a perspective may be adequate for explaining certain aspects of the arts, but it illuminates neither the different skills needed by critics and creators nor the effect of a certain level of comprehension upon the production and perception of the child. For these thinkers, the concept of *configuration* is considered sufficient to account both for the perceptual process involved in gazing at pictures, and for the abstract operations required in mathematical problem-solving; furthermore, the Gestaltists tend to focus on perception of art objects, saying little about the creation of new ones.

From this last characterization one should except Arnheim, who has devoted much thought to the nature of creativity in the visual arts and has commented instructively on the education of the connoisseur in the various artistic realms. His descriptions of Picasso's sketches for *Guernica* and his discussion of visual thinking represent an intelligent and logical application of perceptual principles to the area of artistic and scientific creation. However, in his effort to illustrate the affinities between normal perception and the "leap" characteristic of creative thought, Arnheim has insufficiently acknowledged that the required reasoning may involve mechanisms quite distinct from visual perception, notably the ability to manipulate propositions or ignore perceptual input. As a consequence, his conclusions are more relevant for certain kinds of problem-solving than for others. Taken as a whole, then, the Gestalt tradition has concentrated on the visual arts and, within them, on the nature of object and pattern perception. The school forms a natural complement to the information theory approach, which has proved more applicable to the "temporal" art forms.

A rather different view of arts and the human mind is found among those associated with the psychoanalytic tradition. Perennially fascinated by the arts, Freud devoted some of his most provocative writing to studies of Leonardo, Jensen's *Gradiva,* and certain works of Shakespeare and Dostoevsky. In these essays Freud brilliantly demonstrated how defense mechanisms and character disorders uncovered in his clinical investigations could be used to elucidate the source and appeal of artistic works. Freud discerned neurotic tendencies in poets and artists: He disparagingly referred to art as "substitute gratification" or "an illusion in contrast to reality." Yet Freud felt that, unlike neurotics who are truly sick, many artists are able to find in work the potential for expressing themselves, and thus for alleviating their suffering. The artist appeared to have more ready access to his unconscious, indeed achieving many of the psychoanalytic insights without effort: "it is vouchsafed to a few, with hardly an effort, to solve from the whirlpool of their emotions the deepest truths, to which we others have to force our way, ceaselessly groping amid torturing uncertainties." Perhaps it was Freud's own frustration at this phenomenon—the capacity of artists of every epoch to arrive at the insights that had cost him so much labor—that led to his pessimistic conclusion: "the nature of artistic attainment is psychoanalytically inaccessible to us."

While Freud typically viewed the artist as a neurotic who had somehow escaped his burden, or as a successful sublimator, one of his most talented pupils evolved a separate psychology of the artist that has received inadequate attention. Rank argued that the artist was a gifted individual possessed of tremendous will and ambition who initially molded his own personality so as to make of it a work of art. Particularly prominent in Western society, the "artist personality" preceded the flowering of artistic skills in every art form. Rank generally concurred with Freud on the relationship between art and neurosis, but presented a richer, more rounded portrait of the artist by stressing his conflicts with the culture, his relationship to the previous tradition, his thirst for success, the effect of fame upon his output, and his fears of running dry.

For a characterization of a certain type of mature adult Western artist, Rank's work remains unsurpassed; yet it suffers from excessive emphasis on the artist-as-genius, disregard of the skills an artist must possess, insufficiently considered assumptions about the similarity among arts and artists, and a fondness for slippery notions such as the "will to create." Like others of the psychoanalytic tradition, Rank shows laudable appreciation of the depth and scope of artists and their work, yet he underplays the extent to which participation in the artistic process depends on training, and he fails to elucidate the nature of artistic appeal. Both Rank and Freud can be faulted for an undifferentiated notion of the artistic process and for an unsatisfactory account of the relationship between childhood and artistry.

This modest review of several dominant positions in the psychology of the arts suggests that the field has a plethora of emphases but little concern with the perspectives of various art forms, or with patterns of individual creative and critical development, interest, skill, and understanding. The experimental literature is sparse and scattered, yielding disappointingly few insights about the nature of artistic activity. Research paradigms tend to be artificial, verbal responses are uncritically demanded and accepted, choices are forced, and intricate processes are modeled in tasks lasting but a few moments. Such an unimpressive literature suggests the need for more realistic, longitudinal, developmental studies of the artistic process. However, the major developmental theorists from whom such studies might be anticipated furnish relatively little insight into the particular contours of aesthetic development.

While Freud and Piaget have little to say that bears directly on the question of aesthetic development, the few asides they do make are, as always, superlatively suggestive. Freud declares:

Might we not say that every child at play behaves like a creative writer, in that he creates a world of his own, or, rather, rearranges the things of his world in a new way which pleases him? It would be wrong to think he does not take that world seriously; on the contrary he takes his play very seriously and he expends large amount of emotion on it. . . . The creative writer does the same as the child at play. He creates a world of phantasy which he takes very seriously—that is, which he invests with large amounts of emotion—while separating it sharply from reality.

And Piaget poses in a few sentences the major motivations for the study I have undertaken:

Two paradoxical facts surprise all who are accustomed to study the development of the mental functions and aptitudes of the child. The first is that very often the young child appears more gifted than the older child in the fields of drawing, of symbolic expression such as plastic representation, participation in spontaneously organized collective activities, and so on, and sometimes in the domain of music. If we study the intellectual functions or the social sentiments of the child, development appears to be more or less a continuous progression, whereas in the realm of artistic expression, on the contrary, the impression gained is frequently one of retrogression. . . . The second of these facts, which in part can be equated with the first, is that it is much more difficult to establish regular stages of development in the case of artistic tendencies than it is in that of other mental functions . . . without an appropriate art education which will succeed in cultivating these means of expression and in encouraging these first manifestations of aesthetic creation, the actions of adults and the restraints of school and family life have the effect in most cases of checking or thwarting such tendencies instead of enriching them.

With Freud and Piaget passing over aesthetic development, and learning theorists and behaviorists showing scant interest, only Werner and Kaplan among developmental theoreticians seem to confer some importance upon aesthetic matters. These writers seek to demonstrate that the ability to utilize symbols is critical for humans, and that the manner of symbol use alters in the course of development. Several of their studies convincingly illustrate the extent to which individuals agree about the expressive or physiognomic properties of various symbolic stimuli. Werner and Kaplan also document how a child initially lacks distance from those he addresses and from the symbols he uses. Development is portrayed as the increasing distancing and differentiation among a tetrad of elements: the object, the symbol, the addressor, and the addressee.

Werner and Kaplan's account of symbol formation represents the most significant effort yet undertaken toward a developmental view of the arts. Among developmentalists, only they have captured the interplay between perception and feeling so prominent in the arts, and the role of the body in the apprehension and creation of perceivable displays. Yet their work is incomplete for many reasons. They do not deal with the artist, but only with the ability of normal individuals to engage in symbolic activity. Their studies are limited to a demonstration of the expressiveness of geometric symbolic vehicles, thereby skirting the effects of aesthetic objects. They do not address themselves to the skills needed in the arts, nor to the broader question of how skills are taught or learned. Their discussion of symbol use barely extends through the preschool years, and they do not appear to have a coherent position on the status of affect and feeling. The problems raised by Werner and Kaplan's presentation are myriad and will demand concerted efforts over many years before satisfying solutions can be reached. To their credit, they were among the first to pose many of these pivotal questions, and they have set a sophisticated standard for those bent on solving them.

A DEVELOPMENTAL STUDY OF THE ARTS: QUESTIONS AND ISSUES

It may prove possible to treat in an integrated framework both problems that have been raised here: the relationship between "affective" and "cognitive" approaches to development, and the need for a psychology of the arts. We can look to the works of Piaget, who has shown how many of the issues confronting philosophers can be recast and freshly elucidated by a consideration of the development of knowing in the child. His approach has yielded convincing conclusions on the relationship between the empiricist and nativist approaches to knowledge, perception and cognition, language and thought, structure and function, part and whole. As recent commentators have argued, Piaget's approach represents a wholly new paradigm or theoretical framework for psychology, and it predictably causes assimilatory agonies for those raised upon the old. While the introduction of a new paradigm is not intended here, I have taken inspiration from Piaget's example; I seek to illuminate a whole cluster of questions associated with the arts and development by studying the artistic process as it develops in the lives of its participants.

Why undertake a developmental study of the arts? How can the arts facilitate a rapprochement between affective and cognitive approaches? The importance of these questions has frequently been anticipated by others, and it is worth citing a few items of testimony which, without predicting its success, suggest the widely felt need for such an undertaking.

The relationship between the artist and the child has so often been noted that the study of children would appear a natural source for insight about the arts. On this point (though on few others) artists and psychologists agree. Arnheim comments: "I can think of no essential factor in art or artistic creation of which the seed is not recognizable in the work of children." Jaensch suggests that "the closest parallel to the structure of personality in the child is not the mental structure of the logician but that of the artist." Spitz notes that "adults who have retained the capacity to make use of one or several of these usually atrophied categories of perception and communication belong to the specially gifted. They are composers, musicians, dancers, acrobats." Thomas Mann regards the artist as "a passionately child-like and play-possessed being"; Henri Matisse claims that "the artist . . . had to look at life as he did when he was a child and, if he loses that faculty, he cannot express himself in an original, that is, a personal way." Tolstoy writes about his early years in a way that anticipates my own conclusions:

Was it not then that I acquired all that now sustains me? And I gained so much and so quickly that during the rest of my life I did not acquire a hundredth part of it. From myself as a five year old to myself as I now am there is only one step. The distance between myself as an infant and myself at present is tremendous.

Goethe's note is perhaps the most resonant: "If children grew up according to early indication, then we should have nothing but geniuses. But growth is not merely development. . . . After a certain time scarcely a trace is to be found of many of these capacities and manifestations of power." Pfleiderer, a psychologist, also reflects on this paradox: "What is for the adult a serious and often very arduous task—training head and eye to become absolutely obedient and trustworthy servants of the artist's will—is for the child pure pleasure. The child repeats with ceaseless delight every new work, every new grasp, every new stroke." These and numerous other remarks suggest that, rather than being pure reflections of one another, the child and the artist share a limited though revealing set of features. As in comparisons of parent and child, a careful study of the common and individual features of each will produce a fuller understanding of both, casting new light on the nature of heredity, environment, and their interaction. It is the similarities *and* the differences between the child and the artist that may provide, through a study of both phenomena, clues that will elucidate each.

The claim that affect and cognition are two distinct yet related aspects of child development is at least as widespread as the doctrine of affinities between child and artist. The two aspects are frequently opposed to one another, the young child being viewed as a creature of affect who evolves into a creature of thought and cognition. We read that "the real task imposed on child psychology by general psychology is to describe how the child's thinking frees itself from emotional fetters and approaches the ideal of pure objectivity in a series of conquests of numerous obstacles and mistakes." Students of children's art echo this dichotomy when they contend that the young child painter is guided by his emotions and feelings, while the older artist is controlled by rational thought processes.

More suggestive in my view are certain contemporary psychoanalysts who, instead of contrasting affect and cognition, call attention to constant interaction and interplay between the two systems. Thus Wolff contends that affect may sometimes take the lead in engendering psychological development:

Clinical data suggest that, contrary to Piaget's assertions, affects *are* structure building forces which give rise to semi-permanent emotional predispositions (e.g., mood, character, traits, etc.) and that, when so structured, affects may also serve as defenses to ward off other affective experiences.

And Bowlby, also responding to Piaget, contends that

Any given pattern of behavior can, at different times, vary in the amount of emotional and intellectual activity which goes with it. . . . It is useful to look at the development of behavior patterns, even affectively toned ones, as being possibly independent of cognitive development in their initial stages.

Rather than contrasting affective and cognitive components, feelings and thoughts, it may be preferable to think of them as two kinds of systems or processes that may be operative in the organism at any time and in various combination. However, the confusion attendant upon a dichotomy of affect and cognition has led me to posit a different model of child development, one in terms of *three developing systems,* each of which can spur on or retard the others. In this formulation, cognition is no longer included as an autonomous system, taking on instead a more circumscribed meaning related to logical-scientific reasoning.

The postulation of three systems seems a productive way of describing development. Such a heuristic takes account of the wide range of possibilities open to the young children and indicates how the child may realize important developmental end states, in particular those involved in aesthetic processes. Through this approach the contentions of cognitive theorists, who see development as a series of qualitatively distinctive stages and reorganizations extending until adolescence, can be reconciled with the claims of the psychoanalysts, who perceive of development as a sequence of dominant affects that continue to assert themselves in some form throughout life. My conclusion is that the Piagetians and Freudians are focusing on different aspects of development and, hence, on a different set of problems.

In a child's development, I find one total reorganization of the systems, which takes a number of years and is occasioned by symbol use, as well as a continuity in feeling states best illustrated through the concept of "modes" and "vectors" (see Chapter 3). The continuity in feeling life is consistent with Freud's views, while the reorganization of the symbolic level incorporates the notion of discrete cognitive stages put forth by Piaget. According to my formulation, the child fluent in symbol use may already be thought of as an artist, but he must pass through further discrete stages before he can be thought of as a scientist. Even so, in a deeper sense than the scientist's, the artist's development continues throughout life. Thus a discussion of the possible end states of artistic development necessarily touches upon crucial issues in human growth raised by the complementary investigations of Piaget and Freud.

Of course, no individual can realize all the potentials inherent in the species, as William James lamented:

> Not that I would not, if I could be both handsome and fat and well dressed and a great athlete, and make a million a year, be a wit, a bon vivant and a lady killer as well as a philosopher: a philanthropist, statesman, warrior and African explorer as well as a tone poet and savant. But the thing is simply impossible—the millionaire's work would run counter to the saint's; the bon vivant and the philanthropist would trip each other up; the philosopher and the lady killer could not well keep house in the same tenement.

Yet, despite the counterpulls that prevent simultaneous realization of all possible end states, it seems advisable to posit a set of related end states toward which all development tends. The roles involved in the arts seem to provide a particularly suggestive end state, avoiding the sprawl James warns against, while of relevance to the overall development of all individuals. "Full participation in the artistic process" as an end state seems at least as creditable as the "normal adult" personality generally cited by the Freudians and the "scientific thinker" embraced by the Piagetians, as it allows for a variety of roles and integrates cognitive and affective aspects. Although no single person will achieve all four roles equally, nearly all persons will realize significant aspects of at least one of the roles. While human personalities vary markedly across cultures, and scientific thought differs in status and sophistication in various regions, the arts appear in roughly comparable forms in all known civilizations, and hence are pertinent to human development everywhere. Indeed, participation in the arts is so natural and integral a part of human growth that an understanding of this process should provide important clues to many pivotal questions of human development.

I must indicate at this point that concentration on the arts in this work is in part a strategy. It might be possible to make the desired points about development without mentioning the arts, indeed by emphasizing the sciences instead. Yet the work would be far more strained were I to take the sciences as my end state, because the processes of development are only partially and perhaps distortedly realized in realms outside the arts. Science as we know it, featuring the experimental and hypothetico-deductive methods, is largely confined to post-Renaissance man; art antedates recorded history. Even though there is making, perceiving, feeling, and symbol use in the sciences, these aspects are more fully realized and integrated in the arts by creators, performers, and audience members than by researchers, theorists, and students in the sciences.

In a sense, then, I am writing about the arts because they enable me most cogently to express my notions about development. I outline a specific view of the arts, but whether the arts play for a given individual the precise roles I have described is not crucial. Rather I have outlined an end state, a series of ideal roles toward which development appears to gravitate. I have called these *aesthetic* and have sought to make points relevant to the arts, but if a reader should disagree with my views about the arts qua arts, he should not thereby reject the conclusions about development. By the same argument, a number of the conclusions about aesthetic issues can stand, irrespective of developmental considerations.

A word, finally, about value. I believe that the value, worth, or merit of experiences is important to individuals, indeed that all judgments are inherently evaluative. I have a hierarchy of preferences in the arts, faith in certain canons of judgment in the artistic realm. In speaking about artists, I will mention many, and offer some as examples of outstanding creative individuals. They will epitomize the end state toward which I see the young artist heading, just as other persons will be cited as developed critics, performers, audience members, or scientists. That the reader share all my preferences is unlikely, and in any case unnecessary; but I ask that he at least allow the possibility that some works and some artists are to be valued over others. Development can only be elucidated if some sort of end state is posited; that end state need not be fully delineated, but its general legitimacy and contours must be recognized. Thus there is a sense in which it is necessary to speak of a *developed* artist or critic, just as one would speak of a developed scientist or businessman, not to denigrate other individuals (including children), but to describe an ideal-type or end state toward which development proceeds. The specific individuals cited are examples only; the aim is to define what an artist can do, not to legislate aesthetic merit. The testimony of those actively involved in the arts will often be drawn on; I believe that their words can frequently teach the psychologist and the aesthetician about the kinds of skills, percepts, feelings, and products characteristic of greater or lesser development.

My investigation of the artistic realm has centered on a number of questions and problems that will be treated at various points in the book. What is the nature of the artistic process? Which individuals and objects participate in it and in what manner? What skills are necessary for participation in the artistic process? What is the relationship between child art and adult art, prodigy and master, the personality of the artist and his product? Why are artists so often thought of as being childlike? At what time does the child first engage in aesthetic situations? In what ways are various art forms related? Which aspects of the arts appeal to all individuals and which exercise specific appeal for certain individuals? What is the most useful way to conceptualize such artistic factors as style, tradition, content, and form? What is the difference between "direct experience" and the use of artistic symbols? Why do creativity and even the ability to appreciate aesthetic objects so often decline at certain points in the life cycle? What motivates an individual to choose the arts as his calling? What importance does logical thought assume in the development of various individuals? What is the nature and source of the qualities conveyed in an artistic object? How are the arts and sciences related? The answers to many of these questions remain partial at best, but before they can be properly confronted, my conception of the artistic process should be outlined.

THE ARTISTIC PROCESS

The process culminating in artistic production and comprehension involves up to four roles or modes of participation and a work of art. The *work* may be a concrete object or it may be a performance prescribed by some sort of notation: paintings, sculptures, symphonies, poems, and the dance are all works of one sort or another. The four prototypical participants in the artistic process have been mentioned above; let us now examine their roles in somewhat greater detail.

The creator or *artist* is an individual who has gained sufficient skill in the use of a medium to be able to communicate through the creation of a symbolic object. A poet, for example, may undergo a deeply moving experience, which he seeks to communicate to others through an effective arrangement of words, images, and themes. Likely as not, he will spurn a straight description of what has happened, searching instead for an allegory, character, or pivotal symbol that can evoke the range of mood he seeks to convey. And he will become immersed in the arduous task of selecting and combining words, phrases, and figures of speech suitable to the ideas and tones he wants to convey. Although many others may have shared the poet's moving experience, only one practiced in choosing words, achieving certain moods and rhythms, capturing the highlights of a situation, or creating appropriate tropes will be able to fashion a work that has the sought-for effect upon others. His essential assignment, like that of the composer, sculptor, or painter, is to draw upon his arsenal of creative skills and to make a work of art.

The *audience member* is one whose feeling life is affected when he encounters a work of art. To qualify as an audience member he must undergo affective changes but, unlike the artist, he need not share this experienced affect with others. His principal aim is to follow (or "read") the symbolic communication so that he can be moved in some way, experiencing feelings of pleasure, openness, balance, renewal, penetration, or pathos. Knowledge of the background of the work, sensitivity to nuances and layers of meaning, awareness of alternative styles or performances may enrich his range of feelings; but even a partial grasp of the intent or import of the work can suffice to alter his phenomenal experience in a desired way. Thus the individual who attends a concert has fulfilled the role of audience member when he undergoes a range of affect or feeling (preferably but not necessarily feelings that are pleasurable, stimulating, or otherwise moving). However, whether a concertgoer, gallery visitor, television viewer, or armchair reader, he must appreciate that the work in question has been created by another individual and functions as a communicative symbol, differing in these ways from a naturally occurring event or object.

While any audience member affected by a work of art has fulfilled his role, the connoisseur or *critic* must communicate his reactions and evaluations to other individuals. His task is to make discriminations concerning the works he is contemplating, and, more generally, concerning the art forms in which he is expert. He may be aided in this task by his subjective reactions and his prior knowledge, but these are secondary to his capacity to perceive essential features of the work and the symbolic media under consideration. The critic attending an art show must examine each work carefully; monitor his own reactions and evaluations; assess the painter's technical capacity, conviction, authority, use of color, shape, and form, choice and execution of subject matter. In addition he may relate the works to those of the artist's predecessors and contemporaries, trace the artist's development, and assess the overall originality and importance of the painter's *oeuvre*. But his most important quality is his capacity to discern features and distinctions that might be missed by casual viewers and to convey his insights to others in a logical and unambiguous form. Alone among the participants in the artistic process he must be able to reason in propositional form and express himself in logical language about the realm of the arts.

The final participant in the artistic process, the *performer,* is an individual who transmits a work created by an artist to a larger audience. The roles of creator and performer were once usually combined, but now the performer generally masters the work either through reading the artist's prescriptions or notations, or through intensive study of another's performance. The performer, whether dancer, actor, or musician, must have awareness of the multitudinous ways in which the performance could be carried out, and sensitivity to audience reaction; otherwise he risks giving a stereotyped performance and lacking rapport with those witnessing his performance. He may be aided in his task by subjective reactions to works, by knowledge of the tradition, or by skill in the creation of symbols; but these skills, of primary importance to other participants in the artistic process, come to nought unless the performer can perceive the surface features *and* the underlying themes of the work of art, communicate its essential contours faithfully to the audience, and stimulate the affective potentials of those attending his performance.

For heuristic purposes, the four prototypical participants in the artistic process may be placed around a circle representing the artistic work (Figure 1). In forms like music or drama, the artistic process involves the relationship between these four individuals, as they center about the performance of a work. The creator originally conceives the art work by drawing on his knowledge of the medium and the tradition, as

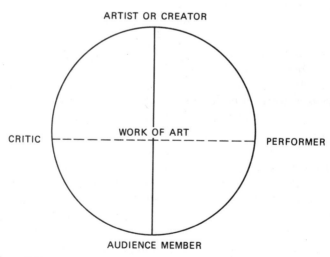

FIGURE 1.   The artistic process.

well as on his own ideas, skills and feelings. He may either realize the work himself, or, if it is a musical composition or drama, he may simply write down indications sufficient to permit performance. The performer reads the notation or follows the instructions drawn up by the creator (unless performer and creator are the same individual). His task is to realize the art work according to the creator's prescriptions, though he will be allowed a certain latitude in interpretation.

Neither creator nor performer can continue to function without an audience, a group of individuals or a single individual who will behold the art work, seek to comprehend it, and in all likelihood have some sort of affective reaction to it. While the audience is essential, the critic (like the performer) may only be present at certain times: His function is to describe, discuss, and/or evaluate the work or the performance and then convey his impressions or evaluations to a public. A piece of criticism may at times be an artistic work, and an artistic work may at times be an effort at criticism. As for the critic and audience, an important distinction is suggested by Arnheim's decree: "The business of the consumer is to consume, that is, to enlighten and enrich his life through seeing and hearing, not to dissect the formal means by which such enlightenment and enrichment is accomplished."

The location of persons about the aesthetic circle illuminates the relationship between the participants. The audience and the creator are positioned opposite one another, for, as the quintessential components of the artistic process, they have complementary functions. The creator should anticipate facets of the audience's reactions and the audience should be cognizant of a creator who seeks to communicate symbolic messages; nonetheless, the audience member and the creator need not possess the same skills and may have little empathy for one another's roles. The line between audience member and critic is much finer, however; nearly every audience member is to some extent a critic, and every critic likely undergoes some of the affective experiences of the audience member. In particular, the informed audience member sensitive to the multiplicity of meaning and the subtle nuances of works blends the roles of audience and critic. Similarly, if there is to be a performer, he requires a powerful sense of his audience in order to communicate the work satisfactorily.

Though less fundamental to the artistic process, critic and performer are also natural antagonists and often have complementary sets of skills. The critic must be able to step back from the work, contemplate it in a disinterested manner, and weigh it in relation to other works and alternative possibilities; above all, he speaks his mind. The performer may feel the need to immerse himself totally in the work, and find his behavior cramped by excessive critical consideration of the work; he suppresses his own views, in order to communicate the ideas of another. Furthermore, the critic seeks to lay bare what lies beneath the surface of the work, while the performer must concentrate finally on presenting surface manifestations. If the critic misses the underlying "point," or if the performer is too intent upon communicating it, both may fail in their roles.

There is, however, a certain kinship between creator and critic, since the creator must be able to adopt the critic's stance while his own work is in process, and the critic has, in most cases, done some creative work in the specific area and may even be an accomplished or frustrated artist. Furthermore, the elements of creativity in an effective piece of criticism may engender in the critic a certain empathy for the role of creator. Nonetheless, criticism differs from creation in that criticism presupposes an art object, while creation involves the manipulation of a symbol system in order to create a new art object.

The description of the four participants in the aesthetic circle is a convenient fiction, of course. Roles frequently collapse or combine in actuality, and some art forms highlight or eliminate one or more roles. Furthermore, this formulation is strongly colored by the Western arts and by the art of the past century. Were one describing preliterate art, or "postliterate" happenings, one would emphasize the merging of performer and creator, or of audience and performer, or the irrelevance of the critic. (Indeed, the history of the drama might be traced in terms of alterations in the dominance of respective loci on the artistic circle.) My purpose in describing an aesthetic circle, then, is not to characterize accurately any particular artistic form or era. Rather I want to suggest *separable psychological functions and skills* which develop in distinctive ways and are distributed in different proportions throughout the population. And I want to emphasize the interdependence of the various participants involved in the communication of artistic symbols. In speaking of development toward this quartet of end states, I suggest that all normal individuals realize in a fragmentary way aspects of each of these roles, that individuals differ markedly in the extent to which one role is highlighted relative to other roles, and that the range of end states involved in the artistic process represents a terminus toward which all development tends. My aim is to describe artistic development, not to prescribe norms, but I will indicate which traits characterize fuller realization of the several artistic roles.

As the artistic process involves persons with distinct skills and backgrounds, it is necessary to indicate the role under discussion at any given time. From now on, unless otherwise specified, I will be referring to the development of the artist or creator. Other roles will be defined in relation to the artist. Art objects may also be of several types depending on the art form, and I will usually specify the form of art to which reference is intended. In addition, art assumes various forms in diverse cultures, and much of our characterization is particularly applicable to Western society. At the most general level, however, I find it valid to refer to the arts, the artistic process, Art. *Every art form involves communication on the part of one person (or subject) to another by means of a symbolic object that the first subject has created, and that the second is able in some way to understand, react to, or appreciate.* This definition may seem to encompass almost everything ever charged with being an art form, from cooking to chess, if not proving theorems or making love. I do not want unduly to limit the notion of the arts, for I have argued that art can be used to elucidate all human development; yet none of the four items just mentioned conforms exactly to my notion of the arts. An attempt to explain why, by listing some of the symptoms or characteristics of the arts, may clarify the definition just introduced and provide a fuller description of the realm of activities I consider aesthetic. For the most part, I shall be contrasting the arts with the sciences, not because these fields are polar opposites, but because they are roughly equivalent in scope, and because scientific skills will be more familiar to many readers.

CHARACTERISTICS OF THE ARTS

Aestheticians have long struggled to provide a satisfactory definition of art, and many have despaired of so doing. Some analytic philosophers have even sought to demonstrate the futility of formulating a satisfactory definition. On strictly logical grounds, these philosophers may have the day—yet psychology can often be suggestive even when it does not unerringly reflect distinctions made by logicians. Accordingly, I shall exploit my lack of philosophical standing and list those criteria which are most diagnostic of a process occurring in normal individuals. This process could be termed "communication of subjective knowledge," but I shall call it *art*.

Communication

The aesthetic involves an attempt to communicate. It is deliberate, intentional. The artist fashions something that would have an effect on someone else. Because the arts involve communication between subjects, human beings must be involved in the artistic process. A view of nature should not be regarded as artistic, though a representation of it may be; nor are a squirrel's scratchings on ground or paper aesthetic, for there is no apparent intention to communicate. (They may be treated as if created by a person, but that is another matter.) On the other hand, a child's early efforts with a pencil or brush, or the dribblings of an action painter may be aesthetic, as these activities typically involve a desire on the part of one subject to communicate some sort of knowledge or understanding to another: "The artist, poet and—in a different way— some scientists . . . have the avocation and the skill to communicate some aspects of what they perceive, beyond the realm of the already familiar, to those who are willing and able to listen to, or look at their communication."

Deliberate communication is emphasized in this formulation because the mature person typically brings a different attitude to a sign that he believes has been intentionally emitted. My reaction to water dripping in the gutter depends on whether I think it is rain dropping, a mechanical failure, a chance happening, or a deliberate attempt to tease me. A randomly produced pattern may be deemed beautiful but it will not function as an aesthetic object unless a communicative impulse has stimulated it. However, all this does not imply that artistic perception depends on determining precisely what it is that the creator attempted to communicate; the work of art will contain numerous implications and it is the perceiver's role to draw out these meanings, irrespective of which were intended by the artist. Nor does it attempt to rule out art as self-expression, though, as a practical matter, I believe all protracted artistic activity is intended, at least implicitly, as communication to other persons.

The invoking of "intentionality" or "communication" potentially raises a vein of philosophical objection I cannot hope to meet. Nonetheless, I hope to demonstrate in the ensuing chapters that a child's behavior, unlike that of most animals, comes increasingly to be permeated by a desire to express discriminations, feelings, and beliefs through a symbolic medium. This demonstration may bear on the "intentional" aspects of the artistic process.

Translatability

An aesthetic object tends to be nontranslatable. As a presentational symbol, an integrated whole without dissociable elements, a work of art is not readily rendered in another symbol system. To be sure, some tales or tunes can be changed somewhat and remain effective, but the changes can only be made by a skilled hand, and so require fresh artistic activity. Altering a picture without destroying its character is highly problematic because of the autographic nature of the medium, and a poem is generally tinkered with or translated at its peril. In general, a scientific product stresses the conceptualization of relevant factors. Once conceptualized, these may be executed or embodied in a variety of equivalent media. But aesthetic messages inhere in the specific medium (sound, plaster) in which they have been realized, and no ready translation across media can be undertaken. Never can translation of an aesthetic work be totally mechanical; rather, the translator must recreate the work, and in so doing may devise an entirely different work.

Unlike paints and tones, words are used by scientists as well as by those engaged in the arts. The contrast between scientific and artistic language is thus of some interest. Although they often favor expression in a mathematical formula or model, scientists can convey their findings in several ways. The constituents of water can be described in numerous linguistic ways or presented in two- or in three-dimensional models, or expressed by formulas such as

$$2 H_2 + O_2 \longrightarrow 2 H_2O.$$

In such cases, the symbols are mere conventions, denoting the elements rather than exemplifying them. The chemical symbols or the words serve to describe a physical process, and the sounds made in articulating them are irrelevant. In contrast, words used by the creative writer are meant to be heard, as they frequently epitomize or exemplify the qualities at hand:

> 'Tis not enough no harshness gives offence,
> The sound must seem an echo to the sense:
> Soft is the strain when Zephyr gently blows,
> And the smooth stream in smoother number flows;
> But when loud surges lash the sounding shore,
> The hoarse, rough verse should like the torrent roar.

And, even if no onomatopoeic effect is intended, various rhythms or tensions, important to the work's effect, may be built up in (and restricted to) the medium of sound.

Textbooks are possible in the sciences because there is a body of information and principles to be conveyed, and the wording in which information is conveyed is flexible, so long as logical connections and relevant factors are preserved. In sharp contrast, trots or textbooks on eighteenth century literature bear no such relationship to the literary works with which they are concerned. As Sapir points out, "one can adequately translate scientific literature because the original scientific expression is itself a translation. Literary expression is personal and concrete . . . it would be absurd to ignore the distinctive qualities of a particular author, or, indeed, of a particular tongue." Science builds up over the years because certain principles are assimilated by the contemporary scientist who makes further discoveries and then revises the principles accordingly. Arts are not cumulative in the same way: Old works, though they may be forgotten, are not superseded; there is no specified meaning that every audience member is expected to attain. Rather, illusion and allusion are important, with audience members returning repeatedly to the same work either for enjoyment or for more complete appreciation. In nonartistic communication, allusions can be quite misleading, and considerable effort may be exerted to exorcise those ambiguities or multiplicities of meanings that are the very life-blood of the arts.

Closely related to translatability is the fact that art forms tend to be presented in a sensory medium, that is, couched in a mode that appeals directly and powerfully to the sense organs. Paintings with their colors, words and music with their sounds contain elements toward which organisms will orient, even before their significance is realized, and which may be found exciting, irritating, soothing, or dramatic. Indeed, the sense organs become the final arbiters of the success with which a quality is conveyed. If one cannot or ordinarily does not orient toward an element, it appears deficient in aesthetic potential:

All art appeals primarily to the senses and the artistic aim when expressing itself in written words must also make its appeal through the senses. . . . My task which I am trying to achieve is, by the power of the written word to make you hear, to make you feel, it is, before all, to make you see. That and no more, and it is everything.

As Conrad suggests, a work of literature, though it may be read silently by an audience member, fails in its effect if it does not arouse sensory images. To be sure, the marks uninterestingly scattered across the page have no more sensuous content than the ciphers in a mathematical formula. Rather, literature seems to stem from art forms that do make strong appeals to the senses: oral storytelling and dramatic art. Perhaps, for a literary work to exercise aesthetic effect, readers must hear the story being told, with accents, pauses, tropes, rhythms, phrasing, or their minds must form dramatic images of characters and situations. Reading a literary work may be analogous to reading a musical score—both can be treated simply as notations, or as aids to the creation (by the reader) of a performing art form having sensuous appeal. Once one is *within* the art work, the play of ideas, themes, forms, and other nonsensory elements will contribute substantially to the artistic appeal of the work. It is in the lack of immediate sensory appeal, and not in the elegance or subtlety of its conception, that a mathematical formula departs from the characteristics of the arts.

In comparing a literary work and a scientific text, attention can again be called to the *litterateur's* greater concern with the manner in which his message is communicated. To the extent that a text is written with an eye toward style, like William James's classic, *Principles of Psychology*, its author is poaching upon the artist's territory. The literary work, with its appeal to the senses, resists reworking or translation, while the textbook strives toward the lingua franca of science—mathematical formulation—and invites further translation. Most novels have an appealing or arresting sound when read, for the words have been chosen so as to sound pleasing even to those of a different culture. Novels thus excite the auditory imagination:

> The feeling for syllable and rhythm, penetrating far below the conscious levels of thought and feeling, invigorating every word: sinking to the most primitive and forgotten, returning to the origin and bringing something back, seeking the beginning and the end. It works through meaning, certainly, and not without meanings in the ordinary sense, fuses the old and obliterated and the trite, the current and the new and surprising, the most ancient and the most civilized mentality.

Subjects, Objects, Distance

Beyond their different presentations, the arts and sciences also exhibit contrasting goals. Scientists strive toward an explanation of the world, the building up of models that can describe and account for natural occurrences. Artists seek to recreate, comment on, or react against aspects of the world or facets of subjective experience, vivifying them for an audience rather than reducing them to fundamentals. Aspects of life that appear inexplicable or ineffable to scientists dominate the aesthetic realm. Consistent with this difference in emphasis, the arts tend to be concerned more with the feelings and thoughts of individuals than with the world of objects, while science has been more notably preoccupied and successful with the latter domain. To be sure, the social sciences seek to produce models of human life; this they do largely by treating human subjects as objectively as possible. In the arts, however, an attempt is made to communicate the subjective aspects of life by the creation of an object that captures these subjective factors. Indeed Tolstoy defined art as "a human activity consisting in this, that one may consciously by means of certain external signs, hand on to others feelings he has lived through and that others are infected by these feelings and also experience them."

The creation of an object in symbolic form is an important component of the arts; unmediated interactions between individuals rarely qualify as artistic. What is lacking in a conversation, wrestling match, or embrace is the possibility of *distance between subjects* raised by the creation of a "third" object. To the extent that subjects are totally involved with one another (making love rather than dancing a ballet) or with an object (devouring rather than viewing), they cannot attain that delicate combination of distance and involvement, of detachment from with appreciation of an object's qualities which appears to be characteristic of an aesthetic attitude.

In some art forms, to be sure, the individual himself becomes an object. One example is a theatrical performance, yet in that case the existence of a script usually provides an additional dimension. The mime or the modern dancer does become totally merged with the aesthetic object, but under such circumstances the relationship between the performing and viewing subjects may still legitimately be considered an aesthetic one. This is because there is the potential for a notated performance (and hence, a separate object), and more importantly because of the audience's awareness of the theatrical (performed) nature of the presentation. It does not however seem useful to term as aesthetic the ordinary behavior of an individual who is in control of his appearance or who is attempting to achieve an effect. The special conditions necessary to creation in the artistic process should not be confused with the attempts on the part of a histrionic individual to "put on" or to "put something over on" others. If, however, all present are equally aware that someone is "performing," one might allow that a performance is underway. Inability to separate an artistic performance from a genuine interaction signifies an incomplete aesthetic attitude on the part of an audience member, epitomized by the rustic who leaps upon the stage to save the endangered heroine. Metaphors of the drama might be useful for some descriptions of human action and interaction, but the difference between a performance that ends at a previously determined moment and an interaction in daily life, with its ineluctable long-range implications, seems beyond argument. Indeed the arts are a pregnant area for developmental analysis precisely because they lie in the middle ground between mundane experience, from which it is difficult to maintain one's distance, and scientific practice, which generally avoids subjective qualities.

The distinction between the world of persons and objects has received little attention in the psychological literature. Yet even cursory observation suggests that individuals think about and behave quite differently toward other individuals than they do toward material objects or even representations of humans. As Norbert Wiener once quipped: "To human beings, human things are all important." This theme is relevant because artists seek to capture in symbols insights about (subjective) life, feeling, and experiences. An appreciation of these presentations is dependent upon the abilities to distinguish persons from material objects, to react to the qualities of each, and to appreciate that aspects of persons can be captured in symbolic objects. Sensitivity to the subjective qualities captured in objects is also necessary if the audience member is to react appropriately to the symbolic work.

The artist, for his part, seeks to place the tools of his medium "into direct contact with all that is felt, seen, thought, experienced, imagined." Crucial to the effectiveness of the work is its capturing of meaningful dimensions of subjective experience: insights about love, tragedy, pride, and aspects of the forms, balances, contrasts, or rhythms characterizing feelings within the human experience. To participate fully in the artistic process, one must be able to embody within an aesthetic object *significant* knowledge or understanding of one's own life, and to discern such knowledge when confronted by such an object.

Summary

We have suggested that the arts involve a communication of subjective knowledge between individuals through the creation of nontranslatable sensuous objects; one may vary one's distance from and involvement with these objects while contemplating the various messages embedded in them. Even though the characteristics described can obviously not be maintained rigidly, the effort to distinguish the arts from play, from science, from "life," may facilitate understanding of the terms "aesthetic development" and the "artistic process."

This view of the arts, in its combination of subjective and objective factors, tends to transcend the distinction between affect and cognition, between feelings and thought. Certainly the arts are apprehended by the intellect, but just as assuredly they marshal affective responses and are concerned with the quality of feeling. Indeed, the differences in human reaction to persons and objects suggest that the quality of affect depends on the kind of object perceived, and its relationship to other persons or objects. Without expecting to eliminate entirely the venerable affect-cognition dichotomy, I have devised a framework that may more

adequately demonstrate the way in which individuals become involved
in the arts.

THE THREE SYSTEMS

Discussion of development can be facilitated I believe, by positing three
systems in the organism which have an independent existence at birth
and which are found throughout animal life. These systems may be
termed *making, perceiving,* and *feeling.* The outputs of the making
system are *acts* or *actions;* the products of the perceiving system are
discriminations or *distinctions;* the results of the feeling system are
affects. More generally, basic units of the three systems can be called
behavioral patterns or *schemes.* The making system concerns the schemes
the organism is capable of performing; the perceiving system concerns
the aspects of the environment to which the organism is sensitive; the
feeling system concerns the organism's phenomenal or subject experience. I can offer no precise, operational definition of actions, discriminations, or affects; the reader is directed to note how the terms are used,
and to employ his intuitions as he does when encountering *stimuli,
responses, operations* or other such building blocks of psychological
theories.

The general approach adopted with reference to the three systems
might be considered phenomenological, though in invoking this label I
wish to indict neither myself nor the phenomenologists. Put differently,
my approach aims to be consistent with common sense and with psychological findings. An affect is, following Langer, anything that the organism feels (which presumably means that it undergoes a discernible
change of state to greater or lesser pleasure, openness, excitement, etc.).
An action is any motion on the part of the organism that is potentially
observable; thus random finger tapping and stomach peristalsis as well
as walking or hammering a nail qualify as actions. (Purely reflexive
actions may be termed *movements* or *motions* to distinguish them from
"intentional" actions.) Discriminations involve all distinctions made by
the subject, either with respect to aspects of the outside world (differentiation among colors, shapes) or his own thought processes (formation
of classes, ideas, fantasies). Perceiving may involve affects, or result
from actions, but neither subjectively experienced feelings nor objectively determinable acts are essential for a discrimination to occur. I may
note that a book is blue or that today is Saturday; electrophysiological
measures may reveal that stimuli presented subliminally have been

perceived. If I experience no phenomenal feelings or change of affect, then my feeling system has not and cannot have been mobilized. If I have not done any action or making (except for the inevitable acts of opening my eyes, breathing, or recording stimuli via neuronal connections), then my making system has also remained at rest. But as soon as I have made any sort of distinction of which I am at some level cognizant, *or* which an investigator can unambiguously specify, my perceptual system has been utilized.

A perceiving system which first attends to the broad, salient properties of the environment and eventually becomes tuned to very fine distinctions, internal as well as external, and a making system which begins with reflexes and gross motor movement and eventually culminates in complex schemes and skilled behavior will be familiar to many, and will be elaborated further in the discussions of the developing systems in infants and animals. A few words of clarification about the feeling system seem in order, however. As used here, it is not possible for an *observer* to determine unequivocally whether an organism is experiencing *affects*. Actions and discriminations can be observed or tested for, and both may exist irrespective of the individual's consciousness. Affects however either exist or do not exist, depending solely on whether the individual has internal "felt" experience, a subjectively experienced change of well-being, comfort, or tension. To be sure, certain behavioral clues may be of use: One assumes an affective state of well-being accompanies a smile, pain or distress a cry. But these affects are not necessary concomitants of these actions. In what follows I will use the terms *affect, feeling,* and *emotion* interchangeably, to refer to any subjective experiences, generalized or highly specific, felt by an individual. The sometimes misleading but usually reliable and unpretentious vocabulary of daily life will suffice for naming these affective states until a new terminology—modes and vectors—is introduced in Chapter 3.

While the status of the perceiving and making systems is relatively secure in psychological analysis, paralleling closely the accepted notions of sensory and motor capacities, the need for positing an autonomous feeling system is not widely conceded. Undoubtedly the difficulty of talking meaningfully about affects, feelings, and emotions contributes to the distaste many analysts display toward such terminology. Furthermore, the difficulty of determining affect (physiological measures thus far proving inconstant guides) cautions against its uncritical use. Yet any discussion of the arts would be unthinkable without a recognition that individuals are deeply affected by artistic works, undergoing powerful feelings during both perceptual and productive activity. If one agrees that "the starting point for all aesthetics must be the personal experience of a peculiar emotion," the need to include feeling in discussions of art and of human development should become compelling. Indeed, with feeling invoked both as the stimulus for an aesthetic work ("Ecstasy affords the occasion and experience determines the form") and as its principal consequence, a psychology of the arts that avoids "feeling" becomes indefensible. Although my steps in this uncharted area may to some extent be uncertain, I am convinced that the effort to incorporate a person's phenomenal experience in a description of his behavior represents a step toward holistic presentation of the individual. Accordingly, in describing psychological development, I will touch on an individual's presumed affective states—his range of feelings—and note how these are influenced by and in turn exert influence upon his acts and discriminations. The concepts of modes and vectors will help explain the child's most primitive feeling states—affects of openness, fullness, introjection, penetration, etc.—and will also provide an explanatory framework for those experiences most relevant to aesthetic perception—feelings of balance (or unbalance), harmony, rhythm, and formal elegance.

The grossness and artificiality of these systems will be manifest because, in the adult organism, these systems and their respective "schemes" occur simultaneously and continually, and may better be conceptualized as portions of one integrated system. All the same, it is revealing to speak of the three systems. The immature organism seems to be equipped with discrete structured wholes or systems, which are programmed at specific rates, which go off independently or even interfere with each other, and which only gradually come to interact smoothly with one another. Schemes of action, affect, and discrimination in young organisms each seem to have a course of their own: the infant undergoes changes of feeling, makes assorted discriminations, and exhibits clumsy and skilled actions, without these initially interacting with one another. The situation is even more acute in lower organisms, where an animal may slowly torture himself or starve to death because of an incapacity to fuse information from his disparate systems; thus a frog will keep pursuing a fly even though his tongue gets impaled on a sharp stake in the process.

Development can be seen as a process wherein the three initially discrete systems gradually begin to influence each other, with interaction eventually becoming so dominant that each system inevitably involves the other ones. The rules whereby each of these systems independently evolves and comes to interact with others are open to study. The succeeding chapters will contain numerous illustrations of how the systems interact with, guide, or interfere with one another at all levels of animal and human life. Though it is but a distant prospect at present, I hope to be able to find physiological and neurological evidence that will support the positing of distinct developing systems and illustrate how the separate systems come slowly to mesh and to function afresh on the planes of symbols. Indeed, it is the physiological evidence in support of anatomically distinct systems that occasionally enboldens me to reify these systems.

The positing of three systems runs counter to much current psychological theorizing, in which the young organism is viewed as an undifferentiated whole, a blooming, buzzing confusion, which only gradually evolves into separate, hierarchically integrated parts. It may well be that, from the point of view of the organism, there is little differentiation at the beginning, and a gradual trend toward increasing differentiation and integration. Furthermore, it may be pointed out that, even in a simple reaction like the tonic-neck reflex, there is an inevitable fusion of perception, making, and feeling. Why, in view of these countertheories, should development be viewed as a gradual integration of three separate systems?

The following considerations seem relevant. A psychological theory should, in my view, be directed toward elucidating situations where the person's biological endowment is affected by his experiences in the environment, his learning, training, and cultural milieu. From this perspective the organism's behavior and reflexes at birth are of less interest than actions and perceptions formed in relation to his environment. When these occasions are studied, it appears that the child has various predispositions to handle stimuli in a certain way, but that only gradually are these predispositions modified by the environment and related to other predispositions. For instance in making contact with an object, the child is predisposed to issue certain actions toward it, to perceive certain distinctions within it, and to receive certain feelings from these experiences. At first, however, none of these dispositions is integrated with any of the others. What is perceived does not alter what is made or felt. In the course of psychological development the initial independence of these behaviors gives way to piecemeal connections and interactions among them, as the child undergoes neurological and muscular maturation, as he assimilates new experiences, and as he structures the relationship among these experiences. Within each of the systems there is continual differentiation, and between the systems there is increasing interaction and integration. The moments of greatest psychological progress come when two hitherto separate systems or subsystems combine into a more integrated and flexible whole, be they the union of perception and making in the child's first successful graspings, or the fusion of perception, feeling, and action in the painter's capture in a symbolic object of a mood or expression.

Although there may eventually be physiological evidence for the initial independence and eventual integration of the system (as there is for the positing of discrete visual or language systems), such "physical underpinning" is not germane to my argument. By using the term *system,* I want only to suggest a psychological organization with a certain coherence, as well as a consistent set of operations and developmental patterns. The terms *structure, unit,* or *mechanism* could be substituted. In psychological terms it makes sense to speak of systems, only when there is some range of choice (conscious or not) available to the organism, or conceivable alternate patterns of behavioral development. Thus the discussion of systems and system interactions is restricted to those points at which a different set of experiences could have led to an alternative organization. It avoids treatment of behaviors (such as infant reflexes or strong drive states) in which behavior is predetermined in all significant aspects by species membership.

Even though the developing systems eventually sacrifice much of their autonomy, it seems that individuals become involved in occupations or pursuits that highlight or draw most prominently on one or another of the systems. The critic is expected to excel in discrimination and perceiving, in discerning similarities, patterns, contrasts. The audience member is expected to feel, to enjoy, to be inspired, or to become disturbed. The performer or creator is characterized by making, acting, and exhibiting practiced skills. These distinctions are of course rough: The most skilled executants of any of these roles are characterized by high development in them all. The relative importance of the systems may nevertheless remain in approximately the same proportion. And it is interesting to note that both common and philosophical language support these distinctions. John Dewey speaks of "doing" and "perceiving" as central in the arts. The historian Janson notes that only in the sixteenth century did people begin to speak of painters and sculptors as "creators"; until then they had simply been "makers." Thomas Mann characterizes his own pursuits: "An author is a man essentially not bent upon knowing, distinguishing, and analyzing: he stands for simple creation, for doing or making."

I will speak of three developing systems, then, because they are consistent with what artists and aestheticians have maintained; because they seem compatible with gross neuroanatomical regions; because their operation, evolution, and interaction seem guided by certain principles; and, above all, because they prove useful in describing development toward a range of artistic end states and in explicating the mastery of skills during the formative years. The making system of the artist, the perceiving system of the critic, and the feeling system of the audience member will concern us, even as the confluence of these systems within each of these individuals will come under scrutiny.

In all but the highest primates, early behavioral and subsequent development is adequately described by accounts of the evolution of each of these systems and the eventual interaction and reciprocal influences among them. Even the complex communications systems of bees and birds seem reasonably accounted for in terms of actions on the part of one organism and a programmed discrimination and action on the part of another. Indeed, nearly all animal development can be described in terms of nonmediated interaction with the world of objects and organisms. But in considering human communication, it seems clear that there is a great latitude in what the individual choses to communicate, with species programming of messages hardly an adequate explanation. Humans become characterized, increasingly, by their abilities to employ new, nonbodily media, such as tools, paints, words, and various symbol systems, in order to transmit knowledge. These messages can deal with any number and combination of topics, with what the organism has felt, discriminated, believed, made. Peculiarly human is the ability to devise more or less arbitrary symbol systems on which an individual can draw to convey such information, confident that another individual can learn to extract roughly the same sort of information from the message. To elucidate human behavior one must describe a level of development subsequent to the maturing and interaction of the three systems, a level in which the three systems have become involved with symbols, and recapitulate their earlier evolution on this new plane. This development commences in the years following infancy and may continue throughout the individual's life.

Until this point I have spoken of the arts as if they were one, a viewpoint justifiable only for certain purposes. To be sure, there are no clear-cut distinctions among art forms, with music leading into dance, pantomime into drama, prose into poetry. There are even attempts to combine poetry with painting, and of course hybrid forms like ballet and opera have long been accepted. Ways of discriminating among the arts do however exist, and these will now be introduced and defined. Similarly, there has evolved a language for dealing with the particular features of art works; this will also be drawn upon below. This terminology has been presented in a separate section so that the reader may return to it as required.

A BRIEF GLOSSARY

In speaking about the arts I include all those forms mentioned above; but examples will be drawn chiefly from painting, music, and literature, as these fields are familiar and representative. Certain differences among them should now be mentioned. Some art forms, such as painting and sculpture, can be termed *autographic* in that the artist acts upon the same physical material that will be subsequently perceived by the audience member. Others are *allographic,* in that the artist makes selections from a code that already exists in the language (the writer from natural language, the traditional Western composer from the diatonic system). These selections can be captured in a notation, so that the (necessarily) autographic character of the original creation is immaterial. Autographic and allographic art forms differ in the amount and kind of information about the artist that can be gleaned from a contemplation of his work. Beethoven's untidiness comes across in his sketchbooks, but not necessarily in the performance of his works. As Ned Rorem has pointed out, "admittedly the musical language is more symbolic than others . . . logicians cannot yet decipher a composer's secret and expose him like Goya or Martha Graham, for indecent motives."

Autographic and allographic forms also differ in the kinds of compositional techniques that are feasible and preferable. Thus, while revision of a word in a poem requires only an erasure, revision of a detail in a sculpture may require reworking of the entire block. Finally, allographic arts frequently require an interpreter or performer, while autographic arts must speak for themselves. Despite such differences, the style of the artist achieves distinctiveness in both autographic and allographic art forms, each of which allows ample opportunity for communication of subtle nuances about the world and the creator.

Through a quirk of language, art objects are spoken of as *symbols,* even as their constituent elements are also called symbols. What is meant here is that paintings, poems, novels, dances, and so forth, whatever their intrinsic interest and appeal, possess the potential of reference to the external world, to the world of subjective experience, and even to themselves. As Nelson Goodman has pointed out, a painting can, when functioning as a symbol, denote a man, express sadness, and exemplify grayness. The capacity to create and to appreciate symbols in a *medium* (such as sound or gesture) or in an *art form* (such as dance or music) is regarded here as the major prerequisite for artistic development, one which may be restricted to human beings.

Even as entire works are symbols, they are created out of elements which in themselves often entail symbolic references. Words, tones, lines, colors, and forms acquire shades of meaning in the course of an individual's experiences; when incorporated in an artistic object, these symbolic overtones play a determining role in adding to (or detracting from) the work's effect. The art forms we are concerned with here will generally draw on sets of symbols which may have traditional referents, and which may also have a characteristic syntax among them. We shall speak of the arts as involving symbol systems (such as natural language, diatonic music, folk dance, etc.), and concern ourselves with the way in which children become able to draw upon these systems in the creation and perception of artistic works.

The compartmentalization of an art work into components should be avoided whenever possible. For example, while it may be appropriate to define the subject matter of a newspaper report or a scientific article, it is much less legitimate to identify the subject matter of a Melville novel or a Chagall painting, let alone an Eliot poem or a Stravinsky chorale. Nonetheless, at least a rough terminology seems required for analytical purposes. I find it useful to distinguish between the *subject matter* (the aspect of the external world referred to, if any), the *content* (the embodiment of the subject matter within the work), the *style* (the characteristic traces left by an artist upon his work and works), and the *form* (the most general properties of the work, which result from the manner in which the medium or art form is employed).

My notions about *form* deserves a brief comment. This term refers to the balance (or lack of balance), the internal rhythm, the relationship of parts to one another, the location of peaks, points of change, continuities, and contrasts within a work. Whereas each art form (such as painting or poetry or music) may lend itself to certain subject matters and contents, the range of art forms includes a common set of *formal properties*. The vocabulary of form may refer equally to a motet, a sonnet, or a portrait. I will argue that children frequently capture in their own creations the formal aspects of the arts (though they may fail to appreciate them in the works of others). Indeed, there is a valid sense in which the child aged 5 to 7 may be regarded as an artist, with his subsequent development largely a heightening of technical skill and greater familiarity with subject matter and tradition. It is in his ability to realize various formal and modal-vectoral properties that the young artist is most impressive.

COGNITION, ANIMALS, AND THE ARTISTIC PROCESS

The claim that young children are, in a sense, artists, is a bold one, to which much of the remainder of the book is directed. Many developmental psychologists may recoil at this idea, for they will have been impressed by the lengthy period of "cognitive development," the series of stages described by Piaget in which the child becomes able to perform various mental operations and, eventually, to reason in propositional form. Yet such cognitive development, vital though it be to the future Western scientist, does not seem of special moment in the development of the creator, performer, or audience member. What must occur to set artistic development into motion is the evolution and gradual interaction of the three systems during the sensorimotor period, from birth to 2 years of age, and then the employment of these integrated systems by the organism in the years following infancy in the skilled use of various symbolic media and elements.

Although the mastery of any symbolic system takes years, I do not feel that a new order of mechanisms comes into play at specifiable times. The groupings, groups, and operations described by Piaget do not seem essential for mastery or understanding of human language, music, or plastic arts. Rather the organism's experience with these symbol systems involves an increasingly complex making, perceiving, and feeling, which draws in a comprehensive way on the mechanisms evolved during infancy. The rate at which a child becomes able to manipulate tones, words, or lines varies greatly, but logical operations play little or no role in these activities. Development takes place within the medium itself, through a concrete exploration and amplification of its properties. Just as there is no need to step outside the medium, there is no need for the artist, performer, or audience member to master logical operations, or to pass through the cognitive landmarks that occupy Piaget.

Because I construe artistic development in this way, I do not find it necessary to speak of cognitive development in the sense of logical-scientific thought, nor to treat of hierarchical stages and operations in the lives of artists and audience members. However, the work of the critic does seem to involve those faculties that have been so expertly diagnosed by Piaget. It is in the role of the critic that the artistic process merges with and lends itself to the same kinds of analysis as the scientific process. Because critics will not be our main concern, however, I will speak of development as consisting in two principal phases: the evolution of the three systems during infancy, and their integration and reintegration with symbolic systems during the years following infancy.

For the remainder of this work, I will implicitly preface the word *cognition* with the term *scientific*, thereby restricting the term to that branch of human activity particularly concerned with the systematic investigation, description, and analysis of the world, in which a set of translatable, logical languages are evolved to permit unambiguous communication of findings. In other words, cognition will serve as a counter-term indicating that class of intellectual processes that do not appear central to artistry. At the close of this work, as I distinguish between artistic and scientific development, I will present further thoughts on the nature of cognition in aesthetics and in science.

Before we can adequately consider the nature of these processes, however, it is necessary to focus on those psychological systems that do not yet involve the use of symbols, an understanding of which should allow us to proceed with more assurance in our inquiry. The developing systems in the young animal and the human infant will be reviewed, with special reference to those activities that seem most akin to the arts. This discussion will again make use of a negative example. By describing animals and infants, we will suggest indirectly the characteristics that are essential for artistic development. We will then be able to examine in a more positive spirit certain aspects of artistic development, starting with the transition from sensorimotor behavior to symbol use, then tracing the development of the three systems on the symbolic plane. In later chapters we will consider the young child as an artist, outline the training required for mastery of an art form, and, finally, treat the relations among the various participants in the artistic process.

THE POOR SWAN

At Christmas it was very very cold colder than it has been for nearly a hundred years and all the ponds were frozen over Dunneys pond was frozen over too. So me and Geoffrey decided to go and skate on the pond. When we got there we saw a Big white thing near the nest so we all skated over and we saw it was one of our swans. So I sat on the nest with it and I put my coat over it. We thought it was dead and it was dead real. So the others went home to get some tools to get the swan out of the cold ice so we got it out with the axe and an hammer and some shovels and a pick and then we took the swan carefully out of the ice put it in a warm cover and took it to our secret cave.

A 7-YEAR-OLD BOY

a little egg
in a nest of hay.
cheep-cheep.
crack-crack.
a little chick
pecked his shell away
cheep-cheep,
crack-crack.

A 7-YEAR-OLD GIRL

My centipede is called Beehunter and he has lots of hands to tickle me with: he has twenty-two hands. He lives under the house and eats dirt. He made his house himself and it isn't very good. His mother lives there too and her name is Sheema.

A 7-YEAR-OLD BOY

A PLACE

When we went for a walk I heard the long-tongued dogs barking; buzzing bees busy in nests. Short-beaked birds were singing sweetly in cool-leafed trees, which reflected in the cool twisted river. I heard the leaves rustling softly and light-winged cicadas singing. I saw the long shadows of trees dancing in the water. The flax flowers hung heavily on broken stems.

I could hear birds singing, popping buds, shivering trees, rippling waters, romping leaves.

I could see bubbles rising, a tree a-swinging, buzzing bees, smooth stones and little chirping birds.

A 6-YEAR-OLD GIRL

NO GOOD

There's nothing that remains,
The house was all in flames,
The rags are all scorched
And nobody thought
What to do with the remains.
Nobody did any thinking,
What to do with the building.
Isn't it a shame.

A 7-YEAR-OLD BOY

FIGURE 2. Piano song by a 7-year-old child.

FIGURE 3. "Serenata," by a 7-year-old prodigy. (From G. Révész, *Psychology of a Musical Prodigy*, pp. 157, 158.)

FIGURE 3. (Continued)

FIGURE 4. Drawing by a 6-year-old boy.

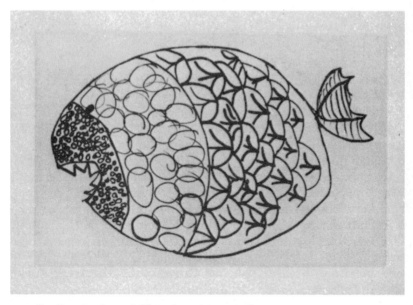

FIGURE 5. Drawing by a child in the primary grades.

51

FIGURE 6.   Drawing by a child in the primary grades.

TWO

The Three Systems in Animals and Infants

When one considers the magnificent plumage of a toucan or peacock, the alluring sounds of a nightingale or hummingbird, it is tempting to conclude that other members of these species are audience members, experiencing pleasurable aesthetic reactions to these displays. Similarly, the ape feverishly at work on a canvas or the parrot playing with sounds may easily seem engaged in artistic creation. We shall examine some of these activities, as well as a more general range of competences, in order to determine whether animals and human infants are participants in the artistic process, and, if not, to specify the reason why they are barred from this pursuit. We will then describe the three systems in animals and young children, specify the mechanisms governing their development, and analyze their relation to the symbolic activity involved in the arts. Just as understanding of the normal personality can be enhanced through a study of schizophrenia, or the phenomenon of language elucidated through an examination of aphasia, so the defining properties of the arts may be revealed through a treatment of activities that resemble in some way, yet are not equivalent to, the artistic process.

PRIMATE PAINTING AND AVIAN SONG

The ethologist Desmond Morris gave his young chimpanzee Congo a pencil and carefully studied his "drawing activity" during ensuing months. Morris found that even the very first scratchings were not random: "[Congo] carried in him, the germ, no matter how primitive,

53

of visual patterns." The chimpanzee passed through several stages characteristic of early child art. He began with simple lines that were poorly controlled, next executed multiple scribbles spread out across the page, then entered a new phase of simplification. He proceeded through the "scribble stage" on to the diagram stage, where he reproduced his own patterns, such as crosses, circles, and triangles. In addition, when given exercises, Congo emitted many of the responses that characterize young children: he "balanced" a page by placing a pictorial weight in the blank portion, filled in figures and resisted drawing outside them, completed those that seemed unfinished, favored the color red, drew on leaves when no paper was available, and made symmetrical marks inside a triangle. The animal invented and then reproduced "fanlike schemes," and, like other chimpanzees whose drawings have been studied, seemed to evolve his own style. At least Morris was able to identify his drawings as well as those of other chimps.

The differences between human and chimp art were equally striking, however. Congo appeared to enjoy the physical activity of drawing more than the results, and often would throw drawings away or crumple the paper without drawing. Environmental influences such as nearby objects or the surrounding scene were never reflected in the drawing, and after a while Congo gave up drawing entirely and just performed the physical exercise. Significantly, while Congo's muscular power appears to have been superior to that of human infants, his calligraphy was much poorer. Where the child becomes a compulsive student of his scribbles, the chimpanzee often preferred just to move his arm vigorously. Morris concludes: "It is thus preference in human infants for calligraphy . . . that leads to the ultimate creation of the first representational images, a phase never yet reached by an ape."

The critical difference between human and ape art inheres in the apparent inability of the primate to perceive representations of objects in his own drawings and his reciprocal incapacity to so arrange his lines that they will be read by others as an object or aspect of the world. It is of course possible that another ape, by accident or through intensive training, might have reached this "representational" stage, where lines come to embody objects and to function as "symbols" for them; but such an orientation toward lines on a page seems beyond the ken of most animals, and counter to the spontaneous evolution of the chimpanzee's graphic activity. Rather than engaging in symbolic activity, the ape is exercising his *making system*; he is mastering motor activities and building them up into more complex skills. He appears to be interested in the marks he has made and to get a pleasurable feeling from the activity and the product; hence his perceiving and feeling systems are being exercised as well. But a close interplay between making and perceiving does not characterize his efforts, and the three systems appear to operate only in relation to the world of natural objects like pen and pencil, removed from the referential or symbolic realm. The chimpanzee seems never to use this making activity to communicate something he has seen or felt. His drawing is a motor or making skill that may improve or atrophy over time, but is never put to the representational service of his subjective experience and knowledge.

If ape drawings vie to be considered paintings, then bird songs contest for the accolade of musical composition. Certainly, to human ears, bird song can be charming, even captivating. Indeed birds were once thought to be transmitting love calls to one another; but now it has been determined that the song has as its principal function the announcement that a territory is already occupied. Bird song is at most communication of a small set of predetermined messages, and the song itself is rather narrowly fixed. It appears to lack the varied reference, reflection of individual mood, and expressive and exemplificatory property of symbolic activity. Even if other birds are not enchanted, excited, or soothed by a song, however, the singing bird may be immersed in an artistic creation or performance. Because bird song is so intricate and pervasive, its relationship to the arts deserves further attention here.

Most readily accounted for is the song of a bird like the corn bunting; any member of the species is able to emit the pattern even if he has never heard any examplars of it. In such cases, the bird song is clearly an innate vocal pattern which, once triggered, emerges in completed form. More commonly, the general form of the song is available to the bird before exposure to a model, but details of its performance must be picked up from other species members. Often birds have inborn ability to sing a song of the right duration, to recognize the appropriate tonal quality, and to sing the song at preordained intervals. They can emit the rough outline of the song—the "subsong"—and then, upon hearing themselves sing, drop out the extreme frequencies and preserve notes appropriate to the final version. All birds practice their songs, some with such assiduousness that they become accomplished warblers.

Experimental manipulations yield insight into how bird song is learned. If members of most species are deafened before attempting the songs themselves—before engaging in making activity—they cannot master the pattern, even if they have already heard—perceived—the adult song. If birds are deafened after they have practiced, however, they continue to perform correctly, for they have already mastered the required motor pattern. The later the deafening or isolation, the more perfectly the song mimics that of conspecifics, or fellow species members. In most cases, the isolated bird appears to be influenced solely by songs of members of his species.

Song birds generally require a learning period in which the species song is mastered. This period is rather short, usually only a few months; there may be a critical period, after which the bird will not learn the full song, in spite of extensive exposure. In the white-crowned sparrow, the critical period is an interval when the crude auditory specification of the subsong (a template or basic "rough plan" whose contents is inferred from the songs of deafened or isolated birds) is converted into the final species version. This task appears to be accomplished over a lengthy period through comparing feedback of one's own song with the model provided by adult males. As stimulation is continued, the template becomes modified and more precise. By the time of adulthood the template will embody not only a complete set of species-specified traits, but even the characteristics of the particular local dialect.

At least in the sparrow, the mastery of bird song depends on the integration of the making and the perceiving system. If deaf, the sparrow can never master his song; he appears to require both his own productions and those of the adults around him. There may, indeed, be certain rough parallels between the mastery of the bird song and the learning of human language. In both cases, there is an initial period of babbling, which ends with sounds that are but loosely patterned though they increasingly reflect the local dialect; a critical period during which the song or language is most easily and "naturally" acquired; difficulty in acquiring the appropriate vocal patterns after the critical period; heightened sensitivity to specific kinds of environmental noises; a predisposition to realize certain rhythmic sequences or patterns; and some experimentation with variations during the period of acquisition. The strongly determined nature of the development process, the predictable emergence of making patterns that are altered in lawful ways by perceptual feedback, and the sensitivity to elements of syntax and dialect during a critical period suggest that certain common psychological and physiological processes may be operative.

The affinities between human symbolic activity and bird song become yet more intriguing when one considers the unusual capacities of certain birds. For instance, there are species with such acute perceptual and making capacity that they can imitate with astounding accuracy. The red-back shrike includes motifs from other species in its songs; the mimicking capacities of parrots have been legendary. The variety of songs found in several species is also striking. Wild male blackbirds use dozens of phrases in various combinations; individual thrushes vary their basic repertoire of 20 syllabic types in myriad ways. Most astonishing are birds that can accomplish feats reminiscent of human choral performance. Henschel tells of a canary and a bullfinch who sang "God Save the King" antiphonally; in this case, "the younger bird died, whereupon the first resumed its performance of the whole."

Despite these suggestive parallels between human language and bird song, a wide gulf exists because of the apparent absence of diverse ranges of meaning in bird song and the apparent lack of a template or "basic linguistic core" in human infants. Yet, as these components are sometimes said to be absent in human music, we are challenged to specify in what ways bird song differs. I would suggest that the primary difference inheres in the "single-mindedness" of the bird song. In the overwhelming number of cases, the species has a single song or a small set of songs; the species member masters this song but is restricted to its use. It is not impossible that humans too have a species song, but what is distinctive is the extent to which such a song becomes submerged, as the particular characteristics of music within a culture and the skills and desires of the individual musician come to the fore. Those humans gifted in the musical realm go on to become increasingly individualized in their productions, conducting ever more elaborate experiments with rhythm, tone, and melody, and affecting others in diverse ways; all this, of course, differs from the vast majority of bird species, where the music is restricted to one form and one message.

Still, in certain cases, individual birds or species have demonstrated versatility and flexibility in dealing with sound. Whether they gain some sort of "aesthetic" pleasure from these experiments is not known; but their capacities to modify components of melody or rhythm may reflect mechanisms related to those that enable the average human to play with sounds in language and in musical activities. In view of the parallels between bird song and human vocal products, it is intriguing to consider that one of the few examples of asymmetrical organization of the nervous system in the animal kingdom appears in songbirds.

Lest it be supposed that birds are artistic practitioners, I want to return to the fundamental differences between bird song and human music. In human music, feelings, patterns, and ideas of one individual are communicated to others; in bird song, however, there is no evidence that the refinements achieved by a particular bird possess special meanings or elicit diverse affects in him, or *a fortiori,* in others. Human music is a symbolic system, characterized by a wealth of expressive and exemplificative properties, adaptable to the communication of varied meanings, possessing a syntax that can be manipulated and transformed in order to achieve certain effects; these characteristics, if not entirely absent from bird song, are present in only the most fragmented and inchoate form. All told, bird song involves intricate interactions among the three systems, but seems bereft of symbolic overtones—hence it falls outside the arts. Finally, the amount of control and flexibility the human musician has over his material is qualitatively greater than that exhibited by the talented bird. The bird operates with what it has at hand, and is restricted to imitating it or to varying its dimensions according to a few innately determined principles. But the human creator has access to the whole domain of sound (including instruments), can select any aspect of it for elaboration, may systematically vary the particular transformation he wishes to test, and incorporate particular messages or forms into this work.

Because the human species song is not a powerful constraint on musical production, given versatile voices and various instruments, the individual has much greater freedom for exploration and growth, for expressing particular ideas and feelings in musical form. And even though music does not have a specific reference for the connoisseur, there appears to be a stage of development during which music denotes particular aspects of the universe; in fact, humans may have to pass through such a "figural" or "referential" stage before a mature relationship to musical works becomes possible. What we have in bird song is an extremely interesting artifact, no doubt related to certain human making and perceiving capacities, yet one qualitatively distinct from human artistic symbol systems.

I have proposed that complex forms of animal behavior can be adequately analyzed in terms of the operation and interaction of three developing systems. We have no evidence that features in animal life that superficially seem related to the aesthetic—displays of color and form, musical or visual productions, play and exploration, powerful affective reactions—involve symbolic aspects. Consequently, they are more legitimately thought of as involving the unmediated perceiving, making, and feeling systems. The human infant, in his first year of life, is also an amalgam of the three developing systems, but certain occurrences during that period suggest that the organism will eventually reach a new level of development, in which elements can come to have denotative reference. Before we can deal directly with symbol use, however, we should describe the operations and mechanisms characteristic of the three systems as they are found in the animal kingdom and in the infant child. In each case we will describe the basic elements and mechanisms of the system, indicate the aspects that are highlighted in animals and humans, furnish examples of the system in operation, and then describe the relationship of the system to later artistic creation and production.

THE MAKING SYSTEM

The making system includes all those behaviors of an organism that are overt or potentially overt and hence subject to verification by an observer. "Acts" or "actions" of the making system include eye blinks, curling of toes, shaking of hands, running, swimming, typing, singing, eating, and mental operations. Certain acts, such as respiring or excreting, characterize most animal life, while others, like preening or talking, are restricted to isolated species. Acts to which we give the same name need not be under the control of the same psychological or neurological mechanisms, nor need acts labeled with distinctive names necessarily be mediated by different mechanisms. Naming apart, all such motor activity features the making system at work and exhibits certain other common properties.

Perhaps its most striking characteristic is the tendency of the making system to combine isolated acts, once they have been smoothed out and mastered, into more complicated sequences, often ones that are hierarchically arranged. In learning to drink from a cup, a child combines the previously discrete acts of grasping the vessel, turning his head, following with his eyes, maintaining balance, and so on. Once drinking has become a single smooth act, it can in turn be embedded into a larger sequence (eating, brushing one's teeth), thereby becoming part of an increasingly hierarchical structure. Although finished actions may be carried off so smoothly as to appear like instinctual patterns, many months will ordinarily elapse before the disparate components of the action are combined in an organized structure. "Skills are mastered on a day-by-day basis and once mastered, they permit the development of new skills, which in time serve, so to speak, as the modules for the development of still higher skill." Such complex human behaviors as writing, playng an instrument, or solving a geometrical problem may be thought of as the skilled integration of many individual modules developed previously in isolation.

The making system, then, consists of behavioral acts, elements, or schemes, which tend to become combined into more elaborate, hierarchically arranged skills. A suggestive account of the relationship between isolated uncoordinated acts and flexible skills has recently been proposed by Fischer. According to this analysis, goal-directed behavior passes through four discrete stages: (1) initially the sequence consists of relatively disconnected and disorganized acts, frequently interrupted and requiring fresh starts; (2) the behavior remains poorly articulated and integrated but is often carried off as a single, pauseless action; (3) the sequence begins to take on the form of an integrated unit yet remains partially dependent upon motivation; (4) the sequence is fully differentiated into parts and yet integrated and wholelike; the actions are flexible, involving less demand on attention, and susceptible to reorganization under appropriate conditions; response segments can be detached and recombined in generative fashion. This description seems applicable to the rat learning a maze, a child throwing a ball, or a pianist mastering a difficult passage.

As with the other developing systems, the making system originally appears to be relatively isolated, but comes increasingly to interact with other facets of the organism. Illustrating this initial autonomy, it has been shown that the motor organs involved in ordinary locomotion can be activated in the absence of feedback from the environment; that is, even when perceptual information has been cut off, the motor sequence will continue to unravel. Such motor sequences seem under the control of a central rhythmical organizer present in the organism at birth; the organizer is gradually modified and integrated with other evolving patterns as the organism becomes increasingly sensitive to input and feedback from the environment. Yet, as Karl Lashley and Peter Wolff suggest, there may be an underlying commonality among the spontaneous rhythmical movements of the isolated nervous system, the elementary reflexes of human infants, the skilled movements of an accomplished musician, and the syntactical structures in human language. What differs among these activities is not the underlying mechanisms of the making system but rather the degree of hierarchical organization, flexibility of segmentation, and sensitivity to environmental and task demand.

While some properties of the making system are constant across developmental stages, certain features are highlighted in most animal species, others are more closely identified with human activity. The "animal pole" is characterized by a greater proportion of completed motor patterns at birth and less difference between infant and adult making; the "human pole" has relatively fewer intact patterns at birth, a longer, more flexible period of learning and development, and less continuity between immature and mature motor patterns. In the learning of skills, humans often take a longer time, but this period does not seem to be wasted; the infant appears to be learning "how to learn," acquiring general procedures for picking up new skills. The intricate evolution in human infancy—mastery of individual acts (primary circular reactions), their combination into more complex acts (secondary and tertiary circular acts), increasingly skilled attempts to preserve interesting spectacles, the invention of new means to solve problems—has been shown by Piaget to be integrally associated with subsequent cognitive and problem-solving activity on the level of symbols. Although the distinction is far from absolute, human infants seem to devote relatively more time and energy to activities not directly related to satisfaction of primary needs; this tendency, variously called *will to exercise, play principle, competence,* or *Funktionslust,* seems an important facet of development closely related to aesthetic and protoaesthetic activities.

If most animals can be distinguished from human infants on these dimensions, the primate group clearly forms an intermediate case. Apes possess an enormous cluster of skills, learned gradually during childhood; these skills are sometimes passed down to succeeding generations, though not in so formal and comprehensive a manner as in human cultures. Incipient tool use has been found, for example, among the apes studied by Köhler. Rods were joined to reach objects located behind bars; boxes were piled upon one another to gain access to a desired branch. Chimpanzees have even done factory work and driven cars. In such complex behaviors, the primate making system reflects a high degree of precision and complexity, certainly including sensitivity to environmental features.

Yet even in the most advanced animals, there seems to be a dependence on the immediate presence of environmental components. What may be lacking is a storage or "coding" system, which would permit usage of elements remote in space or not recently encountered. Furthermore, the finesse and complexity of motor patterns and tool use is limited by the primitive nature of the precision grip and by an inability to sustain a long sequence of disparate acts. In addition to deficiencies in memory, coordination, and integration, the absence of any developed communicative, symbolic, or cultural system inhibits the learning and teaching of complex procedures in interaction with other members of the species, the monitoring of multiple elements, and the voluntary direction of making activity. The most likely exception to these generalizations is the chimpanzee, whose feats in the symbolic realm will be considered at the conclusion of this chapter.

The operating principles of the making system can be seen through a consideration of the pattern of human sucking. At birth the infant sucks in a regular manner, independent of environmental feedback; there are two rhythmic organizations, one characterizing nutritive sucking (1.0 sucks per second), the other characterizing nonnutritive sucking (2.1 sucks per second). So vital a behavior must be built into the organism in order that it will operate in a reliable manner. By the age of 4 weeks, the sucking pattern is no longer just a mass movement; a more skilled form, involving differentiation of parts and sensitivity to environmental events, has evolved, and the child will stop sucking when an object enters his visual field. By the age of 2 to 3 months the child is able to alternate his sucking and his looking: He will suck in bursts and look during the pauses. He will also vary his sucking rate so as to bring a picture into focus, but sucking will generally cease once the picture has been brought into focus; thus he has achieved a sequentially organized set of making activities, alternating with his perceptual activity.

A little later the child will be able to vary this pattern, continuing to suck at a slower rate when the picture is present, stressing either the positive or the negative phase of sucking depending on schedules of reinforcement, varying the length of his pauses in order to process perceptual information. Yet if the regularity of the sucking pattern is strongly challenged, the behavior will lose its flexibility and return to a more intense and unlearned level. By the age of 6 or 7 months the sucking behavior is highly sensitive to a range of environmental forces and can be integrated smoothly into other behavioral sequences. Interestingly, only the child or adult who suffers from severe brain damage can realize the simple, imperturbable pattern of sucking found in the newborn; in the normal person sucking has become so closely integrated with the other developing systems that he no longer has access to the congenital form of the behavior.

Sucking may be regarded as a model of certain aspects of the making system. It is a highly organized making pattern, present at birth, of functional importance, which undergoes definable changes and interactions with other systems, and eventually becomes integrated into diverse behavioral schemes and environmental situations. Yet human skills can develop in other ways. In the case of walking, for example, a primitive reflex present at birth soon drops out, emerging only much later as a result of creeping, crawling, standing, and general neurological and muscular maturation. In the case of composing a musical piece or solving mathematical equations, there are only tenuous relations to primitive making activity and a more elaborate series of intervening steps is necessary. The prerequisites for such symbolic activity will concern us more directly in subsequent chapters, but it should be pointed out here that the early developments in the making system are a necessary component. Symbolic activity depends on the development of an object concept, an understanding that objects exist and endure irrespective of presence in the perceptual field or particular actions upon them. The attainment of the object concept is a culmination of the making behaviors involving objects during the first year of life.

The operations of the making system cannot be divorced from the capacity to define and to solve problems. Once problems have been set for the child, or the child has determined his own goals, he must draw upon his arsenal of acts or skills. Problem-solving involves the choice and coordination of behavioral acts, either with reference to material objects or to symbolic representations. In the former case we speak of acts upon objects, in the latter "operations" (or implicit actions) upon symbolic representations, other actions, or other operations. The differences between transforming compositional fragments in order to produce an effective symphony and varying sucking rates in order to see a picture hardly need spelling out, yet both are examples of achieving effects (or solving problems) through the effective deployment of an arsenal of skills. The task confronted by the artist in front of his canvas and the task confronted by the child at play with a new toy, whatever their disjunction in level of skill or complexity of materials, both require the deployment of a making system. It is in the degree of integration with the other developing systems, and in the symbolic material that the artist works with, that the important differences between the making child and the making artist are to be found.

THE PERCEIVING SYSTEM

The perceiving systems of natural organisms are most impressive and have filled many a naturalist's diary. Numerous species have sensory and discriminative capacities surpassing those of man. The bat can guide its flight by emitting sounds and tracing echoes that defy human perception. A dog can follow a whistle 200 yards to its source, and trace individual human beings by their scent. A salmon can return to the river of its birth at spawning, apparently because it remembers the odor of the water. And some electrified fish are so sensitive that the static electricity produced by combing one's hair nearby is sufficient to startle them. Nor are animals deficient in their visual systems. A fly's eye can resolve light patterns as well as a human's, and the eye of the owl is exceptionally well developed for vision in the dark. Indeed, when the range of perceptual capacities in the animal kingdom is considered, the powers as well as the limitations of the human perceptual system can be better appreciated.

The making system, as we have seen, is a generator and combiner of actions or schemes. The perceiving system, in contrast, may be thought of as devoid of actions—or, perhaps more precisely, as the exercise of one action only, that of perceiving or making discriminations in the external world. Whereas the making system involves the limbs and muscles of the body combined in numerous ways, and the gradual internalization of these actions into mental operations, the perceiving system involves only the sense organs and the differentiations they are gradually able to make, first externally, then internally. The necessity for a division between the making and perceiving systems derives from two facts: the initial dissociation between the physical acts and the sensory discriminations of which an organism is capable, and the respective emphases put upon these two psychological systems by the artist and the audience member, critic, or perceiver. The division is not dictated by logic, since all perception could be considered one form of making; yet the division does seem necessary for a comprehensive picture of the particular skills and capacities involved in the artistic process.

There are various affinities and distinctions between the kinds of perceptual processes involved in the infant's initial attention to sound and light, and the critic's capacity to make fine stylistic discriminations. The difference is the product of a long developmental process. The infant has but one or two perceptual mechanisms, while the critic can employ a range of perceptual proclivities that reflect his developmental level and, perhaps, discrete neurological and physiological mechanisms. I will describe these various perceptual proclivities, indicating which are favored by animals, which by humans, and then illustrate the roles played by the perceiving system in the worlds of the animal, the child, and the artist.

The most primitive form of perception is *orienting* or *tropistic perception,* sensitivity to specific stimuli during the postnatal period. Some of these stimuli have survival value for the organism—because his tropistic perception is predisposed toward certain configurations, the organism is able to locate and respond to its parent while avoiding its enemy. In certain cases, such as the chick's imprinting upon its mother, this discrimination involves only the perceptual system: No motor acts are required for imprinting to occur although, of course, a series of motor actions will follow. In the human infant, tropistic perception seems particularly sensitive to discrete aspects of the environment, such as motion, lines, edges, and contours, apparently because cortical cells fire in the presence of these arrays. Much as the loud noise commands attention, or the overly bright sunlight dictates shielding, tropistic perception has an ineluctable, compelling quality.

The young chick must orient toward its mother (or toward that set of stimuli equivalent to mother), just as the infant child must orient toward black lines and the vertices of a triangle.

Perceptual proclivities at birth, though rigid, are scarcely devoid of flexibility. For example, domestic fowl can be trained shortly after birth to prefer different colors. Chicks can learn to peck at triangles rather than circles at 3 to 5 days; they will orient toward conspecifics rather than food, providing they are not hungry. One may accordingly posit a somewhat more flexible mechanism called *preferential perception*. Among the stimulus dimensions toward which the young organism is capable of orienting, such as light, motion, hue, contrast, and sound, there is a hierarchy of interest, such that, under ordinary circumstances, an organism will view a stimulus having one property more than, or in preference to, a stimulus having other, competing properties.

The hierarchy of preferential perception is flexible and can be altered by training, providing the natural range is respected and the hierarchy not too closely tied to survival. Presumably, at times of stress, orienting perception is dominant, whereas preferential perception is highlighted when needs are largely satisfied. Preferential perception also reflects the previous experience and exposure of the organism; thus, when the organism has responded repeatedly to a certain configuration, it will tend to prefer a novel configuration, particularly one not wholly discrepant from earlier ones. Preferential perception features competition between stimuli and features, rather than a single dominant stimulus. Thus chickens peck more to certain colors, dogs urinate more to certain kinds of contours, and butterflies move to objects of a certain color when feeding, yet are attracted to other hues when mating. Among lower animals these preferences are more rigid, whereas among higher animals there is an increasing flexibility and preference for more complex or more novel stimulation. The preferential hierarchy in humans is of special suggestiveness for the student of aesthetics, who can locate its evolutionary antecedents among animal species.

Tropistic and preferential perception are dominant modes among many organisms, with preferential perception becoming increasingly pervasive in daily activity, and orienting perception remaining as a basic stratum which can be alerted at any time and which may be most closely tied to the fulfillment of basic needs. Both perceptual systems seem sensitive primarily to dimensions that the organism can perceive shortly after birth. Among higher animals, particularly mammals and birds, tropistic and preferential perception are relatively less important than a perceptual· system which develops gradually over time, and which has been termed *gestalt perception*.

As defined by Konrad Lorenz, gestalt perception is the ability to discern and recognize identities among patterns or objects, even when they appear in different contexts or guises. After observing a member of a species, a geometrical figure, or some other stimulus for a considerable time and from various perspectives, the organism becomes able to recognize that stimulus, irrespective of its present surroundings. "Gestalt perception is only possible if the sensory organs are receiving data which are either spatially or temporally determined. It is useless to look for gestalt phenomena in the sphere of the olfactory or gustatory sense." This mechanism is primed to pick out constancies in the environment, but lacks the kind of predisposition toward certain forms of specific information characteristic of the preferential and tropistic systems. Gestalt perception is instead a potential for discerning configurations or forms (rather than simple dimensions) that must wait upon experience with the environment before the specific form to which it will become sensitive can be known. All the same, there may be proclivities ("working hypotheses," in Lorenz's phrase) for picking out certain gestalten.

A good illustration of the emergence of gestalten for which there may be a predisposition is the perception of the mother's or caretaker's face. During the opening weeks of life, the child will focus upon the mother's motion, or will perhaps pick out her eyes for special attention, because of their contrast. However, he will behave in the same way toward other moving targets and toward drawings with eyelike configurations. At about 3 months, the infant's visual system begins to observe a new law of pattern discrimination. "The pattern is no longer just a collection of elements but is, in fact, a whole in a mysterious sense, in a gestalt sense." At this time the infant favors any facelike configuration. It is only by 4 months of age that the child is able to differentiate between the human face and other dummy forms of stimulation that may feature an oval shape or two black dots in the center. And within a month or so, according to most observers, the human infant recognizes its mother alone. At the same time, other constant forms in the child's environment will have been discriminated, and the child will have formed gestalten for a favored toy or mobile, for his crib, or for another member of the family. Soon he will be dominated by gestalt perception, which will enable him to recognize objects, persons, and fine details, irrespective of their size, context, or orientation. Such fine-grained sensitivity to members of a class in indifference to precise physical properties is unlikely to have been programmed into the organism. It probably results from a lengthy education of a complex visual system and cannot be easily deceived or extinguished. Gestalt perception is particularly valuable in dealing with those dense symbol systems involved in the arts whose elements cannot readily be specified, but which present coherent configurations such as recognizable styles.

The organism can continue to apply gestalt perception within any domain, thereby making increasingly fine distinctions and classifications. Much of what has traditionally been considered conceptual behavior—such as the ability to form complex categories, to recognize individuals, to discern artistic styles—seems adequately explained as a reflection of practiced gestalt perception. Furthermore, gestalten are not dependent on tutelage in the course of development; the system as a matter of course makes these classifications and discriminations. (Of course, instruction can predispose an individual to perceive one gestalt rather than another.) If the principle governing the making system is the combination of acts into superordinate skills, the principle governing the perceiving system seems to be increasingly fine discriminations, which follow upon extensive exposure to instances of a class of objects. Perhaps, in achieving these fine discriminations, the perceiving system comes to employ some of the same kinds of skilled sequences, combination of modules, and hierarchization of routines as does the making system. If so, then the perceiving system would contain, as a component, mechanisms embodying principles of the making system.

On might expect examples of visual gestalt perception chiefly among primates, but a most impressive illustration has been reported by Herrnstein and Loveland, who succeeded in training pigeons to respond selectively to pictures that contained humans or parts of humans. The authors claim the pigeon has formed a concept of a human being, in our terms a gestalt for humans or any portion of them. The fact that such gestalt perception is found among birds suggests that this capacity is not dependent upon the other developing systems and evolves independently of symbol use.

Whereas gestalt perception appears rather limited in its pervasiveness and fineness in intrahuman species, human beings particularly excel in the ability to form new, complex, and unexpected gestalts. Indeed Lorenz regards the creative scientist as an individual with heightened gestalt perception, one who can discern new patterns where others have merely noted disparate facts. (No doubt many artists share this sensitivity to configurations and have the further capacity to create strikingly new ones.) While experimenters have had some success in training higher mammals to perceive various gestalts, each species seems to have distinct limitations. Rats have failed to treat differently oriented triangles as equivalent; chimpanzees have been unsuccessful at regarding triangles composed of broken lines or circles as equivalent to euclidean line figures. And, though birds may also have some ability to discern and recognize complex gestalten, it is at least conceivable that pigeons have an innate tropism toward humans or that they are responding to something else in the photograph.

In the human, gestalt perception will continue to make finer discriminations and novel classifications throughout the life of the organism. The child learns first to recognize facial configurations, then the human face, then the face of particular persons, and so on. Similar refinement of perception takes place in every domain, from observation of one's self to tasting of wine. Two- and three-year-olds can discriminate among closely related animal species, identify car makes or product labels, and perhaps even differentiate systems of notations or artistic styles. The potential for this kind of activity may be present in higher animal species, but clearly it achieves its fullest fruition among humans.

Two other forms of perception, however, may be restricted to humans. The first, which may be termed *gestalt-free perception,* is the capacity to look beyond the dominant figure or gestalt in some kind of presentation; the observer pays attention instead to the fine details or microstructure which cut across figure and ground, characterizing both the gestalt and its embedding context. This gestalt-free capacity is crucial in the perception of artistic objects; its existence in animals is at best problematic. The other form of perception is the capacity to treat in an equivalent manner different symbols belonging to the same class, such as handwritten or printed, lower or upper case letters. Here is an example of gestalt perception within a category that belongs to a symbol system. Since the capacity to work readily with symbol systems seems restricted to human beings, perception within symbol systems is necessarily a special characteristic of human beings.

With the exception of these latter perceptual capacities, the difference between perceiving in the animal and human seems to be one of quantity rather than quality. Most animals more frequently employ tropistic and preferential perception, whereas gestalt and gestalt-free perception are relatively more important in human functioning. In addition, most animal perception depends particularly upon proximity, interaction, or tactile contact with phenomena. This trend is effectively characterized by Schachtel, who proposes that animal perception, like that of human newborns, is largely *autocentric.* "The autocentric sensations are generally experienced not centrally nor as a sensation pervading the entire person but as localized in, around, or near the particular sense organ through which the sensory perception takes place." In contrast, human perception becomes increasingly *allocentric*—the human perceives objects at a distance from his whole person and soon contemplates them without direct physical involvement. Autocentric perception exists to ensure communication of messages incorporated in instinctual mechanisms and is concerned with qualities; allocentric perception emphasizes recognition, allows perception at a distance, and relates primarily to objects. Schachtel argues that the development of aesthetic sensitivity rests upon the ability to maintain distance from objects while retaining an interest in the object apart from the gratification of physical needs, the very capacity seemingly undermined by the predominance of autocentric perception in most animals.

While higher animals make many of the same differentiations and form many of the same gestalten, human children are eventually distinguished by the predominance of gestalt perception, and the capacity for gestalt-free and for symbolic perception. Indeed, the capacity to use symbols directs attention to gestalten that may be missed by the perceiving system alone. It is these very capacities that are most critical for the participant in the artistic process. The powerful appeal of art objects comes from the fact that, more than other kinds of stimulation, they excite the full range of perceptual proclivities. The individual contemplating a colorful Mexican gouache may initially attend because his tropistic perception has been aroused by its brightness and contrast. The pleasant use of color and lines will activate his preferential perception, and the familiar forms and shapes will be responded to by gestalt perception, while the subtle nuances that cut across gestalt and ground, giving the work a characteristic texture, will be detected by gestalt-free perceptions. Finally, the symbolic aspects of the paintings, the religious or social elements to which reference is being made, the dynamic properties expressed or exemplified by the work, will be discerned by the symbolic perception of the individual. Naturally the interest in and the final evaluation of the work of art will depend on the particular qualities and quality of the work; but its capacity to arouse the whole gamut of human perceptual systems will contribute crucially to its impact as an aesthetic object. And, though we have focused on the realm of visual perception, an analogous form of analysis and range of perceptual capacities could be brought to bear on a musical or literary work.

THE FEELING SYSTEM

In the discussion of the making and perceiving system, we have drawn primarily on the findings and formulations of other students of sensory and motor activity. While a vast literature on these psychological capacities exists, there is relatively little concerned with the realm of feeling. Thus our task is to justify the need for a feeling system, to point up problems in earlier discussions of feelings, to suggest a few of the characteristics of the feeling system, and to lay the groundwork for a fuller discussion of the feeling system to be undertaken in the following chapter.

The difficulty of describing the feeling system was put succinctly by one biologist: "about the feelings of the animals, we can say very little with certainty." Much the same characterization is applicable to the feeling lives of young children. As for older persons, introspective evidence is available, but even there it is difficult to interpret a person's description of what he feels. As Thomas Huxley asked:

What is the value of the evidence which leads one to believe that one's fellow man feels? The only evidence in this argument from analogy is the similarity of his structure and his actions to my own, and if that is good enough to prove that one's fellow man feels, surely it is good enough to prove that an ape feels.

Given the difficulty of determining feeling life, why introduce it into a discussion of artistic development? The answer, already propounded, is that feeling life has been regarded universally as a crucial component of the artistic process; any discussion of the arts that takes no account of the feelings of individuals runs the risks of completely misrepresenting the phenomena under investigation. If artists speak of communicating their feelings to others, or of portraying feelings and their forms in artistic works; if perceivers and critics have their feelings deeply affected and altered through encounters with artistic works, these are situations that merit study and explanation. Hence our picture of the developing organisms and of the artistic process must incorporate the feelings of the individual.

A century of theorizing and psychological research has failed to produce a satisfactory way of talking about feelings, though it has brought to light certain aspects of *feeling life*. By this term I mean to suggest that which is experienced phenomenally by a person and which he can talk about or reveal to others through his behavior and reactions. One cannot always determine when a person has experienced feelings, or change of feelings, since these need not be conveyed in overt actions or testimony; yet it is implausible that there should be no correlation between a person's subjective experiences and more public signs of these feelings. On the assumption, then, that psychological indices to an individual's feeling life exist, we may draw certain conclusions concerning the development and place of feeling life in animals and humans.

Evidence of feeling life in animals comes from a number of sources. For instance, when physiologists found that stimulation of certain neural structures was a sufficient reward for rats, the conclusion was drawn that these loci produced a feeling of pleasure in the anmial. Further electrophysiological explorations have suggested that other feelings as well may be housed in specific portions in the brain; apparently an animal such as the rat will undergo a range of feelings when rewarded with food or punished by shock.

Another line of evidence in support of the feeling life of animals is the range of expressive gestures and facial configurations, which may correspond to the internal affects. Animals seem to exhibit the same set of gestures and expressions under recurring circumstances, giving rise to the hypothesis that these reactions are tied to situation-specific elements and may involve an accompanying range of affects. Among primates, for example, activities such as courting, fighting, and play characteristically involve certain facial and bodily gestures, which in turn evoke a matching or complementary set of gestures from other members of the species. These gestures are often accompanied by sounds and expressions which, proceeding on an analogy from human behavior, appear to signal feelings of pleasure, distress, pain, fright, or enthusiasm.

Nor are these commonalities restricted to the higher end of the animal kingdom. Lorenz has reported a number of situations in which birds appear to experience the same range of affects as human beings. In a famous passage he describes how "a young female goose that has fallen in love never tries to force her company on the object of her passion." The goose does not follow the gander around, but, as if by chance, turns up in places where she knows he will be. Indeed, when pursued by the gander, the goose pretends not to pay attention. Only the play of her eyes communicates how the male's courtship is being received. Though the goose never looks directly at the gander, and indeed pretends to be looking at something else, she still monitors his activities carefully. Lorenz suggests that this courting behavior resembles that of human beings both in the components of the ritual and in the quality of feeling life of the participants. Numerous other examples drawn from an array of species supports the claim that situations which evoke strong feelings among animals are frequently akin to powerful human experiences.

Given the suggestive evidence for commonalities in human and animal feeling life, analysts have often made two assumptions. First, they have applied the same emotional labels—anger, fear, distress, envy —to animals as to humans. Second, they have asserted that more complex emotions in the adult build up out of simpler ones in the young child.

Thus J. B. Watson posited original emotions of fear (due to loud sounds or loss of support and marked by crying and clutching); rage (due to frustrating experiences and marked by stiffness and a blue face); and love (due to gentle tactile stimulation and accompanied by smiling). Similarly, K. Bridges posited an original emotion of excitement and then traced its gradual differentiation into a series of finer feeling states characteristic of the adult (see Figure 7). The problem with such accounts is not that they are implausible, but that they are difficult to document or even to test. Given the fact that even a 6-month-old exhibits in his facial configurations the full range of human expressions, almost any formulation about the emotions of the child would gain support.

Consideration of the term *emotion* suggests, however, its inappropriateness in a discussion of the affect of the young organism. The emotions of adult feeling life require a context and an interpretation; one loves in relationship to another person, fears a situation or an organism, becomes angry at a target or the thwarting of an expectation. More complex emotions, such as envy or pride, require yet more subtle discriminations and comprehension of human experience. Merging such terms with more elementary states such as excitement and pain, and applying such terms to the feeling life of a young child or animal seems gratuitous indeed. The challenge is to find a language of feelings that makes fewer assumptions about the knowledge of the organism. At the same time, this language should allow for the experiences of older individuals, which merit description in terms of complex emotional states.

The introduction of a new way of speaking about feeling life will be the task of the next chapter. In it I will describe modes and vectors,

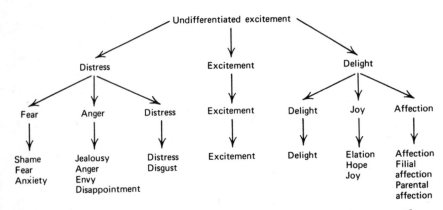

FIGURE 7. One view of the development of feelings. (Adapted from K. Bridges. Reprinted by permission.)

ways of organizing experience that are based in the first instance on the sensations and affects of the body, and that eventually combine into the more complex emotions of human experience, even as they serve as integrators of the developing systems and as transitions to the realm of symbol use. To prepare for this discussion I will suggest some general characteristics of the feeling life of the infant and some of the parallels and differences between animal and human feeling life.

Based on his painstaking studies of young infants, Wolff has posited the existence of a number of "organismic states" (such as deep sleep and alert inactivity), which succeed one another according to specifiable rates and sequences during the first days of life. Each state is characterized by a degree of arousal and attention (with matching physiological and behavioral manifestations), but no necessary claims are made concerning the relationship between these states and subsequent affects or emotions. Wolff does suggest that certain behaviors will occur primarily in certain arousal states, and implies that certain internal feelings are more likely to accompany certain external states. In his view the infant is characterized by changing amounts of available energy, which may be expressed through a number of equivalent modalities. For this reason it is fallacious to link a particular behavior with a certain feeling or energy state; excitement may be equally well manifest through erections, startles, or smiles, and smiles may accompany excitement, mild tension, or rest.

If Wolff is correct, the feeling system is characterized initially by a succession of programmed arousal states, accompanied presumably by felt affects on the part of the infant. Here lies evidence for an autonomous feeling system since, at least at first, these feelings follow one another without dependence on perception of environmental features and independently of the random behaviors of the child. This is not to claim that the child will not have certain feelings when he cries or bangs his hand, only to deny that there is any flexibility in the occurrence of these feelings. These affects will be inevitable concomitants of specific situations, which are themselves determined by a programmed succession of states, over which the child has no control. It is when the child begins to form gestalten, and to have certain feelings associated with these gestalten, when the child has mastered certain motor sequences and can use them in mean-ends situations, that the feeling system will come to have meaningful interactions with other systems.

These distinctions have suggestive parallels with classical studies of learning and conditioning. So long as certain feelings are inevitable concomitants of certain stimuli, so long as responses are automatic and unconditioned, it makes little sense to think of the feeling system as being involved in a genuine interaction with other systems (though in a literal sense many of the infant's feelings will be linked to percepts and to acts). But when the child comes to associate feelings with certain situations, and to alter his acts and discriminations based upon these associations, or when feelings come to anticipate or to follow upon such percepts and acts, then the feeling system is beginning to become integrated with the other developing systems. Such a characterization seems to fit comfortably with our knowledge of conditioning and learning, for in these forms neutral stimuli come to be colored by feelings and incorporated into act sequences because of the way in which schedules of stimuli presentation and contingencies of reinforcement have been arranged.

A useful index of the feeling life of the child emerges from careful observations of his early months. After the neonatal period, organismic states no longer follow each other automatically, reflecting instead the particular conditions of the environment. One child may always cry following one kind of situation, another will cry less frequently, and a third will cry at irregular intervals. A wealth of stimulation may lengthen periods of alert activity, treatment by the caretaker may encourage feelings of comfort, and so forth. The feeling system, no longer autonomous, will become integrated with the discriminations made by the child and with the acts and skills of which he is gradually becoming capable. At this point, it seems plausible to speak of general states of arousal (more or less aroused or quiescent), and of modal-vectoral properties (phenomenal experiences of openness, closedness, sharpness, dullness), as well as experiences of physical qualities (heat, wetness), which the child presumably undergoes long before experiencing the emotions of guilt or jealousy.

As a complement to a study of the situations in which the child becomes involved, one may also look at major behavioral components and emotional expressions; for example, his crying and smiling behavior may indicate something of the quality of his feeling life. Such an examination suggests that the circumstances eliciting facial expressions change dramatically during the first year of life. The response of smiling, for example, appears quasi-spontaneously during sleep and drowsiness or after the newborn has drunk to satiation. But by the age of a month the baby will smile at certain "adequate" stimuli, even when it had previously been whimpering or fussy. During the second month of life, the baby begins smiling as an accompaniment to his own activity, as a response to visual and auditory stimulation, and during exchanges of eye contact with his caretaker. And, in the second through fourth months, smiles are induced by visual sights, such as the appearance of another person, though the expression on the other's face is not taken into account. Games of pat-a-cake or the sound of voices are also effective elicitors of smiles during this period. Later on, the smile becomes restricted to certain persons and certain situations; unfamiliar persons may well elicit frowns or tears, and the same person viewed in an alien context may no longer produce a smile. Clearly, the smile, as well as other facial expressions, can occur in a wide range of situations and may convey a variety of meanings.

If we use the smile as a clue to the child's affective state, we find it to be determined initially by internal factors—the general equilibrium of the body or the reduction of a need. Soon, however, the smile comes to reflect the child's interactions with the external world, the individuals he encounters, the discriminations he makes, and the contours and results of his making activity. The smile seems to follow discriminations (at first gross, then increasingly fine) and accompanies various kinds of making activity (a game of pat-a-cake or a toss in the air). Affective expressions and feelings continue to signal events not under the control of external stimuli, such as a release of gas or a bodily pain, and in this sense the feeling system continues to possess autonomy. But the more striking feature of the first year of life is the extent to which the child's feelings become integrated with the other developing systems.

An emerging aspect of feeling life is the child's tendency early in the second year of life to divide the world into good and bad, pleasant and painful. We know something of the child's attitude toward the world because he displays alternative behaviors toward the same objects and persons under varying conditions, and because he can tell us there is a good Johnny and a bad Johnny, a good mommy and a bad mommy, and indicate why he is referring to persons in that way. The tendency to bifurcate is so pervasive as to make it a principal way in which humans process information and perceive the world of persons and objects. Indeed, it is only when the child begins to speak of his world using such terms of approval and displeasure that one can legitimately speculate on his experienced emotions or feelings. Before this point, the observer is restricted to inferences from the child's expressions and from other indirect behavioral indices; thereafter one has a stronger indication that the child is experiencing phenomenal affects (particularly when they are accompanied by the same "expressions" as in adults), that he is aware of these affects and is attempting to communicate them to others. Given the widely acknowledged temporal lag between practical knowledge of a state and the capacity to capture it in symbols, it is tempting to use the child's initial bifurcation of the world into good or bad, pleasurable or painful, as evidence that these are also the first affective states he experiences; however, I know of no way to test that hypothesis.

We have suggested that the feeling life of young children (and of animals) bears certain parallels with the feeling life of adults, but that there is insufficient justification for speaking of emotions in the developing organism. In some ways, the parallels between animal and human feelings appear close, because of common neurological structures, analogous situations in which organisms are found, similarity of accompanying expressions and gestures, and the pervasiveness of learning and conditioning capacities. My guess is that higher animals may well experience at least some of the feelings (thermal sensations, pleasures, pains) experienced by humans in similar situations. If feeling results from (or is the necessary correlate of) the operation of a physiological system, similarities in the nervous organization of animals and humans should engender similarities in felt affect.

What is lacking in animals would seem to be the ability to alter this feeling, either by labeling it or criticizing it, or by desiring or willing some change. The feelings, in other words, are inevitable concomitants of situations; though felt, they involve no symbolic reference to other situations. Nor are they stimulated or modified by references in a symbolic medium. This does not make the feelings of animals any less painful or ardent—a wound is a wound, frustration is still frustration—but it prevents them from being elicited in other than certain specified situations. While humans can regulate or modify feeling life through voluntary control or allusion to distant events, can rationalize away an affect or produce one in another individual, the diverse feelings in an animal are essentially preordained by the structure of his nervous system and the range of interactions for which his species is predisposed. Animals cannot deliberately withhold or experience an emotion, nor run through the gamut of affective states through contact with symbols: "except perhaps in the highest mammals all signalling behavior is immediate reaction to internal or external stimuli . . . the signalling behavior of animals can be compared with the involuntary expressions of anger or fear in humans of all ages." Tied to the immediate situation, such signalling cannot serve as a comment upon or a personal view of the world. The lack of symbolic systems in which feelings may be captured, and the relative preponderance of ritualized encounters such as mating behavior or threat encounters, presumably limits the potential use of the feeling system.

It is the increasing integration of the feeling system with other developing systems, and in particular its functioning in conjunction with symbolic processing, which causes the feeling system to play a pivotal role in artistic production and perception. The artist frequently seeks in his own work to capture a feeling or set of feelings that he has experienced, and relies heavily on his own subjective reaction in determining the effectiveness with which the feeling has been captured and communicated. The performer also seeks to embody specific feelings in his activities, and measures his success by the extent to which the feeling life of the audience has been affected. Finally, the audience member's relation to an aesthetic work is integrally tied to feeling, for the stimulation of his feeling life in a desirable or interesting way is the principal goal. Only if his feelings have been affected in a meaningful way can his relationship to the artistic work be consummated. For, while the feeling system plays an ancillary role in the activities of the artist, performer, and critic, it is paramount in the experience of the audience member. All told, the development of the feeling life in the years following infancy, when the child becomes capable of experiencing more complex emotions himself and discerning nuances in the feeling life of others, is crucial for participation in the artistic process.

I have indicated in brief fashion the existence and form of the three systems within the animal kingdom and the world of the young child. Development may be viewed as the further differentiation of each system and the increasing interaction among them. Ascending the phylogenetic scale, one encounters multiple instances of interaction among systems. Thus, while the behavior of euglena or amoebas may reveal relatively little interaction between developing systems (except of the automatic sort), the behavior of birds and mammals is permeated by such interaction: We have seen how the primate combines perceiving and making in his tool use, how the bird relies on perceptual feedback in order to perfect his song, and how the rat will learn a maze in order to undergo a pleasurable affect. Similarly, while imprinting seems to require only the perceiving system, infant reflexes only the making system, and organismic states only the feeling system, more complex behaviors, such as imitation, problem-solving, and communication involve a rich combination and interconnection of all three systems. The difference between animals and humans inheres not in the existence and interaction of the three systems as such, but rather in the fact that animals function adequately through a reliance on the three systems and show no signs of wanting, or having the capacity, to use the systems on the symbolic plane.

THE INTERACTION OF SYSTEMS

Although the interaction of systems is a pervasive aspect of psychological development, its importance is such that a few examples should be presented. While those discussed are quite simple, analogies exist at the level of the most complex human functioning, including many facets of the arts. For example, one of the most familiar examples of systems interaction occurs during the first 4 or 5 months of life, when the child learns to grasp objects in front of him. Of course, the child is able to perceive objects, or aspects of them, shortly after birth, and is at an equally tender age able to grasp objects placed in his hand. There may even be a limited capacity for visually guided reaching during the neonatal period. Yet it takes several months for the child's perceptual capacities—his ability to locate objects in space, to estimate their size, to differentiate which parts are graspable—to develop and interact with his making capacities—his ability to hold his hand in a desired form, to move his head and hand the appropriate extent, to position his fingers in a comfortable position, to hold onto and manipulate an object placed in it. An interaction of systems has taken place when prehensile behavior has matured, and this interaction is analogous, in important respects, to other system interactions, as when the older person learns to correct an error made in sketching a scene, to hold his bow in the appropriate position for securing the desired sound, to focus on those aspects of a musical selection that will yield a pleasant feeling, or to write down his impressions and criticisms of a work that was just performed. Analogies can be found on the symbolic plane which correspond to these additional examples of system interaction in the young child.

Perceiving and Feeling

An example of perceiving and feeling is the infant's anxiety when he encounters a stranger. The infant forms gestalten of the individuals whom he regularly observes. After these gestalten have been firmly established, novel sights can occasion extreme anxiety, thus mobilizing unpleasant affects in the feeling system.

Perceiving and Making

1. Children perceive different sounds or rhythm patterns, then proceed to rock or to march in time or out of time with the music.
2. Infants who are sucking will observe a sight and cease sucking.

They later become able to continue the positive sucking component while observing the scene.

Feeling and Perceiving

1. A child suddenly feels extreme discomfort, then notices that he has burned himself, has fallen, or has cut his hand. The unpleasant affect has preceded the discrimination among stimuli.

2. A child who has been exerting himself feels faint. He then notices that it is dark outside.

Feeling and Making

1. An infant feels tired and then begins to cry and to kick.

2. A child who experiences emptiness in his stomach turns toward his mother and lifts his cup for food.

Making and Perceiving

1. An infant knocks his head against a cradle gym, hears the noise, and then begins to hit the cradle gym repeatedly.

2. A child places sticks next to one another, then notices they can be joined.

Making and Feeling

1. A child pulls his hand across his face and hurts himself, thus producing unpleasant affect.

2. A child reaches for a cup on a hot day and pours some cool water for himself, experiencing a pleasant sensation.

Among the examples of system interaction present in early childhood and later implicated in the arts, three stand out: problem-solving, imitation, and communication. As part of our developmental analysis of the artistic process, we will examine briefly the early forms of these systems interactions.

Much of the artist's activity can be viewed as the setting of certain problems and the search for adequate solutions. For example, the achieving of a certain effect poses difficulties for an artist, who then draws upon skills, strategies, and behavioral schemes in order to arrive at an acceptable solution. More generally, problem-setting and solving behavior can be viewed as the definition of a task, a realization that it is not immediately solvable, the recognition of factors relevant for a solution, and then execution of a solution within some kind of medium. This definition can be applied to most higher animals; they can handle a variety of problems that arise in their daily existence, as well as problems set by experimenters in the psychological laboratory. Thus an animal is shown a group of geometrical figures and is rewarded for choosing a certain shape or position; or the animal is placed in a maze or puzzle box and allowed to pursue a reward or avert punishment. By and large gestalt perception is exploited in solving such problems. The capacity to discriminate certain kinds of geometrical configurations, and to perform appropriate actions based on these distinctions, seems to be accounted for by the ability to detect the invariants of such configurations. Yet the rats or octopuses who can handle these discriminations appear unable to solve an oddity problem, where the task is to select the member of an array that differs from the others. (This task requires a more complex, "abstract" form of gestalt perception, which may involve overlooking certain salient perceptual aspects.) Moving up the phylogenetic scale, spider monkeys appear unable to discern equivalence relationships among geometrical figures unless they are directly contiguous, whereas chimpanzees can appreciate such relations irrespective of locus. But even chimpanzees reach an impasse when required to match two ordered sequences; they appear to have difficulty generalizing about ordering per se.

The most impressive form of problem-solving is found among the chimpanzees who, as Köhler showed many years ago, can exhibit dramatic intersystemic behavior. The chimp will display signs of frustration and discomfort as he paces around, picks up items more or less at random, or sits and "ponders." Suddenly the chimp will freeze and then brighten up during a moment of "insight." This affective breakthrough presumably signals discrmination of those aspects that will enable him to achieve his goal—for example, fetching a banana by joining two sticks. The anticipatory affect is followed by making behavior of joining, guided in turn by perceptual attention.

Imitation is another important feature of the arts, since individuals typically learn to master an art form, at least in part, through observation and copying of other practitioners. Most higher animals are capable of some degree of imitation, behavior in which they reproduce the actions of another animal. While an ape's imitation of a hand wave seems explicable, since the ape is able to see both his hands and those of a model, it is more difficult to envisage how the ape can mimic a facial expression of another ape, since the former cannot see his own face. Nonetheless, primates have repeatedly demonstrated their capacity to pick up just these kinds of "blind" imitations. Perhaps they have a representation of their own body, secured by generalization from the bodies of others or through study of their own reflections.

The sensitivity and subtlety of animal imitation is also striking. A finch watching unskilled finches perform an action in an imperfect way will experience deterioration of his own actions just as if he were copying the learner's mistake; no "inhibit" mechanism is present. Kittens who observe their mothers performing acquire a response quicker than kittens who observe strange females. These findings document the close attention paid to details of a model's behavior and the importance attached to the identity of the model. Clearly animal imitation is a highly organized and developed capacity; yet it is not known whether, in the absence of symbol use, the animal's attention can necessarily be drawn to the aspect of the model's behavior that should be imitated. For example, an animal may accurately imitate a model's behavior at a piano without ever appreciating that the tone produced is the goal of the behavior, rather than the physical form of the playing technique. Similarly, a parrot's faithful mimicry of an oral passage, or a monkey's accurate reproduction of a behavioral pattern, may capture many components of the model's behavior, without necessarily incorporating its intended purpose or rationale.

Discrimination of fellow species members is crucial, if one is ever to become sensitive to the creating individual who lies behind every art object. Among animals, a certain capacity to recognize particular species members is undoubtedly present. For example, members of baboon colonies clearly recognize one another. They observe positions in pecking orders of hierarchies, and behave differently toward each member, often incorporating the results of previous encounters. Certainly the feeling systems of animals are affected by these encounters; deeply felt bonds obtain between animals. However, the aesthetically critical creation of an object by one animal and the perception of subjective aspects of the creating animal by a second animal does not seem to occur. The scratchings on the ground by one ape may create pleasurable or unpleasant feelings in a second animal, but there is nothing to suggest that subjective aspects of the first animal have been detected and appreciated. While animals can acquire unmistakable and potent meanings for one another, there is no evidence that creations by animals ever achieve comparable meaning for other animals.

The problem of communication among animals is a vexed one, and of particular import here, given the view of art as a form of communication. Because of our definition of communication, there is no need to consider those expressive behaviors that are exclusively physiological concomitants of feelings. For example, primate cries customarily accompany certain situations and appear to reflect the amount of affect felt, not any additional information. Nor can expressive gestures communicate novel information, for they have a preordained meaning: direct gaze means threat, looking away means submission, lip smacking is neutral. Instead, generalized gestures reflecting a high degree of arousal or disturbance—the tantrum or the attack—are likely to occur when the primate wants to communicate something novel, bizarre, or important. In such cases loud sounds serve to convey a disturbed internal state and produce certain arousal reactions in others, rather than to communicate specific messages; it is possible, of course, that a combination of gesturing and pointing may contribute to the successful communication of a specific item. Interestingly, in the case where a chimpanzee has been trained to use sign language there are comparatively few indications of self-initiated responses, attempts on the part of the chimp to learn new names, or asking of questions. The chimp does not appear motivated to communicate propositions about the world, though it may very well wish to explore it physically or to engage in play; still it possesses considerable capacity to convey motivational information and subtle changes of mood.

Somewhat different, and more puzzling, are those animal communicative systems that transmit explicit items of information, such as the mode found among bees. Through a series of dances, bees convey to one another the direction and the distance of sources for honey. The type of food is indicated chemically, the direction by the straight part of the dance, and the distance by the turns per unit of time. In this case, the bees are transmitting a specific message of the sort that humans might convey in a map or diagram. Such messages stand in sharp contrast to the emotional expressions of primates, which serve to convey moods and sentiments rather than particular locations. Yet, despite the differences between the expressive systems (the infinite range of gradations in primate cries) and the nominal systems (the limited and specific information available in bee dance), both are readily distinguishable from human communication. In each case the kinds of messages that can be communicated from one member of the social group to the other are preordained. If one knows what the species is, one can in effect write out its future messages. Each communication system has its own powers and restrictions. In the case of the baboon, the number of states that can be expressed is not large, but the degree of emotion felt and exhibited is infinitely varied. In the case of the bee, only a few topics (such as location and direction) form the subject of discourse, but the specific information transmitted can be as varied as the possible number of flower beds. Even the most "talkative" animals still have remarkably few topics about which to communicate, and do not seem able to introduce and define new topics.

In contrast, human speech is open-ended; an indefinite number of topics and an indefinite number of messages about them can be transmitted. Humans have an infinitely greater range of possible references. They can devise new languages that perform specialized functions (mathematics, sign languages); they can transmit them to progeny. Indeed, it is in the capacity for system interaction in communication that the gap between animal and human is particularly striking.

Until this point, we have described system interactions in animals which, though possessing certain similarities to human activity, are relatively simple, inflexible, and devoid of symbol use. There are, however, certain animal behaviors, found particularly among chimpanzees, which seem much closer to human symbolic behavior, and which challenge any contention that animals do not participate in the artistic process. To such instances we now return.

THE THRESHOLD OF SYMBOL USE

One of the most characteristic aspects of artistic activity is the investment of particular meaning in certain objects, which can in turn exert a powerful influence on other individuals. While animals can certainly evoke powerful affective responses in one another, the unfolding of most actions that have this result is relatively fixed. The clarity and rigidity of such *ritual* behaviors are explained by the need for nonambiguity between communicating animals. Typically these behaviors involve movements that are slow, formal, exaggerated, conspicuous, and not susceptible to misinterpretation. The subtlety and individual manifestations characteristic of the human artistic performances are generally absent in a courting dance or an exchange of threats.

Somewhat more flexibility and individuality characterizes social interactions of primates, however; baboons groom specific partners and may even cater to one another's whims. Primates also appear to form attachments to vestiges of other organisms and humans. When the cherished organism is absent, the animal may cling to a substitute, such as a tatter of clothing or a favored toy. While such attachment may be elicited purely by the smell of the object, it may also include a primitive symbolic representation of the missing object. For example, the ability of chimpanzees to use tokens to "purchase" certain rewards and to take into account the relative value of these tokens suggests the operation of a primitive symbolic faculty. Like young humans, primates seem able to regard certain objects as symbols, as representations or partial substitutes for the "real thing." This capacity is little developed in apes, yet

Something very much like an aesthetic sense of import is occasionally displayed by anthropoid apes. . . . The earliest manifestation of any symbol making tendency, therefore, is likely to be a mere sense of significance attached to certain objects, certain forms or sounds, a vague emotional unrest of the mind by something that is neither dangerous nor useful in reality.

There are scattered anecdotes about apes who regard objects as if they had special meaning—for example, fear at the sight of toadstools or calming by a favored pair of overalls. Certain apes also show signs of disgust when they have to remove feces from their bodies. "These reactions have just the character of being common yet individual which belongs to aesthetic experiences."

If attachment to tokens occurs sporadically among higher animals, it is rampant among young children, nearly all of whom at one time or another invest special significance in a little bear, doll, blanket, or "mommy's shoes." The capacity to attach special value to such fetishes because of their relationship to others or to oneself is crucial in the aesthetic process. Where the animals and young children remain deficient, however, is in their "reading" of these objects. Members of these groups attach significance to objects merely because of their familiarity with the object or their attachment to its owner; an aesthetic reaction inheres in the ability to appreciate knowledge about the world and about subjective experience that a creator who may be unknown to the perceiver has sought to capture in a symbolic object. Considerable development of the communication system is essential before such an appreciation becomes possible.

Were this book written some years ago, it would probably have been sufficient to mention the use of tokens only to conclude that there are no more convincing signs of symbol use in the animal kingdom. Indeed, except with reference to the higher primates, this statement still seems virtually unimpeachable. Recent studies of chimpanzees suggest, however, far greater capacity to use symbols than had hitherto been imagined; the species may well be capable of human-level perception and making with linguistic and pictorial symbols.

Though there is yet no evidence that chimpanzees can produce a drawing and discern an object represented in it, such animals can look at photographs or drawings and relate them to the world of objects and persons. A chimpanzee appears able to look at a photograph and recognize who is depicted therein, even though, in the absence of personal testimony, we cannot be sure. Furthermore, it appears that learning based on three-dimensional objects transfers to drawings of these objects, though the relevant studies are open to several interpretations. Also pertinent is a primate's willingness to perform a task in order to see a picture more clearly in focus. It remains uncertain whether chimpanzees receive pleasurable feelings from the purely aesthetic aspects of a display, such as texture, style, expressiveness, and use of color; but their ability to read a two-dimensional display as representing objects in the world merits a surmisal that symbolic functioning is occurring.

Even more astounding are the results of recent attempts to teach "language" to chimpanzees. Earlier efforts had been failures, but it now appears that the fault lay more in the analysis made by the psychologists than in the capacity of the chimpanzee. Washoe, from Nevada, has learned a considerable amount of American Sign Language, while Sarah, residing in California, has learned to decode (or read) complex messages expressed in colored, variously shaped tokens. Neither instructional attempt is completed and the documentation on both is still sketchy but, unless the first reports have been misleading (and there is no reason to suspect that they have been), the researchers have demonstrated considerable potential for learning a language resembling natural language through other than vocal-auditory means. Washoe can signal scores of words and handle multiword answers and commands, proceeding at a high rate and with few errors. Sarah can answer questions that appear to involve stimulus identity, conditional probability, and even embedded references—for example, What is the color of the name of apple? These chimpanzees seem to have the cognitive prerequisites for language, can make the necessary discriminations in the world, and can link these to more or less arbitrary symbols (tokens or gestures).

Vexing questions must be answered before determining whether there are significant differences between what these animals do and what humans can do. Apparently, the chimpanzees do not ask questions spontaneously, rarely report what has happened to them, do not "play" much with their elements of language, and do not invent new words; their language use, rather than being communicative, self-initiated, or filled with experimentation, seems part of a game conducted with the experimenter for certain rewards. Nor is there evidence that the chimpanzees can handle syntax in the ready and generative way of the human child. The Gardners have not studied word order, and Premack has made a given word order compulsory. Neither of these conditions allows a determination of whether these chimpanzees, like human children, gravitate toward the correct syntactic relations when combining symbols. Along the same vein, the environment of Sarah is carefully controlled and new instructional methods are systematically introduced when she fails to acquire a concept; thus her powers of inference are not allowed free play.

Finally, there is some question about how far the chimpanzees can develop their linguistic potential. Although both progressed further than many would have predicted, there are signs that the animals have reached the level of language use that is optimal for them (they are at adolescence). They have resisted, at times violently, the attempts to teach them further, or to make them handle complex constructions involving many words with intricate embeddings or propositional reasoning. Like the apes who enjoy drawing but do not create representations, these animals show little if any tendency to take language further or along different paths than those shown. These factors suggest that while the chimpanzee certainly has some potential toward symbol use, it is not the fate of his species, as presently constituted, to become an easy and natural practitioner of a humanlike language, fluent in expressing his wants and feelings, his recollections, and his ideas. Given equivalent environments, a child readily acquires language, the chimp does not. Instead, chimpanzees have been allowed a glimpse of the promised land of symbols, but it was left to their weaker and less agile competitor to enjoy the fruits and the burdens of unrestricted symbol use.

In this chapter, I have generalized about a tremendous variety of organisms and stages, to such an extent as to make nearly every statement open to challenge. In other portions of the book this would be a fatal flaw, but I have been less concerned with describing animals and infants with complete authority than with suggesting, by means of contrast, the crucial characteristics and differentiae of human art. If statements here should be erroneous, if animals and infants could really perceive, feel, make, and symbolize the elements I have withheld from them, my total argument would not be undermined. Rather, I should then be talking about art and attempting to relate it to all of animal or organic development. It is only because I am convinced that the differences between human and nonhuman species are considerable that I have drawn upon animals and infants as a means of introducing the problem of human aesthetic development. That is, I have sought to bring out the characteristics of artistic activity by reviewing behaviors that are not artistic, and have undertaken a developmental analysis of a phenomenon by examining stages where the important features can be only faintly detected.

Despite this emphasis, many of the behaviors described above share affinities with aesthetic creation and perception. For example, human perception of artistic works seems characterized by an ability to focus on diverse aspects of an object—to orient to its most salient features, to note its dominant qualities, to respond to gestalten, to detect those gestalt-free aspects involved in style, texture, and harmony, and to appreciate its symbolic references. Analogously, children and higher animals have developed the capacity to perform complex making skills—to use implements for achieving ends, to treat objects in various ways, to build structures, and to achieve systematic orderings. These capacities are drawn upon when older children construct configurations of wood or lines and interpret them as representations of objects or as exemplifications of properties. The animal and young child also appear to have a diversified feeling life; they can integrate feelings with perceptions and acts. This capacity will be involved when, in confronting symbolic objects, the child or adult experiences changes in his affective life. Finally, we have seen that, even in the first years of life, the capacities to solve problems, to imitate others, and to communicate messages of some complexity have already evolved, and the highest primates have clearly evinced nascent skill in using elements in a symbolic way, in integrating their feelings, behaviors, and perceptions on the level of symbols.

This ability, detectable in chimpanzees but essentially alien to the animal world, will be the hallmark of artistic activities. The artist employs the same developing systems as the young child but with a crucial difference: His actions, perceptions, and feelings are directed toward symbols, elements that have become imbued with a referential significance, that stand for his feelings, experiences, ideas, knowledge, objects, and desires, that exemplify qualities and properties of importance to him. This ability confers tremendous power upon his activity, because no longer is the organism restricted to elements that are immediately present, or to actions and feelings tied to the here and now; instead, every experience he has had, or would like to have, enters into the realm of communicative possibility. Only the symbol user can leave the world of his direct experience and go on to create new worlds in his imagination, or to discover such worlds by "reading" the symbols of others. Why this potential should be available to humans and not to animals is in one sense a metaphysical question; but whatever the reason this capacity for symbol use depends on the developments of the first year of the child's life. In the following chapters we will discuss a number of factors that seem to contribute to the human's unique capacity for symbol use. Of these, none is more crucial than the emergence of modal-vectoral sensitivity, a capacity that arises from the most primitive feelings of the young organism, yet continues to underlie the most sophisticated use of symbols in the artistic process.

THREE

FROM MODE TO SYMBOL

The world of the 5-year-old shares comparatively few features with that of the animal or the infant. The toddler can speak his native tongue clearly and expertly, make most of his wishes and ideas known without difficulty, and follow the conversation of others or a television program while busily engaged in one or more unrelated activities. He is a master of motoric skills, walking, skipping, running about, playing ball, writing his name, climbing trees, perhaps swimming or riding a bike. He knows numerous melodies and sings them as he walks about the house, marching or pirouetting when he hears a strong pulse, inventing variations as he hums a tune during his morning bath. He may be able to read a few words and can make painstaking discriminations among pictures, sometimes astounding his parents by his memory for details or his sensitivity for stylistic features. He is also able to draw objects and construct interesting patterns, to name colors, invent simple rhymes, tell a story, or build a fortress of sand. In nearly all activities he is aided tremendously by the capacity to devise, use, and comprehend various kinds of symbols. This ability distinguishes him from younger children and from all other animals. In this chapter we will complete our discussion of what is distinctive about the early years of infancy and then suggest the mechanism by which the use of symbols becomes possible. Only then will we be able to focus explicitly on the child's use of symbols and relate this capacity to his eventual participation in the artistic process.

CHARACTERISTICS OF EARLY CHILDHOOD

A pivotal characteristic of early childhood is the development of the sense of object permanence, superlatively outlined by Piaget. For the young infant, discrete objects do not exist. Locations and qualities may be associated with certain experiences, but these features lack an existence independent of the limited set of behaviors directed toward them. When the child is in direct contact with it, the breast will stimulate a rooting response and yield pleasurable tactile sensation, but this object will not exist for the child outside the context of feeding. When the child watches an object disappear, he ceases to look for it: Out of sight is, for the 4-month-old, out of mind.

By the first year of life, the child is able to follow an object that has been removed from sight, but if he does not find the object in the place where he first searches for it (which is usually its original location, rather than the place to which it was moved), the child behaves as if the object no longer exists. Only as he approaches his second birthday does the child achieve a developed sense of the object, as things continue to exist for him, irrespective of their temporal and spatial context. The child who witnesses the disappearance of the object now invokes a theory he has constructed, whereby all objects continue to exist in space and time, despite momentary disappearances; the child will continue to look for his doll or his duck, rejecting the possibility that the pet animal has ceased to exist.

Except perhaps among primates, a developed sense of objects seems absent in the animal kingdom. Cats, for example, move quickly to the fourth of Piaget's stages (searching for a hidden object in the place where it had been), but never reach a higher stage. Perhaps this fact helps to explain the absence of symbol use among animals: In order to employ symbols or language, the organism must have a view of the world in which objects continue to exist, or else the symbols cannot have any referents.

Why the object concept should develop and what the object means for the child is not yet understood, but the following considerations seem relevant. For the young infant the object exists only as a sum of actions—a ball is something to be sucked, to be bitten, or to be rolled. Each object has some potential actions it alone elicits, and a larger number of actions it elicits along with other objects. As the child's experience accrues, objects come to acquire a distinctive set of actions and potential actions that are elicited or potentially elicited whenever he comes into contact with the object.

While it might seem adequate to speak of the object simply as the sum of its potential actions (and perhaps as the sum of potential discriminations and feelings as well), there seems to be a further element. As the child continues to work with objects, he will perceive that they possess certain general properties, one of which is that they do not disappear permanently but always reappear. One action appropriate to every object is searching for it after its disappearance. Thus it becomes possible to posit a permanent object, to perform potential actions upon objects even in their absence, secure in the knowledge that they will once again reappear. Once this stage of object permanence has been reached, similarities between objects present and absent become more significant than differences, for the child now perceives all objects as if they continue to exist throughout time and across distances of space. The child has thus evolved from the state where actions and perceptions and feelings are directed only to present objects, to a state where his three systems can also deal with elements that are potentially present. This capacity in turn permits the emergence of symbol use.

Symbolization requires appreciation of an object and the capacity to link the object known to a picture, label, or other kind of element that denotes it. Gestalt perception allows recognition of the symbol across variations in presentation. But the linking of symbol and referent appears to presuppose as well a neurological connection between two regions of the cortex; for example, between the auditory area where the sounds of names are stored and the visual area where objects and symbols are perceived. Geschwind has pointed out that in most, if not all, nonhuman species the capacity for such "cortical-cortical" connections is limited. These animals can learn to link a sound, object, or picture to some kind of behavior, providing that the link obtains between the cortical sensory element and the subcortical limbic system, involved with the reduction of basic drives such as hunger, thirst, or sexual release. However, these organisms do not have the extensive neurological structures that would allow formation of nonlimbic links between sound and picture, between picture and object, or between picture and picture, which are required in symbol use. Recently it has been shown that the highest primates, such as chimpanzees, are able to make associations of this sort, for example transferring a response learned to visual display of an object to a task in which the same object is presented tactually. Presumably, then, such organisms do possess some capacity for cross-modal cortical connections, and, hence, are capable of rudimentary symbol use; nevertheless, only the rich cortical interconnections of the human child would seem to allow unlimited expansion of symbolic function.

A few other differences between human and infrahuman species are worthy of brief mention in our attempt to fix the limits of symbols and art. The lengthy maturation of man and, in particular, the latency period between ages 5 and 10, enable the child to develop at a leisurely rate with greater freedom for individuation. While many animals have critical periods during which specific experiences must occur if certain capacities are to evolve, the human infant seems characterized rather by "sensitive periods," whose temporal and spatial limits are not so rigidly demarcated and whose alternative courses are more numerous. Human culture figures prominently in the normal child's development. Whereas humans can build upon the progress and learn from the experience of their predecessors (with symbols assuming a crucial role in the transmission of culture), the absence of extensive culture among infrahumans means that each new generation must commence development from equally primitive levels. The amount of curiosity, the ease with which new information is assimilated, and the capacity for fine movements of the hand combine to make the human infant a perpetually exploring creature. The extent of sensory cortex enables the human to make increasingly precise differentiations in various modalities: "the potentials for becoming a human being, as compared with a less complex kind of animal, lie largely in this enrichment and elaboration of the sensory and motor ranges of experience."

RELATIONS BETWEEN PERSONS AND THE DEVELOPMENT OF THE SELF

A further attribute of the young human is his intense interest in the world of persons. From an early age the child pays special attention to other people and to manifestations of them—he alerts to the human voice, responds to a smile, focuses upon faces and facelike configurations. These perceptual tendencies may be "wired in" and comprise part of "tropistic perceptions." So compelling are the face and the eyes of other persons that failure to orient toward these targets is viewed as a sign of abnormality. And the possibility that the child is uniquely sensitive to the sounds of human speech is supported by the recent finding that, like an adult, even a 1-month-old child bifurcates sounds within the speech range (for example, at the same physical point between voiced and unvoiced sounds).

Whatever the reason, the child's attraction to other humans seems beyond dispute. Caretakers play an indispensable role in the normal development of the child and can be replaced neither by mechanical apparatuses nor by the peer group. Disruption of the tie between parent and child after the first year of life can upset the child, with a lengthy separation from the loved object having devastating traumatic effects. Perhaps, in fact, the development of a strong emotional relationship to one or more caretakers, and then gradual separation from them for increasingly lengthy periods, is a prototypical experience integral to species survival. At any rate, an affective involvement with other individuals is a pivotal developmental event, probably essential for later fulfillment of the parental role; these primordial ties will be reflected in the involvement with various kinds of symbolic objects, such as those involved in the arts.

The special character of the mother- (or caretaker-) child relation is brought out by recent studies suggesting that Piaget's object concept develops more rapidly in relation to the world of persons than to the world of objects. The child becomes upset at the loss of a person earlier than at the loss of a toy, less readily accepting "out of sight, out of mind" when the departing object is his mother. That the mother-child relationship may be prototypical of subsequent relationships seems underscored by the cross-cultural parallels in its development and in the recapitulation in brief form of its salient features in subsequent interpersonal contacts.

The initial regulation between mother and child involves strong nurturing and feeding instincts; social contact begins within a month or so, the mother and child communicate through looks and sounds as well as through feeding. By the latter half of the first year the mother is recognized as a particular individual and behaviors are directed exclusively toward her; a feeling of possession evolves, and idiosyncratic signs are used for selected communicative purposes. Shortly thereafter, the relationship becomes more differentiated; the child is able to use the mother for fulfilling specific needs, and the child and mother become able to communicate a range of different feelings (pleasure, annoyance, satisfaction).

When the second year begins, the possibilities for communication become enormously magnified, as the child and mother can speak to one another and the child can initiate relations with other individuals. The nuances and the specificities of contacts continue to become more refined, as the child is now able to assert his own desires and to express his displeasure in many ways. And a certain distance between the two individuals will assert itself as the child moves out into the world of others. However, the mother still remains as an anchor point, a place of solace, the primordial figure against whom other persons and experiences are measured. Aspects associated with the mother take on special meaning for the child—a picture of her, an item of clothing, the mention of her name; these activities herald the advent of symbol use and the possibility for art. When the child relates these materials to his mother, or perceives aspects of her personality in the objects she has made, he is adopting an aesthetic attitude.

A pivotal event in the first years of a child's life is his development of a sense of self. The infant is totally egocentric in that he cannot separate his existence from that of others; he is part of their world and all that happens to him perforce happens to (and is known by) all other persons. The sense that the person is a particular individual, with his own name, wishes, feelings, beliefs, and ideas, takes many years to unfold and cannot be reduced to simple factors; it is inseparable from the whole developmental process. (Interestingly, infants and certain animals appear to behave toward their own reflection as if it were another organism. Only chimpanzees raised in the company of others have an incipient sense of self—they will behave differently toward their own reflections than those of other chimpanzees.) The evolution of self seems dependent upon contact with others, observation of social relationships between persons, monitoring of one's own behavior, and growing awareness that persons speak of themselves and of the child himself as a separate entity. Perhaps it also involves the ability to employ metaphor, to posit oneself as a discrete object or person, analogous to others who are more easily known. Finally, the development of the self also seems to be closely tied to the child's ability to imitate. One of the original students of the "self," the brilliant American psychologist James M. Baldwin, was an imaginative student of imitation, and his suggestive account of that process is highly relevant to our understanding of artistic communication.

IMITATION AND THE SELF

All intelligent activity, in Baldwin's view, is stimulated by models that the child can imitate. From an early age the child can make a broad distinction between persons and objects. Material objects assume less importance for the child, because he can treat them in a habitual way, while the ever-changing aspects of persons increasingly attract his interest. Other persons are seen as the ultimate source of pleasure and pain, and thus occupy an increasingly important niche in the child's world. Imitation is directed toward other persons and is the means by which the child comes to understand the subjective aspects of life; he grows to understand what others are like, even as he gains further comprehension and sense of himself.

The distinction between persons and objects was, for Baldwin, the initial factor in determining character, "the child's very first step toward a sense of the qualities which distinguish persons." However, the full understanding of the other individual and one's relation to him took a considerable period of time. Baldwin outlined the subsequent stages through which the child must pass. To begin with, there was a *projective* sense of personality in which the child first discovers individual differences, contemplates other individuals, and notes characteristic behaviors. The child is struck by the irregularity or capriciousness of the behavior of other persons and seeks to organize it in some way: "[the child] watches the face for any expressive indication of what treatment is to be expected: for facial expression is now the most regular as well as the most delicate indication."

In the "projective stage," the child passively lets the other's behavior "project" upon himself. Soon, however, the child attempts to react differently to individual persons, quiet to one, showy to another. The "subjective stage" begins with the advent of persistent, effortful imitation. The subject becomes active, takes the details of the situation into consideration, and begins to separate himself from others. The child assimilates to his own body the other person's physical behavior, and his own imitations cast light upon himself as a subject.

When the child's growing sense of self is now used to illuminate other individuals' behaviors, the child has entered the "ejective stage." The child realizes that other persons' bodies undergo the same experiences that he does. What *he* feels is now ejected onto others. They are also "*mes*," the child realizes, and his ejective self is born. The child's sense of his self grows by imitation of the other, while his sense of the other grows in terms of his sense of himself. "Both ego and alter are thus essentially social." For a time the child's sense of self includes too much—all those about him. Much of development can be viewed as the increasingly accurate (realistic and limited) sense of self. Ultimately, interpersonal understanding involves an appreciation that others are individuals like oneself, that they have typical ways of acting, as well as enduring characters that transcend individual situations. In sum, then, the projective stage involves consciousness of others before awareness of the self; the subjective stage involves consciousness of self; the ejective stage involves consciousness of others as similar to oneself.

Baldwin attributes the child's appreciation of feeling life to his imitation of emotions discerned in the expressive behaviors of those about him. A sensitive correlation process is set into operation. The child comes to realize that when another individual expresses emotion in a certain way, he is apparently undergoing the same affect as was the child, when he spontaneously produced the expression in an analogous context. Eventually the child is able to appreciate aspects of the individual without having to confront him directly. The voice, the face, the signature, or the shoes can stand for the whole person. As the child becomes able to experience and to appreciate complex feelings and emotions, he is able to discern similar states in other persons, to participate in subtle interpersonal relations, and, eventually, to incorporate or appreciate these in symbolic objects. He may also eject feelings onto inanimate objects, such as a stuffed animal, and attempt to recreate significant relations and situations with such "substitute persons." In coming to know his own feelings and the feelings of others, through interpersonal interaction and through contact with various objects, the child will achieve fundamental prerequisites for aesthetic practice.

We have spoken of the development of a "sense of self" and have illustrated the crucial role played by social imitation in the comprehension of subjective experience. Even if the details of Baldwin's account are not completely verified, his general description of the interaction between an individual, other individuals, and the gamut of emotions has the ring of accuracy. Development of the self through imitation and communication is an unconscious as well as a conscious process, and, a person's sense of self—his identity, to use the current parlance—is an enormously complex and subtle phenomenon. Although a conscious sense of identity or self is many years in coming, its roots extend to the earliest experiences of childhood, particularly the special quality of the feeling life of the young child. While any comments about the feeling life or the self of the infant are, of necessity, highly speculative, Erikson's thoughts on this subject are worth consideration in view of their suggestiveness for our inquiry.

GENERALIZED FEELINGS

Let us begin by considering what happens when infants undergo traumatic experiences. Living through a fire, the death of a parent, or some other calamity can have considerable impact even though the event is a unique occurrence. Indeed, such early disasters may cause severe repression or neurosis later in life. In general, however, reactions to such an event depend chiefly on the kind of *general* balance, poise, or equilibrium the individual has obtained in his daily experience. It is generally believed that a "healthy child" can withstand such a traumatic event, but explanations of his "health" or "strength" in terms of reinforcement history or drive states are most inadequate. Erikson, in his discussions of general aspects of feeling life, seems to have provided the most apposite formulation; he speaks of the ratio of *trust to mistrust* that the child develops over the first months of life. Trust results from the mother's love and care for the child, yet is not a direct result of the amount of care administered. The child seems sensitive to the *quality* of love: A genuine and deeply felt caring on the part of the caretaker must somehow be transferred to the child in a clear and convincing manner.

Articulating this point of view is not a simple matter, and one may be tempted (as was Piaget) to translate the notion of "basic trust" into information theory, calculating the amount of uncertainty the child feels from one moment to the next. To prove sufficient, such a metrical formulation would have to reflect subjective aspects of a mother's reactions —whether she feels a genuine and deep attachment for the child or is merely feigning such behavior, whether she has achieved a mutual understanding with the child, or remains disjointed and ill at ease. I believe that, just as the raven can detect irregularities in the locomotion of its prey, the young child is able (perhaps by alertness to rhythms or general configurations) to perceive when the behavior of a parent is natural and uninhibited; his assessment will necessarily have a pervasive influence on his feeling life and his relations with human subjects.

Belief in qualities as elusive as basic trust—in a child's capacity to sense his caretaker's genuine feelings and to incorporate them in his own psychological makeup—rests on the seemingly mystical notion that there are truths in the world, appropriate rhythms to behavior, and prescribed ways for the young organism to sense them, and that when these are violated by feigned, illegitimate, or insecure behaviors, the organism will sense it. According to such a view, normal development can be blocked if the parent fails to treat the organism as valid on its own terms, or if the parents' good feelings are, for whatever reason, not accurately transmitted to the young child (as may happen in cases of infantile autism). Just as there is an apparent wisdom in the evolution of species and the survival of the fittest, so, too (according to this view), there seems to be a coherent sequence to development, which may be realized or thwarted, depending on whether the participants are able to enact their roles properly. Even though I would be most hesitant to maintain that there is one rhythm, behavior, plan, or feeling essential for optimal interpersonal relations, I feel that there may well be a range that is likely to be effective, another that will lead to less happy results. Only future research can determine whether this position is useful and, if so, which evolutionary events have contributed to such qualitative sensitivity among children.

Scientific support for Erikson's position may well be forthcoming. Just as the frog's retina contains cells that respond when the animal perceives an insect, there may be mechanisms that enable the young child to discern the veridicality or degree of trust inherent in a caretaker's behavior. Evidence for such a "truth sense" is found in studies of eye-to-eye contact; this form of direct communication between individuals, vital at every developmental level, has its origin in earliest infancy, is the precursor of social relationships, and can, if impaired, signal the presence of severe disturbance. Such detecting mechanisms can be deceived at times, but if too often misled, the frog or the child becomes "distraught" or "neurotic"; indeed, the autistic child is characterized by his inability to maintain eye-to-eye contact. The kinds of demonstrations presented by the ethologists, such as the profound effects of maternal deprivation on young macaques, and the kinds of explanations ethologists offer in terms of contact, timing of interactions, relations with peers, and sensitivity periods would seem closely related to the phenomenon under discussion here. It seems probable that humans are so constituted that they will thrive in a certain kind of environment. If too many of the expected elements are absent, or too many unanticipated ones are introduced, the organism may be thrown out of equilibrium, and such adaptive mechanisms as "basic trust" will never develop.

Our understanding of these general states—feelings of trust, security, comfort or distrust, insecurity maladaptiveness—is extremely primitive, yet it would be misguided to ignore these clinically demonstrable phenomena merely because an explanation is not yet at hand. Indeed study of these phenomena would appear warranted. Upon it rests the possibility of explaining the general qualities and states crucial in artistic activity, such as the fidelity or sham that audience members detect in particular works; or the properties of liveliness, grace, balance, penetration, harmony that creators instill and perceivers appreciate in works of art. If individuals claim to perceive such qualities in art works, if they declare that one work seems genuine, another contrived, these are genuine reactions that must be explained by any psychological theory of the arts. Indeed, if the arts involve communication of information about subjective experience, the initial manifestation of such communication may be crucial; "truth" or "genuineness" in works of art may reflect the sense of well-being and veridicality also paramount in encounters with human beings. And if the artistic process involves communications between individuals, the particular qualities (be they universal or unique) of persons obviously assume critical importance.

Such talk will no doubt discomfit the scientist, who despairs of ever studying these aspects (if they exist) in unalloyed forms. Yet, such terminology and concepts are rampant in the writings of artists, who are unconcerned about the demands of empirical investigations and are eager to describe their works on a level fully adequate to them. Students of artistic development are consequently confronted by a dilemma, for they want to treat artistic objects with the respect accorded them by artists and aestheticians while retaining the possibility for scientific investigation of the fundamental nature of the artistic process. My solution has been to examine the roots of artistic activity, to capture what is fundamental about the process before its complexity reduces the prospects of comprehension. Since we have held that symbols are crucial to the artistic process and represent an aspect of development that may be unique to humans, it is vital to clarify the ontogenesis of symbol use. In the following pages I will introduce a hypothesis about the first uses of symbols in the human, one which I believe can also explicate what is special (and perhaps unique) about the arts. I believe that symbol use rests in part upon the ability to discern and to capture general properties in objects, and that an understanding of this "alertness to the general" lies at the core of symbol use.

MODES AND VECTORS

What is known about the child's earliest experiences and feelings? Until the child can himself describe them, one must rely on inferences from his behavior, ranging from his physiological reactions to his facial expressions. While efforts to list the child's basic feelings seem destined to remain in part a reflection of the psychologist's extrapolating powers, recent efforts to characterize the overall features of the child's affective life, to focus on the general properties of feelings rather than on the identification of specific emotions, offer greater promise of verification.

A brilliant attempt to bridge the tantalizing gap between the child's physiological functioning and his psychological processes is Erik Erikson's description of the organ modes and zones. Building on a psychoanalytic framework, Erikson outlines the manner in which libidinal energies are focused in the initial months of life upon the mouth, only to be displaced according to a predetermined (presumably genetically based) plan onto the anal region, and subsequently, the genital area. This much is common Freudian conviction; Erikson then proceeds to describe the manner or *mode* of functioning characteristic of each zone, drawing crucial psychological implications from particular patterns.

Beginning with a description of the oral zone, Erikson records its preeminent function of ingesting food, at first rather passively and then

increasingly actively and aggressively. As he considers the purely reflexive to be of scant psychological interest, Erikson directs his attention
to two psychological modalities. One is the modality of "getting" which
derives from passive ingestion; the other, more active modality of "taking"
or "holding on" derives from search for food. The physiological has taken
on psychological significance when the child not only ingests food but
begins to "get" or "take in" tactual experience, visual stimulation, parental love, objects, attention, and approval, and when he experiences
affinities between these formally analogous activities. Separate making
activities are felt to have similar properties, common affective concomitants. Analogous parallels are discerned by Erikson at the times when
other bodily zones are in the ascendancy. The predominant modes during
the anal period are "holding on" and "letting go," primordially in relationship to the feces, increasingly in relationship to other objects, individuals, and phenomena. So, too, the modes characteristic of the urethral-
genital region—intrusion, inception, and inclusion—come to characterize
the child's general approach to experience, figuring in his fantasy as well
as his reality-oriented thought.

While each zone has its characteristic mode, the remaining modes
are also exhibited there; the mouth and the "oral child" may be involved
literally or figuratively in retention, elimination, or intrusion. Furthermore, the whole body or person may come to be permeated by a particular mode. A child with heightened anal retention can also become
tight-lipped, expressionless, and rigid; a patient becomes "all mouth and
thumb, as if milk were running through the body." The several modes
each involve the relationship between an individual and the field or
objects outside his body. Some emphasize keeping portions of the environment within one's own body, while others involve the release of what
is or was once part of the body into the external field. Some involve
contact between parts of one's own body, others between parts of the
body and external objects. The modes may be regarded, then, as primitive means used by the child to communicate or interact with the outside. Despite these intermodal affinities, however, it seems most probable
that each mode has a distinctive affective component. Observation and
introspection suggests that passive taking in of food or events is experienced in a different manner from active biting, and that elimination of
waste or words is not identical to the introjection of organ or other.
Thus, while the modes are akin to each other as various way of relating
the body to the world, reliable differentiation between the principal ones
seems indicated.

Erikson's contribution inheres in his demonstration that physiological
modes (which are not to be confused with sensory modes), initially

related to drive states and bodily patterns, become social and cultural modalities, the child's way of experiencing the world beyond his own skin. A preliminary application of this view to the realm of artistic development suggests that a child not only experiences the mode within his own body and in relationship to the environment in a consistent manner, but also tends to discriminate the same kinds of modal configurations in various stimuli which he beholds, including symbolic objects and to behave in a "modal" way toward external objects.

To be sure, for the young infant, the outside world is coterminous with himself; there is little point in speaking of "inner" or "outer" stimulation. As the child gradually differentiates himself from the environment, however, the sensations and percepts that have previously characterized his undifferentiated self can be brought to bear on objects and forces, which are acquiring a separate existence. Even as the child experiences modal functioning in his own body, he becomes sensitive to such properties as "taking in" and "holding on" in the various individuals, objects, and works he contemplates. Furthermore, the child's own activities in various realms, including manipulation of objects and use of symbol, also involve modal properties that can be appreciated by the child and by others. Modes, then, figure in the child's phenomenal feelings, his perceptions, and his creative activity. Indeed, these general qualities are crucial just because they evoke feelings, because they are realized in the child's making behavior, and because they guide his discriminations. Modes such as "openness" or "penetration" cut across the three developing systems, facilitating their gradual integration into a single overarching structure.

Detailed consideration of a specific mode—for example, taking in—reveals that several dimensions are involved in it. In order to "take in," the organism must either open a portion of his anatomy or, on the psychological level, evince readiness to assimilate new experiences. This "open-ness" or potential for "taking in" need hardly assume a single fixed form, however; taking in may occur readily, with reluctance, widely, narrowly, at regular or staggered intervals, alternating with closing up, uniquely for imbibing massive aliment, or repeatedly for the assimilation of small portions. Likewise, incorporation or introjection may occur intermittently or regularly, forcefully or weakly, with hesitation or enthusiasm. Clearly, the various modes are abstractions, general stances toward the world; any specific exercising of a mode necessarily involves a considerable number of specific dimensions or *vectors* pertaining to the speed, forcefulness, conviction, and so forth, with which the mode has been realized. Not every mode involves every vector; nor are the vectors necessarily manifest equally at each stage of development. Furthermore, they are not completely isomorphic with one another and resist ready expression in language. Despite these difficulties, a list of some vectoral properties of the modes described should help concretize the ensuing discussion (see Table 1).

TABLE 1   MODES AND VECTORS

Zones	Characteristic Modes	Some Vectoral Properties of Modes
Oral-sensory (mouth/tongue)	Passive incorporation (get, take in) Active incorporation (bite, grasp, investigate)	Speed (quick vs slow) Temporal regularity (regular vs irregular) Spatial configuration (wide vs narrow; curved vs angular)
Anal-excretory (sphincter)	Retention (hold onto) Expulsion (let go, release, push out)	Facility (ease vs strain) Repletion (hollow vs full) Density (thick vs thin)
Genital (penis-vagina)	Intrusion (stick into; go into) Inception or inclusion (take into, envelop)	Boundness (open vs closed) Also: directionality, force, depth, comfort, texture

Although the existence of modes is plausible, as is their accompaniment by feelings and their projection to external objects, neither their centrality for the child nor their importance for aesthetic experience can be uncritically assumed. Evidence for the importance of the modes is the same sort as can be invoked for the centrality and sequence of the erogenous zones described by Freud. Observations of the infant and consideration of his principal needs both reveal that mouth activity, in particular the ingestion and the occasional expulsion of food, is of importance in the early months of life, and that anal activity, especially the retention and expulsion of fecal matter, becomes of significance later in the second year. That these modes and their accompanying vectors begin to take on psychological significance is less easily demonstrated. But studies of the young child at play, of rearing in different cultures, and of individuals with emotional disturbances suggest that the extension of modes from physiological functions to social and cultural experiences is pervasive. The modes serve as a transition to symbolic behavior, the vehicles by which the three developing systems evolve from action upon the environment to involvement with various symbolic and cultural forms.

What might be considered as errors or generalizations made by the child are often revealing; evidence about the existence and significance of modal-vectoral (m/v) properties may accordingly be derived from this source. A number of developmental psychologists have been impressed by the generalizations and analogies the infant makes, and their observations may be elucidated by Erikson's concept of the mode. Although it is not possible to review all the evidence, some examples of errors and generalizations made in infant imitation should indicate the extent to which the child appears to abstract the modal or vectoral properties of his environment:

1. At 9 months, one of Piaget's children watches him stick out his his tongue and then raises her forefinger. Piaget comments: "It would seem that the child's reaction can only be explained by the analogy between the protruded tongue and the raised forefinger."

2. On various occasions, Piaget's daughter opens and closes her hand slowly after he has opened and closed his eyes; opens and closes her hands after he has opened and closed his mouth; opens and closes her mouth after he has opened and closed his eyes.

3. While trying to extract a chain from a matchbox, Piaget's daughter slowly opens her mouth as if this making activity aided her in locating the required action—the widening of the slit.

4. Piaget says a given number of syllables and his infant repeats roughly the same pattern. Similar phenomena are reported among children learning to speak.

5. A 4-month-old child "began a curious and amusing mimicry of conversation in which she so closely imitated the ordinary cadences that persons in an adjacent room would mistake it for actual conversation."

6. A child of 13 months rocked his head from side to side in response to movements of other parts of his body. He also "accepted" his father's movements of head or arms as an adequate response to his own soliciting head movements.

7. My wife and I conducted a study of imitation in our 6-week-old infant and found that the child was more likely to imitate the m/v properties of extension/withdrawal and openness/closedness than the particular bodily zone in motion.

Such instances suggest that the young child is sensitive to the m/v properties of behavior and stimuli. These properties, which impress themselves on the preverbal child, are then abstracted from configurations and become a basis for imitation. The errors are crucial, of course, for they indicate which features of the model's behavior are most salient, which of little moment. As Werner and Kaplan suggest:

> [Children] were sensitive to the dynamic properties of opening and closing and expressed these properties through different parts of the body capable of carrying out these dynamic features. . . . The sensory-motor patterns possess qualities which defy a mere analysis of the movements of specific body parts; they have such qualities as direction, force, balance, rhythm, and enclosingness.

It seems likely that a mode is experienced or "felt" initially throughout the body, and that its vectoral properties become increasingly refined and differentiated in the course of development.

A trend from physiological (bodily) modes to psychological modalities of thought has seemed plausible to various observers. Kubie maintains that:

> Since infancy and childhood, cravings arise in body tensions. It is inevitable that the child's thought should begin with his body and that his first concepts must deal with the parts, the products, the needs, and the feelings of the body. . . . The indirect representation of the parts of the body occur exceedingly early in the formation of language in the growing child . . . furthermore, they stand as a fringe and background tonus behind all conscious adult thought and feeling.

Writing from a somewhat different perspective, Lorenz stresses the organism's tendency to generalize, and suggests that responses to specific kinds of stimulation which may have been programmed in the organism are soon projected upon features of the environment that share similar figurative properties. And Wolff, summarizing a developmental trajectory like the one proposed here, indicates that congenital potentialities for psychic structure, each specific to an organ,

> become organizing principles for experiences related to other organ systems by mode displacements and become categories of thought independent of physiological activity by mode estrangement. . . . The formal properties of action patterns rather than physiological activities *per se* are therefore the referent to the mode. . . . What characterizes the mode is its configurational or space-organizing properties, which no doubt are derived from bodily function but extend far beyond these to become styles of veridical thought and social interaction.

The examples and their theoretical underpinnings suggest that the modes and vectors are a flexible set of "dimensions" or "categories" through which the child initially experiences his own body and the world beyond. Precisely because of their generality, they are not restricted to one form of child behavior. Rather, one finds in the child's physical activity, his interaction with others, his imitation, his perception of various objects, and even his own manipulations and creations clear signs of the organizing role played by the modes and vectors. The kinds of generalization and analogies made suggest further that even when particular modes or vectors appear in diverse domains or sensory modalities, they are experienced by the child in fundamentally similar ways.

That the same modes can be experienced in different systems and situations may seem counter to our claim that development involves three initially separate systems. In fact, however, the increasing extent to which modes permeate the child's experience serves as an indication that the once discrete systems are coming together. At first, a mode is a bodily feeling that accompanies only a circumscribed set of primitive behaviors and situations. At this time a particular mode, for example "taking in," occurs only in the region of the mouth during times of feeding. The transfer of the mode to other zones and situations can only occur when the child's developing systems begin to interact with one another, as perceiving, making, and feeling schemes intertwine. The increasing connections between different portions of the nervous system facilitate this generalization and transfer of modes. By the end of the first year or so, taking in can occur in other bodily zones or throughout the whole body, and in novel situations, as in one's relation to a toy, a person, or a pictorial symbol. Only as the developing systems become integrated with one another can a child's own making behavior (as when he builds a structure) or his perceiving (as when he looks at a scene or object) involve modal and vectoral properties.

Such claims are certainly subject to challenge. One might question the extent to which the apparent prominence of modes and vectors is merely a reflection of the kinds of language suited to discussing activity and experience. Indeed, this language is so general as to make it difficult to conceive of analyses that would not somehow incorporate m/v properties.

These objections have a surface plausibility. Indeed, we talk of openness, penetration, depth, and so forth, in many contexts, and feel that such properties permeate our experience. What is striking, then, is the extent to which such a note is almost entirely absent from "hard-nosed" discussions of behavior in psychology. The difficulty posed by modes and vectors is that they are "higher-level" terms; they defy a ready analysis into quantifiable, experimentally controllable dimensions. Most investigators have therefore shied away from m/v treatments, because they despair of measuring reliably openness or closedness, potency or embeddedness. Indeed, current psychological writing conveys the impression that head turning, bar pressing, and other conditionable responses are the child's chief activities, and shape, hue, and absolute size the aspects of configuration most prone to be noticed. Yet observation of children in less structured situations suggests that these quantifiable and operationally attractive dimensions achieve psychological import (if ever) only after sensitivity to general m/v properties has dominated experience.

The psychological literature confirms then, that there *are* varied ways of talking about an infant's world. Traditional investigators might concede the appeal of the more allusive language adopted here, but would reject it as inherently unscientific. Erikson's contribution becomes critical, providing for the first time a basis for considering such properties. The writings of various investigators suggest, in addition, that methodologies more appropriate for uncovering m/v properties are gradually evolving. Only with such techniques, and a set of hypothetical possibilities, will it be feasible to determine whether the m/v aspects outlined are appropriate concepts for discussing children's perceptions and creations, whether m/v aspects can be reliably distinguished from other aspects, and whether their relative importance changes during the course of development.

Until now, aesthetically oriented psychologists (ranging from the Gestaltists to Jung), while sensitive to the salience of general qualities, have tended to equate them in importance. One might say that such approaches use vectoral language indiscriminately to discuss all experience. From the developmental viewpoint, however, there is little reason to expect all modes and vectors to be equally prominent at all times; considerable evidence indicates that certain m/v properties should be ascendant at different times. One would predict, for example, that modal properties of intrusion and inception, and vectoral aspects of force and penetration would become particularly dominant during the years 3 to 5 (the Oedipal period). In addition, some children would be expected to have heightened sensitivity to particular m/v, others relative insensitivity to the same dimensions. These hypotheses ought to be weighed against the implication that all experience must necessarily be described in terms of all modes and vectors.

It may be useful to anticipate the general drift of our argument. At the time that the three developing systems of the child come increasingly to interact, m/v properties play a crucial role for the child. Perhaps because of the proliferation of associations between sensory realms (facilitated by neurological maturation), the child is beginning to discover parallels and patterns in various domains. As yet unable to use ordinary language, he seizes upon the common m/v aspects of these experiences and attempts to express them in some way. In the second year of life he makes groupings based on perceived modal parallels, and his feeling life becomes permeated by such generalized qualities as trust, security, malaise, or imbalance, each of which would seem to reflect a certain pattern of modes and vectors.

At about this time, the child encounters for the first time elements used in symbolic reference rather than as signals—words, musical tones, colors, lines, man-made objects of various sorts. According to a well-established developmental principle, an individual entering a new realm of experience relies upon established procedures and only slowly evolves mechanisms appropriate to the new realm. For example, as the child first begins to use and understand language, he does not immediately supply the appropriate referent or apply words in the correct context. Rather, he makes use of the processes and proclivities already extant; accordingly, the child's sensitivity to m/v properties comes to dominate his initial experience with words, pictures, paintings, musical motifs, and other symbols. We will see numerous examples of how the child first employs symbolic elements in order to express m/v qualities and, similarly, how he anticipates such general qualities from the symbolic vehicles he encounters. Rather than noting specific geometric, physical, or denotative aspects, the child, in his feeling, making, and perceiving of these symbolic elements often stresses the common dynamic and configurational properties that characterize the m/v realm.

A final advantage of the modal-vectoral hypothesis is that it draws the discussion of feeling life decisively away from a list of specific emotions or affects. What one has, rather, is a series of states, in all likelihood traceable to the infantile states of arousal, which may be interpreted as any of a number of specific emotions, depending on the surrounding context. The m/v property of openness may be related to the emotional states of carefree abandon, vulnerable exposure, or neutral receptivity, depending on surrounding circumstances and on individual interpretation. Such emotions as envy, such general states as basic trust, such aesthetic categories as balance or harmony, can similarly be viewed as combinations of modes and vectors. The m/v hypothesis accounts both for the neutral qualities of certain bodily sensations and for the strong emotional tinge of others, without confusing these two strands, as so often happens in discussions of affects.

The demonstration that early symbol use rests on m/v properties, while interesting and perhaps important, does not prove that modes and vectors are relevant for subsequent aesthetic creativity, perception, or feeling. I will argue later that while m/v properties continue to figure in experience in diverse adult realms, forming a backdrop to assimilation of all experience, they are particularly characteristic of and crucial in the arts, which have as a principal goal the capturing and the communication of various general qualities about the world and about subjective experience. Illustrating this point in a discussion of artistic metaphor, E. H. Gombrich indicates that:

> Metaphors are not primarily transferred meaning, linkages established, as the classic theory of metaphorical expression has it. They are indications of linkages not yet broken, of pigeon-holes sufficiently wide to encompass both the blueness of a spring day and a mother's smile. It adds to the interest of these categories that they are so often intersensory; the smile belongs to the category of warm, bright, sweet experiences; the frown is cold, dark, and bitter in this primeval world where all things hostile or unpleasant strike us as similar or at least equivalent.

Further support for our contention that the arts highlight modal/vectoral relations will be drawn from the testimony and experiences of various individuals associated with the arts, from speculations about the training involved in becoming an artist, and from notions about the nature of development, including the further evolution of the three developing systems.

MODES, OBJECTS, AND SYMBOLS

The categories of modes and modal-vectoral experience and the world of objects both play constitutive roles in the genesis of symbol use. Since the modes are the child's principal way of experiencing his own body, and a primitive way of organizing his perceptual and making activity as well, they necessarily figure in the child's early experience in the symbolic realm. Words, pictures, musical motifs, and other symbols arouse modal-vectoral experience in the child from the first, and, particularly when these symbols figure in the arts, they continue to be apprehended in a modal-vectoral way. A crucial issue, then, is the manner in which this aspect of the child's experience becomes intertwined with his growing realization that the world consists of discrete objects, each existing in time and space irrespective of the child's present situation.

My view is that modes and objects form complementary aspects of all symbolic activity. The use of a symbol generally involves both a discrete reference to an object or element in the world, and a more general allusion to a penumbra of associations, meanings, and properties. The word *girl* denotes a young female and connotes such general properties as lightness, openness, brightness, balance, and freshness. Neither of these aspects of meaning need dominate, though as a practical matter the dictionary meaning is stressed in scientific reports or job applications, the connotative aspects in songs or poems. Picasso's *Les Demoiselles d'Avignon* denotes several harlots, while connoting harshness, sadness, sharpness, sterility and degeneration. While it is doubtless an oversimplification to regard all symbol use as involving simply these two aspects, linking denotation to objects and connotation to modes, this framework does provide a rough-and-ready way of conceptualizing the components and ontogenesis of symbol use.

Let me try to flesh out what I am proposing. Initially the modes are limited to a few aspects of bodily functioning—the young infant feels openness or closedness, emptiness or fullness, particularly at the regions of the mouth, but perhaps also throughout his body. Two trends occur during the first year of life. First, he becomes increasingly able to transfer these modal experiences, which occur initially within his body, or in relation to objects in contact with his body, to the perception and making of objects external to himself. Second, he becomes sensitive to subtle nuances within each mode and to a multiplicity of modal and vectoral properties. The modes and vectors become a set of categories that he can bring to bear on the full range of his experience; in addition they come to combine with one another in diverse ways, giving rise to distinct emotions, styles, aesthetic categories, and temperamental strains. A basic set of modes and vectors, founded in bodily experience, interact and coalesce with one another to form a much larger set of general categories through which the child comes to know the world. The child at the threshold of symbol use conceives of the world in significant part as a flux of these different primary and secondary general properties, which have their origin in his organismic experience and which now pervade his experience of objects and persons.

It might seem that once the child appreciates the permanence of objects he has achieved the necessary and sufficient condition for symbol use, since the primary function of a symbol at this time is to denote a particular object, or, better, a class of objects. Yet, as we have seen, initial symbol use does not feature a discrete link between signifier and referent. Rather, the symbol enters into the child's early life as part of a complex amalgam in the experiential world and only acquires clear demarcation after many months of discrimination and practice. At first the symbol arouses a wide range of associations and of meaning, which shares little with the eventual denotation, but much with the set of modal-vectoral properties surrounding its use. *Mama* is not primarily a name of a distinct person, but rather a range of possible actions (calling, desiring, clinging, etc.) and a combination of modal-vectoral properties (trust, closeness, intermingling, satisfaction, comfort, etc.). Indeed initial symbol use appears to divide the child's experience into wide domains (*Mama* may refer to everything positive, *Nana* to all that is negative). Only very gradually does the child's conceptual division of the world come to resemble that of ordinary adult symbol use. Were it not for the modal properties, and their potentials for specific as well as general combinations of qualities, it is doubtful that the child could ever make the transition from the set of actions, perceptions, and feelings characteristic of the sensorimotor period to the capacity to exercise his three systems on the level of symbol use. In a profound sense, modes allow the transition from sensorimotor behavior to symbolic activity.

The roles of modes and objects can also be seen through a consideration of the classical epistemological dyad of subject and object, knower and known. If we think of the infant and the environment as separate entities, we find that the former's task is to come to know the world of objects and persons by means of his actions upon them. Since his knowledge of objects depends in large measure on his contact with them, we need a vocabulary of contact, of the relationships between subject and object, or within an object, in terms of proximity, attraction, contact, interaction, or fusion. This is supplied in part by describing actions the child can undertake (reaching, grasping, sucking), in part by describing the modal relation between the bodily and object surfaces in contact (holding on, letting go, penetration, inception, envelopment, intrusion), and in part by describing the vectoral quality of this contact (how intense, rough, smooth, hollow, active, deep). Only through a combination of actions, modes, and vectors does the object enter into the experiential matrix of the child, forming the basis for further knowledge about the objective and subjective worlds.

The relevance of all this to aesthetic activity is manifest. The individual as a perceiver or creator of art works takes a position at a certain distance from an object, draws certain qualities from the object, invests the object with certain desired qualities. The kinds of properties characteristically associated with aesthetic objects are in large part those that dominate the experience of the young child, though they include in addition properties of much greater complexity and subtlety. The initial modal-vectoral situation of a child in contact with his body or with external objects provides a primordial model of later relationships with art objects.

Such relationships have two facets, both traceable to these initial subject-object interactions: a general stance of distance from or intimacy with the artistic symbol, involving such dimensions as attraction, fusion, and withdrawal, and a more specific capacity to detect it or infuse into a symbolic object a range of qualities, such as hollowness, activity, balance, direction, or closedness. These facets of aesthetic perception and symbolic activity would seem inseparable partners of that capacity to perceive objects per se and to link symbols to classes of objects, which is central in apprehending the denotation of all symbols. The modes and vectors have the peculiar quality that they are in a sense more primitive than objects, since no appreciation of object permanence is necessary for m/v sensitivity, and since such sensitivity is an inevitable concomitant of bodily and extrabodily experiences; yet at the same time m/v categories extend beyond object perception in subtlety and pervasiveness. All symbol use potentially involves a fine-grained and highly differentiated experience, which may include countless arrangements of modal and vectoral properties. The development of object competence and of modal-vectoral sensitivity are thus seen as complementary trends, both essential for symbol use. Understanding of objects is fairly well established by the years of early childhood, and sensitivity to modes and vectors has its foundations in the most primitive experience, yet continues to deepen throughout the child's development.

A CONVERGENCE OF ORIENTATIONS

We have argued that bodily experiences common to young children constitute a foundation of later symbolic "shared" knowledge, with the possibilities for aesthetic communication resting, in part, on common experiences with modal/vectoral properties. In addition to its centrality for the analysis of symbol use in the arts, the modal-vectoral position also appears crucial for developmental theory, since in it various psychological perspectives appear to converge. The Gestalt tradition, for example, strongly affirms the role of modal properties in perception, going so far as to suggest that overall physiognomic properties of objects are the ones perceived initially. Our viewpoint, while consistent with the Gestalt perspective, draws on developmental and psychoanalytic theory in suggesting that there may be a sequence of properties to which the organism successively becomes responsive, depending upon its level of psychosexual (and perhaps physiological) maturation.

The fact that psychoanalysts, Gestalt psychologists, and cognitive theorists interested in development have all been drawn upon in this discussion of m/v properties may be of considerable significance. Perhaps, in the child's sensitivity to such properties and in his tendency to conceptualize experience in these terms, we have a genuine convergence between these seemingly disparate psychological approaches. Piaget's notions of affective schemes, imitative behavior, and figurative perception, the psychoanalytic view of symbolism and psychosexual states, the ethologist's emphasis of gestalt properties and distinctive features, Werner's model of symbol formation all seem to point to, or at least be consistent with, the sketch of modes and vectors introduced here. Perhaps the power of the modal concept lies in the fact that it is neither a cognitive nor an affective construct, or, rather, that it incorporates aspects of both domains. Far from being merely a feeling experienced by the individual, an act made, or a discrimination perceived, modes become schemes for organizing all experience, be it perceived, felt, or made; modes invoke discrimination, involve feelings, and are manifested in motoric activity. Indeed, persons can classify in terms of these categories in perception, produce instances of the categories in making, and experience these categories as affect. The modes and vectors provide both form and content for the child's earlier experiences. They are drawn on as the child proceeds from the sensorimotor to the symbolic stage, and remain as a backdrop and substratum for all later experience.

If, then, the modal approach receives widespread concurrence from principal developmental approaches, without, however, being a logically necessary way of discussing human development, it promises to be a useful tool for describing the ontogenesis of the artistic process. For, as will be elaborated later, artistic objects derive their impact in part from the fact that they capture and convey general qualities of the type experienced by mature individuals, but already accessible to young children. Artists are individuals able to realize within symbolic media those m/v aspects that one apprehends in the world and senses in one's own body. Indeed both preverbal children and artists who reject standard cultural labels or categories are marked by a heightened sensitivity to the general qualities of persons and objects we have termed m/v aspects (perhaps purchased through a neglect of the exclusively object-related features). Young children classify experiences by their physiognomic properties; artists testify that the works they perceive and create are embodiments of such expressive qualities. In neither case need a particular emotion or feeling be at stake; rather, the arts draw on the general forms, rhythms, and combinations that characterize feeling life as a whole—less the emotion itself than the "dynamic quality of emotion." Artistic development of course includes much more than general sensitivity to modes: The capacity to create a unique work, the ability to realize the full implication of a text or score, go well beyond the sensitivity described here. Yet, much of what is distinctive about aesthetic activity may depend on the continued development of modal/vectoral sensitivity.

Unfortunately the experimental evidence on these questions is almost nonexistent, and the modal/vectoral hypothesis is no more than that, though clinical and cultural evidence does support its claims, and some pertinent psychological investigations are outlined in Chapter 5. Important at present is not any particular list or sequence of modal sensitivities, but rather the contention that m/v sensitivity is pervasive, and the hypothesis that specific modes assume particular importance at different developmental levels, and in various symbol systems. Whether these trends are biologically determined, fixed in sequence, or subject to learning and cultural influences can only be determined if sensitive measures of modes and vectors can be devised.

A full exploration of the modal-vectoral hypothesis would probably involve at least the following investigations: a study of the infant's principal ways of imitating and communicating, with special reference to the roles played by various modal and vectoral properties; a parallel study of children's play with physical objects and with symbolic materials; an examination of the relationship between an individual and an art object, both with respect to the individual's distance from and involvement with the art object, and with respect to the particular expressive and representational properties discerned in the artistic object. For each of these studies, it would be necessary to work out a taxonomy of possible modes and vectors, as well as of other properties (geometric, quantitative, denotative, etc.) that fall outside the range of modes and vectors. Observers would examine behaviors in terms of these analytic categories and attempt to pinpoint the role played (or not played) by modes and vectors. A final synthesis would involve a consideration of the particular modes and vectors evident at different stages, in different situations, and within different developing systems, as well as examination of the evolution of a modal category. The mode would be traced from its original location in the bodily experience of the child to its subsequent position as a component of making, perceiving, and feeling on the plane of real objects and in relation to artistic symbols.

As one moves from the child's elementary experiences to the more complex emotions and reactions of adults, a language of greater subtlety and breadth than modes and vectors becomes desirable. Such feelings and emotions do not, to my mind, involve qualitatively different structures, however. I view the specific emotions about which adults speak (pride, jealousy, awe) and the general properties that pervade aesthetic discourse (balance, formal elegance, rhythmic sweep) as combinations of modes and vectors, which recur in a certain range of situations; the individual may correlate his modal-vectoral affects with the elements of the situation he perceives, later declaring that he is experiencing a certain emotion. When the individual is uncertain about the interpretation of felt modes, he will place special reliance on environmental clues. By and large most people probably have experienced in a similar way an array of modes and vectors, and have many combinations of modes and vectors in common. This is what leads to the possibility of experiencing situations and works of art in common ways. The artist, however, may structure his modes in a novel way, thereby achieving a powerful impact on his audience, and perhaps affecting its arrangement of modes and vectors. If, however, his particular blend of modes and vectors is captured in an art work in too idiosyncratic a way, the work of art may be remote from an audience, "leaving it cold," or "failing to touch" it.

The properties we have classed together as modal/vectoral undoubtedly represent a wide range of physiological and psychological mechanisms varying in complexity and manner of emergence. Certain modes may be present within a developing system at birth. For example, the capacity to detect such properties as openness, closedness, or nearness may be part of the brainstem visual system operative at birth and present in lower organisms. The capacity to distinguish such features of speech as stopped/nonstopped, or open/closed may also be congenital, part of the perceptual system of every human. The perception of other general characteristics of objects, such as symmetry, harmony, or expressiveness, or vectoral properties of force, tension, or density, may be quite advanced developments, dependent upon elaborate practice of the perceptual system and considerable experience in the world of persons and objects. And the transfer of a mode from one system to other systems similarly depends on a wealth of experiences and associations. These considerations remind us of the "generality" of the general; objects are multifaceted, and it is most unlikely that all modal-vectoral aspects are available from the first to all persons. Indeed, the very word *mode* remains ambiguous, since the cross-modal associations described by Geschwind do not necessarily involve the sort of general properties under discussion here. Nevertheless, the capacity to discern continuities between disparate objects and experiences, including those drawn from different sensory realms, does seem related to Geschwind's argument; both themes reflect the finding that children have a strong synesthesic tendency involving colors, sounds, and other sensory experiences. Presumably, these synesthesic capacities reflect cross-modal associations as well as sensitivity to the kinds of modal-vectoral properties introduced here. And it is probably in this suppleness of association and generalization that the human differs most pronouncedly from the higher primates.

One further aspect of the modal-vectoral hypothesis deserves reiteration. We have already indicated the crucial contribution of the object concept to symbol use. We should now stress that modes and vectors *are* another way of cutting up the universe, one more primitive in some respects than an "object" approach, yet with greater potential for subtle discrimination and continued deepening throughout the individual's life. Once the child has constructed the object concept, he possesses an extremely useful approach to the world, serviceable throughout life: Classification by objects is the constant tool of the child and scientist. Such an object-orientation may however be limiting, if it implies this is the only way to divide up the world. Consequently, the more supple and variegated approach allowed by modal-vectoral sensitivity is of crucial importance in permitting a more flexible manipulation of symbols. It also provides a powerful tool for the young child who is able to modulate his references by drawing upon modal-vectoral as well as objectlike properties. The modal orientation, stemming from primitive physiological mechanisms as well as complex intersubjective experiences, generalized and diffuse rather than focal and specific, open to many interpretations rather than rigidly determined, derived from and felt in the body, constitutes a useful, perhaps essential, counterpart to the "object" approach to the world of experience. As the scientist develops an object approach to its ultimate level of sophistication and finesse, so the artist and the connoisseur derive the fullest potential from a modal-vectoral stance.

Our general argument having been introduced, it may be advisable to recapitulate it briefly and to touch on one possible difficulty. We maintain that human development is initially characterized by the operation of three systems which soon, however, begin to interact and combine in a variety of ways. Such interaction describes even as it defines the limits of animal development. In humans, however, perhaps because of the capacity for nonlimbic cross-modality associations, a whole additional level of development involving the use of various symbolic vehicles is possible. In this chapter we have introduced the conception of modal/vectoral properties in an effort to suggest how the transition from the sensorimotor to the symbolic stage may come about, to indicate a convergence between various developmental theories, to pinpoint certain aesthetic aspects of symbol use, and to illustrate the manner in which the three developing systems manifest analogous forms and content.

Our view of the arts involves communication of various qualities associated with subjective experience. We now propose that the arts are concerned in large measure with the communication of modal/vectoral properties; since such qualities dominate human experience, we expect humans to have the capacity to produce, appreciate, and experience various art forms as they gain control over symbolic media. The artist's mission is to capture modal-vectoral properties in a symbolic medium. As we have seen, some communication of such general properties appears to occur, even in the initial days of life.

Since art involves communication, we have examined the beginnings of communication between individuals. We have stressed the importance of early eye-to-eye contact, of the feeling of trust between individuals, because of our convictions that such early communication is crucial in its own right, and that a "truth-sense" figures in all interpersonal communication, whether it involves face-to-face confrontation or communication through aesthetic objects. The evidence indicates that while young children are capable of quite subtle communication and appreciation of feelings with those whom they know, they may not yet be able to invest objects with such subjective aspects. This ability apparently involves symbolic capacity and awaits our treatment in the following chapter.

Why, however, should we confer a special status upon objects created by humans? Cannot the perceiver experience openness or boundedness in a cavern or a waterfall as well as in viewing a portrait or hearing a symphony? The answer would seem to be this. Once the organism has become sensitive to modal-vectoral properties, he can relate them to any kind of display or experience, man-made or not. He may even be unaware of any difference between a landscape and a representation of it. Our argument about the primacy of objects produced by subjects rests in the first instance on an assumption that human reactions to displays are always an analogy from their own personal, bodily experience. Humans know boundedness, penetration, or looseness because they have felt these dimensions themselves. When they contemplate another individual or object, they "eject" their own feelings, or the feelings they have themselves known upon the other object, discerning modal/vectoral properties in that object. No belief in conscious or deliberate "empathy" is necessary for this argument; the process of "reading out" modes may be totally preconscious, yet it seems manifest that one cannot find a property or quality embodied in another object unless one has in some sense known this element oneself.

Why confer a special status upon objects produced by others? First, because the kind of communication most important to individuals is communication from or toward another individual. Hence in the course of development objects produced by other individuals are always of particular interest, especially when they embody direct traces of the creator. In the second place, next to ourselves (perhaps even more than ourselves), we know other humans best. Thus, we will treat objects as if they contained humanlike qualities and modes, simply because we understand and respond best to human subjective experience and are sensitive to analogies of it, whatever the realm. The fact that many young children form attachments to animals or to specific toys, far from contradicting our point, offers independent support for it. Children may feel they have much in common with such objects; they treat them in a humane way seeking interpersonal comfort and responsiveness from these ersatz persons.

These proclivities—to value human communication and to interpret it in certain ways—will be influenced by one's cosmology. Belief in spirits or gods leads to the interpretation of natural events and objects as communications from the deity. Hence, by extension, the world of natural objects is treated as akin to objects produced by other individuals—in this case, by a god. The special status conferred by nonreligious persons on man-made objects is extended by religious individuals to any object that has religious significance, just as it may be withheld from all objects unconnected to or in conflict with the deity.

The general point I wish to stress is that objects are treated as manifestations of other persons or subjects, because of the way in which our perception of qualities evolves. Objects that are in fact created by other individuals, divine or mortal, thus possess (at least potentially) a special significance, because they not only manifest modal-vectoral properties but are also, at the same time, communications from other individuals. They are alive, vital, reflective of human thought, rhythm, and belief in a way that naturally formed objects are not. They are the most promising sources of new insights about human life; they give us access to other minds, including unusually creative ones. The capacities to appreciate the relationship between creator and object, and the manner in which an individual reflects aspects of himself and his knowledge in his works require the tapping of the perceivers' knowledge about other persons' feelings and activities, as well as his own qualities and feelings. This understanding of the artistic process is too complex for the young child, but we have seen that each of the components has undergone considerable development in infancy. Let us turn finally, then, to the evidence for art in the protosymbolic period.

INFANT ART

In the first years of life, there is little in the way of literature, music, or painting that anticipates adult forms. Only rarely are there reports of prodigious behaviors, such as the 9-month-old who could sing correctly a tone struck on the piano and who did not speak until long after she had learned to sing on key. Yet an important contribution to later artistic participation occurs even among nonprodigies in the development of sensitivity to modes and vectors. To be sure, the human infant neither differentiates the content and forms of messages in his own behavior, nor will he read such distinctions into displays that he sees. For that very reason, however, the unity in aesthetic experience felt by many adults probably has its origin in the apparent integrity of experience in the young infant; that same tendency in children which has been called egocentrism, lack of distance, an excess of embeddedness provides for the child during the most impressionable period of life a model of a unified experience or wholeness. Failure to undergo such experiences, to develop a veridical or trusting attitude, to witness a model of intersubjective communication, or, alternatively, a premature tendency to categorize or compartmentalize, seem destined to impair the development of aesthetic sensibility and the power to produce a work that coheres.

With the exception of this sense of unity, which has its foundations in the child's simple feeling life, the aspects of infancy directly related to art are scattered. In the feeling realm, one notes the emerging ability to understand communications of mood on the part of another individual, through perception of facial expressions, voice, or gestural accompaniments. The child can appreciate various vectoral properties of the object, but still seems unable to comprehend the existence of a creator behind an art object. And only the simplest expression of his own feelings can sometimes be observed in his communicative use of modes. In the making realm, a 1-year-old child can on occasion maintain regular rhythms or produce very primitive drawings, though these are probably exercises rather than representations. The first drawing strokes are rhythmic, however, a suggestion that the inherent motoric components of skilled behavior structure protoaesthetic activities from the first.

Most making activity in the first year is relatively primitive. Possible precursors of formal elegance in art are nevertheless also found, such as the balanced drawings of young children and the union of affect, subject matter, and intention in initial utterances. Piaget offers an account of variations on a theme in the motoric behavior of the young child:

The child constantly repeats the act of letting go, of throwing and rolling, but it is without knowing what will follow and precisely with the intention of finding out. . . . Jacqueline tries to reproduce an effect already observed (tilting up a box, floating, throwing, pouring water, etc.) but this effect is a theme with variations.

He also talks more generally about the beginnings of inventiveness:

Real invention arises as a function of a sort of rhythmic conditioning by the ensemble of the preceding behavioral patterns. . . . Given this rhythm, invention is therefore comparable to the application of familiar means to new situations . . . being creative also partakes of the process of . . . the discovery of new means through active experimentation.

All told, however, such formal aspects of early making activity seem reflections of general motor development, not direct analogs of aesthetic behavior.

Perceptual discrimination of the sort required in the arts may also have a modest beginning in the first months of life. Many children can by their first birthday recognize pictures of various sorts. Capacity to sing may precede the ability to speak, and some year-old children recognize specific musical examples. Indeed certain youngsters exhibit a proclivity to understand and express themselves musically before they do linguistically. While other parallels between infant discrimination and adult artistry might be introduced, the genuine antecedents of the critical faculty seem dependent upon some degree of competence with symbols.

There is little dispute that the difference between human infants is staggering. Constitutional factors of temperament unquestionably exist and, presumably, inherited differences also characterize the making, feeling, and perceiving systems, their rates of development, form, and efficiency. Of interest here is less the obvious fact of individual differences (consider Galton's precocity or variations found among infant temperaments) than their role in precocious artistic achievement. The data are anecdotal but it is worth noting that some future musicians have sung or reproduced melodies in their first year or so, whereas the necessity for some motor skill has prevented the emergence of promise in the plastic arts at quite so early a time. Nonetheless, perceptual precocity may exist in the realm of painting or music, for example, in the capacity to be deeply moved by a work of art.

Claims of early audience membership or connoisseurship are, however, not reliable, for the ability to divide up or interpret the world in unusual, unexpected ways may be due to assorted factors. The individual can either be a precocious genius or a pattern generator who can discern unanticipated arrangements, or he may simply be ignorant of the way in which his particular culture divides up the world—he may have unintentionally produced unusual and unanticipated categorizations. To children, the world appears as they describe it; rather than imposing systematic order like the scientist or creating novel arrangements like the artist, young children (who do not separate reality and illusion) report what they see. Although in some cases the pattern perceived may be truly original, it is most difficult to demonstrate the child's discovery as other than accidental.

Reports of unusual sensitivity in early childhood are difficult to interpret. Some investigators believed they had detected the precursors of genius in some extremely sensitive children: "Some very young children possessed unusual sensitivities manifesting themselves in several if not in all sensory modalities . . . color, bright lights, noises, animal sounds . . . seemed to have an extraordinary impact upon these children at a very early age." A follow-up examination revealed however that these children were very deeply disturbed; like autistic children, they lacked protective barriers against various sorts of stimulation and so became psychotic.

We find, then, tremendous differences among individual children, and serious difficulties in interpreting the significance of such differences. To the adult a child may possess a mystical ability to see what he and other adults have failed to see, and thus he becomes a perceptual or receptive genius. In fact the child may have simply made a blunder, misstatement, or casual aside. Genetic endowment may contribute to future artistic excellence but it can never ensure it. The difference between the child who will truly become a genius and the one whose genius is ephemeral is a subject for the following chapters.

I LOVE ANIMALS AND DOGS

I love animals and dogs and everything.
But how can I do it when dogs are dead and a hundred?
But here's the reason: if you put a golden egg on them
They'll get better. But not if you put a star or moon.
But the star-moon goes up
And the star-moon I love.

A 5-YEAR-OLD GIRL

MICE

Creeping mice in the garden
And our cat comes
And bounces on a mice.

A 5-YEAR-OLD GIRL

FIGURE 8. "The Santa Fe," by a child in the first grade.

FIGURE 9. "Katharine's Phoebe Song," by a 4-year-old girl.

FIGURE 10.   Drawing by a 4-year-old boy.

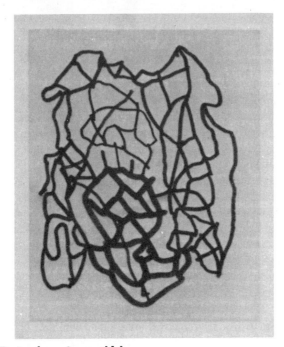

FIGURE 11.   Design by a 3-year-old boy.

123

FIGURE 12.   Drawing by a 3-year-old boy.

FOUR

THE WORLD OF SYMBOLS

THE BROKEN COOKIE

One afternoon my 20-month-old daughter was seated in a high chair having a glass of milk. "Give me a cookie," she asked. She took a bite from the butter cookie, then placed it on the tray in front of her. She took a look at the remaining piece and said, "It's a boat." I took a look at the fragment and thought that, indeed, one could see the prow of a ship on one side. Then she picked up the cookie with both hands and tugged at it, breaking the fragment. "Oh! The boat broke," she exclaimed.

Six months later, while on a trip to the seashore, I sat down with her near the water's edge and we dangled our feet in the surf. Spying a particularly lovely seashell, I picked it up and showed it to her. "Isn't it pretty?" I asked. My daughter looked at it for hardly a moment, scooped it up, and put it in her mouth. I asked her to take it out, reminding her not to put foreign objects in her mouth. She then threw the shell away.

These two incidents help define the extent to which a young child, at the dawn of symbol use, is involved in the artistic process. In the anecdote about the cookie, we have a symbolic and potentially artistic interaction. My daughter was not only correctly labeling the object as a cookie, but was transforming the cookie into a new symbolic object. Her gestalt perception discerned a resemblance between the cookie and a boat and she revealed the new meaning of the object in a public communication. Already she was using the materials of her environment to make a novel object acceptable to herself and to other persons. Then she went on to give the newly-designated object a life of its own by introducing it in a literary context—"the boat broke," even as she was injecting her own feelings into this objectivizing process with the exclamatory "Oh." Here we have the bare but unmistakable outlines of a creating process: making an object, discerning symbolic significance in it, and using the object to convey further thoughts and feelings about the world. To the extent that others could share her thoughts and feelings, and discern analogous information from her "story," my daughter had performed a communicative artistic act. Her behavior was analogous to that of the painter or writer who seizes upon an idea or percept in his environment and then embodies and transforms it in an available symbolic medium.

Lest we conclude that the 20-month-old is a developed sculptor or litterateur, we must consider the second incident. During our trip to the shore, I had seized upon an (admittedly natural) object and remarked on its attractiveness. The meaning of my remark was that, either in comparison with other shells I had seen, or, more generally, in contrast to the general run of objects, this particular shell embodied a combination of color, shape, expressiveness, balance, and delicacy that engendered a pleasurable feeling and invited closer examination. I was adopting an "aesthetic attitude" toward the shell, involving myself subjectively while maintaining a certain distance from the object. My daughter's behavior was most interesting, for she obviously found the shell sufficiently attractive to warrant picking it up. Rather than admiring it from a distance, however, she attempted to know the shell in the way most accessible to her—passing it over the sensitive surfaces of her mouth. While this behavior was not satisfactory to me, it would be presumptuous to term her approach bereft of the aesthetic attitude. Yet, by placing the shell in her mouth, my daughter was prevented from considering many salient aspects of the shell, though she was affording herself the "taste" of it, which I had not savored. The incident underlines the extent to which our relationship with objects is colored by our previous activities. It also reveals that the distance from objects which is considered part of the aesthetic attitude takes time to develop and may be culturally mediated. "Isn't it pretty" is a much less natural approach to an object than "doesn't it taste good," and will probably gain ascendance only after more autocentric forms of perception have declined.

SYMBOLS

These incidents illustrate that the 2-year-old child has arrived at an important developmental milestone—the adoption of symbols in a world hitherto dominated by direct or unmediated relationship to objects and persons. The young infant perceives, makes, and feels in direct relationship to the substances and sights around him: an object is played with; a person is seen; a smile or a delicious piece of candy give rise to feelings such as comfort, openness, pleasure. The developmental progress made in the first year and a half of life is of three principal forms. First, the child slowly constructs a world of permanent objects; second, he becomes increasingly sensitive to the modal/vectoral properties implicit in his feelings and experience; finally, he integrates his three developing systems with one another in an increasingly facile way. Indeed, as various psychologists have proposed, the interaction of systems may make developmental progress possible: "systems seem to develop at different times . . . and may remain in relative isolation from one another . . . gradually they become coordinated into a complex superordinate system which integrates their separate capacities."

We have proposed that system interactions become increasingly important as one ascends the phylogenetic scale, with humans having extensive differentiation within each system, elaborate relations between systems, rich connections among the association cortexes, and, consequently, the capacity for symbolization. Symbol use, as described in the previous chapter, rests upon object permanence, which involves a recognition that the world is composed of objects which endure, and modal-vectoral sensitivity, in which various aspects of contact, proximity, and intersection are felt phenomenally, and discerned in other objects and persons. Once these two foundations have developed, the potential for reference exists, for an arbitrary element or symbol can be linked to a class of objects or properties, and both denotative and connotative aspects of this symbol can be appreciated.

In addition to the referential aspect—symbols denote aspects of the world without entailing immediate action, reaction, or drive reduction—symbol use involves another equally pivotal aspect: systematic relationships among the symbols themselves. While any element can (and in certain conditions does) serve as a symbolic vehicle, symbols found in a culture have typically become organized into complicated systems. Words do not only have relationships to objects in the world but also to one another. The different parts of speech operate in conjunction with each other and more abstract words refer only to other words rather than to nonlinguistic referents. Similarly, in the realm of mathematics, pictures, and music, symbolic elements have a complicated series of associations and organizations among themselves. Mathematical symbols are to be combined with one another in specifiable ways; musical elements are typically organized into scales, chords, harmonies, and rules of composition; lines, colors, and textures are arranged in the plastic arts to produce effects, with certain of these arrangements having superior coherence or power.

Although these symbol systems are not directly isomorphic with one another, referential and systematic properties appear to pervade all symbol systems. For example, music is highly organized and systematized, but has only limited reference (though these referential aspects may be important); alternatively, paintings are clearly referential but lack systematically related components (though there is a systematic progression in the stages of painting and, under various circumstances, certain pictorial and formal arrangements are considered acceptable or unacceptable). Perhaps those symbol systems used in the arts rely particularly on modal aspects and involve a more active systematization, variation, and structuring on the part of the artist than is required with more "scientific" and "object-based" symbol systems. In many cases, the *referential aspect* of symbol use involves associations between different sensory modalities (primarily visual and auditory, or tactile and visual) while the *systematic aspect* inheres in associations within a perceptual modality (between sound and sound, or sight and sight).

To summarize, then, I view a symbol as an element or material, which may but need not be a physical object. Rather than eliciting a specific reaction the part of the subject (as does a signal in the Pavlovian sense), a symbol can denote itself, as well as other aspects of the world—a material object, for example, or a feeling, a concept, or some formal aspect of such entities. In addition to (or in lieu of) reacting to a symbol, the individual may contemplate it or conjure it up in a variety of ways. Rather than being an inevitable concomitant of a particular set of experiences, the response will be determined by the particular form of the symbol and its present relationship to other symbols. Many objects, such as traffic signs, can serve as signals or as symbols, depending on how they are used. If a green light specifies "Go" in the sense of triggering an acceleration, it functions as a signal. If, on the other hand, it is displayed in a gallery or shown in a movie (that is, embedded in these particular symbolic contexts as a representation of authority or order) it is functioning as a symbol; instead of dictating behavior it denotes experience or exemplifies concepts. The capacity to contemplate an element, to appreciate its denotation, to contrast it with other elements and perhaps to pass an evaluation upon it, is characteristic of and perhaps restricted to humans.

While I have contrasted "direct experience" with "symbol use," it should be emphasized that no firm boundary can be drawn between these realms. Certainly symbols are "real" and can be directly experienced, and, equally surely, such "real" objects as balls, bodies, or bullets may operate as characters or elements in a symbol system. What is at issue is not whether certain elements are intrinsically symbolic or non-symbolic, but rather the way in which the individual processes, creates, or responds to the different elements of his world. To the extent that he treats the elements as part of a habitual pattern of action and response, where reference to anything beyond the element is neither intended nor realized, he is operating on a sensorimotor plane. To the extent that he perceives and interprets elements as having reference to something outside themselves, or as exemplifying or expressing certain qualities, the individual is functioning on a symbolic plane. With age and experience, an increasing proportion of our time is spent operating with symbols, so much so that it becomes increasingly artificial to talk about "real" or "direct" experience. Symbols remake our world, and color even those interactions and perceptions that might previously have been judged as "direct" or "unmediated." Accordingly, symbols gradually yet inexorably become our reality, and once the individual has crossed the Rubicon of symbol use, he may never again have an innocent eye, or a symbol-free experience, except perhaps under conditions of brain injury or regression.

Use of symbols and symbolic systems is, in my view, the major developmental event in the early years of childhood, one decisive for the evolution of the artistic process. So long as shells are tasted rather than looked at, so long as objects are accepted as intrinsic to a behavioral act rather than a potential representation of the world, the organism is operating (animallike) purely on a material plane, with the three developing systems in greater or lesser synchrony. Once a sense of objects, a modal-vectoral orientation, and some capacity for systematization have evolved, the use of symbols becomes possible and, within a short period, the world of the child becomes a world of symbols. Operating on the plane of symbols produces a revolution in the child's world, for he is no longer limited to making, perceiving, and feeling in relationship to material objects and events; he can go on to invent new objects and events, adopt a variety of complex relationships to them, and use them to communicate subtle and even imaginary views and situations to other persons. Essentially he confronts a realm of infinite possibility, drawing from it, he may go on to produce unique objects, to embody his own feelings in them, and to become a practitioner or observer of the various artistic forms.

Although the premier use of symbols—the first "mama," squiggle, or tone—already implies these dizzying possibilities, one must avoid the easy assumption that the child is aware of these possibilities. Symbols may well possess special status for the adult—letters, melodies, and drawings seem far removed from and not confusable with physical objects or individuals. For the growing child, however, such elements initially are simply another dimly understood aspect of the universe, requiring no special treatment or understanding. Speech and music consist of sounds, just like thunder; letters and pictures are visual displays, just like trees or mountains; the production of sounds or scribbles is merely another making activity, like clapping or walking. In short, one initially makes, perceives, and feels what will later be regarded as symbols in ways scarcely different from those in which one relates to objects "in the world."

This attitude is not permanent, however, for the child gradually discovers that "symbolic elements" have ways of functioning distinct from other physical or animate elements. People will perform elaborate acts because of words, whereas other sounds do not produce such an effect. Certain line configurations bear significant resemblance to the world of objects (while not being identical to them) and can thus initiate actions, responses, comparisons, and evaluations, which other arrangements of lines do not initiate. Striking regularities obtain among the tones and words others issue, and the child himself has the capacity to discern these regularities, to imitate them, to produce novel instances which nonetheless recapture these regularities, and to partake of the powerful effect such symbolic forms can evoke. The child is introduced to an aspect of the world apart from natural and social objects, the realm of *symbols,* which can refer to or capture aspects of the "real world." Eventually the child can reconstruct the world previously known only in a sensorimotor way entirely anew, upon the symbolic plane.

One may distinguish a formal and a referential aspect in each artistic symbol system. There are various formal relationships that elements may assume toward one another—properties such as balance, rhythm, mood, and tone. Part of development involves an understanding and a mastery of these formal aspects. In addition, one encounters *reference* in each of the art forms. While reference is most apparent in the use of ordinary language and in the plastic arts, where symbolic vehicles can be mapped directly onto the world of object and experience, this aspect of symbolization is also found in the realm of music.

In particular, two aspects of music may be thought of as referential. There is, first of all, the widely sensed relationship between musical patterns and the emotional-feeling life of the individual. Certain configurations are perceived as melancholy or sober, others as sprightly and gay, others as joyous, ceremonious, or saccharine. These referential or "expressive" aspects of music are accessible to young children as well as to adults, and unquestionably mediate the perceiver's relationship to music. Second, music appears initially to function for the child much as language does; it fits into a context and possesses a fairly specific reference. Music without words poses assimilatory difficulties for the child. Because of the context in which they are generally heard, melodies like Brahms's "Lullaby" seem roughly equivalent for the child to "bedtime" or "good night"; the references in "Happy Birthday" or "Santa Claus Is Coming to Town" may contribute to the perennial popularity of these melodies. I have found, furthermore, that young children often give names to untitled compositions and treat the compositions as if they refer to particular events and persons. No doubt the more sophisticated listener adopts an increasingly abstract stance to the work of art and may well sneer at such a referential approach; this does not mean that he himself bypassed the stage where music has specific meaning.

The major changes in the years following infancy involve the child's emerging capacity to create and to interpret symbols, and the consequent changes in his three developing systems as they function on a symbolic plane. Needless to say, these processes have scarcely ceased by the time the child is of school age. The process of integrating the developing systems with symbolic media, well underway by then, continues, and the further evolution (which may well continue throughout the individual's life) will not lead to a qualitatively different stage. I conclude (in opposition to most learning theorists) that there is a major reorganization of the child's developing systems in the course of his life, one involving the transition from direct actions on the world to a plane of symbols; yet I find (in opposition to most cognitive theorists) that the major reorganization occurs in an early period (ages 2 to 7) and implicates processes that will continue to operate in analogous fashion throughout the child's life.

To be sure, the affects and modes felt by the young child continue to be experienced in similar fashion by older persons. The significant change is that the feeling life becomes mediated by symbols. Thus Freud correctly speaks about the continuity of affective development and notes its embryonic progression, but is insufficiently cognizant of the range of aspects that can influence a person's affective state, the changing relations among individuals, or the way in which symbol use can remake one's knowledge of presymbolic behavior. Similarly, Piaget is correct in arguing that the child undergoes a major reorganization of his world following the sensorimotor period. But, in his concentration on scientific thought, Piaget mistakes changes related primarily to that realm for universal shifts influencing all psychological development. And, quite possibly, he overstresses the effect of later shifts (particularly the advent of formal mental operations during adolescence) upon the child's mental life (see Chapter 7).

Through the modal concept, we have seen that the child's initial way of organizing the world continues to color the way in which he encounters experiences with the whole range of symbolic elements. It would be an error to view development as a process in which modal-vectoral sensitivity is increasingly eliminated in favor of a wholly objective and abstract approach to materials. Sensitivity to general properties remains, in my view, an essential part of all human perception and cognition, and an effort to eliminate it produces an artificially restricted view of human nature.

I have proposed an integration of Freudian and Piagetian systems based on the possibility of extending a modal-vectoral and a symbolic analysis to areas that these psychologists have not themselves investigated. Reference to specific domains of cognition and affect has been suspended in favor of a view of three developing systems, which eventually operate upon a symbolic level and culminate in diversified artistic practice. I contend that, as the child develops, he may continue to make, feel, and respond to objects and experiences, both in the direct way characteristic of the sensorimotor period, and on a superimposed plane of symbolic experience. Making a painting involves acting upon objects and performing motor skills, as well as dealing with a symbolic system of great delicacy; similarly, viewing a painting involves consideration of its status as a "thing" in the world, as an attractive object, and as a comment on aspects of the world couched in a symbolic medium. The power and fascination of the arts rests precisely on the fact that individuals become involved with them on both the sensorimotor and the symbolic planes.

Since the development of the child from infancy to artist is our concern, a few general remarks on the nature of development are indicated. Subsequently, some findings of developmental psychology which are reflected in the arts will be briefly sketched. As these findings are chiefly of the quantitative rather than the qualitative variety, a mention of them will hopefully relieve the necessity of recapitulating them in our specific discussion of artistic development. We will then focus in some depth on the symbolic system central for most children—natural language—and attempt to demonstrate the principal events that occur and the mechanisms operative in the the transition to a world of symbols. Following the discussion of language, we will look briefly at the fate of the three systems as they are recapitulated on the symbolic level; at the relationships between early child activity, play, and art; and at the extent to which children of 5 to 7 may be considered participants in the artistic process.

CONCEPTUALIZING CHANGE

The nature of the mechanism by which development proceeds is a question that tempts every fledgling theorist. A theory of development should have its apparatus of change, though the often encountered insistence that there be a mechanism for *explaining* change is no longer so persuasive. After all, in tracing the course of development, many embryologists have found it satisfactory merely to describe the evolution of the embryo from zygote to neonate without endeavoring to indicate what *causes* the cell to divide or the organism to assume a particular form. Signaling this trend, Bellugi and Brown, in describing so complex a phenomenon as language development, are content to point out that "the very intricate simultaneous differentiation and integration that constitutes the evolution of the noun phrase is more reminiscent of the biological development of an embryo than it is of the acquisition of a conditioned reflex."

Following this argument, I see no necessity to postulate a simple mechanism that brings about changes. I am struck by the relentlessness and inviolability of the phenomenon of development, which seems to occur in one direction, or under certain circumstances in the reverse direction, from birth until death, irrespective of conflict, reinforcement, or equilibration. Like the embryo which must unfold if it is to be, the human must develop. The possibility of any organism remaining frozen at a point of development is synonymous with death; those that do not progress to more complex stages will regress. The insistent nature of development suggests one reason why perpetual making, perceiving, or feeling in a given realm tends to produce greater skill and deeper insight. As these systems are exercised, their organization seems to become more stable, their interaction smoother, their precision and finesse increasingly pronounced. Within the organism, at any one time, one encounters different levels of organization; sometimes a more primitive level can assert itself, either because subsequent advancement depends on such regression or because the demands of the situation are sufficiently pressing that a more organized response cannot be emitted. Under hypnotic suggestion, for example, college students may perceive optical illusions as they appear to grade school children; indeed it may be that every percept passes through a more primitive stage before it is articulated.

Regression often appears nonfunctional to students of cognitive development. For understanding of the arts, however, the possibility of the organism backtracking temporarily is quite suggestive. In describing their creative moments, many artists mention reversion to a more primitive period or feeling, and speak admiringly of the lability and flexibility of the child's mental processes. Kris has written at length on the importance of regression in the arts, stressing that it is often adaptive (in the service of the ego) for the organism to return to an undifferentiated or less differentiated earlier state. But he indicates that

> The regression in the case of artistic creation is purposive and controlled. The process involves a continual interplay between creation and criticism, manifested in the painter's alternation of working on the canvas and stepping back to observe the effect. . . . The artist has the capacity of gaining easy access to id material without being overwhelmed by it, of retaining control over the primary process and perhaps specifically the capability of making rapid or at least appropriately rapid shifts in level of psychic functioning.

Innumerable aspects of the world are potentially accessible and significant for man, in part because of the multifarious ways of gaining access to them. The frequently observed originality of children seems due in part to the fact that they are still responsive to the many possibilities of reacting to the world. They are alert to modal-vectoral as well as object properties, less completely embedded in the ways of their culture than the average adult. The greater flexibility of children, their ability to construct materials in new ways and to revive past associations without being limited to them, as well as their rapid progress and capacity for differentiation as they invade new areas will be a leitmotif of our discussion of incipient symbol use.

The myriad ways in which children of various ages respond to problems, tasks, and experimental situations have been the major concern of genetic psychologists for several decades. With age or stage as the major independent variable, developmentalists have done thousands of studies on problem-solving, memory, creativity, perception, and so on. Some theorists find a major watershed at the beginning of the school years; others find the ontogenesis of speech or of puberty the critical points. I feel that such divisions are probably more vital for the purposes of understanding scientific problem-solving "or cognition" than for artistic activities, where the feeling, making, and perceiving systems continue to evolve according to the same mechanisms throughout life. Nonetheless I concur with those who feel that the onset of symbol use at the ages of 2 to 5 brings about major reorganization of the child's developing system; at this time the evolution which characterized the sensorimotor level is recapitulated with various symbol systems, and the child learns to put his acts and perceptions into words or pictures. Detailed reviews of a large number of developmental studies and theories can be found elsewhere, and need not be undertaken here, but it is worth mentioning some of the principal findings of the past decades.

In the most general terms, psychologists have discovered that as they get older, children are better able to handle the diverse demands of psychological tasks. Older subjects are able to organize stimulus materials more efficiently, to process information more rapidly, to attend to a wider range of features, and to focus more rapidly on the area of greatest information. Children of all ages find it easier to work with materials that are meaningful, but older children find more materials meaningful, both because of their more extensive experience, and because of their greater potential for assimilating apparently meaningless stimuli into functional categories. Children adopt a variety of strategies in their effeorts to solve tasks, with older children employing the strategies in a more systematic way, suspending strategies when they are not reliable, and avoiding those strategies least likely to pay off. There are isolated tasks at which younger children perform better than older children, and these will be reviewed later; the few reversals in developmental progress come about either because older subjects are misled by the demands of the task, or because the customary strategies they bring to the task turn out to be dysfunctional. In most cases, however, regardless of subject matter or experimental procedure, developmental studies document a gradual put inexorable improvement in performance from early childhood until adolescence.

The list of developmental changes in children's problem-solving capacity could be lengthened, but such an extension is not necessary for our purpose. I have tried to give sufficient examples to render accessible Werner's terse and useful account of less developed and more developed organization. Werner finds development proceeding from syncretic to discrete, diffuse to articulate, indefinite to definite, rigid to flexible, and labile to stable. All these trends can be discerned in scores of studies. What is intriguing is that the aspects considered most developed, while obviously necessary for the scientist, are not unambiguously beneficial for the arts. Artistic messages may be characterized as syncretic, diffuse, indefinite or labile in certain respects, and achieve some richness of nuance from these "less developed" properties. Yet in order to produce such works, the artist himself must be capable of highly developed behavior, which shows control and flexibility. The artist often uses his more developed skills to capture ambiguous and nebulous aspects of the world; he may even encourage a certain regression or suspension of ego processes in the audience. He must be able to retain contact with and appreciation of less developed states and may indeed have to regress in some measure in order to create an effective aesthetic message. As the artistic process involves more developed as well as less developed states, uncommon flexibility seems to be required; talk of the childlike ways of the artist is best considered in this light.

The developmental principles cited are essentially *directional* dimensions that change gradually over time. One does not pass from lability to stability, from random to systematic scannng in a matter of months; indeed, aspects of both polarities characterize individuals of every age and description, depending on the task. The appearance of a more fundamental shift between the ages of 1 and 7 seems due to the child's emerging ability to handle tasks expressed in words or in other symbolic form. Every 2-year-old knows his left from his right, when it comes to finding his way around the house; but only the normal 7-year-old can point correctly to the left and right sides of various objects about him. By and large, developmental psychologists have traditionally been concerned with incremental changes, Only the cognitive psychologists, in the wake of Piaget's works, have stressed the possibility of qualitatively different stages. Because the qualitative leap in symbol use is of particular interest here, we will concentrate on it; the reader may presume, in the rest of the discussion, that innumerable incremental changes are occurring as well. Armed with this view of development, then, we confront the realm of language, where we will find a suggestive model of how the child moves from a world dominated by and restricted to objects and persons to one permeated by symbolic vehicles and systems.

LANGUAGE

Writing about the first years of his life, Leo Tolstoy asked

> Was it not then that I acquired all that now sustains me? And I gained so much so quickly that during the rest of my life I did not acquire a hundreth part of it. From myself as a five year old to myself as I now am there is only one step. . . . The distance between myself as an infant and myself at present is tremendous.

Tolstoy's belief that in his first quinquennium he had gained more skill than during all his later years poses succinctly the argument of this chapter. The periods of greatest development and progress in the aesthetic realm (though perhaps not in the scientific) seem to be the years directly following infancy, for it is then that the child first becomes able to express himself through the various symbol systems available in his culture. How he comes to use and comprehend these systems is a problem still wrapped in mystery, but even a partial description of the process may be suggestive.

Language development has been much investigated in recent years by a number of psychologists who have assembled diaries of children's utterances. From these studies has emerged the realization that standard models of learning, whatever their relevance for nonlinguistic behavior, reveal little about the process whereby a child comes to speak in a matter of months. Even the more conservative of the linguistic analysts concede that initial utterances have some form or structure. Vocables by no means appear randomly in two word utterances, but rather tend to fall into intelligible pairs, reflecting an incipient sensitivity to syntactic arrangements and basic meanings. Even when first using language, a speaker parcels out the verbal universe in a relatively consistent way, thus communicating with efficiency and reliability.

Exactly what the child might learn from others and what sort of innate linguistic proclivities might merely be unfolding is currently being debated. Numerous examples suggest that whether acquired from imitation, from careful analysis of others' utterances, or merely extracted from a preexisting structure, there is a strong sense of overall rhythm or form, perhaps corresponding to the tonalities characteristic of sentence types, that the 2-year-old speaker imposes on words or phrases he may know. That is, the words and sounds do not merely pour out in a formless, unaccentuated way, but rather seem to be bits in a message that has already been chunked or patterned. Even as he begins speaking, the child already appears to possess the rhythms that customarily accompany speech. Lenneberg, one of the most careful students of this process, comments

> The linguistic development of utterances does not seem to begin by a composition of individual, independently movable items, but as a whole tonal pattern. . . . The child reacts also to a whole pattern rather than to segments and so the intonation pattern of a sentence is the more immediate input rather than individual phonemes.

My own observation of babbling infants has convinced me that even when the particular tokens are random and meaningless, the infant already has assimilated many of the cadences and rhythms of speech. These rhythms seem to be perceived during the first year of life and leave a mark even on the earliest, otherwise distorted, utterances. Speech output can be viewed as a series of slots that can be filled by any sort of token, but ability to employ tokens properly depends on a prior emergence of the slots, appropriately timed and set out.

The first words or *holophrases* seem to constitute the child's effort to communicate a great deal of information in one sound. Such words regularly fit into larger behavioral sequences that help to indicate whether the child is desiring or rejecting something. The child reaches, withdraws, or points in accompaniment to his words. Often these words are natural sounds—bow-wow—adopted from the environment and frequently they are accompanied by relevant gestures. Spontaneous vocal reactions with emotional overtones will also accompany the arrival or disappearance of interesting objects. The first word, Piaget has urged, should be thought of as an action on or toward an object, rather than as a separate, semantic entity with an unequivocal meaning. What reference it does possess is more akin to a general feeling or modal/vectoral dimension than a specific denotation.

> We do not find a particular word connected with a particular thing, but a group of words loosely linked with a group of meanings. . . . The word *mama* isn't only expressive of the child's own state of distress or contentment, but it also begins to express the feelings aroused in him by things external to himself, things in the situation in which he finds himself.

It is only with the two-word utterances that the child becomes able to communicate by words alone, or to convey messages of any subtlety, to capture his thoughts and feelings in symbolic coin. Now he has combinations and choices at his disposal and can more effectively specify what he intends to communicate. Self-consciousness on the part of the child need not be assumed (any more than on the part of the ape who has joined two sticks) in order to maintain that a great deal of additional power has accrued. Nonetheless the capacity to handle two linguistic elements, which emerges sometime in the second year of life, may well serve as a pivot toward greater self-awareness, since the child is now able to postulate a topic (cookie) and then to comment on it in some manner (good), to talk about himself and his own actions (Johnny fell), and to issue instructions to others (hit me) or to himself (get cup). The child with burgeoning linguistic powers can begin to reconstruct experience, and to have an orderly, reliable, usable memory. Indeed, in the absence of some sort of symbolic representation, it is difficult to see how the child's memory could ever evolve from an arbitrary series of isolated images to an ordered series of thoughts and pictures of the past.

The child's growing capacity to use and comprehend symbols can be discerned in other realms. Dreams may occur as early as the first words, with the presence of rapid eye movements in the infant's sleeping pattern raising the possibility that some kind of mental imaging, referring to objects or events, may date from an even earlier period. Sounds and gestures of all sorts come to carry symbolic overtones. While most youngsters begin immediately to speak the language of their parents and peers, there are cases on record of more private languages. Usually such personal languages have clear links to the tongue spoken in the milieu, but these may be more evident to the linguist than to many parents, occurring in the phonological or syntactical rather than the semantic realm. Révész relates the story of a German youth who had a private language, but who demonstrated his assimilation of German by switching abruptly to it at age 3. And Jesperson reports the curious case of two Danish children raised by their deaf grandmother who on their own developed a language with no specifiable resemblance to Danish.

Children raised in bilingual environments have little trouble picking up both tongues and usually do not confound them. Stern indicates one such case who spoke Malayan and German: "His never failing consciousness of which language he was speaking was a special characteristic of this age period." I have even encountered a child whose one parent reportedly spoke only one language to her and whose other parent spoke only a second language to her. Not only did the child respond in the correct language, but she made the appropriate sexual bifurcation, addressing males in her father's, and females in her mother's tongue. It is apparent from these and numerous other anecdotes that the child is exquisitely sensitive to patterns and rules in the symbolic schemes of his culture, and encounters little difficulty generalizing these regularities. His perceiving system, even as it notes gestalten in the visual realm, is able to ferret out analogous regularities in the realm of speech or music. Thus the syntactic aspects of symbol systems pose no more problem than the semantic facets.

Early language use is a form of making activity which initially functions simply as another way of dealing with the object. One pulls an object, throws it, says words to it, and only somewhat later confers a name upon it. Yet within a short time children bring their understanding of interpersonal relations to bear on linguistic practice, distinguishing in a variety of ways between communication meant for others and that not used to elicit responses. And, from early on, language increasingly interacts with the developing systems. With regard to the feeling system, for example, most children employ *whys* affectively, the word expressing the child's feeling of disappointment or letdown, rather than his curiosity about a phenomenon. That language use draws on perception, labeling what the child has discriminated, is clear. The reciprocal relationship is equally striking, as the child's words increasingly guide what the child perceives or discriminates. And, of course, speaking is both a making activity per se and a guide, punctuating other forms of making activity.

Although an incipient sense of self is not dependent exclusively on language, the increased use of language undoubtedly contributes to the individual's sense of self, his ability to control his own behavior, his setting forth of plans and goals. With the advent of language use, the child becomes better able to conceive of himself and to regard himself as a separate entity having both typical and unique experiences, an entity that acts, feels, perceives, and enters into relationships with others. Language (or an equivalent symbolic medium) allows the child to represent to himself (and to others) the fact that he is doing things. The "I" is a linguistic metaphor for the behavior and perceptions of a subject, and the capacity to speak of "I," "you," and "our" signals the child's discovery that he is a person, like those about him, capable of entering into relationships and describing them. Accompanying this realization is a growing awareness that his behavior is under his own control and that he can regulate it by talking to himself, initiating programs, altering them in necessary ways, and evaluating his own success. Naturally the development of this capacity takes some years; the young child has difficulty in inhibiting ongoing behavior and in executing complex commands issued by others. Still, language does seem a tool sufficiently powerful to guarantee that eventually the child will be able to set up goals and to regulate his own activities. Then, once these capacities have evolved, the child can regulate his communications to others and set out deliberately to convey a certain emotion, mood, or idea in a symbolic medium; similarly, once he has confirmed that the world is composed of others like himself, he has the potential to discern subjective aspects in the works of others. Thus the child's emerging self-consciousness and voluntary control over behavior form a necessary precondition for a developed participation in the arts. While it is probable that these capacities are not explicitly tied to the use of language, with other symbolic systems also contributing to growth in self-awareness and decrease in egocentrism, there seems to be little doubt that language is a medium splendidly suited to achieve these purposes.

LINGUISTIC PLAY BY THE YOUNG CHILD

One of the most fascinating and revealing behaviors of young children is their tendency to play with words. As a child enters his second year, he is beginning to understand the communicative function of his language; at the same time, he is becoming aware of the sound combinations permitted in his language, the preferred arrangement of consonants and vowels, and incipient word meanings and senses. As in other realms of development, considerable progress and learning results from a playful repetition of various schemes. The child tries out the numerous words that might fit into one slot or another, varies the rate of production, then inserts another set of words and experiments with them. He invents likely and unlikely sound combinations and juxtaposes them in every conceivable way. The child's tendency to play with words (in more than a babbling sense) has often been noted by observers, but Ruth Weir is one of the few to have made a systematic study of the phonetic, syntactic, and semantic aspects of this drill. A few examples of the word play she found rampant in the nighttime monologues of her 2½-year-old son Anthony are reprinted here, followed by summary of Weir's observations.

1. Wonderful
2. What
   What
3. Ha what
4. What
5. He want to play
6. Play
7. Cobbers not night-night
8. Yellow blanket please

Notice repetition of /wa/ sound; alternation of /h/ and /w/; /n/ and /t/ together; the general aura of pleasure which unites *wonderful, play, please*.

1. Shoe fixed (4 times)
2. Fix it (3 times)
3. Shoe fixed
4. It took it
5. Bring it back
6. Took them
7. Took it down (4 times)
8. He took it (2 times)

Notice placement in utterance of various forms of *fix;* and of *it;* alteration of /t/, /k/; substitutions in the frame around *took;* theme of taking a shoe to be fixed and bringing it back (referring to events of the day before, or to forthcoming events); alliteration of *bring back,* with the /k/ referring back to *took;* attempt to substitute plural pronoun *them* and then return to the more comfortable *it,* while *them* is echoed in the alveolar and nasal of *down*. As in the first monologue, the experimentation operates on the levels of sound, syntax, and meaning.

Finally, citing one of the longest monologues will convey the flavor of such recitations.

1. That's for he
2. Mamamama with Daddy
3. Milk for Daddy
4. OK
5. Daddy dance (2 times)
6. Hi Daddy
7. Only Anthony
8. Daddy dance (2 times)
9. Daddy give it
10. Daddy not for Anthony
11. No
12. Daddy
13. Daddy got
14. Look at Daddy (falsetto)
15. Look at Daddy here
16. Look at Daddy
17. Milk in the bottle
18. I spilled it
19. Only for Daddy
20. Up
21. That's for Daddy
22. Let Daddy have it
23. Take off (2 times)
24. The
25. Turn around (2 times)
26. Look at donkey
27. That's the boy
28. That's the donkey
29. [daen] Daddy [daen]
30. Pick up the [dɔn]
31. I can pick up
32. I can
33. How about
34. How about the Daddy
35. OK
36. Daddy's two foot
37. Daddy had some feet
38. [bí:bɔ̄]
39. Put on a record for you
40. What Daddy got
41. Daddy got

42. On the plane
43. Look at pillow
44. What color pillow
45. What color
46. Is not black
47. It's yellow
48. Daddy dance
49. Ah, Daddy
50. Take it to Daddy
51. Daddy put on a hat
52. Daddy put on a coat
53. Only Daddy can
54. I put this in here
55. See the doggie here
56. See the doggie
57. I see the doggie (2 times, falsetto)
58. Kitty likes doggie
59. Lights up here
60. Daddy dance (3 times)
61. With Bobo
62. What color's Bobo (2 times)

Again Weir's comments on this protocol are worth citing. She reports that the monologue had occurred shortly after the child had been put to bed and after he had been visited by Daddy; hence the underlying theme. *Daddy* occurs at regular intervals throughout the lines, and the phonic properties of the word are played on with such other terms as *Mamamama, donkey, that, had, hat, can, doggie,* and above all the lovely *Daddy dance.* Words of great importance and possible sources of conflict to the child recur as well; *bottle, milk, Kitty, Bobo, Anthony,* and *Mamamama* lend to the monologue an epic quality, as the child reviews the central themes of his young life. Fragments from daily reports and conversations recur, as in lines 6, 11, 18, 35, 53, and 57. Role play also seems prominent, as the child plays with the adult use of *I,* and takes the part of various animals as well. After noting the unusual number of grammatical and phonetic experiments, Weir concludes:

The rondo-like construction of the paragraph is clear. Here are more examples: the important *for me* of the first line reappears as *for Anthony* in line (10); in lines (16) and (21) it is *for Daddy,* and the *for you* in line (39), which brings this circle back to its starting point, is only linguistically different from *for me* in line (1) due to the imperfect learning of pronouns. *Only* in line (7) finds its counterpart in lines (19) and (53), but first it is *Anthony* then twice *Daddy; what color pillow* of line (44) reappears as *What color's Bobo* in the last line of the paragraph.

A more explicit illustration of practice with symbolic schemata currently salient in the child's perceiving, feeling, and making systems is difficult to envision.

Perhaps because of the dominance of modal properties, children possess a general sense of word relevance and reference long before they have satisfactorily worked out precise semantic markers. This occurrence leads to interesting confusions and poetic creation. Sometimes what is regarded by adults as a sign of potent imagination turns out to be the child's misuse of words; at other times the child seems aware that he is sketching or playing with ordinary usage. With a twinkle in his eye, the child may speak of an "angry automobile" or a "middle-aged piece of cake"; having seen the beak open and close, he may label a crow as a scissors. Such imprecise uses indicate how the rule-sensitive child has seized upon some element of the word's reference and is using it relentlessly in every context where the usage might possibly pertain. "The child also seems to be aware of inappropriate (semantic) extension as an early example of verbal humor illustrates . . . his laughter indicates that he was aware of an inappropriate and therefore funny extension of the meaning (22 months) . . . By the time he was thirty months old, deliberate semantic deviation—especially in the form of imaginative play—was very common." Younger children required to imitate are more likely to make spontaneous corrections in sentences than are older ones: "the younger the child, the more frequently does he hear and reproduce sentences in terms of their rules disregarding their exact form."

Just as the child learning language is given to overgeneralizing rules, he is also given to overusing words in a variety of contexts. For little Hans, the 4-year-old studied by Freud, many objects had "widdlers." His vivid imagination extended the term to any situation where it might conceivably be relevant. This tendency is enriched by the child's Gestalt perception and his proclivity to perceive modal aspects. Indeed the child sometimes hits upon the very m/v similarities among objects that have impressed literary artists: the poetic links between flower and woman, stars and eyes, sleep and dying, battle and fire. When he captures such qualities in a symbolic medium, he will be viewed by some as engaged in creative activity.

In records of children's conversations and spontaneous speech one finds frequent illustrations of various figures of speech, often reminiscent of the deliberate efforts of skilled writers. How planned or accidental these "figures" are is very difficult to determine. But even if these figures should not be deliberately planned, they may well be noticed and appreciated by the child as speaker or hearer. Language has a life of its own, and in an important sense all the resources and the potentials of the language are present in the simplest utterance; it is thus futile to isolate a moment in time or a "stage" when a particular function of language is first appreciated or exploited. Rather, the various resources of language are differentially exploited over the course of development, depending upon the rate of development, the interactions of the child's three systems, and his increasing command of a symbolic medium.

A careful study of one young speaker has revealed that every hour-long sample of his speech contains a number of usages that on the face of it qualify as figures of speech. It cannot be determined how many of these figures are accidentally or deliberately selected; evidence contained within the protocols themselves suggests that perhaps one-half of the figures involve a deliberate effort to play with a word's sound or reference in order to achieve a desired meaning or effect. We find that Adam, when 2 years old, can "drive" a record that he is turning around and see his cocoa "dancing like cowboy coffee"; a few years later he speaks of a "lonely old crayon," "punishing" a stubborn block, and compares the replay level of a machine to a windshield wiper. In each case supporting data suggest an awareness of the literal and metaphoric meaning of the terms employed. Sometimes, on the other hand, purely phonic considerations come to the fore: " 'Who dat Mommy?' (Mother: 'That's the tattoo man.') 'Too man, tattoo man, find too tattoo man, tattoo man. Who dat? Tattoo. Too man, go Mommy? Too man. Tattoo too man go? Who dat? Read dat. Doctor dere, tattoo man, tattoo man right dere. Too tattoo man. Funny too man, funny. Tattooed man.' "

Comparable outpourings of figures of speech are found in nearly every collection of young children's speech that I have seen. There are similes ("I have a blanket like a lipstick") metaphoric personification ("The clouds go very slowly because they haven't any paws or legs"), augmentation ("On the plane, look at pillow, what color pillow"), variations on a theme ("Careful broke the rami, careful broke Anthony, careful broke it"), metonymy ("His tail . . . dat a duck"), syncope ("rubband" for "rubber band"), and even stream of consciousness ("Or a donkey. Shepherd. Lambs, God, give. Dese are given. Gifts camel. Dat a barn/ dat a tur/ . . . key. I don't know. Who Dat.") These examples highlight the extent to which literary devices pervade children's language. Whether these figures of speech are spontaneous, planned, or accidental seems less crucial than the unarguable proliferation of them and the clear pleasure the child gains from uttering them. While similar examples could be gleaned from many art forms, the literary arts may serve as the paradigmatic art form, in which infinite creativity, indefinite variability, and experimentation with referential and formal aspects are clearly manifest. Poetry, at least as much as music or pictorial art, is accessible to the making, feeling, and perceiving systems of the young child, and so there is a sense in which language may serve as a model for all symbol use and all art.

MODAL PLAY

The child's imagination is not limited to verbal references. Countless examples can be found of the child who will seize upon an object and use it for some other function, where the only relationship obtaining is a perceived modal affinity. A toddler will make a train out of animal cracker boxes, use a paper roller as a tunnel, dress himself in leaves, or wrap a spaghetti necklace about his neck. Personification is typical, and children will talk to or pretend to be objects, dolls, or animals. Such fantasy for its own sake is also a valuable way of learning about the world. These transpositions and analogies not only indicate the flexibility of the child's perceptions, but also reveal that the child (like the adult) finds it easier to relate to and learn about objects if he can integrate them into the categories and feelings that have already evolved. The world is alive and vibrant for children, and they extend all available categories to novel phenomena.

Synesthesia, or the capacity to perceive a stimulus in several modalities or senses, predominates in children, seemingly as a manifestation of modal-vectoral perception. Many children report feeling colors, seeing tones, and hearing visual patterns; such anecdotes have been confirmed in the experimental literature. I recently discovered to my amazement that, when I casually played passages on the piano, a 5-year-old could effortlessly and appropriately relate the motifs to the letters of the alphabet. There may be some consistency across individuals in these intermodal associations. For example, nursery-school children regard yellow as a happy color and brown as a sad color, and will so color figures in stories of these moods. In addition, there is growing evidence that children of this age can apply in a consistent manner qualitative labels (such as hot and cold, strong or weak) to elements drawn from various sensory realms. One also finds among children a proclivity to respond to an object physiognomically, as if it had a life of its own. These capacities of synesthetic and physiognomic perception usually atrophy later in childhood but may be revealed under certain experimental conditions, and are thought to endure in the practicing artist.

What may seem rather separate (and even conflicting) functions are naturally and indiscriminately combined by children. For example, many children will recite verses or sing while drawing. As has been said of many preliterate peoples, children discern magical significance in material objects, undergo synesthetic experiences, and are given to metaphoric expression. Although modes and modalities may begin in bodily experience, "they have a highly symbolic quality from the first. Mode fragments in the human become integrated only by becoming symbolic at the time they become real, i.e., they become social, aesthetic, and moral modalities at the same time they become an expression of the organism."

The early years of symbolic expression, when the child is gradually converging upon adult categories and classifications, are particularly marked by these interesting usages. The young child has an abundance of labels, ideas, schemes, and concepts competing for his attention, though he is but dimly cognizant of many of them. He learns new ways to refer to things, develops refined actions toward them, and discerns novel qualities in arrays. He is swamped with behavioral schemes he cannot fully control and often appears to be headed in all directions at the same time. During those periods when the child's energies are not completely marshaled for one activity, the child may run through these schemes for practice. Given a brush or a toy, he will do everything to it that he can; when lying in his crib he will review, practice, "wear out" all the new sounds, patterns, and rhythms he has heard.

To witness a child making, feeling, and perceiving in the symbolic realm is a marvelous experience; the practice, expansion, and deepening of symbol use seems connected in a fundamental way to the kinds of phenomena first described by Freud. Dreams, play, and sleep may be adaptive activities that allow for the exercise or practice of symbolic patterns which, either for accidental, practical, or defensive reasons, have not been sufficiently exercised during the waking hours. The child achieves versatility with a symbolic medium, just as in his play with objects he achieves versatility in sheer making activity.

The discoveries of Freud and the psychoanalytic school suggest that certain of these symbols and affects should take on additional significance. As energies center on different bodily regions, the child's physical and psychical attention becomes fixed on related zones and modes. The 2-year-old is therefore likely to be preoccupied with problems of holding on and letting go and may be prone to anal imagery.

Often a preference for opposites or contrasts asserts itself at this age, as a norm is rejected for the sake of contrariness, or in order to test limits. Similarly, the child of 3 to 5 appears to be preoccupied with the dimensions of intrusion and rejection; genital imagery may predominate, and behavior may be characterized by vigorous action and extreme fluctuations of feelings, from the heights to the depths. These bodily regions assume a special significance for the child; they are important in his daily life, and they facilitate communication of general socio-psychological themes such as the relationship between family members or the question of authority.

Concern about these areas may well be expressed only in fantasy, because a direct reference has produced too much anxiety or censoring by parents. Such trends are most clearly delineated in sick children (who may try to hold on to or to expel everything). For this reason, the universality claimed for the epigenetic progression has sometimes been challenged by nonanalytic observers. Yet the games and play of normal children are filled with numerous examples of the important role played by symbolic allusions to these modes. Kubie cites the 3-year-old child who looks at her father's genitals, then declares offhandedly. "Oh I was just looking at a mouse." A little girl shows her father her genitals and says, "Come, let's play you're a snake." He also reports that girls tend to repeat "in and out"; this is a typical reference to urinary openings, but that when challenged they declare, "Oh I meant in and out of the little holes in my shoe. . . . I wish I were married." In a discussion of bananas, carrots, and bombs, Adam provided this lovely illustration:

> It's gonna get bigger and bigger and bigger.
> If you keep on going, it's gonna get bigger on this side
> And bigger on that side, right . . .
> It grows and grows and grows . . .
> Keep on growing and I wanta see what happens . . .
> What do you mean, get very thin? I don't want it to be.

Piaget, hardly committed to the Freudian position, produces a raft of examples of the centrality of genital modes during the ages of 2 to 5. Within a handful of pages I noted several dozen samples of children's spontaneous speech that focused on sexual or parasexual matters, and that highlighted the modes and vectors cited by psychoanalysts. Thus one box on top of another is "sitting on a pot"; a mountain is seen as turning into a little long thing with a hole at the end for water to come out; two statues are commended for having penises, "if they hadn't they'd quarrel"; a little boy's legs grow too long and "then he had a little sister who became a mummy too, suddenly without noticing it";

a baby inside a mother is seen as having sharp, pointed teeth that later became smooth; a child is frightened of a horrible lady who stood with her legs apart and played with her feces; a child is chased by a tiny man with a very big head. Piaget's children dream about chimney sweeps, having and eating babies, pouring water and urine, cutting off heads, people suddenly becoming larger or smaller, hiding inside Mommy's stomach, and a "bean that was so big that it quite filled it. It got bigger and bigger all the time."

Such instances are of course open to several interpretations and only systematic research can reveal whether children are really pre-occupied with sexual matters, and whether the Eriksonian model of favored modes at certain stages has validity. Nonetheless, the protocols that I have seen indicate that the hypothesis of modes and zones of special importance, like that of basic trust or the sense of identity, deserves to be taken seriously. Clearly, the content of children's utter-ances and the particular modes and vectors alluded to are not random. Rather, they appear to reflect the current status of their bodies and their daily experiences. Naturally the m/v properties that dominate the child's consciousness (or unconsciousness) are reflected in the making, perceiv-ing, and feeling of the child, both upon the world of objects and upon the symbolic domain. Similarly, the mature works of artists will reflect their dominant modes, which not infrequently involve a sexual element. In proposing, then, that sundry m/v properties gain ascendancy during various periods of development, reflecting both bodily and social changes, we may take another step toward synthesizing the Piagetian, psychoanalytic, and ethological approaches.

The child's use of symbol systems will reflect oscillations in his life of feeling due to psychosexual factors and other potent events in daily experience; that these alterations in feeling influence the perceptions children have and the creations they make is documented by children's symbolic inventions at times of severe stress. Studies of children's draw-ings and stories done in a concentration camp or at the time of President Kennedy's assassination or in the aftermath of the riot in Washington, D.C. following the shooting of Martin Luther King, have indicated that these periods of stress often supply powerful themes and evoke strong feelings in the youngsters. Keen powers of discrimination and some developed technical skill are obvious prerequisites if the child is to interpret a traumatic experience meaningfully and communicate it effectively, but even children who seem only dimly aware of the sig-nificance of events are still able to capture elements of their feelings in poems and pictures. While the child is still engaged in the traumatic experience, the creative powers are less likely to be effectively mobilized, but later, when the memory is still fresh and the tension of the moment has somewhat abated, it can be put to creative use. Perhaps in those moments where "emotion is recalled in tranquility," when defenses are lowered and the child is mildly aroused, he will make significant artistic progress or become better able to create an interesting, viable aesthetic object.

In preceding chapters I have proceeded by describing the three developing systems in animals and young children. At the time when symbols first begin to be employed, these systems are scarcely fixed, and they will come increasingly under the influence of ordinary language and other symbolic forms. Reciprocally, powerful feelings, enhanced skills, and novel discriminations will exert considerable influence on the use of language. Because these systems continue to evolve, both in relation to the world of objects and to symbolic elements, it is worth touching upon the course of development of the three systems. The principal emphasis in the remainder of this chapter and in the following chapters will however fall on the development of those symbolic systems prominent in the arts, and on the way in which the symbolic systems influence the three systems of development.

FEELING

The period following infancy is marked by continuing differentiation of affective states. The child notes the recurrence of particular combinations of vectors and modes in given situations and comes to regard these phenomenal configurations as discrete emotional states. One combination, occurring while he is engaged in an enjoyable activity, may be termed happy, other situations and their accompanying modes will be deemed sad, unpleasant, thrilling, or heroic. As the child becomes increasingly sensitive to other individuals, he becomes capable of experiencing and interpreting those emotions that depend on a relationship to another individual: guilt, shame, jealousy, pride, empathy, altruism. Many of these feelings remain diffuse for a long period, as the child's self-differentiation and self-consciousness is still in embryonic form; but the child who is most precocious and sensitive or who undergoes stressful experiences may experience the same phenomenal states and reach the same interpretation as older individuals.

Gradually the child's range of feelings and emotions, the interpretations he places upon his dominant modal and vectoral affects, come to form a more or less coherent pattern. The child not only senses these regularities in his own feeling life, but becomes increasingly aware of analogous consistent patterns in the feeling life of others. These patterns of feeling life viewed as a whole may be thought of as an individual's *temperament* or *personality*, his enduring modes of behavior and his characteristic reactions, which involve not only regularities in action but also continuities in feeling life. Eventually these patterns become reflected in the child's creation of objects and contribute to his *individual style;* analogously, as his sensitivity to other presons deepens the child becomes able to perceive in works created by others these underlying constancies of feeling life.

Although the child's affective life undergoes continuous alteration, consistencies in the temperament and emotional reaction of individual young children are already apparent at the nursery-school age and may even be discerned in the symbolic products (speech and drawings) of individual youngsters. The severe neuroses that may befall such young children also signify the emergence of a consistent emotional tone. Yet, while the child himself may be able to experience a wide range of emotions, and though his particular temperament may be readily noted by others in his play or in his art work, the child's own ability to perceive such aspects of emotion or feeling in the work of others is still undeveloped. This immaturity in interpreting expressions embodied in objects accounts for the primitive nature of the young child's appreciation of works of art. He may well, at the age of 3 or 4, be able to discern his parents' or friends' feelings by noting their general expressions and behaviors; he may be able to discern certain expressive features in natural and artistic objects. But the capacity to fuse subjective knowledge of individuals with an appreciation of their role in creating a particular object is rare in a child of this age. Further insight into the communicative nature of artistic works waits upon additional experience in personal relations.

Attempts to study the development of specific or "perceived" affects felt by the child as he is engaged with symbolic objects are nearly as perilous as speculations about infants' affects. One must depend on expressions, behaviors, and correlations of such indices. Still it is probable that by the age of 3 or 4, children can experience discrete emotions as well as general modal-vectoral sensations when exposed to symbolic objects. Thus they undergo amusement or experience pain as they listen to a funny or tragic story, hear a piece of music, or behold a visual work. Usually they only become able to discuss their feelings about a work, and to use emotional words properly, at a somewhat later time.

To the adult, the feeling life of the child may seem irrational. For example, children report fears of being attacked by lions, tigers, or snakes, even though the objective probability of this happening is nil. However, it would be wrong to assume that these fears are not deeply felt; in fact they may be even stronger than adult fears, for the young child has difficulty in distinguishing illusion from fact, and that is in itself a cause for anxiety.

The child's inability to differentiate "real" action from that which has only an artistic or illusory status has important implications for our study. When children attending the theater cover their eyes until the hero has been saved, they reveal that they have not yet achieved the status of an informed audience member. The latter can retain distance, and participate in the feeling or quality being described, without ascribing to it the same reality status of his own life experience. Aesthetic maturity involves an increase of distance between the perceiver and the aesthetic object, so that the perceiver can discriminate between "real" and "pretend" and appreciate the work as the product of another individual working in a symbolic medium.

In distinguishing children's affective relationship to art objects from adults', several points should be made. First, the child may be involved with art objects not only as he creates them but also when he beholds them; he may lack the ability to suspend or scrutinize his emotion. Then, too, the child may well experience affects different from those felt by most adults, since his range of experiences and discriminating capacity is much more limited. Thus he may enjoy, fear, laugh at or become uneasy in the presence of displays that produce subtler reactions in adults, or he may produce idiosyncratic "works" when beset by these feelings.

The child's immersion in such affective states does have a positive dimension. Because of its unity and potency, an affect may well have an integrating and structuring effect on the child's experience, influencing both his perception and his creation of objects. Stories told by young children in conjunction with their art work may be permeated by an affect that unifies diverse aspects, just as a child's phenomenal experience in observing a complex array may be limited to a single unified emotional response. Furthermore, the works of children may appear to be affect laden, since youngsters are less likely to obscure or disguise strong feelings. The child will also come to treat situations, displays, and works as similar because they possess the same modal properties, and this single-mindedness and intensity may add to the power of their aesthetic experiences.

In all, affects operate as solders, welding together the child's experience, sometimes too insistently or in too rigid a way. For example, a child expresses fear that a teacher late for school will miss the policeman who helps one cross the street. The response is charming in its sensitivity, but inappropriate for the situation. At other times, however, an appropriate response with a unifying affect can lend a formal elegance to a product. Indeed, one of the reasons why the works of the young so often possess grace is that, unlike those of older children, they are neither stereotyped nor do they reflect inconsistent and unworked out emotions. Rather, they convey directly both the form and the substance of the powerful affect that inspired their construction. "Feelings of great joy which may be aroused by many unusual circumstances give winds to the child's conversation and cause speech performances which would be unthinkable at any other time." That the child reacts to works primarily in terms of evoked feeling need not detract from his aesthetic perception. At least, as I. A. Richards indicates: "Most readers will admit the full sense analyzed and clearly articulated never comes to their consciousness; yet they may get the feeling perfectly."

One final feature of the child's feeling life as it comes under the influence of symbols is his continuing ability to become deeply involved with objects in a modal-vectoral way. The child attending to a piece of music or a story listens with his body. He may be at rapt attention and totally engrossed; or he may be swaying from side to side, marching, keeping time, or alternating between such moods. But in any case, his reactions to such art objects is a bodily one, presumably permeated by physical sensations. Adult musicians often indicate that their involvement with music entails intense kinesthetic reactions—pulls, strains, tensions, and directional strivings—which accompany, enrich, and integrate the musical experience. Perceivers of literature and works of plastic art often report similar involvement of the bodily scheme and activation of modal-vectoral perception. Whereas this somatic involvement may be absent in many adults, who no longer react physically and affectively to objects, it seems present universally in children and may be a pivotal component in the feeling and perception of art objects. The intricate way in which the feeling system becomes enmeshed with various symbolic vehicles is not yet well understood, but the potential capacity of symbols to activate sensory feelings and modal-vectoral properties seems powerful indeed. The possibility that this bodily reaction to symbols may at first be universal underlines the extent to which integration of feeling life and symbol use may have an important adaptive function in human perception and performance.

We conclude, then, that the child's simpler affective life and temperamental patterns may enable him to perceive artistic works as organic wholes, to become fully involved with them in an affective way, and to produce works that often have unity and coherence. Yet the child's restricted range of experience ensures that his particular feelings will not coincide with those of most adults, and that he will be unable to interpret many artistic works (perhaps including his own) in an appropriate way. Knowledge of love, jealousy, anguish, torment, empathy, irony, while certainly not totally absent from the child's works, will necessarily deepen and expand as his worldly experiences accumulate. It is probably in this area that the child's development is least advanced; a child's ability to interpret emotional expressions, at first directly from persons with whom he interacts, later from objects created by individuals and manifesting analogous properties, takes years to unfold and, in many cases, remains gross and approximate.

In the course of development, the child's feeling system retains the modes, vectors, and dominant affects of the sensorimotor period, combining them into complex affects that depend upon more subtle personal relations; the system becomes increasingly characterized by those modes and vectors associated with later psychosexual maturation, those interpretations that derive from accumulated experience. Predominant feelings and affects tend to coalesce with and modify one another, giving the child an increasingly individualized yet integrated temperament. The feeling system develops epigenetically. Modes and feelings never disappear totally, nor are they completely restructured; rather they integrate increasingly with one another, operate in conjunction with later developing affects, and are differentially emphasized at various stages. However, they retain something of their original primitive flavor irrespective of the organism's developmental level. Their interaction with symbol systems can become complex, while the manner in which they are felt by the individual will retain elemental and primitive aspects. Even as the feeling system never ceases to evolve, the individual's "perceived affect" retains the flavor of the earliest years; aesthetic objects arouse primitive as well as more developed affective states.

PERCEIVING

By his third or fourth year, the child's gestalt perception is already quite well developed and has mastered many of the perceptual discriminations made by the adult (male vs female, and different colors and letters, for example). Of tremendous assistance in conceptualizing the world in a manner acceptable to the community is the acquisition of language, which serves as a guide to the percepts, actions, and feelings of others. The acquisition of language also aids in remembering information and solving problems, even as it may curtail the originality of the child's discrimination. Early reliance on language seems to have characterized certain geniuses. J. S. Mill and Francis Galton, for example, spoke and read at an early age, but other creative individuals, such as Albert Einstein and Artur Rubinstein (whose work was to become less tied to language use), used the language of their society only at a much later age. Perhaps their unique perspectives derived in part from their abilities to devise and divide their world in a deeply personal way, before the uniforming tendencies of language could channel their perceptions.

Children learning to speak are particularly oriented toward the "thing" property of objects and become very skilled at picking out objects, ranging from cars, birds, and trees to facial expressions and gestures. They also develop some ability to recognize abstract geometrical forms, including numbers and letters, often surpassing chimpanzees in this respect by the age of 3 or 4. In addition to these manifestations of gestalt perception, the child may be exquisitely sensitive to fine details and is likely to notice when an object has been moved in a room or when a new word has been slipped into a story. The rules governing this sensitivity are obscure, but it appears to involve certain implicit standards of what is relevant (and not subject to change) and what can be changed. It is also probable that many if not most young children have a keen auditory and visual memory (in some cases approaching complete fidelity), so that they are more aware of (and more disturbed by) small changes than the adult, who is relatively insensitive to fine details, and primed to overall meaning.

Children's perception of pictorial representations has been subjected to some scrutiny. Youngsters in their second year of life are often unable to appreciate certain of the many details in a picture. They notice parts only when explicitly asked about them, and make many strange mistakes. By the third year, however, the child is able to recognize a great many objects represented in pictures (without equating them with real objects), and shows interest in the stories connected with pictures, even those visible only in outline. That the ability to appreciate and read pictures as representations is to a large extent a maturational process, though one which may involve some symbolic sophistication, is supported by the finding that even when children have had no previous exposure to pictures or photos they can "read" them with no trouble by age 2. Picture reading is dramatic proof of the child's growing capacity to recognize representations, to realize that lines on a page may denote without being equivalent to objects; the perceiving system has become integrated with a symbol system, that of graphic representation. Requiring more tutelage, but also accessible to the preschool child, is the reading of various conventional symbol systems, such as numbers, words, and other notations.

As the child gains facility in using language and reading pictures, he manifests a very strong tendency with respect to these symbols. Put directly, the child searches for meaning or reference in every perceived symbol or object. He is unwilling to accept something as just a form or pattern, insisting on calling it a shoe, boat, dada, or "something." Ehrenzweig has claimed that this object orientation or "thing perception" is so strong as to render the child insensitive to nonrepresentational aspects of perceptual displays:

Thing perception, with its syncretistic grasp of a total object, has to be firmly established before the analytic awareness of abstract patterns can come into its own around the eighth year of life. . . . Thing perception in general allows little or no awareness of pure forms . . . and the young child knows only of things which, because of their highly undifferentiated structure, appear to us as queer abstractions.

Ehrenzweig does not provide empirical support for his claim that "thing perception" precludes attention to abstract and gestalt-free aspects of works; my own research suggests that he may have overstated his case. Nonetheless it seems clear that the child who has "caught on" to symbol use has a strong tendency to name and label all kinds of symbolic objects he comes upon, and appears to assume that pictures, tones, and words each have specifiable meanings (while at the same time he remains sensitive to their general modal/vectoral nuances).

This object orientation, though valuable in mastering a symbol system, may be antagonistic to an aesthetic response. As Ehrenzweig has argued, it is often the gestalt-free aspect of artistic works—subtle nuances of representation, the detailed brush strokes, and the chiaroscuro of a painting; the overtones, vibrato, and subtle harmonies of a musical composition—that account for much of the aesthetic impact of a work. While it is not true (as Ehrenzweig would imply) that these gestalt-free aspects of the work are missed completely by the child, object orientation is a powerful counterpull, which dampens his ability to focus on texture, expressiveness, balance, composition, and other more "purely artistic" aspects. Perhaps many adults never lose this object orientation, and so remain imprisoned in a world of representation and denotation, blinded to the contents of a work that is not readily classifiable and codifiable. Just because they have not yet adopted the categorical system of the culture, children are perforce more open to these gestalt-free aspects, even though some of them appear to be rushing headlong away from it, toward the comfort of ready category labels. The pull toward gestalt and object perception is extremely strong for the young child, making it difficult for him to take adequately into account gestalt-free aspects. Nonetheless, with a short period of training, children can become much more sensitive to aspects of texture. This finding suggests considerable adaptability of the perceiving system during early childhood and points up the child's impressive capacity to make extremely fine discriminations, whether gestalt or gestalt-free.

An extremely interesting occurrence, in all probability related to gestalt perception, is the rise in the capacity for incidental learning during the middle years of childhood. A number of studies have now established that when a child is shown a complex pattern and asked to attend to certain specific aspects in it, younger children (ages 7 to 9) and older children (ages 13 and above) show less capacity to pick up details incidental to the required task than do children of the intermediate age groups (ages 10 to 13). It seems that these incidental learners, either because their attention is less focused or because their capacity to take in intricate displays is greater, recall a significant proportion of details of the display toward which they were not explicitly directed. Perhaps these children are able to escape the attraction of the young subjects to the few salient objects in the display, and also the tendency of the older subjects to focus on well-established gestalten and to attend literally (and narrowly) to instructions. The prominence of incidental learning during the years of middle childhood may be one reason why children of this age have sometimes scored as well or better than older children on tests of aesthetic perception, where the capacity to assimilate a great amount of nongestalt information is at a premium.

The mechanisms of the perceiving system have already unfolded by the time the child begins to work with symbolic media. What has yet to mature is the child's gestalt perception, which will enable him to make finer classifications and categories. Nor has a kind of supragestalt or gestalt-free sense that will allow him to notice the finer nuances, which tend to cut across societal categories (such as those that mediate style detection, or help in decoding symbol systems) yet matured. The capacity to relate differences between works to differences between artists, to realize that what is distinctive about a particular work derives from the hand that produced it, is also late to develop. The perceiving system continues to draw upon tropistic and preferential sensitivities, even as these more complex systems are exploited; and the child's experience with aesthetic objects is marked by a simultaneous or successive exploitation of the various perceiving systems. Indeed the most effective aesthetic objects contain not only those primary elements seized upon by tropistic and preferential perception, but also a variety of gestalt and gestalt-free aspects for the perceiver to savor. As with the feeling system, the principles permitting development of the perceiving system remain the same throughout the organism's life, but are greatly enhanced and newly directed by the child's increasing capacity to handle symbolic systems.

MAKING

The capacity to direct and control one's making activity is qualitatively enhanced by symbol use. During the sensorimotor period, the child is only able to make simple things or to imitate the display in front of him; the ability to use and to understand language and other symbolic systems enables him to realize and build up a wide number of motor skills by the expedient of listening to instructions, or devising models of the process. Before long, the child directs the sequence of actions by overtly issuing instructions to himself. The acquisition of language is not without its pitfalls, however. For careful *perceptual* attention to a phenomenon, the child may sometimes substitute attention to verbal descriptions, which he may not understand or which give him a misleading or incomplete notion of the object at hand. In such cases, careful viewing followed by making may result in a more accurate comprehension than attending to the symbolic description. Yet, simple observation without any direction may cause the child to focus on completely extraneous aspects.

It is useful to distinguish between those behaviors in the preschooler that seem dependent on maturation (such as the ability to run, climb, or hop) and those motor behaviors in which training and tutelage seem necessary or helpful (such as fine motor movements, writing one's name, threading a needle, hitting a baseball, tying a shoe). Even in these areas where training is relevant, instruction seems pointless until a child has reached a certain physiological stage. As simple maturation may however be insufficient for accomplishing the behavior, well-timed and competent instruction is of help.

Acquisition of motor skills is a carefully researched area, which helps illuminate the nature of the making system. At times, training makes little difference, as in a game of hitting a moving target with a ball:

For the complex skill studied . . . extra practice . . . resulted in but slightly more improvement as compared with the control groups. . . . For the development of complex motor skills in preschool children, maturation and a general environment in which many experiences are possible are more important than systematic practice.

But in skills like using a tracing board, performance improves if drill is frequent. Across disparate tasks certain principles of skill development can be discerned. For example, new skills tend to emerge when less complex ones have been mastered, and increments in skill are often saltatory rather than gradual. The principles of making activity evinced in early development continue to be manifest during the symbolic stage; they are brought to bear on the manipulation of various symbolic elements, and are in turn influenced in a variety of ways by the child's use of symbols.

When a child has practiced a certain skill, he becomes able to perform it more smoothly and to cut out, if he chooses, all excess waste motion. This process leads to a shortcut in motor performance, to an increased efficiency and versatility in the behavior. Particularly in the case of drawing, the child will hit upon schemes or motor patterns that can serve to achieve desired effects. Once mastered, such schemes can be used at will for a variety of functions to which they are suited. Whereas at first a child will use the scheme of a circle to represent nearly any object or part, later on different geometrical shapes take on more specifiable and apparent meaning. When functions arise for which the particular scheme is inadequate, pressure develops for the use of a new scheme. Naturally those who engage most frequently in certain activities are most likely to find it necessary and advantageous to evolve new, less ambiguous schemes. Although the basic modules of a skill may still be ascertainable after they have been combined into a smooth melodic movement, the new act becomes a component for a yet more elaborate skill. Ultimately, new hierarchies of organization emerge, and the original components are no longer evident. This process, which takes considerable time, leads to the phenomenon where highly skilled behavior appears qualitatively different from the behavior of a neophyte, and may in fact become controlled by different neural mechanisms.

The attainment of motor skills is obviously crucial for a wide variety of occupations and avocations, not least among them the performing arts. Such attainment of skill is long in coming, and a great deal of motivation may be necessary before the child masters an activity. Because of the length and complexity of this process, the study of intact skills has not been a popular subject with psychologists. A problem inheres in this field, since skills needed for specific tasks are highly individual, and a study of how they are acquired may not necessarily reveal how different skills develop. Nonetheless, investigations of the acquisition of simple motor skills may at least supply a tentative model of later, more complex skill acquisition.

In the years following infancy, the making system becomes increasingly integrated with the symbol systems of the culture. Certain early behaviors, such as babbling or scribbling, are simply new forms of making activity for the child. Very soon, however, these making activities acquire symbolic overtones as the child comes to relate what he has "made" to objects or aspects of his experience: sounds to discriminated concepts, lines to objects, tones to feelings or to other sets of tones. The making system also increasingly reflects the prevalent symbol systems of the culture—a child begins to talk at a year and jumps or bounces in relation to a perceived rhythm as about the same time. He becomes able to move his hands and fingers in certain ways, and in time he will draw figures, play an instrument, or edit a film. The dynamics and contours of his motor activities come to reflect the forms that he perceives and the instructions he receives.

This mastery of the symbol systems of the culture has diverse effects. Competence in the symbol system of the culture is a necessary prerequisite for effective communication within that symbol system to other members of that culture. And skill with the symbol system is a necessary antecedent for creative efforts in the arts. All the same, this fluency may be purchased at a price, for the child comes to construe his experience in terms of the symbol system and may miss aspects not encoded by that system. Paradoxically, too close an identification with one symbol system may thus blind the person to features that can be detected by one less schooled in the symbol system. It is the individual who has mastered the symbol system, while still maintaining the flexibility to step outside it, who is likely to have the freshest percepts, the most original acts, and the unique blend of feelings.

Although the principles of the making system are implicated in all manner of symbol use, the making system may have specific adaptions to particular symbol systems. It seems most probable that the feeling system involves analogous reactions to tones, pictures, or words, and that the perceiving system makes analogous kinds of discriminations irrespective of the symbol system employed. In contrast, neurophysiological evidence indicates that language use (and perhaps also music use) is mediated by unique laws of unfolding—specific syntax— which may not be the same as those employed in other motoric activity, even the sort involved in dancing or in drawing. Characteristics of language like embedding, incursion, and transformations, while germane to temporal media, do not have exact analogies in the spatial or praxic realm. Linguistic symbol systems may draw on one set of making skills, nonlinguistic or "dense" symbol systems on another. While not enough is known to determine whether each symbol system involves its own principles of making, it is at least arguable that there is less universality in the principles of the making system than in the others.

By the time the child is able to speak with ease, to sing a known melody, or invent new ones, or to portray something he sees, his making activity is operating on a new plane—that of symbol use. In drawing, he seeks to achieve a certain effect, to represent a specific object; in speaking, he refers to experiences, desires, concepts. He employs many of the same skills in manipulating lines and words as he does in walking or hitting, while also acquiring whichever making modes characterize a particular symbol system. Just as he has learned to discriminate and feel aspects of the symbolic realm, he can also employ and expand these symbol systems. Most of the principles governing making activity and skilled motor behavior in the sensorimotor stage are brought to bear in symbol use. The child achieves increasing distance from the symbolic medium and is able to recapture or recreate in some kind of symbolic medium what he has perceived or felt on the sensorimotor level. Choice of medium in which his making activity will continue to develop will be influenced by his culture, but his proclivity for working with symbols, imbuing them with his subjective feelings, percepts, and knowledge, is determined by his species membership. Related thoughts have been eloquently expressed by the poet Valéry:

> I have a habit, or obsession, of appreciating works only as actions. In my eyes, a poet is a man who, as a result of a certain incident, undergoes a hidden transformation. He leaves his ordinary condition of general disposability and I see taking shape in him an agent, a living system for producing verses. As among animals, one suddenly sees emerging a capable hunter, a nest maker, a bridge builder, a digger of tunnels and galleries, so in a man one sees a composite organization declare itself, bending its functions to a specific piece of work. Think of a very small child . . . he will explore the possibilities of his faculty of speech; he will discover that more can be done with it than to ask for jam and deny his little sins. He will grasp the power of reasoning; he will invent stories to amuse himself when he is alone; he will repeat to himself words that he loves for their strangeness.

INTERACTION OF SYSTEMS

As the child enters his third year, the notion of separate systems has become a fiction; interaction of systems is overwhelmingly the rule. The normal organism increasingly becomes an integrated whole able to deal directly with the world and equally with the realm of symbols. At this stage, the various symbol systems—such as drawing, everyday language, and music—begin to convey the child's knowledge of the various developing systems as well as their properties or components. That is, in subsequent development, the child symbolizes about his

feelings, percepts, and actions, and looks to symbolic vehicles for manifestations of these systems. Already at the age of 3, the child can manipulate a pencil with some skill. And about this time, his making system
and his perceiving system are sufficiently developed to allow him to see
objects in what he draws. Once he has achieved this point, it seems
valid to consider him capable of representing and of appreciating a
representation; he has become a participant in the artistic process of
painting. He is beginning to realize the potential to draw what he has
seen or made, and to reflect in his drawings what he has felt. Similarly,
as language use and musical sophistication continue to develop, the
child can reflect aspects of the three developing systems in his symbolic
use. His feelings, perceptions, and actions come through in his words,
rhythms, or melodies. The contents of the three developing systems become referents for the symbols the child creates. In words, drawings,
melodies, he captures aspects of his discriminations, makings, and feelings. We encounter a hierarchical structure; the systems that have developed in direct contact with the world become the content for the
symbolic systems, which have developed later in accordance with the
same principles.

As the child becomes able to handle symbolic media, to make and
to perceive symbolic expressions, his awareness of his feeling system is
tremendously enriched. He comes to label experiences as pleasing or
painful, as good or bad, and to hear and appreciate how others have
labeled a range of experiences. Merely being informed that something is
dangerous, safe, harmful, or exciting becomes enough to mobilize a
child's affects and may even cause him great pleasure or disturbances.
Feelings can be evoked by symbolic experiences as well as by direct
interaction, thereby conferring upon the feeling life a new dimension;
reciprocally, powerful yet mysterious feelings can exert great influence
on one's making activity in various symbolic realms. Language will
become increasingly integrated with the feeling system as the child
becomes able to appreciate plays on words, to secure affects from viewing paintings, hearing stories, listening to music, and so on. Both the formal
and the semantic aspects of these media—the arrangement of sounds
as well as the plot of *Goldilocks* and *Peter and the Wolf*—can affect
the child.

It is because the young child's feelings are so readily mobilized by
exposure to the arts, by incipient comprehension of meaning, by sheer
pleasure at tone and rhythm, that I find it sensible to think of the child
as acquiring the capacity to be an audience member. After all, to join
an audience, he need only be able to have feelings aroused by some sort
of aesthetic object—the specific nature of the feeling being, for this

purpose, irrelevant. His modal-vectoral sensitivity, his intensified feelings, his tendency to immerse himself bodily into works strengthens his
affinity with the more mature audience member. Capacity to retain distance from the object will not have evolved fully at this time, but this
fact will not seriously impair the child as audience member, particularly
as he becomes aware that cartoons, stories, or songs are just "pretend-
ing," and as he acquires some competence in interpreting the prevalent
symbol system.

While the young child already has attained audience member status, he does not yet qualify for participation in other aspects of the
aesthetic process. The ability to become a critic is a much later development, since it calls upon the capacity to compare objects on the level of
propositional reasoning, skills well beyond the ken of the 2- to 5-year-old.
Although there is a sense in which we will speak of a young child as
a performer and as a creator, his development in these areas is still
primitive. Mature performances require both the ability to observe and
understand some sort of object (often one embedded in notation), and
to communicate this object to an audience. A sense of distance from
one's audience, which cannot be assumed in the young child, is also
needed. Analogously, the creator needs some mastery of a medium and
some capacity to communicate particular forms of subjective knowledge
to other individuals. This, too, seems remote from the first storytelling
or drawing of the young child. To the extent that the child has an
appreciation of a symbolic medium, however, and is not merely orienting
to the painting or story because it is there, one may legitimately regard
him as an audience member. Further growth will be matched by increasing coordination of the child's developing systems with the symbolic system of his culture.

Just as we considered the nature of symbol use by comparing the
three systems in animals and man, we may find it helpful, in understanding the beginnings of children's art, to contrast the realm of play
with that of art. To be sure, any attempt to delineate a firm boundary
between play and art is misguided. Nonetheless, relying to a large extent on the common connotations of these words, I shall try to locate
the play of children in relationship to their artistic productions.

PLAY

Play may be viewed as the undisciplined operation of the making system.
A child has a great variety of acts that he can perform at any stage
in his development. In his play the child experiments freely with these

making activities, combining them at will, transforming, rearranging, modifying them. The purpose of play is contained in its unfolding: The child is guided less by a desired end result than by the proclivity to explore exhaustively the implications of his schemes or actions. This view is consonant with other descriptions. In Piaget's terms, play is complete assimilatory activity; the child adjusts his world to his actions, rather than his actions to the constraints of the world. In Lorenz's formulation, play is the chaotic combination of instinctual activity. And, as Bender and Schilder put it, "Children are never satisfied with any form that is reached. One form is merely a transition to a chaos that is putting the toys in an unorganized heap. But . . . new organization is immediately sought again."

Play is more than a random exercise of the child's making activity, however. Such activity is also a crucial component of development, for, through play, the child is able to make manageable and comprehensible the overwhelming and perplexing aspects of the world. Indeed play is an irreplaceable partner to development, its prime motor. In his play the child can experiment with behaviors, actions, and perceptions without fear of reprisal or failure, thus becoming better prepared when his behavior "counts." Indeed, for the analyst, the danger in focusing on play, rather than art, is that play covers too much ground; while the arts are a delimited process, which can be contrasted with the sciences or with nonsymbolic activity, play is all-pervasive. It is difficult to maintain one's distance from it, or to base a developmental analysis upon it.

Two other formulations about play help to highlight its crucial role in development. According to Klinger, play is the novel application and combination of preestablished behavioral elements, such as specific responses, rules, grammars, and transformations. Play contributes to the mastery and integration of overwhelming emotional experiences by enabling the child to reenact them under controlled conditions. Thus the young child who has been admonished for spilling ink on the floor, but does not comprehend his parents' reactions, can reenact the incident using his dolls; this recreation may allow him to master the components of the interaction. He may discover new aspects of behavior and interpersonal relations, for he will be able to vary the conditions of the interaction at his own pace and level of comprehension.

For Vygotsky, play is the leading source of development in the preschool—the primary means by which rule-learning is mastered. This form of behavior is invoked when there are unrealizable tendencies in the environment. The child creates an imaginary situation and proceeds to operate according to rules observed in the real-life situation, or formulated expressly for the play situation. Objects that have had one meaning in "real life" become modified so that a fresh set of rules can be adhered to. Rather than regarding one meaning or significance as inhering in an object, the child confers a meaning on the stick (doll or house) consistent with the demand of the rules in his play.

These meanings are not, at first, totally arbitrary: A stick could not serve as a rock for a 2-year-old. But, with time, the attribution can become increasingly free, as the child comes to understand the nature and conventions of symbol use. Play thus is a means whereby the child's intended meaning comes to predominate over the physical object, reversing the ratio initially dominant in the child's mind; during play the meaning of a word becomes separated from the object. For the first time the child becomes free from situational constraints, and is subject instead to restraints he himself imposes. The rules themselves produce a type of affective pleasure, and so the child resists the lure of immediate gratification in order to gain the subtle but more enduring pleasure from adherence to the rules of the play. Indeed, the rules are often adhered to more faithfully during playtime than during mealtime or bedtime.

These descriptions help specify the distinction between play and art. Play emerges as a developmental phenomenon more dominant but less focused than art, more subject to rules but also freer. The importance of play stems from its efficacy in encouraging further development of the child; the child may try out a variety of roles, define and solve problems, understand more fully the structure and functioning of objects. In this sense, play is virtually synonymous with development, the route to competence. On the other hand, the lesser aspect of play is that it need not be (and usually is not) organized in relation to external constraints; it is a free combination of acts, discriminations, and feelings, as often as not leading to a disintegration of a structure or to an increasingly chaotic and meaningless situation, where acts are performed purely for their own sake and no progression or productivity results.

To be sure, any line between "play" and "art" is in the last analysis a definitional matter. What should be stressed here is that both play activity and artistic activity are firmly grounded in the making system, but only the arts involve, in addition, the continuous interaction between the different systems necessary for any kind of communication. Artistic activity and the artistic process are precluded if the communicator is overly egocentric or involved in exercise for its own sake. Furthermore, the creator can only communicate what he intends if he exerts control over his product. Only when the child becomes aware that the object may become other—or more—than its manifest significance has he understood that diverse aspects of knowledge can be located within an object. Similarly, only to the extent that he becomes aware of rule systems can he devise his own set of constraints, place an art work within its appropriate tradition, appreciate how a creator has responded to the various constraints of creating. In sum, the arts, though not the principal mode of development, tend toward the integration and organization of experience in a more comprehensive way; art is a goal-directed form of play. Play differs from the arts in its source and in its ultimate fate, for it derives directly from the circular reactions of infancy and eventually merges with (if it does not disappear in) the most structured kinds of rule-guided experience, such as formal games and mathematical systems.

The arts never become merged with everyday experience, for there is a sense of distance inherent in the arts, a feeling of tentativeness about the communication. While play is an amplification of all experience, the arts are restricted to a certain form of interpersonal communication for which specific symbolic media are suited. Perhaps we should think of play as a necessary antecedent for participation in the aesthetic process.

> The play impulse becomes the art impulse (supposing it strong enough to survive the play years) when it is illumined by a growing participation in the social consciousness and a sense of the common worth of things, when in other words it becomes conscious of itself as a power of shaping semblances which shall give value for other eyes or ears and shall bring recognition and reknown.

As adults are not at ease with goalless activity, they tend to play relatively little: and, when at play, they impose the kinds of constraints associated with formal games or with artistic activity.

THE YOUNG CHILD AS ARTIST

Although useful for expositional purposes, it is most difficult in practice to distinguish play from art in the activities of young children, and perhaps in those of many adults as well. Equally challenging is the discrimination between the child as audience member and the adult as audience member. In both cases, all that is required is that the individual confronting a symbolic object undergo affective changes, a possibility open to both young and old. Even so, however, an adult audience member generally differs from the child who is unable to appreciate the illusory quality of art. The adult audience member has differentiated reality from fantasy to the extent that he realizes what is being portrayed is but a comment on life—an attempt to describe or to communicate one person's messages—not an actual event that will affect the lives and deaths of those on the stage in the indicated way. And because of his greater familiarity with the symbol systems of the culture and his richer experience, he can discern more elements within the works of art.

In discussing children's symbolic activity I have emphasized the distinctions between child activities and adult arts. I feel, nonetheless, that the young symbol-using child is clearly involved in most aspects of the artistic process. At an early age, he has the general sense of unity of experience so crucial in the realm of presentational symbols. Because of the centrality of modes and vectoral properties in his perceiving, feeling, and making, the child also has access to the kinds of messages frequently transmitted in aesthetic objects, and can phenomenally appreciate the way in which such messages are transmitted. A sense of rhythm and harmony too, though in need of much further refinement, is already sufficiently differentiated so that a certain balance characterizes his own activity and appears to contribute to his enjoyment of diverse phenomena. These properties all are examples of the formal aspects of the arts. They appear in the child's making and perceiving and cut in apposite ways across the realms of music, painting, and literature. They are less pertinent to the particular objects being painted, the characters or actions described, the motifs of music, or the individual properties of a given text, and might rather be said to be molds or forms into which the content of the various arts naturally fall.

An additional aspect of these formal properties is that they seem inadequately characterized by the standard dichotomy of cognition and affect. While one might be able to speak adequately about a child's conception of number, using only Piaget's model, or about the child's problems of identification or trust, using only psychoanalytic formulations, such distinctions fail to characterize the verses the child invents or the kind of painting he makes or prefers. These capacities depend not merely on his knowledge nor on his motivational state, but rather on a combination of what he is able to discriminate, feel, and make— in other words, on general sensitivity, which originates in modal-vectoral perception and which continues to be embodied at the level of symbol use. As the child becomes able to express in symbolic coin such knowledge as he has gleaned from these systems and to appreciate other individuals' expressions of their knowledge, it will become appropriate to speak of the child as a developed creator, performer, or critic. Such development depends, however, on a greater familiarity with experiences, codes, and styles; on more developed technical facility; on a finer appreciation of the interpersonal communication process; on a continuing elaboration of relationships between individuals, which proceeds from fairly rigid forms to extremely sensitive nuances. These are questions of crucial importance that need investigation; we need to understand the nature of interpersonal contact and the aspects of these interactions that may be reflected in symbolic objects.

As for the artistic process, then, it is my contention that the child of 5 has already achieved the status of audience member. He can undergo feelings when contemplating symbolic objects and can appreciate the line between reality and illusion. Within the next few years, he will also achieve the status of a youthful artist and a youthful performer. When he is capable of expressing within a symbolic medium those ideas, feelings, or experiences that have affected him, he has realized the essential function of the artist. When he is able to contemplate a work of another person, and to perceive fundamental aspects of this work, then communicate it through his own actions to other persons, he has achieved the essentials of the performer. To be sure, many refinements and improvements in his artistic practice will be necessary, but I find that the average 7- or 8-year-old child has the makings of a creator, performer, and an audience member. Subsequent development is likely to lead him toward the fuller realization of one or more of these end states. It is only in the realm of criticism that a further qualitative change, brought about by the advent of formal-logical operations, would seem essential.

RESEARCH ON GENERAL ASPECTS OF THE ARTS

One task for the remainder of this book is to provide some support for the contention that the young schoolchild is already a participant in the artistic process. Some evidence will come from studies of developing capacities in the specific art forms, though the more powerful evidence comes from the words and the works of children themselves, only a few of which we are able to present between the chapters of this book. At this point I would like to review the little evidence that has been accumulated on the child's sensitivity to some of the general, formal aspects of the arts.

Children's sensitivity to artistic form comes through far more clearly in their own works than in their perceptions of the works of others. This may be because, to achieve balance, harmony, or rhythmic effects in a work, a child need only work with symbolic media; in contrast, he can only demonstrate his perception of these properties in the work of others by speaking of them, and this is a verbal and "meta-aesthetic task," more demanding than simple practice. With this proviso in mind, I will summarize the evidence on formal properties of the arts in children's development.

One area in which children's performances clearly surpass their own perceptions is the expression of feelings or personality in their art work. Particularly in those cases where the art is autographic, for example in painting, observers can discern which child executed a work or what his personality configuration might be. The child expresses himself through his art, though he cannot yet appreciate how others thereby express themselves. Indeed, some commentators have even claimed that children fall into a number of discrete artistic types, and that their works can be classified on that basis.

While such expression of one's personality and feelings occurs most directly in painting, even in the allographic arts, where the artist expresses himself chiefly through his choices from a code, discernible differences among individuals emerge at an early age. In styles of verbal recall, one can distinguish between the *levelers*, individuals who ignore differences and the *sharpeners*, more active individuals who heighten distinctions and structure their materials. In the endings they create for stories as well as in their repetition of stories, individual children exhibit definite stylistic consistencies; there are equally striking differences across individuals. Such differences in patterns of choices manifest themselves somewhat later (at ages 7 or 8), but one can find some consistent pattern even in children who have yet to enter school. For instance, the stories of one 3-year-old are consistently characterized by sharp sentences, violent actions, alternation of affects, and repetition of the beginning; while those of a 4-year-old contain colloquial speech, impersonal comments, concern with locale, and recurrent themes of loss and danger. These stylistic features even survive over the passage of a year, though the stories naturally change in other ways during that lengthy span of time.

Reasons for these persistent individual differences across works are difficult to specify. No doubt available models exert some influence, as do other aspects of personal background. Yet it is difficult to avoid the speculation that some of these temperamental differences, heightened or modified though they may be by experience, have a strong genetic component. Whatever the reasons, the phenomenon remains: Even the early aesethetic works of children display a notable range of individuality.

Although their own styles may be distinctive, young children are often quite poor at tasks requiring them to detect individual differences or styles in the works of others. Whether the task, or the entire phenomenon of style, has eluded the child may be difficult to determine; it seems likely that, in focusing on paintings, children are struck by the subject matter that has been presented, not by the manner in which it has been represented. Similarly, when asked to indicate differences in the way stories are told, they cannot supply convincing answers, but in completing such stories they do not perform notably worse than older subjects who are explicitly aware of stylistic differences. A heightened alertness to differences among other persons (which may await additional experiences in living and further insights into the way in which these may be captured in symbolic objects) may be a prerequisite for enhanced style sensitivity. Still, with modest training, 7-year-olds can learn to sort paintings by style. And in their spontaneous behavior in classroom situations, they clearly can differentiate pictures drawn by Johnny from pictures drawn by Billy. This behavior reveals that, at least on an intuitive level, the child is able to perceive subjective aspects of the creator in an artistic object.

There have been numerous studies of children's rhythmic capacities, but these usually deal with rhythm as an isolated capacity, rather than with rhythms as embodied in artistic works. Generally speaking, these studies have documented an improvement with age in the ability to duplicate a rhythm, as well as wide individual differences. A talented 7- or 8-year-old can duplicate rhythms as accurately as the average adolescent. Ability to notate rhythms and to appreciate rhythmic notation naturally improves with age, but even young children show considerable ingenuity in devising notations for rhythmic configurations. Efforts to train rhythmic sensitivity have not been notably successful; motor involvement during the perception of rhythm does seem to aid some children.

One interesting finding is that, while younger children spontaneously move while listening to rhythmic patterns, older children often hesitate to display any physical reactions. Although the older child is better at various circumscribed tasks involving rhythm, he may have less of an overall rhythmic involvement with what he does. Chukovsky's findings on children's spontaneous language certainly suggest that a type of strongly rhythmic utterance reaches its height during the first years of symbol development; reasons why this potent proclivity may decline are discussed in later chapters.

There has been virtually no research directly concerned with modal and vectoral perception, but the literature on synesthesia and on cross-modal matching documents that the 5- to 7-year-old has little trouble detecting parallels between different modalities and experiencing input to one sensory modality in his other modalities. Even 5-year-old children can match the brightness of a light with the loudness of a sound in the same manner as adult subjects. With proper methodologies one might even be able to find evidence of intermodal sensitivity at an earlier age.

Honkavaara has marshaled impressive evidence to the effect that, as they grow older, children become more successful at discerning the expressive aspects of a variety of stimuli. She suggests a developmental progression in perception from an appreciation of dynamic-affective properties, to the ability to perceive objects and humans in a literal manner, to an appreciation of physiognomic properties and emotional expressions. When shown pictorial displays, younger children (ages 5 to 6) merely react to them by showing fear or joy or by describing their contents, while older subjects are able to describe the *qualities* contained in the array. The rise of the curve for expressive answers is regular and smooth. While the general vectoral (or dynamic-affective) properties may be detected first, the ability of subjects to articulate the expressive content of pictures appears to mature slowly. Impressed by such evidence, Frijda concluded in a review that

> The "immediate evidence" basis does not explain recognition of emotion. . . . Large stores of knowledge need to be acquired: situational meanings, one's own emotional categories, an experiment conserving the moments and actions of others in the environment . . . physiognomic perception and recognition of emotions do not constitute inborn, immediately available givens. . . . Even the intuitive recognition of emotion upon which we may assume a monkey's performance is based, depends on social experience and is absent in monkeys reared in isolation.

Apparently, skill in interpreting expressions when they are captured in works or other forms of symbolic material takes considerable time to unfold.

Such findings indicate that young children cannot, at least in the experimental laboratory, consistently evince the sensitivity to form, rhythm, modes, or expressiveness found among mature artistic participants. Experimental psychology is the psychology of task execution. The difficulty of conveying to young children the particular task being investigated effectively undermines efforts to measure the child's competence in a controlled setting. Nonetheless I shall try to demonstrate that, as a rule, a sense of the formal aspects of the arts can be detected in the spontaneous creative efforts of children of school age. It is hoped that this finding will emerge in a consideration of studies of aesthetic activity on young children, and in samples of the works of young children. Before turning in the next chapter to the specific art forms, a brief summary of my view about aesthetic development may be apposite. Those who are not interested in a review of empirical literature and the artistic works on which such conclusions have been based may then read Chapter 5 in a less than exhaustive way.

SUMMARY

Let us first retrace our course. After reviewing the development of the systems of perceiving, making, and feeling among animals and infants, an attempt was made to specify the principles upon which these systems continue to unfold. We have seen each system developing in characteristic ways, and have discussed the reasons—among them the development of the object concept and the sensitivity to modal-vectoral properties—that allow the human being to recapitulate sensorimotor development on the level of symbols.

Following a description of symbols and symbol systems, much of this chapter has been devoted to an examination of the early flowering of one symbol system—language—and a consideration of how the three developing systems operate on and are influenced by the use of symbols. Consideration of specific symbol systems will continue in the following chapter, but we have already seen that the same principles that govern perception, making, and feeling in relationship to the world of objects are probably adequate to account for the organism's experience with various symbolic systems and media.

When involved with the arts, individuals create and perceive symbolic objects that can affect others on a variety of levels. Each of the developing systems has both primitive aspects (elementary affective states, tropistic perception, simple motoric schemes) and more complex and integrated forms (subtle modes and affects, gestalt-free textures, intricate skilled behavioral patterns). Artistic objects are unique in the extent to which they draw upon the varied aspects and skills of the individual—primitive as well as advanced—and the way in which they reflect the complete, multifaceted individual as well. Whereas interaction with physical objects seems to require primarily primitive mechanisms, and scientific reasoning emphasizes complex forms of discrimination and symbolic operations, the arts have the unique property of drawing broadly and fully upon all systems at each stage of development. Objects are treated as objects and as symbols; individuals are seen in their simplicity and their complexity; symbol systems are drawn on for their formal properties, their elementary perceptual features, and their intricate nuances, details, references, and subject matter. Human perceivers and creators have the unique property of alternating between levels of functioning, of regressing and progressing, as they become involved with artistic objects. They can intentionally vary their distance, immersion, and stance toward displays.

Our picture of the arts is suited to the reconciliation of different developmental views. We have recognized the importance of the difference between sensorimotor organization and the semiotic systems described by Piaget, while bringing out as well the continuities of experience, the persistence of affective states, and the epigenetic aspect of developing systems as formulated by the psychoanalysts. In particular, the concept of modes and vectors has given us a way of analyzing the connection between the sensorimotor and the symbolic stages, the relationship between the three developing systems, and the varieties of information that comprise the first referents in symbolic communication, and which remain as an important background phenomenon in all artistic communication. Furthermore, our hypothesis that developmental periods differ in their emphasis on specific modes and vectors and that interpersonal relations acquire a special status enables us to advance beyond the Gestalt approach, combining Piagetian, ethological, and psychoanalytic viewpoints in a promising manner. While scarcely resolving all controversy between the psychoanalytic and the cognitive-developmental perspectives, we may have shown how the stage-sequence notions of Piaget can be comfortably integrated with the epigenetic model of the pschoanalysts. I believe that a focus upon the arts has facilitated this conciliation.

Our notion of the artistic process stipulates communication between individuals through some sort of symbolic object; among the various kinds of information communicated is that reflected by modes and vectors. Research about communication during the early symbolic stage is still fragmentary, but it seems evident that symbol systems confer enormous power upon the child, including resources he cannot always adequately deploy. At the same time, the child is experiencing new feelings, more subtle and complex perhaps than those of infancy, making finer discriminations, and evolving more intricate motor patterns. All these will eventually be combined with the various symbolic systems, potentially producing an enormously rich and varied creator, perceiver, performer, and/or audience member. At the stage under examination, however, all of these systems and processes are still undergoing development and are not necessarily in harmony with one another.

All the same, the affinities between the child who is becoming versed in a symbolic medium and the adult participant in the artistic process are striking. By the time the child has achieved some mastery of symbolic media, one may discern genuine continuities between his practices and those of the artist. My claim is that all youngsters have some characteristics of the artist and can from an early age participate to some extent in the aesthetic process.

This claim is bolstered more by the experiences of watching children, contemplating their works, and considering the components of the artistic process than by experimental evidence. While the empirical evidence does not refute my contentions, the pressures of the experimental situation, the difficulties of communicating instructions, and the predominantly verbal nature of psychological testing all militate against producing a revealing and comprehensive picture of the young child's abilities. Only in a relatively unstructured situation, where the child has materials at his disposal, and is essentially able to use them as he sees fit, can the aesthetic aspects of his behavior emerge. Not surprisingly, such a situation closely parallels that of the artist at work.

The child engaged in problem-solving is, on the other hand, in a situation fairly representative of the scientific process and of scholarship, areas in which explicit stringencies and external controls are more relevant. In probing a child's modal or rhythmic sensitivity in the laboratory, the experimenter is imposing a specific problem on the child. Naturally, any limitations on the general problem-solving ability or task comprehending will be reflected in the child's performance, irrespective of his modal or rhythmic sensitivities. Ultimately, I feel that conclusions about the child as artist will have to be drawn from longitudinal studies of children involved in play and in the arts; the experimental laboratory will not yield satisfactory answers, though it may clarify specific questions emerging from observational studies, and adjudicate between competing theoretical interpretations.

Studies of children using aesthetic materials in unstructured environments suggest that they have absorbed much of the formal aspects of the arts by the time they enter schools. By no means are they masters; but rhythm, balance, and overall harmony seem to characterize works, particularly of the more skilled or talented children. They have the capacity to utilize the formal aspects of various symbolic media, and to create objects that have a universal appeal. Their perception of art objects may be less mature, but under the appropriate conditions children are seen as sensitive to the formal aspects of works created by others.

To summarize, then, children realize general aspects of the modal-vectoral sort in all three of their developing systems; they perceive, feel, and make in terms of such variables as openness, penetration, forcefulness. Their perceiving system is increasingly dominated by gestalt perception and becomes capable of fine discriminations; their making system is able to combine small units and skills into larger, more integrated wholes; their feeling system covers the range of modal/ vectoral properties, the flux of organismic states, and the incipient feelings of trust and security (or their opposites) characteristic of inter- personal relationships. As children begin to use symbols, they first treat them simply as objects having general meaning; only gradually do they learn the specific properties of various systems and their rela- tionships with one another. As the child becomes able to manipulate a specific symbol system, his self-consciousness and his powers of organiza- tion and direction increase enormously. Nevertheless, it should be em- phasized that, essentially, symbol systems develop according to the same principles followed by the three developing systems in relation to the world of physical objects.

We conclude, then, that development is both continuous and discon- tinuous. It is continuous as regards the functioning principles of the developing systems, but discontinuous as regards the realm in which the functioning occurs. The sense of form and balance that has charac- terized early making and perceiving is transferred to the realm of symbol use. Here is the source of the notable aesthetic quality of many early productions; children become increasingly skilled in discriminat- ing, making, and feeling activity on the plane of symbols, even as they come to appreciate the formal properties of aesthetic objects.

The young child of 5 to 7 has special claim to an affinity with the practicing artist. He shares the spontaneity, the natural sense of form and balance of the accomplished artist, and lacks the inhibitions about product, the self-consciousness about technique that may well impair the work of his older peers. The bulk of the evidence in support of this contention will come in Chapter 5, but its flavor is conveyed through the following illustration.

Recently I attended a presentation where films made by children of various ages were shown. We viewed footage taken by youngsters aged 6 and 7 with no film experience, who had been given cameras and allowed to shoot whatever caught their fancy. Much of their footage was extraordinary, at least as good as work one might anticipate from untutored adults.

What particularly struck members of the audience was the fact that the films shot by these youngsters were of better quality than those shot by older, comparably naive youngsters ranging from ages 8 to 13. Although one could not specify all features that contributed to the superior quality of the younger children's films, a researcher who had seen all the classes indicated that the younger children were not self-conscious about the camera; they used it (as would a skilled film maker) as an extension of the eye and of the mind, to capture what interested them, to linger where there was a story, to ignore the boring and the unintelligible. While the older children tended to take pictures of moving things, or to focus on the antics of their friends, the younger children moved the camera about like careful and objective observers, exhibiting little bias toward staged displays or friends. They seemed to light naturally upon a scene, panning across individuals and objects, moving steadily, patiently looking back and forth until the story was clear. Jerome Bruner suggested that the children had spontaneously discovered a basic insight about communication through any medium—that a topic must be isolated and comments on it conveyed to others. This insight may have evaded older children who worried instead about the apparatus—what the camera could or could not do—and paid insufficient attention to the living drama before them. The younger children also appreciated the importance of a completed scene and did less flitting across unrelated areas.

Whether the age group, the kind of school, the teachers, some coincidence of factors, or pure accident produced these intriguing results will remain a mystery. Yet the films stood as a compelling confirmation of the child of 5 to 7 as one with a natural sense of pacing, balance, and harmony, the capacity to identify and communicate interesting messages, and the feelings of freedom, flexibility, and unselfconsciousness that appear to characterize both young children and many creative artists. Presented with a new (symbolic) medium, they employed their old technology (looking and perceiving about the world with a freeness of feeling) to produce impressive results.

One of the few general formulations about artistic development was made nearly a century ago, but as it fits suggestively with my own formulations of the artistic process, I would like to recall it. William Stern, the pioneering developmental psychologist, suggested that children at first were very sensitive to properties in art objects that yielded pleasure, such as colors, brightness, and pronounced rhythms; the young child could be regarded as a member of the audience. From the purely *receptive* stage the child moved quickly to an imitative state where "he says and sings the song with or after the singer tells the little tales again, records them in dramatic forms and reproduces optical figures in accordance with the copies." Thus, making activity follows in prominence in aesthetic development, and the child may come to possess the characteristics of *performing* or creating before too long. He performs as soon as he begins to imitate, but becomes a better performer to the extent that he can take his audience into account; the child becomes creator as soon as he begins to experiment with and inject his own personality into his songs, words, or drawings. The child is most deficient in the attitude that one should have toward aesthetic objects—the capacity to replace "I want that" with "that is nice." He has yet to progress before he can become a critic; as Goethe knew, "excellence of youthful creation is easier to achieve than excellence of youthful judgement."

Appreciation of the communicative process in the arts, mastery of the tradition, ability to embody subjective knowledge in objects, and a growing sense of self are longest in evolving. The child becomes capable of adopting the critic's role in the aesthetic process only after he has passed through the stages of audience, creator, and performer. We turn now to a study of several art forms in an effort to discover the extent and the manner in which the child is able to participate in each; we begin with a review of previous methodologies and then turn to a discussion of alternative strategies for answering the questions that concern us.

FIVE

EXPERIMENTAL RESEARCH ON
ARTISTIC DEVELOPMENT

In this chapter research on the development of skills in three art forms—music, literature, and painting—will be reviewed in an effort to specify the extent to which children are participants in the artistic process. I will argue that, by the age of 7, most children have achieved essential facets of the roles of audience member, artist, and performer, though not the role of critic. In particular, proceeding from the evidence introduced earlier, I will contend that children of this age are sensitive to formal aspects of the arts; both experimental results and selected examples will be used to illustrate this point. Although such a review has not, to my knowledge, been attempted before, I have been aided by several earlier examinations of the psychological literature, among them those of Werner, Shuter, Read, and Child.

METHODS, PROBLEMS, AND PROSPECTS

Before turning to the experimental literature, I would like to relate my thoughts concerning the possibilities of gathering more useful information about aesthetic development. Previous research in the arts touches on aspects of perceiving, feeling, and making, but suffers from a variety of defects, methodological as well as substantive. Furthermore, other sources that might have illuminated artistic development, such as accounts by teachers in the arts or works by aestheticians, have generally been disappointing, revealing little. New approaches are needed in the study of artistic development, and several will be proposed here. I hope that my discussion of potential research strategies will indicate that ignorance about aesthetic capacities is not a necessary condition, and will encourage investigators to explore this enigmatic domain.

A popular form of investigation in the area of perceiving art objects involves independent judgments of aesthetic *quality*. Once the judgments of experts have been collected, subjects are exposed to pairs of art works and asked to choose the better or the preferred. Higher scores are generally found among older age groups, though agreement between expert and lay judgments are rarely pronounced. Also common are training programs that seek to make choices of individuals more consistent with those of connoisseurs. Either established works of art or randomly generated abstract patterns may be used. Subjects' performances are then compared with experts' choices or with the preferences of individuals of different ages, and general conclusions concerning the increased taste for complexity, order, or subtlety are drawn.

There are two major difficulties with such "preferential studies." First, as reasons are seldom explored, one usually remains ignorant of the rationale governing a choice. This raises the possibility that, in the training studies, individuals may not have their aesthetic sensitivities educated, but may merely be choosing the item they find least appealing, having learned from previous feedback that this choice yields rewards. The experimenter has determined that an individual can discriminate differences in works (which one knew beforehand); he has not determined that the subject is considering relevant components or refining his ability to evaluate works. Second is the historical fact that judgments made by connoisseurs in one epoch are not always shared by succeeding generations. Indeed, change in taste is likely, with the preference for complexity and imbalance that characterizes one generation being replaced by a swing toward simplicity and balance in the succeeding one. Since the artistically inclined person is frequently the individual with an eye toward the future, his selections may well differ from the experts'. (The ordinary perceiver may share the preferences of the "experts" to a higher degree.) The fact that psychologists can rarely induce the most skilled artists or critics to provide norms for such tests, only increases the likelihood that preferences elicited will be for mediocre, conservative, or "popular" works. In general, aesthetic tests that use consensual judgments are controversial, since the whole area of aesthetic value judgments is confused, and its importance perhaps overrated. Nonetheless, the fact that experts from different cultures do show a fair degree of agreement in judgments of aesthetic value is an intriguing one, which merits careful scrutiny. And the way in which the average person acquires the tastes of the connoisseur is certainly a question of considerable importance.

While preference tests only require subjects to choose among works, many other studies require more active participation. Sometimes these discrimination tasks remain within the perceiving realm, as when subjects are asked to group works according to style; at other times the possession of particular skills in the making realm forms the area for investigation. The role of feelings in the creation and appreciation of art has proved particularly refractory to empirical study. Introspective accounts are of limited use, in the absence of methods of systematizing them; checklists of adjectives (of the type used in the semantic differential) provide only a rough measure, while invoking a raft of assumptions regarding the relation of verbal descriptions to aesthetic objects. There is suggestive research in the analysis of Rorschach and TAT responses, and some of the methods might be applicable to studies of responses to art works. Thus far, however, little such work has been undertaken with objects of art. Some consensus is usually found when subjects are asked to label the feelings or affects they experience, or which they find embodied in art works. These agreements prove difficult to interpret, however, and may well be due to convention or suggestibility.

The psychological literature contains numerous studies of a child's ability to duplicate a rhythm, arrange a pattern, draw a circle, match colors or forms. These "making" studies differ in method, type of analysis, depth, and breadth; this variation is unfortunate, because in the absence of long-term case studies, little is known about the relationship of a child's performance at one historical moment to his performance at other times. Equally lamentable is the fact that psychologists have often hesitated to study more intricate skills such as writing a poem, composing a song, or making a series of drawings, because such complex activities are very difficult to analyze using the standard psychological paradigm. And when psychologists have collected children's paintings, poems, and songs, they have shown little imagination in interpreting these creations, either ignoring aesthetic considerations altogether, or relying on traditional techniques (such as critics' assessments) for analyzing them. As a result, a good deal of information is available about the dissemination and range of individual skills, but very little about the combining of these skills and their relationship to the production and understanding of works of art.

An additional problem with many aesthetic investigations is the kind of end state or "right answer" sought by experimenters. All too frequently, "naturalism" is set as the goal for painting development, or "average adult performance" as an appropriate terminus for the evolution of the child's capacity. Certainly such equivalences involve unwarranted assumptions about aesthetic development—is the best drawing the most realistic? Is the average adult competent in aesthetic matters?—which call the interpretations into serious doubt. Then, too, some investigators tend to focus on the reasons given by individuals for their aesthetic evaluations, without sufficient awareness that a person who is unable to put into words aesthetic judgments and experiences may nevertheless possess the requisite understanding and sensitivity to make well-motivated choices or creations. Verbal reasoning about an area is well worth exploring, and has been interestingly examined with regard to moral judgment; it should be recognized, however, that moral judgment occurs largely on the plane of verbal reasoning, while a close relationship between language and choice in the aesthetic realm remains to be demonstrated. Hence studies involving aesthetic objects that focus on reasons rather than on behavior are likely to provide valuable information about rhetorical skill and level of logical thought, but little that is conclusive about the child's relationship to aesthetic objects.

In our review of the empirical literature in the various art forms, we examine and comment further on many of these studies. At this point I propose to indicate the kind of information it would be desirable to have about the arts and development, minimizing for the moment the very real difficulties attendant in securing such information. I will also recommend some techniques for securing reliable information about these questions.

Of particular moment are the following materials and kinds of information:

1. Examples of completed art work done over a long period of time by children from various cultural settings, including stories, plays, and drawings. These should be systematically described and their changes over time analyzed. The relationship between these artistic products and those in other realms (such as interpersonal communication, humor, game playing, or ritual) is also of interest.

2. Suitable categories with which to analyze artistic products. The quantitative categories customarily employed are often the least informative; they appear to have only tenuous ties with the crucial facets of the arts as ordinarily perceived and created. Perhaps one should analyze artistic products in terms of the schemes—the predominant making acts—whereby they are created, the dominant perceptual aspects that are perceived, the figures prevalent in the cultural tradition, and the modes and qualities that pervade the work. If modes and vectors become the bases for such analyses, it would be particularly desirable to avoid simple translation of these aspects into words. Perhaps equivalences in various sensory modali-

ties could be found. This sort of qualitative analysis will have to rely initially on interjudge agreement, though it may eventually be possible to score those categories in a reliable manner. Structural analyses of the sort done by linguists and anthropologists on myths or dreams might well capture much that is distinctive about children's works; perhaps these analyses could also reveal developmental changes by pinpointing the transformations that characterize works produced at different stages of development.

3. Records of children's normal development (both within and without the arts) kept by parents and teachers to supplement the actual works of art, which are more readily accumulated. To the extent that these accounts can be directed toward questions of particular interest to psychologists, they will become more useful. Of help would be books containing problems posed and products collected by art teachers. It is amazing how scarce sources are in this area; the long-standing tension between pedagogy and psychology must be at work here.

4. A framework for analyzing a series of works produced over time. Instruments should be sensitive to changes in the degree of complexity and the kinds of schemes used. Yet the notion of analytic instruments that change as products change is a new one, and will have to be critically examined.

5. Information about the manner in which predominant modes, forms, styles, and schemes change in the work of children over time and the extent to which perceivers also change in their sensitivity. Within an age group, children may have similar modal sensitivities and preferences, but vast individual differences may also obtain. Determining whether sensitivity to principles of construction is characteristic of all 3-year-olds or only of extroverts requires considerable data and appropriate instruments. I would suggest, as a start, that very simple physical environments be set up and that observers note the preferred modal configurations of different groups of children.

6. A critical attitude toward generalizations so overarching they could have preceded the testing, as well as findings so specific that their relevance to the arts is dubious. The level of modal-vectoral qualities suggests meaningful yet manageable categories.

7. Some way of evaluating the works of children. A rigid scoring system is neither necessary nor desirable, but the ability to realize particular qualities and to choose forms appropriate for selected messages is germane in assessing talent. The criteria by which children evaluate works is also of considerable interest and can be systematically investigated.

8. Information about the child's emerging critical awareness of his and others' works. The extent to which the child regards his participation in the arts as problem-solving, work, self-development, or recreation is also of interest. Children's motivations for undertaking artistic work, for continuing to be involved, and for achieving mastery need to be correlated with their conceptions of the realm of the arts. Do they see the arts as a skill,

entertainment, source of prestige, way of life, or some combination of these factors? To answer these questions about motivation and self-consciousness would probably necessitate some intervention on the investigator's part. Considerable care would have to be taken to devise a nonthreatening and noninterfering method for eliciting such information.

9. The reason for children's preferences and opinions. Verbal questioning can be quite revealing, but one should not assume that the child can articulate all his intuitions about an art work. Nonverbal means, preferably involving the medium itself, would seem preferable for determining the full range of the child's competence. So far, nearly all our evidence on these questions is anecdotal and thus of questionable reliability.

10. Biographical information about individuals who go on to become great artists. What kind of personality and temperament did they have at early ages? What skills? What skill seems important early in development, and which can come at any time. Is sequencing of skills important? What is the nature of training for the prodigy? To what extent does he educate himself? How great are differences among prodigies in various arts?

11. Experiments on the development of perceptual and making skills in the linguistic and nonlinguistic arts and means for facilitating them. The effects of training must be followed up to determine transfer and future participation in the artistic process.

12. A picture of the child's changing affective life. Does he experience different feelings when looking at the same works at various ages? How do powerful experiences affect his artistic output in the short and the long run? Is the epigenetic approach useful in studying the development of feeling? Why is there some, yet not high agreement, among judges, about the formal aspects of feelings? What is the developmental trajectory of interpersonal relations? Of individual tempo and temperament? What range of feelings does one have toward other persons at various phases of the life cycle? How does one become able to perceive subjective aspects in objects? Under what circumstances does distance from aesthetic objects first emerge?

While this recital of questions and problems is already staggering, ready extensions are possible. My desire is not, however, to produce an exhaustive list of research needed, but rather to indicate the sort of topics desperately in need of intelligent investigation. The specimens of children's art works, the quality of youngster's stories, the folk singing of second graders in a Kodaly classroom remain the most impressive testimony to the skills and abilities of the young child; it is lamentable that psychologists have made so little progress toward fixing and understanding the nature and development of these artistic proclivities. Furthermore, so long as psychologists insist on letting their present paradigms dictate the questions asked and the methods of answering them, progress on the above issues will be impeded. Having suggested some of the questions I think psychologists and educators should be asking, I would like to propose some sources of information that could be more effectively tapped, and to suggest some methods of analyzing the products, which might yield novel and valuable information.

Millions of children's paintings have been collected, but few psychologists have secured paintings from the same children over a number of years, and fewer still have kept systematic notes on the child's comments, or on the various models that influenced him. Information on children's literary creations and children's musical performances and compositions over a period of years is virtually nonexistent. Perhaps a principal reason for such lacks is the fact that many psychologists feel they are unable to analyze art works properly (and in this they may be correct). One must therefore try to convince those most capable of analyzing aesthetic works to accumulate children's works over time and systematically study them.

In addition to artists and educators, it may be possible to draw on parents as a source of information about aesthetic development. One could devise diaries and systems of data accumulation that would enable trained parents to supply extremely valuable (perhaps even comparative) data about their children's development. This method would alleviate the temporal and monetary constraints involved in a psychologist's acquisition of such data, and even prove enjoyable and informative for the parent. Certainly psychologists who are parents should be encouraged to study aesthetic development, to assemble notes and make analyses of the sort done by pioneers in child development.

Analyzing poems, stories, paintings, and music is a challenging task. In the absence of a systematic framework it is difficult to go beyond common sense observations. Perhaps our discussions of the nature of skills and of the evolution of the three systems will suggest some kinds of observations about artistic development that might be revealing and susceptible of systematization and comparison. My hope is that the language of qualities as introduced in the discussion of modes and vectors can prove valuable in the analysis of children's preferences and works. Lists of such qualities provide useful first steps, but a realization that these qualities are nonverbal in character is mandatory if the investigator is to avoid conceiving of qualities as a closed set of terms. I have found that children's stories can be described and evaluated in terms of modal qualities; judges are simply required to answer Yes/No questions about their own perceptions of the work. When agreement is high, it is reasonable to claim that a work embodies liveliness, openness, penetration, or some other quality. Description and evaluation can either include a positive characterization of qualities or employ a series of negative questions; the judge eliminates descriptions that seem forced or irrelevant. The principle of the semantic differential is potentially applicable, but the choice of nonverbal alternatives would require care.

While verbal characterizations of the qualities of works seem a useful way to begin, such characterizations can never do justice to art works, particularly in media where words are inadequate. Analytic systems that dissect works, note improvements, or consider alternatives *within the media themselves* are needed. Individuals with developed skills in the media, preferably practicing artists and skilled critics, would be logical candidates to achieve this goal.

Rather than asking a child to describe his feelings upon hearing a work of music, or to express his impressions of its principal qualities, the experimenter might offer the child various alternative selections or solutions and ask him to place together works that "feel" the same, or to improvise or transpose a theme that affected him in the same way. If choices were given, responses could be analyzed in standard ways; when the child is allowed to create freely, it would be important to sketch out the range of possible choices and to outline ways of evaluating unanticipated solutions. Similarly, in the realm of the visual arts, children could be shown a variety of works and asked to group them according to their perceived impact, or they could be given oil and brush and asked to make alterations that might produce works with effects similar to or contrasting with an initial set. Of course, unless the developing of specific making skills is the focus of the investigation, one should ensure that an individual's undeveloped motoric skill not impede his response. Methods that would aid the child in producing a work, such as having an artist available who would draw according to the child's directions or a machine that sketches upon manipulation of a lever, are conceivable ways of circumventing irrelevant motoric difficulties.

The innocuous procedure of discussing art works with adults creates decided difficulties with children, whose tendency is to deal directly with materials rather than to introspect about or comment on them. It is therefore advisable to find *materials* that can substitute for the labels ordinarily used by adults. For instance, a child asked for his perceptions of a piece of music might be given series of colors or paintings that he could match to the work under consideration. Particularly if superficial and irrelevant similarities (such as identity of size or colors) are avoided, one may be able to get at the kinds of m/v properties shared by stimuli in different realms. Data available concerning synesthesic perception in children suggest that they should be able to undertake such matching activity and that their responses might reveal something of their involvement with aesthetic objects.

Regrettably, little work has been done in fixing the appropriate units for analyzing children's making behavior. Where the art of painting is concerned, there is a tradition of searching for basic visual schemes; but in the telling of stories, writing of verses, or creation of music, there exist only the units that are employed in analyzing adults products, units which may be inappropriate for studying children's productions. Enlightened trial and error seems to be the preferable approach for an investigator confronting "making" data; one must intuit what schemes have been used, search for evidence of them, and then attempt to write out the rules for scheme alteration, modification, or elaboration. Transformational analysis of the type used in grammatical studies may be relevant for the syntactic aspects of the temporal art forms, but hold less promise for illuminating changes in subject matter, dominant mood, or style. Another potential source of information lies in studies of children's informational processing capacities—for example, the number of units a child can work with or the kinds of operations he is capable of performing under various conditions. The difficulty with such approaches is that they cannot readily account for imitation, prior experiences, familiarity with the tradition, or potent affect states, all of which may temporarily expand the information processing capacity of the child, allowing him to produce works seemingly beyond his capacity. So too, these atomistic approaches bypass the powerful affective forces and the pivotal symbols that permeate artistic works.

Another area in which investigations have been infrequent is that of interpersonal relations, that is, the ways in which individuals come to interact with and understand one another, achieve mature relationships and communicate through symbolic objects. Even less is known about the way in which individuals come to regard objects as embodiments of personality traits, forms of feeling, or other aspects of a creating individual. Studies of the ways in which individuals react to and evaluate natural objects or objects created by other persons or by the individual himself would seem crucial if we are to gain understanding about distinctive aspects of the aesthetic process. Some of the methods suggested for analyzing art objects may prove relevant in the analysis of interpersonal relations.

Two other sources may prove illuminating. The first is careful biographical studies of individuals who became artists, who did not become artists despite great promise, who became artists despite little promise, or who may yet become artists. A vast amount of biographical data about artists, much of it reliable, is available; but with the exception of psychoanalysts, few psychologists have made use of it. Also available are the works done by great artists when they were young, and notebooks and sketchbooks that illustrate the evolution of important works. These rich sources of information are replete with examples of early mastery, partial command of a medium, or rigidity. However, a cursory inspection of material will not suffice. Rather, the analyst will have to undertake the kind of intensive and comprehensive study done by Arnheim in his examination of Picasso's *Guernica,* by Lowes in his study of Coleridge's writings, and by Erikson in his biographical studies of major political and religious leaders. Such efforts take years, but their results can amply repay investment. Again parents and teachers can be called on for recollections and for diaries about the productions and experiences of their young artists; in this way, crucial causative factors and skills involved may be isolated.

A final laboratory for the investigation of artistic development is provided by different school systems and classrooms. Through varying curricula or analogous interventions, one may determine with some precision what effects various teachers, models, environments, traditions, prevalent styles, or training techniques have on the perceiving and making activities of a class. Of course not every factor can be controlled in such elaborate studies; yet feedback on a large number of children as they interact with the same artistic models and go on to produce works of their own cannot fail to be instructive regarding the factors involved in the development of artistic excellence. The drawback of this kind of investigation is the impropriety of manipulating instructional milieus so as to produce deliberately inferior or unartistic individuals. However, there exist enough such environments owing to natural conditions to make this stricture an academic one.

Having viewed the kinds of sources one would ideally draw upon in a study of artistic development, we shall turn to the actual sources—children's art work that has been collected, and the studies themselves. These sources will seem sketchy and incomplete, compared to what one would ideally want. Nevertheless, they suggest that, in the arts, a child of 5 to 7 has already required sufficient mastery and comprehension of a range of formal properties, such that it is valid to think of him as a participant in the artistic process. Before we can examine the further development necessary for the child to become a mature artist, critic, performer, or audience member, the evidence on which this claim is based must be examined.

MUSIC

Music has been termed the most formal of the arts, to which "all arts aspire." Scholars generally agree that a large portion of musical ability or capacity is inherited. For example, in families where both parents were gifted, two-thirds of the offspring showed talent; whereas in families with an outstandingly talented child but in which neither parent had talent only one-fourth of the offspring were talented. Such facts are evidence that there is a sizable genetic contribution to musical competence.

Further evidence of the strong hereditary basis of musical talent comes from a number of sources. Most outstanding musicians are discovered at an early age, usually before 6 and often as early as 2 or 3, even in households where relatively little music is heard. Individual differences are tremendous among children, and training seems to have comparatively little effect in reducing these differences:

> Individual differences are perhaps more marked in aesthetic expression than in any other field of behavior. Greatest variation is shown in musical ability. A child of 21 months may sing songs accurately while some adults may never attain this ability. Lack of ability, unless dependent upon physical handicaps, may not show itself during the pre-school years, but giftedness in artistic expression may be detected very early.

Musical ability is also found quite frequently among children who are not outstanding and may even be retarded in other areas. Many intellectual idiots have a "good musical disposition," and few are altogether devoid of musical learnings. One commentator has even suggested that the special gifts of certain musical prodigies is "the result of a mechanical process in the brain which has no significance for the intellectual value of the individual." And a recent newspaper article tells of a teenager with an IQ of 55 who plays seven instruments, composes excellent music, and can perform about a thousand songs from memory: "When he seats himself at the console of an electric organ a miracle happens . . . poor coordination disappears, replaced by excellent independence in the use of all four limbs, playing keyboard, and pedal board."

Perhaps the most striking evidence for the inheritability of musical skills appears in accounts of autistic children. These grossly disturbed youngsters, who often avoid interpersonal contact and may not speak at all, are reported to have unusual musical capacities. To cite just a few instances: an 18-month-old child sang operatic arias, though he did not develop speech until 3 years of age; a 2½-year-old child listened continually to phonograph records, but skipped over the parts that used the human voice; two autistic children went on to become professional musicians, despite deep personality and intellectual disabilities; among 30 autistic children only one did not show a deep interest in music; and among another group of four autistic children one had extraordinary knowledge of recorded music, two were considered in the class of "musical genius," and the fourth had "an extensive repertoire of popular and classical music." The reasons for this coincidence of autism and musical capacity remain obscure, but it seems possible that the children are reflecting a rhythmic and melodic capacity that is primarily hereditary, and which needs as little external stimulation as does walking or talking in the normal child. Indeed it may well be that musical ability is as localized in the brain and as "primed" to go off as these other skills, with the difference that musical talent is restricted to a certain proportion of the population, while speech and motor activity are virtually universal. As Lévi-Strauss has remarked:

> We do not know what the difference is between the small number of minds which secrete music and those, vastly more numerous, where no such phenomenon occurs even though such minds show musical sensitivity. The difference is so clear that we suspect it implies properties of a special nature which are doubtless to be found at the deepest levels . . . by right, if not by fact, any reasonably educated man could write poems, be they good or bad. Musical creation presupposes special aptitudes which cannot be brought to flower unless the seeds are already there.

Reports of composers who sang before they spoke or who composed in early childhood are legion, but there are hardly any careful studies of the early years of a composer or musical performer. One exception is an intensive study by the psychologist Révész of the Hungarian musical prodigy Erwin Nyireguházi, whom he observed closely for some time. Révész found that Erwin, the offspring of two singers, resembled the infant Mozart, having "intelligence, wit, devotion to teacher and parents, and a youthful manner." When not yet 1, Erwin already exhibited a tendency to imitate singing; in the second year of life, he could imitate melodies, even though his capacity for verbal expression was yet poor. (In fact, he did not begin to speak until about the age of three.) Of course he had absolute pitch. At the age of 4, before he had ever taken lessons, Erwin could play on the piano all that he heard, and by 7 he was able to transpose, to sight-read difficult pieces, and to remember complex ones. He memorized Beethoven sonatas after a few hearings and interpreted them well, though his most skilled interpretation occurred in his own work. He began to compose at age 6 and his early compositions showed decided promise. Only after 12, however, did his creative genius emerge in his own compositions.

According to Révész, such precocity exists only in musicians and does not seem particularly dependent on the mental level of the child. His study clearly suggests that at a young age certain gifted children can be accomplished musicians in the perceiving, creating, and feeling realms. Whether this phenomenon is due to a very rapid development on all levels, or to a particular flowering of capacity in one artistic medium is not clear, however.

A vast gulf exists between the few children who display musical precocity and the majority of children, who have some capacity in the musical realm. Only a few psychologists have made an effort to describe the course of general musical development; their evidence is mostly anecdotal, but I shall attempt to summarize their findings here.

Within the first year of life, most children will alert to a musical stimulus, and within the first two years, they will become activated as they listen to music, rocking back and forth, marching, rolling, or attending intently. Selections with words, and simple themes with strong and regular pulses are the most compelling. While a general inclination to attend to music and to hum along is quite common, children differ enormously in the manner and age at which they begin to sing or to produce sounds on some instrument. Early babbling and speech of course contain musical properties, and some children sing quite clearly before they speak. More commonly, however, the musical component drops out of speech after a year or so, and the child's singing and talking can be readily distinguished. Children with some musical aptitude are able to reproduce melodies quite accurately by the age of 2 or 3, but most others achieve only a rough approximation to the model until the ages of 4 to 6. What is very common, however, is for children to take a song or a musical pattern they have learned and then alter various aspects of it. This kind of symbolic play with music, seemingly akin to the linguistic play characterizing all children, is very instructive. It reveals the aspects of the musical stimulus that are central to the child's perception (usually a predominant rhythm, a lalling syllable, and certain salient intervals), and which of them are missed or minimized by the child (details of orchestration, ornamentation, and so forth).

By the age of 5 or so, most children have little trouble recognizing and singing a large number of songs and motifs. They become actively involved with the musical stimulus and their feeling systems appear to be activated by their contact with music. Indeed, music is primarily a kinesthetic experience for the young child, and his use of instruments should perhaps wait until he has had ample experience immersing himself physically with the music. Reading of notation and playing of instruments is restricted to a small segment of the population, and generally begins only with the school years. However, many children can learn to play instruments (including even the violin) at an earlier age, and can read simple notations as young as 2 or 3. Nor need instrumental performance be confined to a minority; in many primitive societies, everyone plays.

Most studies of musical development focus on changes in particular skills during the first years of life. Even as Gesell and his associates were collecting data about the norms of growth and intellectual performance, Seashore and his colleagues were determining norms of musical development. What emerges from these studies are three primary findings: there are vast individual differences among children; training studies have only limited effects, never transforming the average child into a musical virtuoso; and development of particular musical skills appears gradual rather than abrupt, a peak usually being reached before adolescence.

Consider a study by two of Seashore's students of children's singing capacity. This study, whose results are summarized in the accompanying table, indicated that the average 4-year-old performs very poorly when given an explicit singing task to perform and that improvement is graded, but that the 9- or 10-year-old can execute the task flawlessly. It was found in this investigation that the most talented students were already performing at adult level by the age of 5 or 6. (Table 2.)

TABLE 2   DEVELOPMENTAL TRENDS IN SINGING ABILITY

Age	Sing in Right Direction	Sing Intervals Accurately	Sing Up/Down without Practice	Sing Up/Down with Practice
4	1/10	0/10	2/10	2/10
5	2/10	1/10	2/10	4/10
6	6/10	15/100	2/10	5/10
7	8/10	4/10	7/10	9/10
8	8/10	4/10	5/10	6/10
9	9/10	5/10	8/10	9/10
10	9/10	6/10	8/10	9/10

Dozens of studies of this sort have been conducted by those schooled in the Seashore tradition. It is not necessary to review these investigations here, for they converge on the same conclusion: Rhythmic sensitivity, pitch sensitivity, singing ability, and other particularistic skills develop slowly but inexorably in most children.

The question of the extent to which these capacities can be trained has provoked heated controversies. In general, studies show that, with intensive training, a child's performance can be improved on one of these tests, and that he can retain the improvement over a period of time; however, the extent of improvement is usually not dramatic, and a child almost never moves from below average to the ranks of the very skilled. Motoric involvement on the part of the subject and some indication on the part of the teacher that music is an important area are helpful in achieving maximum effects in training. A particularly intriguing question is whether training can lead to absolute pitch. Recent studies have indicated some success in getting subjects to recognize the concert pitch A, but there is no evidence that the more remarkable faculty that permits a few individuals instantly to name or produce any tone can be trained. There may be a critical period for learning absolute pitch; once this period (perhaps the age of 7 or of 12) has passed, it may be that no amount of training can produce perfect pitch. This suggestion is intriguing, but it would be difficult to support it conclusively.

Rather than recount more findings in this piecemeal area of research, where neither stages nor qualitative changes have been discerned, I would like to focus on a few examples of research in the making and perceiving of music that are more suggestive about the distinctive features of musical development. Many years ago, the pioneer developmental psychologist Heinz Werner looked at the kinds of spontaneous melodies produced by children. In less skilled hands, such an investigation might have only yielded a general conclusion about "gradual improvement." But Werner focused on the *musical* aspects of children's melodies, and was able to discern a discrete series of stages through which all children passed (see Table 3). Werner examined the ascending and descending movements of melody, the role of repetition, the emergence of cadences, and the handling of phrasing. This fine-drawn analysis revealed which aspects of melodies were most salient for children at a young age, and which aspects appeared spontaneously; such a description has interesting implications about the relation between musical development and other aspects of linguistic and cognitive development. One finds, for example, that resting on a lower note is a constant throughout melodic production, presumably reflecting a fundamental tendency in vocal production, but that ability to use and vary cadences waits upon the ability to repeat a simple motif. Werner demonstrated that even a study of this simplicity can yield considerable information about music and general development.

Many years elapsed before other studies of equal suggestiveness were undertaken. One such series was launched by Pflederer-Zimmerman, who examined the relationship between musical perception and the kinds of conservation studied by Piaget. Pflederer hypothesized that the ability to appreciate certain aspects of music—such as the inversion or transposition of a melody, and the identity of a melody

TABLE 3   MELODIC DEVELOPMENT ACCORDING TO WERNER

Age in Years	Direction of Melodic Movement	Gestalt	Ending	Ambitus (total range between low and high)	Number of Different Tones in the Motif
2–3	Descending: \ (rare form: monotone:—)	"Whole-Form" (The motif as a whole is repeated without repetition of parts: ‖ or ∧∧)	On the lowest tone	Minor third	Two tones
3¼	Ascending-Descending ∧		On the same tone as beginning	Major third	Three tones
3½				Fourth, fifth	More than three tones
3¾		Repetition of descending part: ‖			
4			On a middle tone between low and high		
4¼		Repetition of ascending part ∧			
4½			On a tone toward which the low tone is leading upward		
4¾	Double-Form ∧∧ x (tone x belongs to both parts)	Overlapping steps in ascending part: ∧			

193

played on two different instruments or at two different speeds—presupposed a specific intellectual ability: the capacity to focus on underlying structural continuities between seemingly disparate stimuli, which had been first investigated by Piaget. She found that when properties of melodies, such as tone, rhythm, or harmony were changed, 8-year-old subjects were able to appreciate that the two specimens were in some sense the "same" melody; young subjects, aged 5, were unable to "conserve" meter, tone, or rhythmic patterns. Pflederer examined a range of transformations and found an ordering of difficulty, with oldest children finding transformations in which rhythm and harmony were varied simultaneously the most difficult to "conserve." More recently she has investigated the effect of having children themselves produce the patterns and the limits of changes tolerated by subjects.

Pflederer's investigations have raised intriguing questions about the organization of musical sensitivity in the child and its relationship to other kinds of capacities. One may argue that there is a sense in which *any* change in a musical stimulus makes it different and that, as a consequence, analogies with Piaget's research are forced. However, there is clearly something in the fact that older persons acknowledge certain identities among configurations, which apparently escape younger children.

Following an analogous line of inquiry, Bamberger has sought to discover how young children approach musical stimuli. Not content merely to say that 5-year-olds cannot handle musical conservation, she has tried to determine the child's own perception of music at that age. Even though her investigations are not yet complete, she has uncovered a number of fascinating phenomena. Young children (7 or under) will not spontaneously realize that a melody played on a certain series of bells can be played on a smaller set of bells, if all repetitions of specific tones are played on the same bell. For them, the musical configuration seems to be identical with the spatial configuration, rather than inhering in a sequence of pitches that can be realized in many equivalent ways. Bamberger has also examined the development of notation, finding it a useful way of getting at the child's perception of the musical stimulus. The youngest child who hears a simple pattern (say, two quarter-notes followed by three eighth-notes) repeated several times will simply put down a series of circles or squares, with no differentiation between them. At a later time, there will be some distinction between longer and shorter durations, but scant appreciation of recurrences, limited consistency in size relations, and no effort to break down the motif into measures. Only the preadolescent (aged 9 to 12) is able to evolve a notation that captures the time values, repetitions, and "underlying beat" accurately, and that can be reliably and accurately interpreted by someone else. Most recently, Bamberger has been studying the way in which children combine components of a tune in order to produce the target melody; preliminary findings suggest that a tendency to break the piece down into individual notes is less productive than a capacity to handle entire phrases as gestalten.

A final bit of research has been undertaken by Donna Bridgeman and myself. In this study, concerned with children's sensitivity to musical styles, children heard pairs of musical stimuli and were asked to judge whether the two stimuli came from the same composition (in half the cases they did, in half they did not). We found that even first graders perform at better than chance level, that preadolescent subjects tend to focus on the dominant figure (such as a voice) in selections and to base their decisions on whether the same figure is included in both stimuli, and that a second hearing of the series does not enhance performance. Of particular interest was the finding that sixth graders had scores equal to (and in some cases higher than) sophomores at Harvard and Radcliffe Colleges.

In accounting for the high performance of elementary school pupils (there was no significant difference between the scores of 8-, 11-, 14-, and 19-year-olds), the reasons given by the subjects for their responses proved informative. These explanations suggested that younger and older subjects were approaching the tasks in different ways. The preadolescents were immersing themselves in the musical selections, noting their affective and kinesthetic effects, making free associations to previous experiences, and were then basing their judgments on whether the two parts "felt" or "seemed" the same. They were proceeding from the musical event to a final decision. In contrast, the adolescent subjects appeared to approach the task from the perspective of their musical knowledge. They had some familiarity with musical history and terminology, and they looked for examples of prior categories in the music they heard. Thus they would label one fragment as baroque and then see whether the other selection appeared baroque as well; they were proceeding from a structure (their knowledge of music) to the particular musical event being evaluated. These different approaches to music seem consistent with other findings and provide evidence that, with the advent of formal operations and an "abstract attitude," subjects assume a new kind of "distanced" relationship to aesthetic works, one which may be less effective in revealing the work than the unmediated relationship younger children have. The study also points up the surprising amount of musical competence found among subjects at a very young age.

Perhaps the largest number of studies in the area of music probe preferences. I will not review these studies here, as their findings are unexceptional, but a few random findings from this and other areas will be provided, in order to convey the flavor of previous research. It has been found that seventh graders prefer music with fast tempo, variety in volume, and melodic repeats to music with loud volume, jumping melody, and a minor mode. In contrast, 6- and 7-year-olds apparently do not care whether the music is in a major or in a minor mode. The attitudes of younger children toward music are more rapidly altered through repeated exposure to a work, though familiarity does not ensure acceptance. Musically talented youngsters are more sensitive to a rhythm when it is contained in a melody, while children without musical proclivities are more sensitive when the rhythm is simply communicated in pure tones.

There is an interesting and, I think, important convergence among researchers on the importance of the ages 6 to 7 in musical development. During the first years of childhood, the child acquires a general familiarity with music and begins to experiment with perceiving and making, imitating songs he has heard, elaborating them, and recognizing pieces and motifs, for instance. By the age of 6 he has already achieved a working relationship with musical symbols, playing and performing and perceiving with some accuracy. We find Révész testifying that 6-year-olds:

> listen to the piano, are always alert when there is any music, have their favorite songs played over and over again, and try to play familiar tunes on piano. . . . Children's songs are no longer sung at haphazard but are controlled, supplemented and improved. . . . In this period, a gradual transition from playful music-making to a conscious assimilation and correct reproduction of musical impressions is unmistakable.

Another commentator concluded that children aged 6 or 7 are capable of

> a surprising intellectual grasp of music. . . . The children could apprehend music, single out tempo, melody, and rhythm . . . they tend to think of music as being 'about things,' i.e., as telling stories, expressing ideas, and so forth.

Such testimony and the range of research reviewed, from Révész's study of a prodigy to Pflederer's findings about the perception of musical changes, all point to one conclusion: At least for children with adequate musical potential, it is possible to be a participant in the artistic process by the ages of 5 to 7. Noteworthy are both the extent to which abilities of the majority of children have unfolded by that age, and the particular capacities of the most talented. A few examples of compositions by young children, some of average ability, one a prodigy, will illustrate this point.

The average child is capable of a competent musical performance and understanding at an early age, but may never progress significantly beyond the level reached by the close of his eighth year. His information processing ability will increase somewhat, but his ultimate potential for rhythmic and harmonic sophistication should already be manifest at this age. With the gifted child, a different set of capacities seems to be at work, which allows much early progress without noticeable training— as is more universally true in the case of language learning. So powerful are these generative capacities that only those adults who were self-taught are likely to continue playing a musical instrument in their adult lives. It would be deceptive to contend that we understand the nature of these musical abilities, which, in the most illustrious cases, make an individual appear like a member of different species, yet more deceptive still to pretend that these unusual capacities for listening, mastering rhythm, and interpreting music do not exist. The music of a culture is a symbol system with its own aspects of form and content, and if a child is allowed some contact with examples of music and is not devoid of musical potential, he should be able to assimilate if not master the general properties of his musical system. Familiarity with and mastery of a musical system will of course continue to expand indefinitely, but what evidence we have suggests that a "working familiarity" with and understanding of the general mechanisms of this symbol system is within the ken of the child of 6 or 7. Impressive support for this contention comes from a study of musical development among the Balinese, in which it is shown that youngsters aged 8 are able in a short period of time to become full-fledged performers and participants in the subtle musical life of the culture.

It seems valid to conclude, then, that certain formal properties of music can emerge in the making activity, be noticed by the perceptual systems of children, and involve the feeling system of children at a young age. That is, a reasonably competent 7-year-old should understand the basic metrical properties of his musical system and the appropriate scales, harmonies, cadences, and groupings, even as he should be able, given some motifs, to combine them into a musical unit that is appropriate for his culture, but is not a complete copy of a work previously known. What is lacking is fluency in motor skills, which will allow accurate performance, experience with the code, tradition, and style of that culture, and a range of feeling life. This lack renders children's musical performances and compositions somewhat limited and superficial, even though they are not without charm and spontaneity.

That prodigies appear most frequently in the art of music may reflect the preeminently formal nature of the medium and the fact that music is more self-contained than painting. One critic has speculated that "the ear can develop independently, the eye can only develop as one's understanding of the object seen . . . thus the boy Mozart probably did play as finely as anybody else alive. . . . Picasso at 16 was *not* drawing as well as Degas."

LITERATURE

Language is an articulated symbol system, with discernible units, rhythmic patterns, sequences, and transformations. Accordingly, some of the generalizations made about music apply in significant measure to language and literary development. Like music, language begins as a purely making activity, which gradually becomes related to personal and environmental elements and to the aesthetic tradition; formal aspects and syntactic arrangements are the first to be assimilated by the child. A major difference between language and music inheres in the fact that language is used to communicate messages of various degrees of specificity, with each word and phrase having a particular referent. Thus the formal properties of language, its syntactic structure, rhythms, and accents, comprise a relatively smaller proportion of what is discerned as significant in literature. To be sure, music is in no way simpler than language; a composition's reference to its parts or to other works may be enormously complex; yet perhaps because music's complexity is directly built on formal elements and need not rely on the allusions that characterize ordinary language, precocity is more likely to be found in music than in the literary realm.

Students of language development have demonstrated that the child is remarkably sensitive to the syntactic properties of language, and that he has indeed mastered most of them by the age of 4 or 5. Some of these data have been reviewed earlier, along with evidence of the rhythmic components in language learning and examples of the appealing confusions that often appear when a child's syntactic precocity outflanks his semantic maturity. Even when the child's own processing tendencies are primitive, he shows a beginning control of certain longer utterances (by completing those of others and mimicking their characteristic intonational patterns). Linguistic competence appears to begin with an ability to appreciate the phonological structure of the language; phonology is accessible even to retarded children, while the levels of syntax and semantics are restricted to the normal child. Revealingly, the more musical aspects of language learning merge first in the child's developing systems.

The child's linguistic precocity (particularly in the syntactic realm) has struck many psychologists, but it is a Russian writer of children's stories who has emerged as the most sympathetic and sensitive observer of children's utterances. Chukovsky maintains that the ages of 2 to 5 mark a period of linguistic genius. He has compiled numerous examples that illustrate the child's possession of the varied patterns, rhythmic sounds, rhyming forms, images, and structures associated with the great literary artist. Chukovsky gives numerous examples of the devices the child relentlessly uses in his efforts to master his native tongue and to communicate his rich supply of notions, ideas, and questions. Parts of the body are often transposed with those of animals ("Mother, cover my hind leg"); affect is transformed to objects (pants are "sulking"); qualities are transferred to new realms (a "middle-aged piece of cake"; a naked child is "barefoot all over"); metaphor is taken literally ("Why don't you say *pencil* knife"); an adult who says "I'm dying to hear this concert" is asked "Why don't you die then?"; word play is rampant ("more himselfer than you"; "good health" to a sneezing kitten; "get up so early it will be late"); actions are transferred (the locomotive takes a bath); numerous anomalies are introduced (the geese should be killed lest they get cold; the horse is pitied because it can't pick its nose; worms are bisected so they won't be lonesome); whole sets of contrary activities are listed (he rode on a doppled wagon tied to a wooden horse; he sat with his back to the front as he rode to the hunt).

Such literary mockeries and gems reflect a variety of conditions—the child's vivid imagination, his sense of fun, his embarrassment at not knowing something, his experimentation with the potential of the verbal making system, his ardent desire to master the language perfectly. To be sure, inadequate knowledge of the referent of word figures in some of these anomalous expressions, yet these transfers of meanings often reveal a certain wisdom or malice and are not made in total naivete. The playing, exploratory aspects of speech emerge in such experimentation. Chukovsky also notes an inherent poetic sense, however. Youngsters experiment with sounds and regularly produce phonic marvels such as this

Kossi minie, kossi koi
Lieba kussi, lieba koi
Ioka kuku, shubka koi
Lieba kusia, shubka koi

That this piece is meaningless for adults is beside the point; the youngster, like the poet, it attracted to the regular, driving rhythms and the alternation of hard and soft sounds. The deviation from reality is important in Chukovsky's view, because the child can only know reality by testing what its limits might be. Language is excellent for such experimentation; it is readily manipulated, flexible in its reference, and suited for devising situations difficult to realize in life.

The linguistic genius of the child derives in part from his ability to discern underlying structures of the language (a necessary factor if he is to master his native tongue). Chukovsky is not surprised to find the child inventing words that exist in other regions of Russia, generalizing rules where the language features exceptions, applying a relentless logic both to the syntactic structures and the particular contents of the language. Even if the child should make erroneous assessment of cause and effect, this is insignificant in light of the fact that he now believes, as must any good scientist, that effects do indeed have causes. The appreciation of opposites is characteristic of child speech—the child often assumes each word has its opposite in meaning and in quality. Evidence of that assumption appears in the verses and the lines that pepper his daily discourse. The younger the child, the greater his attraction to the regularity or rhyme, and so at the beginning, all are versifiers. Verbal creation is so intimately involved with action that the child is typically in motion when he composes jingles.

As for children's first verses, Chukovsky notes that they are spontaneous and inspired by merriment. They are not so much songs as melodic exclamations, spoken with an accompaniment of slapping and dancing, in trochaic form, brief, repetitive, and infectious. There are close ties in the child's own activity between three kinds of making—speaking, maintaining a rhythm, singing—an association that suggests a common underlying formal basis. Perhaps indeed these regular rhythmic linguistic configurations form a substrate to which all normal humans are sensitive. Such formal traits may, however, be evoked only under special conditions akin to those in which regression typically occurs. In illustration, Chukovsky cites the example of the Russian peasant woman, whose speech was normally unvaried and banal. As her month-old infant lay on the bed and made bubbles with its mouth, the mother, seized with sudden ecstasy, smothered him with kisses and rhapsodized:

> Butsiki, mutsiki, dutsiki
> Rutsiki, putsiki, book!
> Kutsen'ki by, tarakutsen'ki,
> Putsen'ki by, marabuk!

Lines of this sort, like children's verses that have survived the centuries (migrating across continents on the wings of their aptness of sound and meaning) appear to draw upon a general framework of balanced rhythm and form that may underlie literary production everywhere.

Chukovsky concludes his lovely book by indicating the characteristics he finds essential in poetry for children. Poems must be graphic, imaginative, musical, lyrical, and filled with rapid changes; the rhyming words should carry semantic weight, the number of adjectives should be small, trochees should dominate, verses should be suitable for play and attractive for individuals of every age. These characteristics are consistent with the discoveries he has made, and perhaps can be viewed as an attempt to outline the basic forms of verse.

Why does linguistic genius stop at 5? Largely because, according to Chukovsky, the 7- or 8-year-olds have no need for the techniques and pyrotechnics the younger child exploits in expressing himself. He has mastered his own language and can rely upon it to communicate messages. He also has an incipient critical awareness of his speech, and probably does not want to appear babyish to peers. Children at this later age read considerably, thereby assimilating the styles of other writers, and a few will write their own creative poetry. During early childhood, poetry is inseparable from other linguistic creation; but in this later phase, it emerges as an autonomous activity, reflecting self-conscious intentional efforts to achieve rhythmic and rhyming effects. At this level, the child has begun to be in control of his gift, is aware of problems of composition, and is no longer a child versifier. He is a fledgling poet.

Although no other author has explored children's linguistic capacities with Chukovsky's thoroughness and imaginativeness, some investigators have detected the characteristics to which he so compellingly alludes. Carlson and Anisfeld have noted the inventiveness of the young child who deliberately manipulates segmental phonemes in songs, substituting one for another, as in "I Pin Purkin on a Pail Poad." These authors highlight the child's capacity to make utterances longer by employing songs or poems as frames for substitution games. They also cite numerous examples of figures of speech. Burling analyzes nursery rhymes in a variety of languages and finds that they consist of four lines, with four major evenly spaced beats in each line. The verses are usually marked by stressed syllables, and rests occur at regular intervals. "The similarity between languages seems greater for nursery rhymes than for more elaborate forms of poetry. It seems difficult to attribute the cross-linguistic similarities to anything except our common humanity." Stern provides many illustrations of the child's linguistic talent, cautioning, however, that "it is very marked in many children but scarcely existent in others. It shows itself by an arbitrary enrichment of vocabulary in the form of derivatives and of compound words (of their own making)." Stern emphasizes the importance of repetition for the child who "asks for little songs, not to learn them, but to hear them, and to take over new pleasure in the hearings; but all the same at last he learns them." The repetition stage is eventually replaced by a more active phase in which the child gushes forth with those lines which he has learned. "Children from about their fourth year on become capable of learning poetic texts and it can afford them the greatest pleasure to tattle out the verses attached to the illustrations in their picture books, to sing . . . to learn poems." Chukovsky's findings seem to be confirmed across cultures.

A number of authors have surveyed literary development and sought to pinpoint the principal stages through which children pass; both the child's perception of literature and his ability to create literary specimens have undergone scrutiny. Because of the difficulty of separating literary development from general language development, commentators can be faulted for not always discriminating between the two. Nonetheless a few accounts are sufficiently intriguing to merit mention.

The perceptive child psychologist Karl Bühler outlined the general progression of taste in the child. The 4-year-old preferred stories dealing with daily, mundane functions, the 6-year-old liked stories of the supernatural or the mystical, and the 8-year-old favored stories of adventure and excitement. These findings have been confirmed in several other studies of childrens' preferences. A finer-grained analysis of the early years of childhood was made by White, who discerned the following phases in her young child's reactions to storybooks.

AGE 1   The child throws or chews books.

AGE 2   The child likes pictures of babies.

AGE 2½   The child begins to quote from books; imitates characters; recreates scenes; finds pictures everywhere, even where adults miss them; identifies with Peter in Peter Rabbit.

AGE 3 to 3½   The child asks many questions in an effort to understand stories; needs stories which she can easily understand; finds something new at each reading; objects to the illustrations in "it might have been" situations; sits and talks contentedly to a book for long periods of time; repeats phrases; appears to be taking in the content even when not attending exclusively to the story; investigates every detail; is already able to make up a story which draws on fragments of ones she knows. For example: "It's about James Jones and he went marching in the forest. And in the forest do you know who he met? Mr. Jones and he was very very fat." Four stories were drawn on in this creation.

AGE 4 to 4½   The youngster is bothered by inconsistencies between stories; is deeply disturbed by sad parts; often does not look when being read to; becomes more interested in peers, less in mothers and stories.

AGE 5   The child's approach to stories comes to resemble an adult's approach.

The child advances rapidly from a completely inappropriate response to an ability to follow plot, experience pertinent affective reactions, and make his own little stories. His developing systems are able to operate effectively on the symbolic level. My own observations confirm those of White's for the most part; I would only underline the extent to which story hearing and telling is a very special, almost religious experience for the young child, one which commands his absolute attention and seems crucial in his mastery of language and his comprehension of the world. The child identifies fully with the characters and episodes in the stories and integrates them with situations encountered in the remainder of his working day, even as he incorporates names, events, rhythms, melodies, sounds, even entire passages into his nighttime monologues. The central role played by story hearing and storytelling in the lives of most young children leads me to speculate that the narrative impulse plays an important role in organizing the child's world; and the auditory and vocalizing systems may require a certain amount of stimulation which, though available from many sources, seems particularly well satisfied by literary experience.

Several psychologists have performed the valuable service of collecting a large number of stories told by children. Generally speaking, analysts have been interested chiefly in individual differences, the variety of themes, and the psychodynamics reflected in the stories, all of these being of secondary interest from the aesthetic point of view. I have examined these stories from a literary perspective, and have found that, by the age of 5, the average child has passed through six discernible stages in his production of stories. Because the stages are instructive about general artistic development and because examples will help to convey the nature of stories produced by children, I would like to review my findings in some detail.

Of considerable use in analyzing the stories has been the notion of epigenesis, wherein the first stories are seen as possessing (in embryonic form) all the literary traits realized in subsequent development; at each stage a particular feature is highlighted, presumably because of important psychological events of the period and the informational processing capacity of the child. Characteristic of the literary realm is that all its potential devices and resources are present at the very beginning; in a sense the simplest set of utterances exploits (to a limited degree) the manifold resources of the language and the literature, just as the young possess in embryonic form the characteristics of the mature organism. The development found in children's storytelling features a greater complexity, intricacy, cogency, and sophistication as the child practices with the verbal medium and acquires additional knowledge about the environment; these trends persist over many years in the normal child and characterize his overall intellectual and social development. Various literary aspects are also highlighted at the appropriate developmental level; these different emphases reflect changes in the social milieu of the child, alteration in his own physical and mental capability, and, above all, a fuller comprehension of the limitations and potentials of medium of literature. Erik Erikson has described eight central life crises and illustrated how each crisis exists throughout life but is highlighted at a specific psychosexual stage. In an analogous way, I wish to demonstrate that literature contains a series of pivotal elements that figure in all storytelling, but become stressed at particular stages in the storyteller's development.

Table 4 sketches in general terms the six aspects of literature that dominate storytelling in the young child:

Aspect I.   Occurrence of Events
Aspect II.   Counterforces
Aspect III. Control of Resources
Aspect IV. Role of Organizing Affect
Aspect V.   Creation Related to the Literary Tradition
Aspect VI. Creation Related to External Events

I contend that these aspects can be found in every story, but that each becomes emphasized during a specific stage of literary development. Although deviations from the norm of development (the diagonal of the chart) are not wholly worked out, I have touched on the way in which these aspects are handled during stages when they are not a central concern of the child. For example, counterforces exist in each of the stages, but are manifest as a simple statement of opposites or crisscrossing in the first stages, and as "good vs bad characters," "meaningful dialogues," "complex interactions," "themes and counterthemes," during the latter stages of epigenesis. Similarly, the other aspects of literature are manifest even when not stressed. Illustrating this, in the original studies, stories that exemplified each of the deviations from the diagonal were included. Throughout the study of literary epigenesis it should be possible to describe the relevant features of modes and vectors, but the details of such an approach can only be hinted at here.

Here, then, are brief definitions of each of the aspects, accompanied by examples of stories in which they are stressed.

Aspect I. This aspect deals with the actions contained in the story, the things that happen, the relation between the actions or events described in each sentence. Nearly all fiction deals with events that either happen to characters or unfold in the character's mind; column I is particularly concerned with the evolution of that aspect.

I-1. The most primitive form of literature is characterized by a simple notion of events happening. In the typical 2-year-old's utterances, things merely "happen," one after another, in rapid succession without a compelling relationship. "A" does this, then "A" does that. Relationship between ideas remains undeveloped.

> Dale S., 2;5. A bus. He went up a hill. He crashed. He down. He went down in the water and he swammed. He went round and round. He crashed on a mountain. Then he went up in the air and crashed.

Aspect II. This aspect deals with the existence of counterforces or polarities in literature. The creation of interest, directions, and tension generally depends on some dialectic between two diverse parties, characters, emotions, events, or forces. A greater awareness of the relationship between subjects, objects, and ideas is apparent.

II-2. Until the passive events of I-1 are placed in some sort of relationship to one another, the story will lack a sense of direction or movement. II-2 contains the first clear signs of such tension between Peter and the lion.

> Porteus B., 2;10. (Peter vs lion). Once there was a house. Peter lived in the house. He has a lion. The lion ate him up. Peter hit him. Then he eat him.

Aspect III. This aspect deals with the coherence of story, the extent to which the acts, actions, and scenes hang together, possess continuity, and seem reasonable. At III-3, unbridled action predominates at the expense of continuity and coherence. It is as if the child had too many materials available and could not organize them; syntax seems more precocious

TABLE 4   THE EPIGENESIS OF LITERARY CREATIVITY

	I. Occurrence of Events	II. Counterforces	III. Control of Resources
I	things happen; no clear relationship among events	two happenings criss-cross (X up, Y down)	short, jerky sentences; tenuous relations among topics and characters
II	snowball; A acts on B, B acts on C, etc.	polarities; two characters or emotions vie	summary sentences; beginnings, endings
III	more snowballing; one character undergoes numerous experiences	negation included; good vs bad characters or forces	inadequate control of resources; sheer action, syntactic versatility dominate over coherent meaning
IV	events patterned; characters have similar or complementary experiences	relations among characters established; meaningful dialogues	more continuity and coherence because of organizing affect
V	incidents developed; characters begin to have "mental" or "subjective" experiences	characters developed; complex interactions	expectations created and resolved; continuity
VI	scenes with developed characters interacting; multiple themes and motifs	duality sometimes breaks down; characters followed through changes in fortune; themes and counterthemes	attempt to establish and maintain complex equations; ability to switch styles, genres

TABLE 4 (CONTINUED).

IV. Role of Organizing Affect	V. Creation Related to Literary Tradition	VI. Creation Related to External Events
affect neutral; all items receive equal emphasis	parallel structure of sentences	quasi-realism; semblance of coherence due to limited resources
primitive modes; bodily language; occasional signs of logic	word play; rhythmic repetition	stories often implausible (dog eats man)
good and evil forces; much enthusiasm; affect intrudes	onomatopoeia; some description; fragmentary traces of literary devices	free fantasy; impossible events; switch between story, play, simple conversation, and self-expression
affects, modes organize thematic material; tension introduced and managed	stress by repetition; name play, humorous refrains; rhetorical questions; extended description	some sense of audience discernible; characters still implausible; jumping about among events
infusion of affect contributes to forceful style; ability to disguise, create mystery; audience's affect manipulated	stage of classic plots, formulas, literary devices, planning; awareness of "kinds of stories"	emerging realism, sense of audience; differentiation of story from nonstory
control of emotion; feelings coded in plot; commentary and irony emerge; affect is sometimes neutral	sophisticated devices; transformations of classic stories; deliberate metaphor; emergence of style	creations related to individual's experiences; possibility of creating according to formula, reporting objectively, and creating imaginative fantasies

than semantics. Action is more salient than affect, except for the generalized affect of uncontrolled energy. All the elements of a story are present, yet unorganized.

> Ed R., 3;9. A little girl lived with her mommy. And then she got spanked. And a bear came in and he was a long one and he ate the girl up. And then the mommy and daddy came home and the bear flied away and they said, "Where's our little girl?" and they were sad.
>
> And then an eagle came, flied in their house. And Little Red Riding Hood came in and said, "That's a naughty eagle." And then the princess cut off the eagle's head. And the little girl thanked the princess for taking her home. And then the basket broke and her mommy said, "Oh naughty girl Little Red Riding Hood." and the mommy said, "Naughty Girl, Little Red Riding Hood."

Aspect IV. This aspect deals with the presence of an affect, mode, or feeling about which the story is organized. Literature differs from scientific or journalistic writing in that it highlights the communication of subjective aspects of experience, such as the kind embodied in modes and qualities. Hence, the ability to use affects or modes in order to *organize* a set of experiences becomes crucial.

IV-4.   Although all elements of a story seem to be in some sense present in III-3, they are only organized by some dominant affect at IV-4. This affect may be stated or implied, but it should be conveyed to, if not aroused in, the reader. Ideally, a certain feeling such as delight, revenge, or jealousy should pervade portions of the story. "Metaphoric" modes may also predominate, as in Carter's story, where a wooden feeling pervades the conclusion.

> Carter F., 4;8. . . . and when he got home he painted a box. Then he painted a house and then, a big, big church. And then he builded a table and then he went to this house and he built a nice big bench for his mommy. And then he painted his chair green. And that is the end of his story.
>
> Kenneth A., 4:1. . . . (anger and revenge). Once there was a boy who had a bow and arrow. He shot everyone. He killed even his mother and daddy and brother. He killed everyone else . . . the next night the boy's mommy and daddy were away at a party. Then the little boy got out some paints when the Mother and Daddy didn't tell him to do it. They were very angry when they came home and they slapped and they didn't know what to do and they slapped him and spanked him. Then he got in an airplane and rode away when his mother and daddy didn't tell him to do it.

Aspect V. This deals with the place of a story within the literary tradition. One views a story in terms of its uses of literary devices, classical themes, plots, characters, and stories. The ability to use such compositional forms involves both some *planning* and evolution of one's own *style*.

V-5. This is the stage of classic plots and little details. The stories often resemble ones heard elsewhere; there is evidence that the child had planned his story (the first sentence contains implications about the rest), paid attention to details, and is developing a characteristic way of self-expression. By V-5 the unilinear evolution described here is already starting to break down; stories are differing in their originality, use of literary figures, and relation to the literary tradition.

> A developing style: Monica H., 4;8. Today is a special day for me— Boy Scout day. Means stores are closed. Have a big celebration. Have a party. Some of my neighbors come—just have a party. We dance, we eat, everything like that. . .

> Effective beginning: Barry M., 3;10. I'm going to be Dr. Andrew M. I'm gonna have a real stethoscope, real watch, real treatment machine, real band-aids, real, real, real, thermometer. . .

> Little details: Kent W., 4;10. He had hot coffee and then he had lunch and then has dinner—three sandwiches and some coffee. . .

> Classic plot: Trudy B., 4;0. Once upon a time there was a mother and a daddy bear and a baby bear who lived in a little house in the woods. One day the daddy and mother went out for a walk, leaving the baby at home, and they got lost and couldn't find their way home. Then they met a leaf and climbed on its back and were blown home by the wind. And on the way the leaf set them down by a river to have a drink because they were thirsty.

Aspect VI. This treats the extent to which stories reflect an imaginary world, the outside world, the world of phenomenal experience, other stories, or the individual's own life history. The analyst attempts to ascertain whether the child's utterance is a factual report, a realistic description, or the product of his fancy. Excellence or mediocrity can be achieved in each of these forms. Also relevant for Aspect VI is the extent to which the child is aware he is telling a story to an audience with certain expectations.

VI-6. There are several alternative story forms at this level. The story may be merely a soppy *formula*, the repetition or slight modification of a story or formula already known; or a story may be original, yet subordinated to a well-known formula. This form is a comparatively stagnant one, with little room for later imaginative development.

Deidre W., 5;6. Once upon a time there was a pussy cat that wanted to be a Christmas present. . . . In a minute Santa Claus came dashing through the sky and the kitty called up, "I want to be a Christmas present." And then Santa called, "I think I know where to put you." So the next morning he wasn't in Santa's sleigh any more, he was in a little girl's house. And then the little girl said when she saw him, "I guess Santa knew what I wanted for Christmas."

The story may simply be a *factual account* of something that happened to the child, something he saw, or something he wants to be or do. Although imaginatively told, it is principally a *report*.

Everett S., 5;6. If I really decide to take a trip to outer space it would be difficult decision. No one knows anything about these things, you know and it really isn't safe. . . . then we will hurry back to earth and go in the laboratories with our samples and film to be developed.

Fictional creations build on the elements of earlier developmental levels, reformulating them in a creative way. The child, having better control of his resources, can plan his stories; they should strike a responsive chord in his audience because of his knowledge of feelings, modes, and the audience's expectations. The child who tells a story of this type may become a creative writer; further advances can be expected along the developmental path.

Lila P., 4;8. Once there was a fish named Flower. She went down in the water and said, "Oh, my gosh, where's my lover?" She went down in the cellar where my house is. She saw a big father fish which had a sword in his nose. She ran away from the house and hid in another house. She ran up the water and flapped out. She ran away. She went to another house in a deep, deep river. She saw her own home which had her lover in it. They kissed each other. That's the end.

Audience psychology: Keith M., 5;7. So she had it up her nose and her nose hurted. (Really it does hurt and it makes you sneeze really; cause I had it up once.)

This epigenetic view of literary development has, I hope, indicated the vast amount of resources the child has in the verbal realm, the difficulty he initially experiences in deploying them satisfactorily, and the impressive way in which some young schoolchildren can produce cogent and imaginative tales. One sees a productive interaction between the child's making system in the realm of language, the use of feelings to confer unity and tension upon his productions, and the increasingly fine and appropriate discriminations captured in his creations. Perhaps similar epigenetic examinations of productivity in other art forms could be undertaken, and the parallels between these trajectories noted.

Naturally, the 5-year-old is not yet an accomplished storyteller. The themes he can work with are few, his command of poetic devices yet immature, the complexity and subtlety of his productions rather limited. Nonetheless, it is my feeling that the poems and the stories of the 5- to 7-year-old reflect a mastery of formal aspects of the literary realm, and I have collected examples from different sources which give substance to this claim. Some of these have been reprinted here.

What, then, of children's capacities to handle a more structured task in the literary realm? One of my studies explores this area. Children ranging in age from 6 to 15 were told two "stories without endings," asked to make up an ending appropriate for the story, and instructed to retell the story to another experimenter. Unknown to the children, the stories had been composed in two radically different styles, and so the task provided information not only about comprehension of meaning, memory for details, imaginativeness, and complexity of endings, but also about children's capacities to sustain and to remember a style.

From the enormous amount of information collected about children's capacities in the literary realm, three of the findings are worth noting here. First of all, as in the task of sensitivity to musical style, the greatest gap in performance on the variety of measures occurred between the 6-year-olds and the 8-year-olds. In addition, in nearly all facets of the test, the sixth graders had higher absolute scores than adolescents; they possessed the keenest memories, produced the most complex and appropriate endings, and recalled the style most faithfully; this finding supports the hypothesis that formal operations in adolescence may dull a subject's imaginativeness and sensitivity in the aesthetic realm. Finally, each of the age groups exhibited a characteristic approach to the task. The 6-year-olds tended to give a *brief*, one sentence ending to the story, completing it in the simplest possible way, as if supplying the last strip in a comic. The 8-year-olds gave *picaresque* endings. These were long, detailed, complex, often filled with high adventure, drama, and excitement, but not always appropriate to the demands of the stories. The sixth graders appeared to be at the *watershed* of literary creativity: they revealed a great deal of promise in their endings, and the best of them were extremely sensitive to the style of the original, clever in their endings, and faithful to the original. The ninth graders were, as a group, competent, even *professional* in the task;

they executed it adequately, but few, if any, revealed notable originality or sensitivity to style. They gave what was called for, nothing more, and appeared to have lost the promise of the sixth graders.

It is interesting that these findings mirror the epigenesis of story-telling, though of course the stages are realized at a more leisurely pace. In both cases, the first stories are very simple and direct; the next ones are filled with literary resources that are not adequately controlled; succeeding stages feature an organizing affect and much promise; the final stage features a variety of competences, only a few of which directly reveal literary excellence. The question of why so many children come to the threshold of literary flowering, only to turn away and be-come competent "hacks" is of course a crucial one for our enterprise, and one that will concern us directly in the concluding chapters.

As with the other artistic realms, most studies on children's linguis-tic and literary development are of limited interest, for they focus too narrowly on an area of dubious relationship to literary creativity (such as free associations) or because they are limited to the recitation of piecemeal increases (for example, in memory) or uninformative observa-tions on children's discriminations (preference). Again I will review a few representative findings, pausing somewhat longer on those of more than perfunctory interest.

It has been determined that children remember better those stories that possess continuity and lead to an ending; when an incompleted story is told, youngsters will tend to resolve loose threads. Intelligent children find more of the humor latent in literary materials. Children aged 7 to 9 show the greatest interest in heroes whose subjective con-cerns are reflected in their activities. The heroes' own reflections are of interest only when they appear as overt behavior. Children are unable to understand the subtleties of proverbs until the years preceding ado-lescence; a comprehensive mastery of metaphor is also a late acquisition of the child, though instances of spontaneous use of metaphor can be found even in the earliest utterances.

Two studies that yield substantive findings about literature have concerned the child's conception of literary emotion and the child's understanding of irony. In the former study, children heard portions of the *Iliad* with all affect words deleted, and then listened to other vi-gnettes, which were similar to the *Iliad* in certain ways. Children under the age of 7 considered as more similar to the *Iliad* stories that had some objective elements in them (a suit of armor, a person with the same name); only children past this age were able to overlook super-ficial similarities in the stories and focus instead on the underlying emotion or affect with which the particular vignette dealt. As one of the principal aspects of literary perceiving and feeling involves the ability to appreciate the emotion embedded (or having its objective correlative) in a series of events, the capacity of the 7-year-old to appreciate this element is of considerable interest.

An investigation of a more sophisticated aspect of literary comprehension focused on the ability of high school and college students to appreciate the ironic aspects of various passages. Subjects were given statements that might be viewed as ironic (for example, "There are two kinds of truth, a deep truth and a shallow truth, and the purpose of science is to eliminate the deep truth"), and asked to reason aloud as they sought to comprehend these statements. Only the more sophisticated high school students and some of the college students were able to appreciate fully the ironic aspects of the passages. Irony is viewed here as the ability to hold in an "awkward embrace" two conflicting emotions or ideas. Sensitivity to irony appeared to involve a series of perceptual stages. Students first realized that there were two conflicting elements in the passages, and then gradually hit upon the particular relationship between them intended by the author.

This study illustrates well the enormous potential for investigation in the literary realm. In addition, it highlights a major point of our discussion, that in the arts, and particularly in the literary realm, a work can be appreciated on an indefinite number of levels. Even (or perhaps especially) the youngest child can enjoy "Jabberwocky," while the most sophisticated adult will discover ironic or subtle aspects in *Alice in Wonderland*. Throughout literature, one encounters works that can be appreciated literally, figuratively, and allegorically, or at all of these levels. Naturally, literary appreciation may be enhanced by an ability to respond on all of these levels, but is not dependent on it; one who misses the ironies in *Huckleberry Finn* may still enjoy and respond to the story. Appreciation of literature is subject to refinement that can continue throughout life, but is also accessible in incipient form to the young child.

Our discussion of literary development should include an acknowledgment that the works of young children are often remarkably effective. A number of teachers have documented the extent to which young school children can even produce works that honor certain formal constraints. For example, they can pen limericks

> There was a young man called Steve
> Who got married on Christmas Eve
> His new wife called Linda
> Burned his socks to a cinder
> That unhappy man called Steve

and can parody familiar poems:

The rain comes
Plattering down plip, plop, plip
Running rivers overflow
It slides down
The window pane and sounds like
Pattering feet.

Even in so demanding a task as imitating or assimilating a prevalent style, elementary school children can turn out creditable products.

This review has suggested the notable achievement of the child of 5 to 7 in the literary realm. While his making behavior may be rather more advanced than his ability to discriminate among various forms of literature, his general fascination with stories and his alertness to rhyming patterns, play of words, stylistic features, principles of narrative, rhythmic patterns, and figures of speech suggest that both his perceiving and his making systems have assimilated salient formal elements of literature. Certainly, many children will not progress beyond this level, while those with distinct talent will soon reject their childish efforts, as they go on to master the traditions of their culture, gain increased control over their skills, and communicate specific messages in their work. With language a natural vehicle for man, the linguistic mechanisms will sometimes tend to proliferate and overwhelm, so that the child is unable to handle the raft of devices and forms he has assimilated or produced; the mere capacity to regulate this literary resource collection may pose a major problem for subsequent development.

Whereas music may seem like a foreign tongue to many children, the vehicle of poetry is a common property—speech. "Theoretically, if not in fact, any adequately educated man could write poems, good or bad." All individuals pass through a stage of poetic sensitivity and creativity. According to Chukovsky, the preschool child's own verse making and his irresistible attraction to poetry—his need to hear and to memorize it—are temporary and soon to pass, but are strong spurs in his mental growth. "Under the influence of beautiful word sequences, shifted by a pliable musical rhythm and richly melodic rhymes, the child playfully, without the least effort, strengthens his vocabulary and his sense of the structure of his native language." Shortly after this point, many literary faculties tend to drop out of the child's repertoire. Perhaps they have been in the service of language learning; and having achieved their purpose, they atrophy.

Why some individuals may go on (or continue) to be literary geniuses is a crucial query that will concern us later. For the present, one may simply note that the preschooler certainly possesses very strong appreciation of certain formal properties of language. Indeed, with regard to his own work and those works that do not demand a subtle grasp of meaning or unusually fine discriminations, nearly every child seems to have the sensitivity and even the genius that is afforded only a certain elite in music. Yet those gifted in music have a somewhat less perilous course to pursue in order to achieve artistic excellence; they are not constantly confronted with the nonaesthetic function of their symbolic medium, while those involved with language must attend increasingly carefully to the content as well as the form of their utterances and those of others. Literature is not an autonomous artistic realm, and consequently the linguistic arts involve a peculiar set of problems stemming from their functional importance in the culture.

MAKING OF PICTORIAL ART

Of the arts reviewed here, only painting requires that the child master complicated manual skills in order to become a creator. While making music or literature need pose little more strain than speaking, producing a painting presupposes a certain dexterity. The capacity to draw or paint grows out of directed motions of the hand and is, in that sense, a very primitive activity, no different from those making activities of early speech that precede symbol use. Indeed the discussion of animal art points up a similarity between the products of Congo the chimpanzee and of the young child. In a formal sense, with reference to such qualities as balance and rhythm, the ape compares favorably with a young child. But even the most gifted chimpanzee has not yet exhibited awareness that his scratchings relate to objects or individuals in the world. Perhaps because of cross-modal limitations, the ape is incapable of combining a product of his making system with the kind of discrimination realized by his perceiving system. In contrast, angular straight lines drawn by children become curves and one-way movement is reversed, and by the time the child is 2, 3, or at the latest 4, he perceives a resemblance between the lines he draws and aspects of the external world. In this capacity he surpasses all other organisms; the ability to produce and read an image from a line may indeed be a distinguishing characteristic of man.

Although the difference between representational and nonrepresentational art is marked, the child does not from one day to the next begin focusing on objects in the world and draw what he sees. Far more frequently, others around him ask what he has drawn, and if he had nothing in mind, he may simply name whatever occurs to him. Even without the pressure to name, however, early drawings of children appear to follow a regular sequence that leads, seemingly ineluctably, to the production of representations. And once the child begins to represent, even his purely geometrical figures take on a referential meaning of some sort for him.

Rhoda Kellogg, a thoughtful student of children's art, has assembled specimens of drawings from scores of cultures and has cogently argued that children the world over proceed through the same series of stages in their first years of drawing. Her discussion, in essential agreement with most major formulations, is worth recapitulation. The child begins by making scribbles, straight or curly lines, back and forth across the page. Twenty basic types of scribbles used by the youngest "artists" have been identified. The scribbling stage is followed by the placement stage, in which children place lines at least 17 basic ways upon the page. At this time the child's drawings are not attempts to draw specific objects. Rather, Kellogg suggests, children gradually realize that certain objects resemble their own designs. During the following stage, the child masters certain shapes, such as crosses, circles, and mandalas, which are built out of the basic scribbles and lines, and spends his time placing these particular patterns upon the paper. At about the age of 4, the child evolves from drawing suns and mandalas to drawing individuals; he reaches the design stage in which he explicitly presents aspects of the world, notably faces, persons, buildings, animals, vegetation, and transportation. Scribbles are incorporated above circles to serve as hair for people, leaves for trees, smoke for chimneys, clouds for the skys. Certain basic visual schemes are exploited, with the child depicting animals as people with ears extending from the tops of their heads, trees as people without arms, boats as triangles atop squares. The various pictorial building blocks (scribbles, placements, shapes) are systematically or haphazardly combined so as to produce representations of objects and persons—the principles of the making system are certainly exemplified in this realm. At the age of 5 or 6 children's pictures begin to suggest stories; reciprocally, children tell stories about their pictures. Children will then squeeze every object they can represent into a single drawing, which becomes replete with animals, kites, houses, and the sun. Kellogg believes that the unfolding of pictorial art in the child most closely parallels that of biological phenomena. If the child is left alone to develop his art, he should evolve his own individual expression of concepts found in the works of all children.

While Kellogg's account is based on her personal observation of completed drawings, her claims have recently been supported by more systematic experimentation. Such studies indicate that the child at 12 months will make marks on a paper, at 18 months can do so without a demonstration, at 27 months can distinguish a line from a scribble, and at 30 months can distinguish a line from a circular stroke. On the average, a circle is drawn at 3, a square at 4, a triangle at 5, a diamond only at 7. Children are sensitive at an early age to such topological properties as straight/curved, vertical/horizontal, long/short, intersection, closure, symmetry, and continuation, a finding explicable in terms of modal-vectoral properties.

Nearly every psychologist interested in children's art has described the stages of drawings by children; some investigations have covered the same early period as Kellogg, others have extended into the adult years. Perhaps due to the availability of so many concrete examples of the phenomena, there is surprising agreement in their general formulations. Of particular note is the universal conviction that general schemes (circles, squares) precede the representation of objects. The human figure is generally the first and most popular representation. The child initially draws what he knows about objects and only gradually comes to realize that he may attempt to draw directly after nature; attempts to draw in perspective do not generally emerge until 9 or 10 years of age, though some preschoolers already attempt the practice. There is a period of preadolescent regression, in which the child either ceases to draw altogether or draws in a more primitive manner. A Renaissance occurs for some young artists who, upon reaching adolescence, resume drawing in a stylistically more sophisticated and original manner. And in our culture there is a general shift to verbal means of expression and to ornamentation in writing after the years of middle childhood.

Particularly suggestive about the development of the making system in the manual arts is Schaefer-Simmerns's claim that all artistically untutored individuals, young and old, pass through essentially the same stages in their early work. He cites this progression: (1) simple circles, figures against a ground; (2) extended circle with greatest contrast between the highest and lowest segments; (3) figures begin to touch or overlap but no shading or lighting effects yet; (4) ability to use shade and light, and to appreciate proportion. The last phase, in Schaefer-Simmerns's view, can be obtained only by adolescents, but I have not found support for this claim. It is worth determining whether his model of universal skill development withstands critical examination.

As in the other arts, one finds that the child of 5 to 7 has already acquired some fundamental aspects of the art form. In the case of painting, however, this realization, rather than being primarily formal, features the shift from drawings in which only formal aspects are stressed to attempts to represent nature or the social world. Because painting is a manual activity, it necessarily entails powerful formal characteristics, even for animals less coordinated than man. Thus the ability to participate in pictorial art involves a realization that the formal activity may be linked up with the representation of objects. But in the perceptual realm, the ability to read pictorial patterns as referring to objects is apparently a natural occurrence, common in infants and pervasive among 2-year-olds. What is more subtle in the perception of paintings is the capacity to overlook the purely surface manifestations of what is being drawn, and to concentrate instead on the drawing's deviations from nature, appreciating the subtle characteristics of an artist's touch. These realizations are not found in most young children.

In view of the child's smooth entry into the circle of painters, it is scarcely surprising that many observers consider paintings by the young child the most exciting works of any group other than professional artists. The 5- to 7-year-old has achieved some formal aspects of drawing —a sense of balance, harmony, composition—as well as an appreciation of the fact that drawing may be used to represent aspects of the world. Works embody color in imaginative ways and have a rhythmic quality. Several elements are, however, missing from young children's drawings; motor skills so that the child can fully execute his intent; control over subject matter so that he does not flit from one theme to another or from monotony to uncontrollable flights; and appreciation of the tradition so that the child can view and perhaps modify his paintings in relation to others executed before. Some of these capacities, like motor skills and self-control, can be acquired by the 6- to 7-year-old, which may account for the mastery commonly obtained at that level. Only lacking in such cases is familiarity with the tradition. To be sure, ignorance of a tradition does not necessarily indicate that a person's art works will be inadequate. The difficulty implied by such naivete emerges when the child finally discovers that others have drawn in specifiable ways, and have achieved enviable success or proficiency. If, when the child arrives at this realization, his own work appears inferior to or inconsistent with that model, he may cease his artistry altogether, being content merely to contemplate works. He becomes fearful of failure at this suddenly more demanding pursuit. A desire to compare one's own work with that of others, both contemporary and from the historical tradition, is quite natural, and constitutes an important experience for growing individuals. Its absence may signal a somewhat incomplete relationship to the arts.

While the child may not be sensitive to subtle features of others' paintings, his own personality and feelings will necessarily be conveyed in his art from the first. Indeed, as soon as he first wields the brush, his natural rhythms, amount of pressure, pacing, sensitivity, variety of feelings, and so forth become part of his drawing activity and can be perceived by those who study his drawings. There are differences between types of individuals that a practiced observer can readily detect.

The relationship between painting and the personality of individuals has occupied many individuals associated with the psychoanalytic tradition, most notably Alschuler and Hattwick, who devoted two volumes to a thoughtful consideration of the relationships between a child's traits and the nature of his artistic productions. These commentators, with numerous others, have found it natural and informative to relate the particular traits of a child's artistic works with the contours of his personality and his emotional life. Indeed, paintings have been used as a projective technique because they so readily allow the analyst access to dynamics of the child's feeling life. Presumably allographic art forms, such as music and literature, are less sensitive to the specific nuances of behavior than such direct, expressive forms as painting and drawing.

In striking contrast to the situation in other arts, there is a slew of studies on children's perception and making in the painting realm, and we may select rather than lament. We will look first at those studies that deal with the child's making behavior, turning later to studies of perception and preference in the painting realm.

When children are shown models and asked to copy them, they tend to simplify, exhibit closure, and impose increased symmetry. They attempt to organize what they see and, if possible, to give it a representational quality. Incompleted models are usually completed by the child, and anomalous figures are modified so that they become easier to handle and to remember. These practices reflect an overall tendency to organize visual input through one's making behavior, even as one imposes meaning on it.

Children's feelings are reflected in their spontaneous drawings and in their copies. They will devote more attention to subjects they care about, and will highlight those features in drawings about which they have strong positive or negative feelings. After pleasant affective experiences, investigators have discovered improvement in children's drawings; conversely, high anxiety conditions produce more rigid drawings, devoid of playfulness and humor. Modal aspects are frequently included in drawings, sometimes directly, as when a child attempts to incorporate a circular bodily movement into his drawing. We see, then, a close interaction between the child's developing system and his youthful artistic works.

The sequences followed by children when they are making a drawing and the stages through which children pass over the course of time have both been examined. When asked to copy a model, the youngest children just get the overall form. Somewhat older children master a few of the details, but only the oldest children reproduce the entire drawing accurately. This lengthy development reflects the difficulty of focusing on and mastering the part and the whole simultaneously. Older children also tend to outline the entire drawing first, while the younger child will pile detail upon detail, operating in a mosaic fashion. Attempts at perspective emerge in some children as young as the age of 4, but concerted efforts are frequent only among 8-year-olds; by the age of 11 to 13 the average child has some mastery of the principles of perspective. Similarly, the representation of spatial relationships (ability to represent relationships "on top of," "underneath," or partially blocking) is uncommon before the middle years of elementary school. Such mastery of technical aspects appears to require a decline of egocentrism and the capacity to synthesize various points of view and relationships, a complicated achievement seemingly dependent on concrete operations. One should note however that these features, while increasing the acceptability of products by Western standards, do not reflect the quality or interest of an artistic work.

During the years from 4 to 9, children's drawings tend to exhibit increasing mastery in their technical aspects (perspective, use of color, accuracy of representation) while remaining visually interesting and formally satisfying. But with the advent of the preadolescent and adolescent years, there is a notable decline both in the amount of drawing and painting by the child and in the quality of his productions. A number of investigators have noted regression in the skill, interest value, and technique of drawings made by children in the 11 to 14 year range. Generally speaking, this regression appears to involve a growing insecurity about the quality of one's own products, coupled perhaps with an increased interest in other people and in experiences outside the aesthetic realm. The onset of puberty is undoubtedly a factor, exhausting much of the child's attention and energies or, at the very least, deflecting them to other activities. The increased reliance on verbal communication and propositional thought also makes drawing less necessary, and may contribute to lessening of attention to the artistic realm. Furthermore, "as children grow older their drawings become less and less self-expressive. Children tend gradually to portray the realistic details of seen objects or to adopt popular schematic or usual pictorial methods of depicting them."

Individual differences in artistic making are vast. Not only does the child's temperament and heredity influence the skill and frequency of his production, but the attitudes of those about him can be decisive in determining whether a child chooses to pursue the art form. Sex differences are found, for example, in the quality of drawing: In representing houses, boys emphasize the functional aspects (smoke emerging from the chimney), girls the environment (gardens and trees) and the details (curtains); furthermore, girls employ thinner lines and more delicate colors. Work with blind patients has suggested that there may be two complementary approaches to the plastic arts. The haptic approach is expressive of the child's inner feelings and responsive to tactile properties, and the visual approach is a reflection of what the child perceives with his eyes. While there may be an overall trend from haptic to visual perception and production, individual differences seem to remain consistent. Investigators have focused on the differences between artistic and nonartistic children, retardates and nonretardates, children with emotional problems, and the effects of different media, but we will not dwell upon their findings here.

A final aspect that bears on children's making activity involves attitudes toward drawing. The young child appears to have little distance from his drawing, expecting it to express directly what he feels and perceives; as the description of child movie-making demonstrated, this tendency has its advantages and pitfalls. The young child, rather than communicating aspects with subtlety, through textural or compositional means, will express his intent directly. Even toddlers are sensitive to the communicative aspect of drawing (as opposed to its "exercise" facet), and will cease to draw if they do not get visual feedback from what they are doing.

The relationship between the child's drawing and his handwriting is very complex. At first the child makes no distinction between examples of drawing and handwriting by adults, but by the age of 3 or 4 he is usually aware that these are two separable activities. He will speak of "making a picture" and of "writing something." It generally takes a few more years, however, before the child understands the communicative function of handwriting and the fact that it relates explicitly to spoken language. By the age of 6 or 7 the child ceases to consider writing a variation of aesthetic practice and, in the coming years, he concentrates on expressing himself clearly and unambiguously in his writing. Yet, from time to time, and particularly in adolescence, the ornamental aspects of writing may return, and writing activity may be undertaken as much for its formal pleasure as for its communicative value. Writing would seem well worth study, since this activity involves many aspects of the arts, including the autographic communication of linguistic information.

Most observers regard drawing as extremely important for the young child. It provides a natural, unfettered, and satisfying means of expressing whatever ideas or feelings the child may have. Restrain-

ing the child from such activities might well have damaging consequences, and access to drawing materials may be especially vital for
disturbed children. At first, drawing seems to be guided by physiological
forces, but soon it comes to serve emotional and communicative needs.
Clarity in drawing is propelled by the child's desire to communicate
unambiguously, and schemes are differentiated accordingly. The child
at age 5 wants to draw familiar things important to those concerned
with his life, items he values. In Herbert Spencer's words of a century
ago, "What is it that the child first tries to represent? Things perceived,
that are large, things that are attractive in color, things round which its
pleasurable associations just cluster—human beings from which it has
. . . so many emotions: cows, dogs, . . . horses."

While at the ages of 5 to 7 drawing is vital to the child and
stunting of his self-expression might be damaging, artistic activity thereafter recedes in importance. The child becomes able to express himself
more adequately and rapidly through other media, and he becomes
increasingly critical of his own work. Most children scrutinize their
drawings critically at the ages of 8 to 10, but more talented children
may criticize their work at an earlier age. I have certainly found evidence of planning, revision, and evaluation in talented 5- to 7-year-olds.

Even if the child's critical faculty is dormant until the age of 8
or so, children can produce various qualities deemed aesthetically satisfying at a much earlier age. The most thorough experimental studies of
this problem were done by Meier and his students, who sought formal
aesthetic qualities in the work of the very young. They found evidence
of rhythm, balance, and harmony in the childs work; yet when themselves asked to identify or classify works on the basis of these qualities,
children were not very successful. Young children did choose to build
the more balanced of two structures and were able to detect the rhythm
of some very simple patterns. The most sensitive 4-year-olds could match
colors in combination as well as adults could, but had no consistent
appreciation of unity in an arrangement. The difficulty with Meier's
research, a most damaging flaw, is that his operationalization of these
aesthetic qualities was sufficiently dubious, his assessment of which
arrangement was most balanced or unified sufficiently debatable (or
provincial) as to suggest that he was probing children's capacities to
determine Meier's standards rather than their sensitivity to canons of
formal elegance. I feel that the best evidence of children's ability to
evince and discern formal and modal properties comes from a study of
their on-going artistic activity and from an examination of their final
products. These have been collected in many places, and some typical
examples can be seen in this book.

PERCEIVING OF PICTORIAL ART

Having reviewed some major studies in the realm of children's making activity, I would like to describe briefly some investigations of children's perceptions in the pictorial arts. Much energy has been devoted to an investigation of children's perceptual preferences; it has been found by Child and his colleagues that children generally do not share the preferences of adult art experts on a large set of pairs of paintings, but that some training in the direction of the adult connoisseur's appears possible. The children tend to prefer simpler and more representational works, where the experts incline toward more complex and formally elegant works. Interestingly, a slight trend toward aesthetically superior taste emerges from looking at a large number of paintings, even in the absence of information about which is supposedly better. These studies show consistency in judgment among various subject populations. They also provide evidence that experts in different cultures agree on what is aesthetically satisfying, a finding any psychologist interested in the arts is challenged to explain, and they raise the possibility that training, and perhaps even mere practice in looking, will naturally result in a convergence of preferences between naive and tutored subjects.

Several other findings in the literature of children's preferences are of interest. Machotka has done a careful study of the reasons children give for their choices. The younger subjects tend to base preferences on colors; subjects in the middle elementary years refer to realism as a major criterion and also mention harmony and clarity. Only at adolescence are style, composition, and perceived affect cited as a basis for aesthetic preferences. Machotka holds that these reasons reflect various Piagetian stages, a hypothesis probably true in a general sense. Other investigators have confirmed the preference of the young child for bright colored pictures of familiar objects, and the preference of older subjects for more allusory, fragmented and diversified subject matter arrays. Younger children are also prone to call attention to the displeasing parts of pictures (those which are more abstract or which contain subject matter that is not liked), and to refer to them as "ugly" or "ikky."

Generally speaking, when less "purely aesthetic" considerations (such as subject matter) are allowed to influence responses, younger children tend to fix upon them as bases for classifying and evaluating works of art. The number and range of criteria competing with the aesthetic is dramatically revealed by the finding that the 3-year-old often chooses the prettiest picture in an array on the basis of position, and the favorite

color as the one at the end of the tray. Children will alter their preferences if an "expert's opinion" is introduced, and will tend to choose
pictures by older children, because they know they are "supposed to
be better." Often the child will choose the painting that on adult standards is at the next highest developmental level; this is an intriguing
confirmation of the hypothesis that development is accelerated by exposure to products that are somewhat but not too far advanced along
the target population. Only at the beginning of adolescence do children
direct their principal attention to the works of their peers.

While neither adults nor children emerge as particularly sophisticated connoisseurs, young children are clearly able to appreciate certain
central facets of paintings. Certainly, by the time they enter school
their visual acuity and ability to differentiate forms approaches that of
adults. In my own studies of sensitivity to painting styles, I have found
that when subject matter is absent or controlled, 6-year-olds are able
to group paintings by the same artist nearly as well as adolescents.
When subject matter functions as a miscue, only adolescents are able
to resist the temptation to group by subject matter. If, however, 6- and
7-year-olds are explicitly trained to overlook dominant figure or subject
matter, they are able for the most part to sort consistently by style.
And interestingly enough, this sorting capacity does not depend on the
achievement of operational thought (as measured by Piaget). Thus,
while Machotka's Piagetian analysis may account for the reasons given
by children (their "critical comments"), it does not explain their perceiving behavior and capacity. These results suggest that, as in the
musical and literary realm, children tend to focus on the dominant
figure or subject matter, but that with some training they can be encouraged to consider those more pervasive textural aspects, which play
a salient role in style detection and aesthetic sensitivity.

A number of other findings also testify to the aesthetic precocity of
young children. Seven-year-olds asked for their preferences among geometrical forms gave the same ones as did adults. A similar convergence
of tastes has been found using other nonrepresentational materials, such
as textiles. There is, finally, a growing body of evidence suggesting that,
with proper training (direct tutelage or sufficient exposure to pictures),
children's discriminatory powers can be significantly enhanced. Such
training will increase the amount of information children include in
their drawings, the way in which they approach artistic works, the
amount of attention paid to sensory and qualitative aspects, and the
ability to perform certain standard perceptual tasks. It appears possible
to improve children's perceiving powers as early as nursery school or
first grade. This is because sensitivity to the fine aspects of visual arts

appears as a dividend from simple exercising of the perceiving system in the symbolic realm, and does not demand more complex interactions among systems.

An important question is whether children are sensitive to the communicative potential of artistic media. In a recent study it has been demonstrated that, by the age of 7 or so, children are able to modify their representations so that these can be interpreted by the artist's peers. When told that others cannot identify what he has drawn, a 5-year-old child will typically claim that the fault lies in the perceiver. At this point he is unaware of his contribution to (and control of) the communicative process. A slightly older child will realize, however, that the effectiveness of the communication depends primarily upon his representational skills, and he will continue to initiate changes until the desired communication has been effected. This study, especially when considered in the company of other findings on the emerging communicating skills of children, lends support to our claim that the young schoolchild has mastered a basic component of the artistic process.

GENERAL REMARKS

Even though they may lack the manual dexterity needed for skilled drawing, children of 5 to 7 possess many of the characteristics of the artist. In their paintings, young children evince considerable mastery of formal aspects and an adequate sense of control; and in perceiving aesthetic objects, children are often able to appreciate formal properties, particularly if the mesmerizing subject matter is omitted. Indeed Lansing asserts that the educated child on entering first grade is able to behave like an artist because he possesses the following skills:

Making his own understandable symbols for his concepts
Communicating his emotional reaction
Producing a configuration related to an area of experience the child intended
Arranging his visual symbols to produce a pleasing structure
Perceiving symbols in which the technique is pleasing
Achieving his results independently
Recognizing and naming formal elements
Recognizing an especially displeasing composition
Responding to meaning and qualities of objects
Responding to formal qualities
Recognizing a variety of styles in art

Talking about the nature of art
Using a basic artistic vocabulary

While the claims of others are not so explicitly spelled out nor so ambitiously formulated, there is an impressive concord on this assessment of child art. Schaefer-Simmern concludes that

> Children's drawings are not yet distorted by external methods of teaching or by imitation of nature, they possess a definite structure and order which in essence is that of more developed works of art. . . . A child's spontaneous drawing possesses instinctively . . . the distinctive form, even though in a modest way. . . . the creation of unity of form is his way of reaching visual cognition.

And in support, Duquet declares that

> A child who does not draw is an anomaly, and particularly so in the years between 6 and 10. . . . It is at the age between 6 and 10 that the child's individual instinctive bent, an integral part of his emotional make-up and one which is to determine all aspects of his future life, practical, emotional, and intellectual, first comes to light and begins to develop toward self-realization.

This testimony again calls to mind that the reason why the average child does not become an artist is as intriguing as the question of how the gifted child goes on to become a mature and skilled practitioner.

Our principal contention—that the young child is able to realize in his objects, discriminations, and feelings the basic components of adult participation in the artistic process—is somewhat stripped of its dramatic quality by the recognition that the average adult's level of aesthetic perception is so dismal. Indeed, citing the evidence accumulated here, one might go so far as to claim that the young child has a more appropriate rhythmic sense, makes more formally elegant pictures, and is nearly as sensitive to aesthetic properties as most adults. These proclivities, due in part to the type of physical and emotional balance which naturally evolves in young children, and to the opportunities for self-expression in our culture, also seem to reflect the striking degree of organization in the human species which guides what is seen, felt, and made into accessible and appropriate channels: "In the young child we find a natural poet, a natural musician, a person who is accustomed to responding to aesthetic values by his very nature . . . one finds the supreme sensibility in the young child . . . the capacity to respond to life has not yet been dulled or tainted by a set of imposed verbal symbols."

Syntax and rhythm in the temporal arts and schematic balance in the visual arts are but the most salient examples of this potent tendency toward formal excellence in the symbolic activities of the child. Elegance, indeed, is particularly characteristic of the child's making behavior, though he need not himself be completely conscious of this feature. The child speaks and sings and occasionally composes in aesthetically pleasing ways; he dances, plays, and cavorts with grace. The choices he makes are often inspired as he places together certain sounds or colors, invents tonal combinations, or creates metaphoric expressions. Yet in the art forms that involve choice from a code, particularly in literature, the child cannot yet be a master, because he does not have sufficient familiarity with the semantic markers of his language, the traditions within art forms, or the experiences about which individuals can speak, to enable him consistently to invent satisfying literature. Sometimes he hits, sometimes he misses, and in neither case is he controlling his material. The same signs of immaturity are evident in music, preventing him from producing work of a consistently high quality. Further, the sustained effort required to execute an integrated work, with its length, complexity, and detail, is beyond most children until the years before adolescence.

In the area of painting, knowledge of the code and the tradition is a necessary acquisition, and yet the child is less restricted in his expression because communication of subjective aspects will result merely from his behavior. The child's style reveals information about himself, and there is accordingly less need for the subject matter to possess the subtlety or intricacy characteristic of the allographic arts. Rather, the child can portray what he sees (a tree) without embellishment, whereas if he simply said "tree" he would not create a literary effect, or if he simply repeated the same pitch thrice he might not achieve a musical effect. Furthermore, the child may draw a green, red, or blue tree, and, provided it is well executed or arranged in an original manner, many observers will regard it as a pleasing object. Still lacking will be sufficient motor skill required for complete control over the medium, but this handicap should not be seen as crucial at that moment in the child's development, particularly in an era where works of primitive artists (from our culture and from others) are esteemed.

As a perceiver, then, it appears that the child may be slightly more precocious in allographic arts, where he can more readily orient toward the purely formal aspects; subject matter is of little note in music and may, for reasons of necessity or choice, be disregarded in literature. However, exclusive interest in subject matter or mere orientation to bright lights or contrast are sufficiently powerful pulls on the young child as to prevent him from being a mature perceiver of the plastic arts. When subject matter is not a factor, however, the child may become sensitive to formal aspects, displaying the same preferences as knowledgeable adults. The dimension of perceiving in which the child is least advanced involves his capacity to appreciate aspects of creating subjects, the artist's knowledge of feelings and objects as embodied in the object. This area, dependent on experience and on an understanding of the aesthetic process, takes time to develop, though an incipient awareness of the relationship between an artist and his product can be discerned in many 7-year-olds.

In the making realm, the child has some formal sophistication in literature during early childhood, and the gifted youth possesses it in music at an equally early age, but it is the direct making behavior of the young painter or potter that is characterized by sophistication in both formal and subject matter aspects. Making in music and language soon become activities conducted wholly on a symbolic plane, but making in the visual arts remains the kind of activity directly involving objects for which the young child is especially suited. The mechanisms whereby the 6-year-old is able to relate colors and tones synesthetically, or create a bit of verse or set up elaborate and pleasing constructions, are not the results of instruction, at least no more so than the mystifying faculties that permit certain youngsters to intuit mathematical principles, chess rules, or optical phenomena at a very early age. Yet, the existence of such abilities can scarcely be denied.

The progress of the child's feeling life with reference to the various symbolic-artistic media is most difficult to chart. That the child is affected by, gains plasure from, and is sensitive to the several art forms seems plausible, but which aspects are the most powerful and which affects are manifest during a given period is presently only a subject for guesswork. The reasons why children continue to participate in the arts and the impressions they form of their own works remain to be spelled out. By the age of 7, to be sure, most children do have a clear delineation between the real and the illusionary; they can appreciate art forms on their own terms and not merely as a substitute for or imitation of "real experience." Children's preferences change frequently at this time, suggesting that their comprehension and discrimination capacities are constantly expanding; yet the perennial popularity of certain art works among individuals of different ages suggests the presence of universal affects or modes, which these works tap or elicit. In sum, then, the child of 7 or 8 may well have achieved formal sophistication in the arts; in the realm of making, he is likely to be somewhat more precocious in painting; in the domain of perceiving his precocity may be more evident in literature and music. But in each case he has attained the level achieved by most adults, and is able to experience a wide range of modes and affects; within a few years, as his training progresses and his familiarity with the code increases, he may be able to attain the level of the accomplished artist or connoisseur (though his development need not cease at this time). In the likelihood of early excellence and the possibility for a lifelong development and deepening, he differs significantly from the scientist.

It is regrettable that the experimental literature does not more strongly test the pattern of artistic development that has been proposed. As should be evident, my claim that the 7-year-old has attained sufficient mastery with symbolic media to be a participant in the artistic process rests on the actual works produced by children and on their reactions to the arts, rather than on a set of clear-cut experimental findings. We began the chapter by discussing why earlier findings were inadequate, and there is little point in repeating the strictures. But I want to suggest that too few of the investigators have entered the area of the arts with clear hypotheses in mind. As a result, they have favored data collection over the testing of competing theories, and their findings can be used to support a variety of theories, or no theory at all. Admittedly, many of the propositions I have introduced here will be difficult to test, particularly since the arts do not lend themselves to investigation through explicit task setting or verbal interrogation. Nonetheless, the securing of reliable data by which such claims can be tested is clearly necessary before the tenability of my theory can be determined.

The task of reviewing scores of studies and fitting them into a rather tight set of claims has its Procrustean facets, and only others can determine the plausibility of my overview. While conceding that the child of 7 can be quite fluent with a symbolic medium, one might still claim that what the accomplished artist does is of a different order. I would agree that the accomplished artist, audience member, performer, and connoisseur is indeed a different creature, but I do not believe that he has necessarily evolved new logical structures or entered into a qualitatively different stage, as would be the case on Piaget's analysis. Rather, artistic development after the age of 7 appears to include an increasingly fine development of various skills and sensitivities, greater familiarity with the tradition and code and more sense of oneself, of others, and of the process of communication, all of which take time to evolve, but all of which may develop within a symbolic medium, according to the processes outlined in earlier chapters. Unlike the shift from sensorimotor behavior to symbol use, no total reorganization is necessary; qualitative differences result from the gradual buildup and interaction of discrimination, feelings, and acts, rather than from a complete reconstruction of a world view. How the child becomes the artist is the subject for the concluding chapters; but let us turn now to a brief consideration of another aspect of development—the significant differences obtaining among individuals.

INDIVIDUAL DIFFERENCES

Individual differences are vast in each art form. They come through most vividly in painting, since the child expresses himself directly through his behavior, but the child also reveals himself in a decisive and characteristic manner through his choices from a literary code. True, he may learn to use the code at a somewhat slower rate than he learns to wield a brush; accordingly, it is more difficult to recognize young children by the stories they invent (limited as these are in their syntactic variability by sheer constraints on rules learned and information processed) than by the paintings they draw.

Among the benign influences on aesthetic capabilities of the young child are a good memory or the possession of eidetic imagery. These capacities open up a greater range of subject matter or allow easier access to past experiences, though they by no means dictate success in execution. Similarly, the possession of an eye or ear that effortlessly picks up details can greatly enliven a literary production. Maladies such as color blindness or early traumata, while scarcely facilitating, do give the child an idiosyncratic set of experiences that may also yield interesting subjects for artistic presentation, unusual feelings for communication, and creative mechanisms for realizing the presentation. The importance of interesting experiences for the developing artist should not be minimized, as the lack of attractive and powerful themes or subject matter can prove a stumbling block for many promising young artists.

Outstanding promise or genius, as well as notable insensitivity, characterizes all areas, including the arts. At an exceptionally early age, some children evince delight at musical sounds, others possess a keen feeling for harmony, color, light and shade, and "there are many children who display almost complete lack, not only of the productive impulse but of the aesthetic sense of the artist." We have reviewed some examples of early precocity in music and have indicated the linguistic "genius" that seems characteristic of all children. All the same, some children are obviously more verbally gifted than others, talking perpetually, experimenting with rhymes, puns, metaphors, and grammatical constructions. Some ability in early painting seems widely disseminated, but a strong sense of form or a heightened gestalt perception probably belongs only to a select few. Picasso could draw before he could speak, and Preyer describes a 3-year-old genius who used all that he saw in his pictorial art:

> I have had information of a child that only in its fourth year, without instruction, could cut animals out of papers with the scissors (giraffes, greyhounds, horses, lions, camels and fishes) in such a fashion and draw them on the slate with a pencil that everybody knew at once what the lines imposed (even the cases where he had sketched a man sitting). . . . This boy of three and a half, however, bites animals out of bread . . . draws them with a stick in the sand, models them in clay, sees animal forms in the clouds and devotes himself with the greatest perseverance for months, without direction, without the least stimulus from parents or brothers or sisters.

Such a child is reminiscent of youthful Picasso, who was tantalized by forms, or of Leonardo who saw suggestive shapes everywhere in his environment and exhorted his students to search for them. Gestalt perception, though present in all higher organisms, has obviously developed at an extremely precipitous rate, and quite likely to an absolutely higher level in such prodigies. Nonetheless, individual differences in genetic endowment are, at most, one contributing factor to the eventual level of artistic accomplishment. While a deficient hereditary history may preclude high achievement, only arduous training and development of skills can convert the potential for excellence into its realization.

As for the aesthetic process, we have proposed that the young child who orients toward certain objects and who undergoes pleasant feeling in contemplating them may be considered as a young *audience member*. Rare is the child who is not delighted and fascinated by pictures, verses, tales, or songs. Certainly his appreciation of works will deepen as he becomes acquainted with the tradition, as he perceives aspects of life and feeling in art works, and as he comprehends their multiple levels and ambiguities, but he may never get any more pleasure than does the toddler listening to Chukovsky's nonsense verses. I have suggested that it is most plausible to think of the child next as a youthful *creator*, since the line between creating and making cannot be sharply drawn, and since the communicative capacity asserts itself so early in life. Certainly, in a sense, the child is a *performer* too, but he is less the performer of another's works (whose notations or notions or messages he would be expected to grasp and communicate) than a copier of others' performances or a transmitter of his own feelings and ideas. This form of performing, I submit, is really a variant of creating without the separate existence of an aesthetic object. Greater sense of self and of other persons seems required in order for the child to earn the title of performer, and a decline in egocentrism such as Piaget finds in the early school years appears a necessary antecedent. Only during those years does the child become aware of his own work and of its relationship to the works of others, so that he is now alert to questions of quality and style.

In general, critical acumen will not fully emerge until adolescence, when the child is able to reason with propositions and to engage in hypothetical thinking. The ability to understand the nature of the aesthetic process, to value objects because of their communicative aspects, to appreciate the subleties of interpersonal behavior is unlikely to develop before that time. The child as an individual inevitably involved in the artistic process becomes a critic or commentator last, only after he has sampled in some guise the roles of creator, audience member, and performer.

A question to be investigated is the extent to which children realize the various roles in the artistic process. While it would be theoretically possible for all children to realize in equal measure every role, the available evidence suggests that different emphases become dominant, particularly after the age of 7. My observations suggest that most children realize aspects of the creating, performing, and audience roles by the years of school; but that within a short time, developmental paths diverge. Some cultivate their making skills within a medium and others highlight their discriminating powers, while the remainder, probably a majority, come to rely increasingly on their feeling system.

While generalizing about the entire process of artistic development is an ambitious and risky undertaking, some of the aspects that have been stressed here are presented in Table 4. This formulation suggests the two broad stages of development: the presymbolic or sensorimotor period, and the period of symbol use. In the sensorimotor period, there are some simple schemes suggestive of early music making, speech, and drawing. These are, however, difficult to separate from the kinds of activities found among other animals. Humans seem to differ, first, in the extent to which these schemes differentiate, and second, in the tendency toward modal-vectoral expression, perception, and feeling.

The second stage of development—that of immersion in a symbolic medium—also involves a number of facets. Initially, the various neutral symbolic elements become linked to content, to referents, and, in the case of music, to the *code* of the culture. Next, these symbolic media become increasingly explored and amplified, as symbol use is differentiated and brought into accord with communal standards. Finally, a sense of competence, balance, and integration comes to characterize the child's interaction with the symbolic medium so that it becomes plausible to think of him as a participant in the artistic process. Skill develop-

TABLE 5   A SCHEMATIZATION OF AESTHETIC DEVELOPMENT

Music	Literature	Painting

I.   Presymbolic period: Sensorimotor Development (ages 0 to 1)

    1. the three developing systems unfold (animal heritage)

    2. differentiation of these basic forms: emergence of modal-vectoral sensitivity; interaction of three systems

II. Period of Symbol Use (ages 2 to 7)

    3. immersion in symbolic media; arbitrary elements become symbols as they are linked to content, cultural norms, and aesthetic codes to form symbol systems

schemes of music learned; tunes related to experienced situations; elementary rhythmic skills	meaning and reference supplied to patterned forms	initial representation

    4. exploration and amplification of the symbol; increasing relation to code

flexibility in singing; mastery of familiar motifs; experimentation with instruments	stage of literary genius; storytelling; word play; syntax mastered	exploration of different formal and representational schemes

    5. sense of aesthetic form a product of development and familiarity with culture's code

sense of balance among youthful composers and performers—conservation of musical properties	aspects of literary epigenesis coalesce; assimilation of basic poetic forms	competent drawings; sensitivity to formal properties

developed feeling life; spontaneity; incipient command of the medium; experiencing the works of others

III. Later Artistic Development (age 8 on)

    6. skill development, code undergoes familiarization and manipulation; cognitive sophistication, greater experience, critical acumen, self-consciousness, possibility of regression, loss of interest, loss of ability to create, perceive, and feel; final fruition of gifted participants in the artistic process and competent symbol use among normal individuals

ment, familiarity with the code, accretion of experience, and greater sophistication may all follow (as may a less desirable atrophying of aesthetic sensitivity), but as Tolstoy saw, the child of age 7 has taken the decisive step toward aesthetic maturity.

By the conclusion of the second stage of development, the child has become a participant in the artistic process in two senses. He has exhibited sensitivity to the formal aspects of the arts, both in his own aesthetic productions and in his ability to perceive aspects of the works of others. Then, too, he has realized the essential components of three roles in the artistic circle. By experiencing pleasurable sensations and changes of affect in the presence of symbolic objects, by appreciating the difference between artistic illusions and real experiences, and by achieving some understanding of the symbol system, he has attained the status of audience member. Through gaining familiarity with the possibilities of a symbolic medium, and exhibiting the capacity to communicate his own ideas and feelings in a symbolic object, he has realized the basic components of the artist's role. And by appreciating the independent status of works of art by another, while achieving the capacity to communicate aspects of another's work to an audience, he has fulfilled the requirements for performing. Only in the capacity to capture his impressions of artistic works in words, and in the ability to integrate these verbal propositions into a systematic presentation, does he still require a further stage of development.

In attributing to the young child the essential attributes of the artist, performer and audience member, I make no claims as to the overall excellence of his artistic products, perceptions, or feelings. The question of quality in the art of the young is not the most important one, since it is the process or practice of art that plays the significant role in the child's life. Indeed, it may even be injurious to introduce critical suggestions or judgments at too early a point in the child's artistic evolution. With increasing critical acumen, however, and with instruction "in the tradition," the child's ability to realize particular qualities in his work and the overall level of quality in his work becomes of greater importance to himself and his community.

In the last analysis, the quality of the experiences and the feelings the artist communicates *are* of crucial importance in any art object. It does not suffice to be technically competent: The artist must also have something significant to communicate. The knowledge of feelings and their forms which he is to communicate must be knowledge worth embodying. In this area, more than in most others, a deep, meaningful, affect-rich life seems to be a prerequisite for the formation of the significant artist. The young child certainly has insight into some aspects of life and will partake of such universal percepts as may exist. His art may be formally pleasing and charming. But in essence his work is enjoyable and diverting rather than profoundly disturbing, tragic, magnificent, or sublime. A whole developed life lies behind a masterpiece, be it *Don Giovanni, Faust,* or *Guernica.* How a child becomes capable of leading such a life and of penning such a work is our preoccupation for the remainder of this book.

I am fainty
I am fizzy
I am floppy.

A 6-YEAR-OLD BOY

In the market on monday morning
It is busy as busy can be. With laughing
And shouting and screaming from end to
End. With clanging and banging and
Wanging. On pottery stores. Up and down
Round about. Up to the full and dirt streets.
The dustmans van came lumbering down
Bumpety, Bumpety Bump the cars came rackiling
Down the street chacl chacl chacl I
Never got use to the market on monday
mandy morning.

A 6-YEAR-OLD GIRL

Snowdrops are like little, little lights in a town at night time, only
they would be in a very, very little town. Snowdrops are umbrellas
for flies. They could be dresses for spiders and things like that.

A 7-YEAR-OLD GIRL

CAVE MEN

Once upon a time there was two cave men with brims on their
hats, and they went to a little stream to get fish, and one day a
typhoon came and the two cave men had to take everything into
the cave so it would not get blown away, and they had to live in the
cave for ninety-nine years. And when they came out it was sun-
shining and they went to the stream to get a drink and some fish,
and they caught twenty apiece, and they had forty altogether. And
in the light time they would have a swim, and then they would fish
for tea, and then they would lie down and go to sleep and dream,
and their dreams came true.

A 7-YEAR-OLD BOY

TREES

The grass is a rug for the trees to dance upon;
The branches of the trees are arms
Gracefully pointing to the blue-pillowed sky,
Waiting for a partner.

A 7-YEAR-OLD GIRL

FIGURE 13. "Bill's Green Bird," by a 5-year-old boy.

FIGURE 14. "Funeral March for Violincello and Piano," by a 7-year-old prodigy.

FIGURE 14. (*Continued*)

FIGURE 15. "Indians," by a 7-year-old girl.

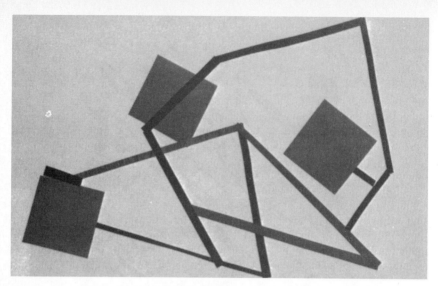

FIGURE 16. Construction by a 7-year-old boy.

FIGURE 17. Drawing by a child in the primary grades.

FIGURE 18. "The Pirate," by a child in the primary grades. (From Irving Kaufman, *Art and Education in Contemporary Culture,* New York: Macmillan, 1966, p. 185.)

SIX

ACHIEVING MASTERY

SARTRE'S CHILDHOOD

Jean-Paul Sartre's recollections about his early childhood, gathered in *The Words,* include experiences common to many creative individuals in the arts. Descended from a cultivated, well-to-do family, which included Albert Schweitzer in its ranks, Sartre was born of a short-lived union between a naive, forlorn girl and an errant naval officer who was soon to die. Most important in Sartre's early life was his patrician grandfather, a writer and scholar of some repute, who, while personally unappealing, was nonetheless a formative influence. Grandfather Schweitzer introduced Sartre to the world of books, displayed him before company, and provided an atmosphere of strong demands, rewards contingent upon good performances, and that model of diligence that has characterized productive creative artists in recent Western history.

The lack of a father is a common feature for artists, who not infrequently have lost one or even both parents at an early age. Sartre grew up in a household that had many visitors, including widely diverse relatives and associates, rather than in a restricted nuclear family that might have sheltered him from the world. At a very young age, Sartre was already entertaining the visitors. While his grandfather pointed out the child's brilliance (thereby appearing as a worthy progenitor), the future author held these audiences spellbound.

I'm a promising poodle: I prophecy, I make childish remarks; they are remembered, they are repeated to me. I learn to make others. I make grown-up remarks. I know how to say things "beyond my years" without meaning to.

242

These remarks are poems. The recipe is simple. You borrow whole sentences from grown-ups. You string them together and repeat them without understanding them. In short I pronounce true oracles and each adult interprets them as he wishes . . . my words and gestures happen to have a quality that escapes me and that is immediately apparent to grown-ups.

Sartre made himself into a spectacle. "I keep creating myself, only one mandate: to please: everything for show." But though he entertained others, he did not appreciate or comprehend the performance; he merely provided that set of behaviors, those making activities, that would secure him rewards.

As a youngster Sartre was surrounded by books. He was attracted to them and listened attentively as they were read, but only slowly began to unravel their meanings. He eventually taught himself to read, having feigned the capacity for some time. Learning to read was a great joy; the boy read what he could get his hands on, found himself whirling in words, and made books his religion. He felt that by giving things names he was gaining power over them. This naming activity gave him his first sensations of dominance, other than those achieved while entertaining others. He was relating to (and receiving from) objects, just as he had previously related to people.

Sartre's world of imagination became populated by all the famous writers, read and unread, collected in his grandfather's study. Much taken with this world, he began to write. He would never have written, he recalls, without the fundamental illusion that naming was creating. Sartre remembers that even in solitude he was putting on an act. He would sit before a desk reading or writing feverishly, and later report to his family what he had accomplished—the simulation of the behavior of the artist continued to be important. He gained pleasure reading classics but reveled in romantic and heroic junk. Like many future writers, Sartre was considered sickly and treated like a delicate child. Until the age of 10, he was jealously guarded by an old man and two women. Only at a fairly late age did the literary prodigy enter school, where he immediately got into trouble because of a lack of basic skills— he was a poor speller.

With no father and a very weak mother, Sartre had an overwhelming feeling that he was superfluous. He feared death tremendously, up to the point of neurosis. The young writer came to sense the loss of an audience that had formerly adulated him. He overplayed, sounded false, knew the "anguish of the aging actress." Sartre realized that he could no longer play the know-it-all, as people were increasingly detecting his lack of sincerity. That others had unmasked him became apparent when a woman who had formerly admired all that he had said rebuked him for his insincerity. "I had given the wrong role. My mistake was glaring. She had asked for the child prodigy, I had given the sublime child. . . . Since nobody laid claim to me seriously I laid claim to being indispensable to the Universe. What could be haughtier? I had been born in order to fill the great need I had of myself." No longer able to impress the circle of his family, Sartre became convinced that his own circle must be the wider audience of the world.

Sartre's mind was the arena for all his activities. An "imaginary" child, he defended himself in his imagination. His first stories were simply repetition of others. He wrote out what he had read. Later he touched up these relics and injected himself into them. Sartre became a hero in his child works, rescuing maidens and slaying enemies. Seeing many movies exacerbated his melodramatic tendencies. He became possessed by the idea of a mission, preoccupied with the notion that certain individuals were great. He led a double life; publicly he was an imposter and a famous grandson, privately he was an imaginary moper who did good works.

Although Sartre belittles his family, he was clearly enriched by the cosmopolitan atmosphere of his grandfather's home. Ideas, words, and thoughts were prized there; music, art, and talk of them was prominent. Sartre's grandfather, who wanted the boy to become a scholar, not a writer, blanketed him with opportunities, engaged him in intellectual games, and exchanged versified letters with him. Sartre feels, however, that this education was at a cost—while all children had individual genius, he had none. He wrote in imitation for the sake of ceremony, so that he might be like a grown-up.

Sartre centered his dreams in the scratchings of his steel nib. He mostly rewrote stories, but saw himself as an original, because he touched things up. Continuing to play the role of the writer, he would pause in feigned thought, then write furiously. Eventually, as his family rejected the puerile output, Sartre's writing became a secret enterprise, carried on for his own pleasure. His stories suffered a temporary decline, since he was no longer copying what he had read; but with the need to devise connections, his stories became more original. Sartre did not see himself as inventing the horrors in his books. Rather, they came to him, like dizzying invisible beings. He found them in his memory, and in order to see them, to freeze them, he had to describe them. His writing now served as a means of capturing the fantastic sights he saw in his imagination.

I was not yet working but I had already stopped playing. The liar was finding his truth in the elaboration of his lies. I was born of writing. Before that there was only a play of mirrors. With my first novel I knew that a child had got into the hall of mirrors. In writing I was existing. . . . I existed only to write. . . . In any case I knew joy.

For the first time Sartre had the feeling he was engaging in a legitimate activity, no longer posing, no longer copying: He was realizing his original thoughts in words. Now that Sartre had taught himself to see, observe, and describe, he stopped writing for a time. He went to school and came to identify fully with the schoolwork. But the lapse, which for many creative children signals the end of the artistic productivity, was temporary. Sartre had come too far to stop writing. He made the writer himself a hero, conferring upon him sacred powers. Sartre saw himself as the author for whom the human race was expectantly waiting, and he promised to meet their demands and rescue them by writing. (For all his identifications with the literary craft, it still had not occurred to Sartre that one might write in order to be read; his notions of interpersonal communication were immature.) At the age of 9, Sartre resumed writing. His pen raced as he wrote in order to write, not to be read. Being clandestine, he was finally being true. He dreamt of his output by 1955, at which time he would be 50 years old: 25 volumes, 18,000 pages of texts, 300 engravings, including a portrait of the author. He found a book about young prodigies with which he identified totally. Thereafter everything in his life became premonitory. Sartre's vocation had been imposed on him.

Now that he knew his fate, Sartre could afford to take chances. At the age of 10 he stopped writing again, this time for 2 years, and according to his recollection, he became totally average. School left no time for writing. Yet Sartre no longer feared the unforeseen, so convinced was he of the happy ending. Of course he began to write again, and of course he became the great writer. Today he indicates that he still finds in the man of middle age many of the traits of the child, even though most of the time they remain dormant. He writes because he has nothing else to do. He lives from day to day, always believing that the one on which he is working will be his best book.

A famous man, a gifted writer, one of the founders of an influential circle of philosophy, Sartre is keenly aware of the great tradition of French self-characterization that preceded him, from Rousseau and Montaigne, to de Beauvoir and Lévi-Strauss. One may assume that, despite (or perhaps because of) his attempts to be frank, there is much license, contrivance, or misremembrance in his work. Symbols have a way of reworking early experience, giving it undue coherence and cogency. Yet one is well advised, I feel, to consider such works seriously, for even if they do not chronicle accurately the events of a single writer's life, they may well help sketch the lines of the artist personality. Even if the facts do not exactly jibe, the broad themes are compelling and have a conviction about them. Indeed, the richness of Sartre's account may well convey more of the essential nature of artistic development than do the scores of studies reported in the previous chapter.

THE ARTIST'S BACKGROUND

Sartre's self-portrait also supplements the picture of the young artist presented in the last chapter, since it emphasizes the self-consciousness and doubts of the young child as he contemplates the nature of his activities and his gift. The complementary roles of developing skills and basic personality constellation are also dramatized. While a picture of the young artist's perceptions, affects, and intersubjective relations cannot be built from one such example, Sartre's account has impressive confluence with a number of archetypical sketches of the artist, drawn up by the clinically interested over the years.

Consider the psychoanalyst Rank's portrait of the artist. Rank feels that, whatever his medium, the modern artist has a special blend of personality, stemming from a heightened consciousness of self and a sense of mission with regard to the world. The artist first molds himself into an individual, a powerful and self-confident personality, who wants to convey his experience and his person to others. In Sartre's case, he anoints himself a writer. Only after he establishes a sense of self can the artist successfully put to use the technical skills he has or will develop. Rank's argument is supported by Sartre's account as well as by other autobiographical works; the young author's growing sense of becoming a writer, of having a mission could be a case study from the pages of Rank. Perhaps, indeed, these accounts supply a partial answer to the question raised in the closing lines of the preceding chapter. The artist in possession of a message of striking quality and interest is an individual who has undergone distinctive experiences and has constructed a persona that can initially attract the interest of an audience and will subsequently evoke deeply felt responses in them.

Certain characteristics of Sartre's background are particularly representative of the artist. Pivotal is his heterogenous background. Young Sartre was steeped in the cultures of two powerful traditions—Gallic and Teutonic—and was suspended between several special groups: the *haute bourgeoisie*, the professionals, representatives of the world of the arts, and his two hapless parents. Sartre's marginality is characteristic of the multitude of ties many artists have experienced. Dickens, for example, was caught between the comforts of his early life, the extreme

poverty of the years his father spent in debtor's prison, and the possibilities for high social prestige that followed his publishing triumphs. Other
kinds of marginality have also provided backgrounds for later artistic
careers—a number of writers from a fairly modest social class were
treated as members of the upper class because they were raised away
from home in a land having colonial or "inferior" status.

Unusual religious backgrounds have contributed to a feeling of
uniqueness on the part of many artists. While strong religious strains did
not characterize the Sartre household, the combination of Protestant
and Catholic influences in his milieu certainly had some impact on the
young author. Concern with religious matters can be found in the
backgrounds of many artists, be they composers (Stravinsky), painters
(Van Gogh), or writers (Mary McCarthy, Simone de Beauvoir).
Others who did not themselves experience a strong religious up-bring-
ing have turned later to religion (T. S. Eliot, Robert Lowell, W. H.
Auden). Sartre's ardent devotion to various political causes and his
proselytizing on their behalf seem akin to a religious attachment. The
belief that matters of the spirit are of great weight—a feeling religious
or ideological background may promote—seems conducive to the development of aesthetic sensitivity and productivity.

Spending one's early childhood in a home where assorted personalities appeared and were housed has been important in opening the
minds and imaginations of future artists. Thomas Wolfe was deeply
impressed by the diverse motley boarders—salesmen, wanderers, harlots
—who lived in his home when he was young. His exposure to many
different kinds of persons was crucial in his literary development: "a
novelist may turn over half the people in a town to make a single
figure in his novel." As his spokesman Eugene Gant put it, "I am part of
all that I have touched and that has touched me." One of Proust's novels
opens with a lengthy description of the deep impression made on the
youthful hero by dinner guests at his home. Dickens, Balzac, Zola, and
other chroniclers of the life of the nineteenth century encountered an
assortment of characters as they wandered the streets of European
capitals, just as those who went on long sea voyages, such as Melville,
Conrad, and Twain, were impressed by the sundry personalities they
encountered.

While travel at an age when the personality has already coalesced
encourages disciplined observations and formulations, contact with
varied individuals during early years probably has deeper effects on the
child involved. Individuals who grew up in homes filled with intriguing
figures may well have developed multiple identifications when they were
young. Rather than having a strong bond merely with parents or with a

single individual, many future artists were strongly impressed by a number of individuals or visitors. They seized upon aspects of these fascinating personages, introjecting their traits into their own developing personality. One can imagine a sensitive young child like Keats or Shelley perceiving and then duplicating the activities of a variety of individuals, practicing them, contrasting them, and attempting to recapture them in their youthful works. Nor need the individuals with whom the child identifies be living persons. Sartre and Emily Brontë built up their world in the imagination, incorporating the impressive fictional heroes they read about, and the famous writers whom they would seek to rival or emulate. Experimental evidence affirms this connection between multiple identification and creativity. Multiple identifications lead to greater creativity scores among certain kindergarteners, children with imaginative companions tend to become adolescents who are creative in literary tasks, and creative architects have had a "plentiful supply of diverse and effective models."

A particular sort of malady or a pivotal event in childhood seems to have been formative for a number of artists. Some artists have been orphaned at an early age (the Keats brothers) or have been raised by a cruel stepparent (the Brontës). Others have been sickly, like Stravinsky, or were so regarded, like Sartre. Being singled out in this manner may have convinced the children that they were very different or special, or were soon to die. Fear of imminent death may have impelled some artists to greater achievement, including such writers as Percy Bysshe Shelley and Stephen Crane, who died in their twenties. A traumatic event or series of events in the young artist's life could have powerful effects—consider the writer whose youth was spent in war or in a concentration camp. Similarly, the possession of a remarkable gift could, when discovered, have decisive influence upon the child. Perhaps supporting this speculation, art products of interest and complexity seem more likely to emerge in primitive societies where socialization procedures are particularly severe than in those with mild regimens.

The setting of the early years can also have a decisive effect. Stravinsky indicates that his earliest memories were of sounds sung by local peasants. Persons around him were impressed with the precision of his ear, even before he had begun music lessons. Joyce, Shaw, and other Irish writers grew up in homes (and taverns) where language was used abundantly, wildly, and poetically; they were enchanted by words from an early age. Music played a major part in the households of many musicians, painting prodigies like Picasso lived in the houses of artists, and an impressively high number of artists grew up in craftsmen's homes. It is my impression, nonetheless, that the strong sense of form characteristic of painters is less often a family trait than the musical or verbal skills of future artists. While musicians and writers most frequently come from households rich in song and words, painters have often been discovered in less likely locales. Perhaps the fact that painting begins with gross motor activity (rather than with imitation of symbol use by others) is significant here. Of course we may simply not know where to look for the sources that stimulate excellence in the plastic arts.

In the past, when little biographical information about artists was available, writers would simply invent a background for their subject. Kris has presented a portrait of the typical painter as seen in those ancient hagiographies.

The youth of the artist is viewed as a period that prefigured his adult career. His paintings demonstrate his special talent, whereupon the youth is suddenly and mysteriously discovered. In the classic example, Giotto, the son of a farmer, is said to have watched the flock of his father and to have drawn pictures of the animals in the sand. One day the great Cimabue came by, recognized immediately the boy's magnificent talent, and took the lad with him. Under the master's guidance, Giotto came to be the next genius of Italian art. Prototypical sketches of this type have often been adopted by biographers lacking data. Although it would be foolish to treat such tales as a standard, the fact that they have been adopted by many writers and have survived for thousands of years does suggest their usefulness as a speculative model. Like Sartre's biography, their details and emphases can prove suggestive about the development of the artist. Since nearly all the evidence we have about the development of particular artists is fragmentary and anecdotal, it would be appropriate to regard the testimony summarized here as tentative hypotheses, which need to be carefully scrutinized and tested.

A brief consideration of other, commonly held views may help to flesh out the composite picture of the artist I have been proposing. One image of the artist, dating back to Plato, represents his mission as the surpassing of reality—combining the features of all beautiful women, for example. Chateaubriand recalled that in his adolescence, he would hypothetically combine the most attractive attributes of all the women he had known. An analogous strain is the belief in the artist's magical powers; as creation is universally considered the prerogative of the divine, those who steal the fire of the gods become targets of ambivalence. They have, like Faust, entered into pacts with supernatural forces. They may be permitted to perpetrate eccentric acts and to indulge in sexual license; they may be allotted tremendous stamina, but they may also suffer serious wounds or an early death because of the power contained within their bows. Even when such themes are not apparent in the circumstances of an artist's life, they often become major concerns in his thoughts or in his work. Sartre is neither supernatural nor in league with the devil, yet he believes in his own magic or gift. Thomas Mann was relatively staid in his personal relations, yet dwelled on the mystical aspects of the artists' life in his various writings.

Reflecting the Kris tradition, other psychoanalysts speak of the artist's need to come to grips with his own unique and mysterious abilities, and his keen sensitivity to conflicts and events. The division of self into a personal (normal, real) and a creative aspect (mystical and perhaps demoniacal) is a common defense on the part of the artist, who strives to reconcile his unusual gifts with his humanness. Often the artist believes in a golden childhood in which adults were Olympians and the child could partake of their special privileges and unconditional love without special demands. But later on artists come to feel they are imposters, that their creative self is a separate entity over which they have no conscious control. This constellation of feelings and perceptions does much to lend a distinctive personality to individuals involved in artistic careers.

So far I have suggested that the absence of a relationship between an artist and his parents may contribute to his feeling of insecurity, his greater willingness to assume all for the sake of career, and such individual reactions as loneliness, estrangement, sexual deviance, or identification with one's fellow man. Not a few artists, however, have had extremely powerful or torturous relations with their parents. Sometimes this relationship has been productive, most notably for certain young prodigies such as Mozart, Picasso, and Goethe. Even here, however, the relation is often marked by ambivalence. As Greenacre indicates, the artist's assumption of a position of importance depends on his seizing the identity of his talented father, who is symbolically killed. Sometimes the father is himself an individual with some accomplishment in the field —Leopold Mozart, Blasco Picasso y Ruiz—but one who took longer to master the medium, excelling only at a late age; these stern taskmasters may feel personal frustration at their own failure, while having a keen understanding of how one learns and what mistakes must be avoided, contacts made, and skills developed. They make ideal initial models for extraordinarily talented youngsters. Reflecting the forces operating in such relationships, Picasso's father symbolically handed over his brush to Pablo at age 14, and never painted again.

More frequently, the child enters into heated conflict with the parent, usually the father. For Proust and Kafka the relationship with their fathers was crucial. As children, these writers experienced little identification with their powerful fathers, who left home early each day and rarely played with them. Their mothers, on the other hand, were kindly individuals who carefully tended their offsprings and indulged their fantasies. The oedipal conflict was pronounced, the psychological costs severe. In Kafka's case, his father continued to dominate his mind. The much tormented youth wrote a 50-page letter, seeking to determine why the father had rejected him and had made him feel guilty, and lamenting the fact that the father was strong and successful while the son was fearful and withdrawn. Because writing served therapeutic purposes, becoming a famous author was less of an obsession with Kafka than it has been with many other artists. Proust was attached to his mother and distraught by his inability to relate to his father, but, taking the opposite path from Kafka, he self-consciously converted his personality into that of the writer or artist, embraced homosexual relations, and sought to become the great novelist. All the same his alienation from others, particularly during his most productive years, was extreme.

Unusual family relations also characterized the Brontës, particularly the lonely and hapless Emily. Children of an eccentric father who was to die young, the Brontës were raised alone. They lived together in a room, and had to be quiet and mannerly. "Here they read, told each other stories in a low tone, and, as soon as they were able to write, began to compose little magazines and books on their own." This peculiar isolation, with intensification of family relations and preservation of the emotions of infancy, may explain much that is extraordinary in the character and the genius of the sisters. By the age of 13, Charlotte had written 22 volumes on her own. Emily, whose mother died when the girl was only 3 and whose father was harsh and unsympathetic, retreated into a world of her own, writing many secret poems as well as an incomparable novel. She sought sustenance from material objects, rather than from people, and formed especially close ties with the region of Yorkshire, where she grew up. Like certain other writers, she lived out her secret life on paper, creating one of the great love stories in English literature out of the life of her fantasy. The Brontës had a strangely impoverished yet productive childhood, where a group of siblings raised each other; drawing on technical skill and prodigious imagination, these deprived artists were able to develop distinctive personalities and produce evocative works.

In considering retrospectively those who became illustrious artists, it is perhaps too tempting to find maladies or special circumstances that contributed to their success. After all, one may ask, whose life has been wholly free of untoward circumstance or fate? Misfortune or special circumstances are scarcely sufficient causes for greatness. Most often, probably, they produce only sadness and failure. However it does seem that *some sort of unusual circumstances in early life,* particularly ones that heighten the individual's definition of himself either by confirming him in his loneliness or by exposing him to significant individuals, may constitute an important formative influence, especially for the future writer. If such atypical circumstances are not sufficient to produce the talented artist, they may be necessary, or at least of considerable help, in suggesting to him themes on which his developing skills can be exercised. A feeling of uniqueness pervades such "special" individuals, who often stand apart from others, working and playing by themselves. The specific nature of these unusual circumstances does not appear critical. Shaw lived midst chaos; the Mozarts were well traveled and thoroughly engrossed in music; Sartre's family represented several cultures and was heavily involved in the arts and in scholarship; Thomas Mann sought constantly to reconcile the artistic and the political-bourgeois tendencies of the family; Goethe was blessed with many talents; Van Gogh or Beethoven had to nurse the one they had. In each of these cases, the combination of talent and an unusually rich or striking personal situation combined to produce individuals of skill and originality.

Regardless of whether the unusual family circumstance precedes and facilitates the gifted child, or, conversely, he finds or "makes" his problem, the great artist must acquire a tremendous range of knowledge about life and experience in feeling if his works are to have significance. Perhaps the young artist is particularly sensitive from the first. "Some persons see much more than others of the natural shapes and colors about them. The artist's world is filled with shapes and colors that go unnoticed by the less perceptive." A natural sensitivity, discernible in the earliest days of life, an ear for sound, an eye for form, would certainly constitute a tremendous asset for the future artist. The novelist Hudson conveys the rich feeling and perceiving life of one young artist.

I rejoiced in color, scents, in taste and touch: the blue of the sky, the verdure of the earth, the sparkle of light on water, the taste of milk or fruit, of honey, the smell of dry or moist soil, of wind and rain, of herbs and flowers: the mere feel of a blade of grass made me happy: and there were certain sounds and perfumes, and above all, certain colors in flowers, and in the plumage and eggs of birds which intoxicated me with delight.

No matter how exquisite the child's sensitivity, however, he cannot communicate to others unless it is cultivated; if blocked or mischanneled by incompetent or well-intentioned parents, the child will never become an artist. Raw gifts alone will not suffice.

In considering the ways in which the sensitive young child may become an artist, a number of developmental possibilities stand out. Most stunning are those children who seem gifted in a multitude of arts and disciplines from the first. Goethe is the classic example, staging plays and writing poems at 5, while relentlessly pursuing other arts and sciences. He was receptive to everything beautiful and epitomized Freud's view of the firstborn: "a man who has been the indisputable favorite of the mother keeps for life the feeling of a conqueror, that confidence of success that often induces real success." Goethe's mother was a cheerful woman, his father a political activist, artist, and generally harmonious person. Their son may be considered a model of the individual precocious in a variety of domains, who may indeed be oppressed by his multitude of talents but who, if successful, is remembered as much for his unique character as for his undeniable artistic and scientific achievements. Other individuals who shared his competence in a variety of fields, fabled universal geniuses, include William Blake, Leonardo da Vinci, and Michelangelo, versatile individuals who confronted tormenting decisions about which medium to focus on. Richard Wagner, for example, was talented in painting and poetry, as well as in music.

Sharing some features with the universal genius is the individual who is prodigious during his youth, but whose efforts are concentrated in one domain. Many young musicians blessed with a golden ear know they will devote their lives to music. They then must decide whether to concentrate on performance, composition, or conducting (though a few, like Leonard Bernstein, Igor Stravinsky, and Gustav Mahler, have achieved success in more than one of these pursuits). On occasion, an artist's gifts in one domain have been so prodigious as to dampen the ultimate brilliance of accomplishment. Consider this assessment of Camille Saint-Saens:

> He was the most remarkable child prodigy in history and that includes Mozart. . . . At the age of 2½ [he] was picking out tunes at the piano. Naturally he had absolute pitch, he could read before he was three. At a little over three, he wrote his first piece. . . . At age five he was deep in analysis of "Don Giovanni," using not the piano reduction but the full score. At this age he also gave piano recitals. At seven he was reading Latin and interesting himself in science. . . . At ten he had made his official debut. As an encore, at his debut, he offered to play any of Beethoven's 32 sonatas from memory. He had total recall and if he read a book or heard a piece of music, he never forgot it.

Apparently, Saint-Saens was too gifted. "He had the kind of mind that absorbs music like blotting paper and everything came too easily for him. He was a wonderful workman and always avoided bad taste. But he may have lacked the difficulties and the sense of tragedy necessary for greatness." Perhaps this is why Berlioz quipped, "he knows everything, but he lacks inexperience." That an individual's superabundance of talent or precocity may preclude greatness is dubious, but it may render the greatest accomplishments somewhat more elusive. At any rate, some of the most remarkable prodigies have grown up to be mediocre practitioners. Perhaps their making system, having unfolded with such rapidity, began to turn on itself, thereby failing to achieve the necessary degree of integration with the other developing systems.

Among those who possessed early talents in one area, John Keats could read and analyze poetry effectively while still a youth, and greeted his interlocutors with laughter and rhymes. Picasso certainly qualifies as one who from the first had the agility, grace, and sense of form characteristic of great painters; he could draw before he could speak. Norman Podhoretz describes the phenomena of a possession of early talent in a medium:

> The desire to write, if real, arises in the first place from the ability to write. A child, for example, may show himself to be unusually articulate on paper, and will then be encouraged by teachers or parents to exercise this power. I choose the word "exercise" deliberately, for articulateness on paper is a gift which does not differ greatly in principle from the gift of physical coordination we call athletic skill: like a muscle it needs to be exercised not only for it to develop, but because it exerts a pressure of its own on the possessor to use it.

Podhoretz suggests that the urge to write is there long before there is anything to write about and will persist even in the absence of anything substantive to say. Here the making apparatus is primed to go off, in the absence of sufficient motivation, energy, or appropriate subject matter. The desire to continue to explore the symbolic medium, to construct more elaborate schemes, to flex one's artistic muscles is inexorable. For young persons in this position, possessing skills but lacking themes, the imitation and elaboration of others' works may prove useful during an interim period.

A third artistic prototype, the most romantic if not the most frequent, is the individual suffering from a warp, wound, or malady, either imagined or genuine, which causes him painful early years but may supply motivation and materials for later creative products. A pattern frequently reported is the memory of happy earliest years, a Nirvana where all wishes were granted, followed by years or even an entire life of great misfortune and poverty, during which the artist sees himself as mistreated, rejected, or abandoned. A rich fantasy life often develops from this feeling of rejection, serving to some extent as a compensation; eventually the fantasies may become embodied in the artist's works.

Numerous writers have described such a wretched period. Kipling's childhood was marked by bad eyes, a nervous breakdown, and severe maltreatment in school; he felt strongly that his parents had deserted him. Henry James, in the shadow of an older, more precocious, better-adjusted brother, spent a withdrawn childhood, and nursed a life-long wound, possibly sexual in nature. Strindberg could get along with neither parent. He was, however, close to his mother and was never able to break off completely. Having deep guilt feelings and bisexual tendencies, he sought refuge in a world of his own creation. Embittered about his family, he came to suffer from extreme paranoia.

The belief in a childhood of rejection is not restricted to creators, and may indeed find its fullest realization in creative performers. Charlie Chaplin tells of a golden period when all things were possible, but then records a childhood of increasing hardship, frustration, and sadness. Both his parents were alcoholics; his father died when he was young, his mother was placed in a mental institution. Another childhood marked by considerable unhappiness befell John Lennon, formerly of the Beatles. His father deserted his mother shortly before birth. The mother in turn soon left John in the care of an aunt, returning only when John was about 13. This depressing and debilitating childhood created a potent need for play, where no event is truly consequential: "I used to live *Azalee* and *Just William*. I wrote my own *Just William* stories with me doing all the things. . . . After I'd read a book, I'd relive it all again. . . . I wanted to be a gang leader in school. . . . I'd want them all to play the games I wanted them to play . . . childhood was all imagining that I was *Just William*." Like Chaplin, Lennon was on the verge of a life of depression, flippancy, and sterility when he met a congenial group of performers, and was able to achieve close relationships with them and to capture some of his feelings in the songs he wrote and the parts he acted. Other contemporary artists have described similar patterns, and have indicated how a theatrical life was therapeutic.

One writer with a markedly aberrant childhood was Lewis Carroll. Born Charles Dodgson, Carroll was a quiet, withdrawn child who invented games, plays, stories, and magic to amuse himself and his brothers and sisters. His father was a domineering individual, who wanted his son to join the ministry. In a series of pointed acts, Carroll rejected not only his father's aim but also his name. Leading a double life as writer and don, Carroll sought to recapture a primitive infant state where adults were barred and the sordid conditions of life eliminated. His extreme ambivalence and antagonism toward the worlds of males and adults, and of rationality, came through in his writing and his letters, where reversal and identification with the young, the feminine, and the absurd predominated.

ARTISTIC TRAINING DURING MIDDLE CHILDHOOD AND ADOLESCENCE

Although the circumstances surrounding the lives of young artists vary markedly, depending on the child's talent and the conditions of his home life, there may nonetheless be a progression through which any future artist will pass on his way to accomplished mastery. At the ages of 5 to 7, universal artistic tendencies may be discerned. Similar drawing schemes, story types, and musical patterns may well emerge in diverse cultures and social groups. Future artists are likely to experience these stages in a fuller, more abundant way than other children. They will perhaps be blessed with especially sharp ears, rich vocabularies, diverse verbal skills, and with a heightened sense of form or motor abilities. And they are likely to be particularly sensitive to their own experiences, either because of inherited disposition and unusual training, or because of special circumstances in their home, family, or own person. Even more so than those of other playful youngsters, their minds are bursting with sights, concepts, images, and notes. Luxuriant making activity, discriminations, subtlety and fullness of affective type can be expected. At the ages of 4 to 7 nearly every child with a supporting environment is overwhelmed by his own creativity and is full of inventiveness. For all youngsters, these are the free years.

In the latency period, ages 7 to 11, artistic productivity typically continues for a time, even among children who are not particularly gifted. Many an 8-year-old still draws, hums, composes, or rhymes spontaneously without appreciable self-consciousness. The future creative child may be characterized at this time by greater sensitivity to sensory stimulation and to the works of others; unusual capacity for awareness of the relationship between stimuli; heightened fluency of ideas; predisposition to an empathy of wide range; and keen and agile sensorimotor equipment. The identification of such tendencies is a vital task, for it is desirable to identify creative youngsters and to encourage them in their pursuits; otherwise, by the age of 9 or 10, creativity among the nontalented and among some talented youngsters may already have started to wane. At this point, many youngsters will curtail their making activity in favor of the roles of critic or audience member.

Each art form has its own perils during this period. In music the demands for technical skill are sufficiently stringent as to discourage many. As verbal skills unfold, children find less need to rely on graphic arts to express their feelings. They can express themselves directly, in words, rather than through nonverbal symbols, and they become more keenly aware of their artistic limitations or failings. They may take a hand at writing prose or poetry, but typically they are interested chiefly in communicating rather than in developing an effective use of language, and their writing approaches a transcription of their casual speech. Furthermore, a sharpened critical sense tends to discourage those whose skills have not developed.

The latency period is a critical time in the development of the young artist. He must make enough progress during this period so that, when he becomes capable of self-criticism, he will not find his own work too wanting. His personality traits are coalescing, but are not yet rigidified; his sensitivity to other person's needs and abilities has increased but is not yet overwhelming.

The years before adolescence may even constitute a sensitive period for artistic development; failure to develop skills during this period may thwart the child during adolescence, when he will be especially critical of his products. Support from his elders and from others in the community are important factors in maintaining the child's participation in the arts. This sensitive period in symbolic processing may be reflected in the ease with which children can learn second languages before the onset of adolescence. Lowenfeld suggests that "if we can stimulate the child's unaware production to such an extent that it reaches in his unaware style a creative maturity which will be able to stand the critical awareness which once will set in, we have kept the child from making a sudden change and have protected him from disappointment or shock with regard to his changing imaginative activity." The ability to acquire skills seems particularly impressive at this time. As V. S. Pritchett states in his autobiography:

> That eager period between ten and fourteen is the one in which one can learn anything. Even in the times when most children had no schooling at all, they could be experts in a trade; the children who went up chimneys, worked in cotton mills, packed coster barrows may have been sick, exhausted, ill-fed, but they were at a temporary height of their intelligence and power.

Many a youngster will devote himself fully, almost compulsively, to the achievement of excellence during the latency period. At the same time, the youngster's comments may suggest that he does not enjoy some of the great works of the past, that he is ambivalent about his own products, and that he fails to appreciate many of the nuances that are so important for his elders. Why he should nonetheless continue to participate in the arts is a complex question. In some cases, no doubt, the child is reinforced by his parents or community for this behavior; prestige, reward, a feeling of competence attend his continued pursuit. In other instances, the child may enjoy the actual involvement with art objects or the chance to attain technical virtuosity. Most frequently, perhaps, the involvement in the arts provides its own motor and motive for continued involvement, as each step of progress opens new possibilities and poses new challenges, which intrigue the youngster. At the same time, the child becomes increasingly conscious of the subtlety and complexity of works of art and thereby derives some of the open-ended satisfaction of working with artistic objects which also characterizes the adult participant in the artistic process.

Various tendencies may characterize the child who continues his artistic output during adolescence. He may focus on a single subject, theme, or narrow field and totally exhaust it; or he may strongly identify with one artist and copy all of his works. He may pursue at a feverish pace the total gamut of experiences: "he would get up in the middle of the night to scrawl down insane catalogs of all that he had seen and done: the number of books he had read, the number of miles he had traveled, the number of people he had known, the number of women he had slept with, the number of towns he had visited, the number of states he had been in."

With the coming of adolescence, for reasons not entirely understood, the young artist may either give up creative activity altogether, regress significantly, or fully embrace the art form and immerse himself into it professionally. There is a "universal change that occurs around puberty from a natural enjoyment and easy identification with artistic behavior to one of inhibition and lack of satisfaction in experience and creating art." In the more normal child, talented but not highly motivated, creativity usually regresses or drops out. H. Read describes this phenomenon, while claiming it is not inevitable:

At about the age of eleven . . . the child acquires the power of breaking up, or disassociating his first unitary perception, and logical thought begins with the capacity to isolate and compare component details. . . . Visual or plastic (imagist) modes of expression may show a tendency to disappear but it is certain that a code of esthetic expressions can be retained by every individual beyond the age of eleven . . . if we are prepared to sacrifice to some extent that exclusive devotion to the learning of logical modes of thought which characterize our present system of education.

A range of psychological findings suggests that during these years the final intellectual gap between child and adult disappears, as the youngster begins to reason and to approach tasks in an "adult" manner. Perhaps the emphasis in our culture on abstract thinking and on rigorous logical reasoning causes a decline in sensitivity to aesthetic properties, though it is also possible that such a decline antedates (or even causes) a shift to more abstract modes of expression and communication. At any rate, assorted studies, including my own, have documented the extent to which the adolescent child appears handicapped in tasks requiring sensitivity to nuance and suspension of abstract thought.

In our culture, the adolescence of the artist is often arduous. At a time when a large expenditure of energy and a reorganization of psychological and physiological components occur, skills may be hampered. Stravinsky writes of his early adolescence as a most unhappy period, when he hated school and had no friends. Other adolescent artists have been neurotically introverted, with symptoms of anxiety, low self-esteem, lack of social skills, and isolation from peers. At a time when social interaction, sexual prowess, and athletic accomplishments are considered vital, the adolescent dedicated to mastering a fine motor skill or to evolving an artistic personality will be estranged from his fellows. Indeed, excessive sensitivity to others may be a hindrance rather than a boon to smooth interpersonal relations at this time. Late adolescence, however, may be a more pleasurable period for artists, as they may already see some fruits of their work. Furthermore, as they gravitate toward artistic circles, they will meet others of like mind, discuss and devour the trends and themes of the day, and plot the next revolution in the arts.

Because the period of adolescence is a turbulent one in the life of the artist, as it is for most individuals in our culture, the individual who suffers from neurosis at that time seems more likely to recover than one who becomes neurotic earlier or later in life. Extremes of behavior and feeling are frequent. In general, the young artist may vacillate from belief in his genius to feelings of despair, from conviction that he will be a great artist to fear that he will amount to nothing. Those who have had a relatively stable background and those who have confidence in their skills are the more likely to remain artistic and to continue producing works. However, a lapse in adolescence need not entail inevitable repercussions later.

Formal education may be a thwarting rather than a facilitative influence in the development of the artist. Artists have often disliked schools, and schools have reciprocated this feeling. Sartre indicated how his schooling kept him from writing for some time. Stravinsky, increasingly involved in music, found school offensive and could not stand to be there. Thomas Mann considered his schooling a waste. Nonetheless, training in their preferred art forms may be advisable and helpful for artists. In particular, instruction seems helpful in arts that involve motor skills. More writers lack formal training (or have only the training of having written school exercises) than painters. And yet even in literature or music, some form of discipline seems to be valuable.

Academic and didactic training may have beneficent effects, and may help the student to identify fully with the tradition, to control his skills, and to discover interesting problems for investigation. The discipline to which the student is subjected may help him strengthen his own method and expression, and also provide a needed spur toward rebellion. The painter Hogarth indicates how the young artist can train himself to observe and remember: "I therefore endeavored to habituate myself to the exercise of a sort of technical memory and by repeating in my own mind the parts of which objects are composed, I could by degree combine and put them down with my pencil . . . the early habit I thus acquired of retaining in my mind's eye, without coldly copying it on the spot, whatever I intended to imitate." The ability to observe carefully and retain what has been seen is obviously a vital skill, best picked up during early childhood. Explicit training does not seem essential for the refinement of the perceiving system, but extensive practice does. The manner in which such essential perceiving and making skills are mastered may vary, but the importance of having them is not in dispute. The eventual rebellion against the tradition, which may be pivotal for the great artist, is facilitated by a strict training, and by possession of skills useful in tackling a novel domain.

Our knowledge is insufficient to permit conclusions about the optimal background of artists, but the above evidence suggests at least one possibility. The future artist is one who progresses sufficiently during the latency years, so that when he becomes critical of his own work he will regard it as acceptable and continue to produce artistic works. This perception can only come about if the child has worked with exceeding diligence, mastering technical skills and studying the examples of the past, so that he will have achieved genuine competence by the age of 11 or 12. Strong motivation seems crucial here, and is most likely to occur in the case of children who are tremendously gifted to begin with, who have striving parents, or who suffer from a disturbance which encourages them to sublimate.

PERSONAL AND STYLISTIC ASPECTS OF THE YOUNG ARTIST

Some personality traits of the youthful artist are worth noting. Frequently the child artist forms a close relationship to his playthings;

these objects become vehicles for an imaginary life and are often cherished as fetishes. Such objects seem of considerable importance, for they are material elements into which the child has invested a part of himself, and which can represent or complement him. They differ from legitimate artistic objects in that the child is tied to the idea and identity of the object rather than to knowledge or formal aspects embedded in it, and in that the communication is more personal than interindividual. Yet this ability to form close ties to objects, which have within them aspects of oneself and which are often treated as if they undergo feelings and experiences, may be a necessary antecedent to a full appreciation of art objects. Only later can a child instill aspects of himself in objects in such a way that others can appreciate the object as well; only later can he assume such an attitude toward another's creation. The personal relation to the object precedes the valuing of it as a communication to others. A gradual distancing from the object, declining egocentrism, and an increasing understanding of the processes involved in aesthetic objects are all products of the middle childhood years, which culminate in a mature and realistic capacity to appreciate aesthetic objects.

Another important aspect in this period is a growing awareness of one's own personality, gifts, and characteristic ways of expression. Sensitivity to one's own style and its relation to the styles of others may not yet have developed; but awareness of oneself as a young artist, as a hero in touch with great ideas, as an individual with rare gifts should emerge toward the end of the latency period. Sometimes, indeed, this self-consciousness begins much earlier: "When I was a young child— before I went to school, I think—I already knew what my life would be like; not of course, that I could guess what my future would be, what economic situation and what political events I'd get into: but from the very beginning of my self-consciousness, I knew what anything that could happen to me would have to be like."

During the preadolescent period the young artist undergoes partial reorganization of his feeling system and deepens his understanding of interpersonal relations. New experiences are cultivated by the child, who experiments with his roles and his relationships to other individuals. Lacking a developed personality or predictable reactions to each new encounter, the child explores a range of behaviors and feelings in an effort to arrive at that life style which is most appealing. Experimentation with different artistic styles is also the norm, and through such play, the child becomes aware of the wide range of individual behavior and of his own considerable potentials and degrees of choice. The child becomes increasingly aware of the dominant traits of those about him, and learns to color his behavior toward these individuals in an appropriate way. His perception of individuals becomes increasingly veridical, a reflection of age and accumulated experience as well as of intelligence. He slowly evolves characteristic ways of reacting to and interpreting experience, so that a dominant personal style, tempo, and temperament begins to emerge.

During adolescence, the tentative organization of personality may once more shatter, and the child will again experiment with roles and behavior. But the range within which he experiments will have been determined by his preadolescent experience, the level of initiative and competence he has achieved, and his personal ambitions; and the child's behavior in his preadolescent years may serve as a more useful guide to his later personality and career than his turbulent activities during adolescence. Finally, the adolescent acquires a growing appreciation of rule systems, of reciprocal relationships between people, and of the norms and nuances of interpersonal behavior; this steadily increasing comprehension serves as an essential underpinning for his own communicative aspects, both in direct personal confrontations and in his perceiving and creating of symbolic objects.

The child's relationship to the styles and works of the past is of some interest. Initially, most children will examine works that are readily available, and almost inevitably will esteem them. In acquiring competence, children will imitate these models, often with much fervor, thoroughness, and success. The future artist may select one or two "guardian angels," great artists of the past whom he seeks to emulate and with reference to whom he will one day define his own unique contribution to the arts. Within a year or two, the young artist may have sufficiently mastered a particular style, that, using it, he can embellish a work—an ability to extrapolate from the style will have evolved. Finally, the style is assimilated to such an extent that the child—by now an adolescent—can introduce his own subject matter and compose original works in that style.

An analogous process often occurs with respect to a cluster of styles. In imitating a range of styles, the youngster becomes better able to appreciate the potential of the whole medium. After mastering a number of prevalent styles, a reaction to the predominant style of the period and the evolution of one's own style should follow. But at the time of the artist's initial works (Stravinsky's first symphony, Picasso's harlequins, Schoenberg's *Verklaerte Nacht*), it seems fair to say that these works are splendid realizations of the current tradition, rather than substantive contributions to any tradition of the new. As the composer Günther Schuller remarks of his own development, he first identified with Schoenberg and Stravinsky's ideas, next combined them in his earliest works, and now recasts them in his own language.

An accomplished style is a late appearance of the artistic process, since the young child has not developed an integrated personality and so can realize only fragments of his person in his work. By the same token, in order to appreciate the style of a work, the person must have undergone enough experience and be sufficiently worldly about the artistic process, that the work can represent to him a manifestation of another individual, as well as a simple tone sequence, story, or rhyme. Thus a developed sense of interpersonal relations, dependent on previous experiences, and their potential embodiments in a work, is a prerequisite for the comprehension of style. Yet explicit cultivation of style on the part of a maker is not necessary, as Shaw indicates: "I have never aimed at style in my life . . . style is a sort of melody that comes into my sentences by itself. If a writer says what he has to say as accurately and effectively as he can, his style will take care of itself, if he has a style." Nonetheless, it is only through considerable experience with a medium (and considerable experience in living) that a distinctive, viable style can develop. Neither the ability to notice stylistic aspects nor to develop one's own style seems dependent upon reaching a new stage of development; yet until a person has achieved fluency with a medium, he will likely lack the distance that permits noting its stylistic aspects.

With the passing of adolescence, the individual who has continued to master his symbolic medium becomes an artist in the full sense—he has become familiar with and is now able to appreciate and to contribute to the tradition in his art form. Earlier, he knew the art as a single form, and such invention as he had done had usually been in one style at a time. Now he becomes intimately aware of the variety of artists and styles that preceded him. No longer are these merely remote names for him. With increasing understanding of the world of persons, the artists of the past emerge as individuals like himself who responded to the challenges, motifs, and feelings of their epochs and captured information about such elements and about themselves in their own art work. Only at this point does the artist achieve sufficient distance—adequate decentration—so that he can perceive himself as engaged in the same kind of activity as his predecessors and can begin to contribute to the tradition. Malraux emphasized the importance of this phenomenon with his bold claim that "artists do not stem from their childhood productions but from their conflicts with the achievements of their predecessors." One paints in relationship not to what one sees but rather to the ways in which others have represented before. Capacity to appreciate the *code* of an art form draws on a developing critical faculty that enables one to make discriminations in a consistent intelligent way, and to appreciate the different goals, means, and tools artists have had at their disposal. Not surprisingly, the greatest artists have immersed themselves in the works of the past; Keats, for example, spoke of being overpowered by the brilliance of the past. Goethe rejoiced that he was not born an Englishman, for he would have had the intimidating example of Shakespeare before him.

The individual who chooses the arts as a career will continue to develop in numerous ways in the years following adolescence. He will devise novel schemes, seek to convey new forms of discrimination and feeling in his works, deepen his understanding of individuals and experiences, and create works in response to those of others and to his own previous work. Only a very few of those who choose to become artists, however, will go on to make substantive advances in techniques or to create works which will have a significant impact on future generations. Such artistic geniuses may be noticed at an early age, because of their unusual skills and precocity, their sensitivity to events, and their capacity to capture significant qualities in some medium. Other indications include unselfishness toward duty at the expense of health, the dim foresight of immortality, total mastery of craft, universal interests, depth of perception (and intense reactions), keen memory, high degree of perseverance, and prolificness. The achievement of originality and uniqueness is a particular goal in our culture, rather than a universal feature of the artistic process. Nonetheless, even in those cultures where maintenance (rather than rejection) of the tradition is prized, individual differences in skill and achievement will be evident, and certain artists will be distinguished by the special way in which they realize (or epitomize) the communal standards of excellence.

Of particular interest is the self-confidence of many promising artists. In the view of many Arnold Schoenberg was inadequately recognized during his lifetime. Yet he had an unshakable belief in his own greatness, which may well have sustained him during periods of dejection and rejection. He wrote that "in ten years every talented composer will be writing this way—it will not be possible to prevent the young and gifted from emulating my style." As early as 1910, before he had invented the serial technique, he was asserting that "even now my name belongs to the history of music." Kahn alludes to the determination and singlemindedness of artists: "Art is obsession: it is one-sidedness. The artists I know are immodestly committed to their own viewpoints and quite consciously put blinders on, to be the better able to trot along their own roads . . . artists treasure their fetishes, prejudices, passions, oddities of taste—all useful motive forces in making art."

While the average artist may cease to display originality after a certain point and be content to repeat himself, the gifted artist continues to develop, to deepen his techniques, to make new discoveries and produce works of greater interest, significance, and profundity, to pose wholly new solutions to aesthetic concerns. Art is integrally related to human development precisely because an individual's art may continue to undergo deepening and enrichment; this progression reflects parallel deepening processes in that person's psychological existence, as he confronts the crises of young adulthood, middle age, and old age.

Révész notes that "the history of art and science show unequivocally that, as a rule, age implies no decrement. . . . In all fields of intellectual endeavor, highly gifted individuals, as they grow older, manifest a heightened productive efficiency usually in quality but also very frequently in quantity." And Henry Moore asserts that "one does find the best artists do their greatest work as they grow older . . . painting and sculpture have more to do with the outside world and they're neverending. As long as the artist remains open to new experiences, in touch with his own feeling life, in command of his medium, one may expect perpetual flowering of his work."

UNIVERSALS AND MODES

While most artists operate within the general code or set of norms devised by their culture, not all aspects of the code are learned by, nor derived from, the works of specific other artists. There appear to be deployments of various media that are more or less tolerable, and arrangements of words, notes, lines, or colors picked up not from special study but from a general facility with a medium. Perhaps some of these sensitivities or tendencies come to the artist by simple virtue of his being human. Certain symbols, motifs, or arrangements may be natural products of the human mind, and thus inevitably present and discerned in aesthetic objects.

The controversial claim that there are universal aspects of art, available to every individual by virtue of his species membership, has come from commentators in many realms. Jung spoke of archetypes that were implanted in the collective consciousness of all humans by virtue of their racial heritage, and he devoted many years to a specification and description of these universal patterns. The Gestalt psychologists recognized that certain forms were indeed ubiquitous, but attributed them instead to a natural correspondence between the arrangement of elements and forces in the world and the operation of the human nervous system. Other observers have been less eager to provide a rationale for such pervasive symbols and percepts, but have nonetheless attempted to document their existence. Scholars have noted the ubiquity of the 2:1 ratio in musical rhythmic patterns; the basic metrical form of folk verses, the relationship between literary forms and the seasons, sensations, and rhythms of life; the perennial interest of children in questions relating to birth, animal life, and the reproductive process; the widespread appearances of certain metaphors in the poetry of the world, such as the relationship between time and a river, stars and eyes, nightmares and monsters, women and flowers, battles and fire, sleep and dying.

Such psychological claims have an interesting confluence with the work of the anthropologist Lévi-Strauss, who, in his description of the "savage mind," proposes that certain issues—among them life, death, and the relationship between nature and culture—form the bases for mythic thought, and hence raw thought, in every human culture. Lévi-Strauss suggests that the way in which these themes and factors are treated reflects the structure of the human mind. He notes how the myths in a wide range of cultures express the same dualities (filled—empty; dark—light; raw—cooked; thick—thin; noisy—quiet) and explore every permutation of such qualities. The individual has little choice as to the form and the subject matter of these myths; they are an inevitable product of the perceptual capacities of man interacting with the elements contained in his environment. The myth teller is simply a mouthpiece through which the unconscious structure of the human mind is made public.

The nature and source of elements and symbols found in disparate cultures or in the works of all children is an issue far too vexed to allow resolution here. Yet the evidence about modal-vectoral properties does suggest that the functioning of the body, its phenomenal concomitants, and its formal qualities may lead to the creation of categories in every normal individual.

I want to raise the possibility that *modal-vectoral properties*—which pervade the functioning and the experience of the young child—form a substratum upon which all experience is initially assimilated. The common elements discerned in myths, poetry, imagery, and visual art may reflect the modal-vectoral qualities perceived and realized by men, women, and children everywhere. What has been regarded as innate qualities by some may be properties that emerge as a natural consequence of human development.

Whereas their centrality diminishes in other realms, modal-vectoral properties remain an important, indeed essential aspect, of the significance and impact of artistic works. The qualities are important because they constitute individuals' experiences of phenomena, which are later communicated to others, and because they represent a way of knowing which, due to common trends of developmental history, is available to every individual. Numerous psychologists have found agreement among subjects as to the modal-vectoral qualities embodied in linear configurations, and have demonstrated the frequency with which individuals exhibit common reactions to symbolic or natural displays. Further, a tendency to describe the perceived world in terms of opposing qualities (of the modal-vectoral sort) is increasingly manifest among scholars interested in the proclivities underlying disparate realms of knowledge (Jakobson and Lévi-Strauss, for example). Finally, there is considerable agreement among experts from different cultures concerning the aesthetic qualities of disparate objects; this fact underlines the extent to which common perceptual capacities may characterize individuals, because they have undergone analogous developing and deepening processes.

While modal-vectoral perception serves as a point of departure for assimilation in every realm and order of experience, it persists with special force in the artistic realm. Even as science strives to eliminate the generality, suggestiveness, and vagueness of modes, vectors, and other qualities, the arts thrive on these allusive properties. The capacity to embody them in a medium in an interesting and significant manner becomes a chief burden of the arts. We have established that the sensitivity to these aspects characteristic of the young child enables him to realize certain formal aspects of the arts at an early age. Yet the ability to convey them to others, to embed them in a symbolic medium, to convey them within compelling subject matter is only a consequence of considerable practice and training. Furthermore, the likelihood that specific modal-vectoral qualities are more salient during certain life stages or cultural epochs and that various media lend themselves differentially to these qualities ensures that artistic mastery is not an automatic consequence of incorporating any mode into any medium; incorporation of modal-vectoral aspects into a given work can be an infinitely subtle and complex process.

INSPIRATION AND DISCIPLINE IN THE CREATIVE PROCESS

As the child evolves into the skilled artist, he must maintain the ability to generate ideas and to integrate them into a finished, polished product.

This capacity is important to consider here, because the creative process as manifest in the mature artist is an end state toward which the training of artists should presumably be directed. In accounts of the nature of artistic activity two aspects predominate: the place of inspiration, and the role of disciplined craftsmanship.

Some of the artists who have left records of their thoughts about their work have emphasized the effortless ways in which ideas flow from their unconscious and are then mysteriously organized; creation emerges as an autonomous process requiring little will or intention on the creator's part. A paradigm case of the inspired creator is found in this passage:

> The poet . . . is put into a passion, at least into a certain mood, by his objects: he can not resist the violent desire to utter his feelings; he is transported. . . . He speaks, even if no one listens to him because his feelings do not let him be silent.

Goethe echoes these sentiments in writing of Mozart:

> How can one say, Mozart has composed *Don Juan* as if it were a piece of cake or biscuit, which had been stirred together out of eggs, flour, and sugar. It is a spiritual creation, in which the details, as well as the whole are pervaded by one spirit, and by the breadth of *one* life, so that the producer did not make experiments and patch together and follow his own caprice, but was altogether in the power of the daemonic spirit of his genius, and acted according to his order.

And Mozart himself fuels this view of creation:

> When and how [my ideas] come I know not; nor can I force them . . . provided that I am not disturbed, my subject enlarges itself and becomes methodized and defined and the whole, though it be long, stands almost complete and finished in my mind, so that I can survey it, like a fine picture of a beautiful statue—at a glance nor do I hear in my imagination the parts successively, but I hear them, as it were, all at once. What a delight this is, I cannot tell. All this inventing, this producing takes place in a pleasing lively dream.

Such descriptions of creativity abound among individuals who have been prodigies, who have created effectively from so early an age that they could not have been self-conscious about their output. Individuals with highly inventive minds, like Picasso and Mozart, have generally been considered to be founts of originality, whose every thought is unfailingly original and artistic. The prodigy is "visited" and must follow his instructions. Coleridge spoke of being in a trance as he composed "Kubla Khan"; he was so rudely interrupted by the gentleman from Porlock that his train of thought was forever lost.

A closer look at these supposedly spontaneous creators uncovers evidence of effortful labor upon their works. Mozart may have had little difficulty generating melodic lines, but he slaved over his works, writing a number of drafts of his operas and choral works. His mind was continually involved with thoughts about music, which may not have pained him but which certainly required effort and concentration. He wrote to his father: "You know that I am knee-deep in music, so to speak; that I busy myself with it all day long; that I like to speculate, study and ponder." Picasso may have a playful attitude toward his paintings, but he produced over 200 separate drawings in anticipation of *Les Déjeuners* series, and almost as many sketches for *Guernica*. Even when he completes it, Picasso does not regard the work as a point of stasis, but simply as the most recent in a never-ending series of experiments. "Paintings are but research and experiment. I never do a painting as a work of art. All of them are researches. I search constantly and there is a logical sequence in all this search." Coleridge may well have composed while in a stupor, but his research and preparation for each work was astonishingly complete. In his *Road to Xanadu*, J. L. Lowes is able to track down a large proportion of the images and references in Coleridge's masterpieces through an examination of the poet's notebooks. Coleridge doggedly followed up references he encountered, eventually weaving them into his works.

Individuals with superlative ears, like Mozart, Coleridge, or James Joyce, seem to have or hear a tremendous number of sounds, ideas, and schemes swirling about in their minds. When they are producing a work, any number of these notions may emerge in a variety of combinations and juxtapositions, even as the nighttime monologues of infants produce unexpected combinations and oppositions. Since ideas necessarily appear to emerge from the unconscious, such artists understandably think of themselves as receptacles from which compositions simply emanate. Yet, while the basic themes and selected details may not need the artist's sustained attention, the finished product is invariably the product of painstaking concern with the final form, and with the exact details and embellishments that contribute to it. Furthermore, it must not be forgotten that sustained practice and training preceded creation of the seemingly spontaneous work. Some artists have even conceded that talk of spontaneous creation is more a reflection of a reluctance to introspect, than an accurate description of a creating process. Nietzsche, Poe, and Schoenberg, to name a few, have noted the perils of overzealous self-examination; Nietzsche candidly acknowledged that "it is to the interest of the artist that others should believe in sudden suggestions, so-called inspiration. . . . All great men were great workers, indefatigable not only in invention, but also in rejection, sorting out, revising and arranging."

PROBLEM-SOLVING IN A MEDIUM

Given evidence of the hard labors and years of training and development even among the most fluent creators, it seems convincing to think of artistic creation as a practice of problem-solving within a given medium. At scattered points I have alluded to the arts as involving problem-solving, and have posited parallels between the perceptual discriminations accomplished by young humans or animals, the more intricate skill deployment of growing children, and the accomplishments of mature artists and scientists. Since I view much of aesthetic development as the increased ability to solve problems that emerge in the exercise of skilled behaviors, it seems advisable to give a general definition of a problem, to justify speaking of problem-solving behavior in the arts, to contrast artistic and scientific problem-solving, and to consider which problems contribute to the development of the young artist or connoisseur.

Fixing precisely the definition of a problem is an elaborate assignment, which cannot be effectively undertaken here. Speaking generally, I find it useful to contrast tasks with problems, maintaining that a task is an assignment that involves no difficulty in either conceptualization or execution, while a problem is an assignment that involves difficulty in one or both phases. Conceptualization of relevant factors (hereafter conceptualization) involves determining the elements of the problem, defining in advance some kind of a desired end state, and undertaking the restructuring and reintegration of factors essential for the desired end state—the solution. Execution in a medium (hereafter execution) is the phase of problem-solving in which the problem-solver fixes whatever notions he wishes to communicate, whichever ideas he wants to realize, in some sort of medium. Conceptualization emphasizes perceiving or discriminating (thinking or rethinking), which occurs internally, while execution is primarily *making* or *acting*, which occurs externally. Problems, therefore, are assignments in which either the "thinking through" or the "acting out" involves some sort of difficulty.

Although the use of the term *problem-solving* seems natural in the realm of science or business, it may seem somewhat out of place in the arts, where one does not think of setting problems with correct answers, or looking up solutions in an answer book. Indeed, the procedure of the artist seems far removed from the logician or scientist who, in tackling a proof, must specify his steps precisely, abide by canons of logic, and allow for independent veification. Yet it is plausible to speak of problem-solving in arts, not only because many involved with the arts so describe their activity, and because much of aesthetic education involves the setting and solving of problems, but also because a view of the arts as a problem-process obviates a number of difficulties. If the arts are construed as inspiration, as sheer creativity, as intuition or uncontrolled spontaneity, the chance to gain an analytical handle on the aesthetic process is sacrificed. Viewing the arts as solely a product of unconscious processes effectively removes them from the realm of scientific investigation. If the notion of a problem is sufficiently broadened so it is no longer merely the textbook variety encountered in grammar school, the analyst retains some assurance that he is still close to the phenomena of the arts, while at the same time he can entertain hope of analyzing the artistic process.

Instead of continuing in this definitional vein, it may be helpful to consider an assignment made in a first grade classroom, and to describe the responses given by the children. Consider the array of circles and squares in Figure 19. The teacher presents this array to his students, and then issues instructions of the following sort: "Here are some groups of circles and some groups of squares. I want you to join the group of circles to the group of squares which has the same number of figures in it. Do the same with each of the group of circles and squares." Such an assignment poses no problem for adults, who can treat it as a pure task—it involves difficulty neither in conceptualization nor in execution. For the first grader, however, this assignment is not so simple, for he is often unfamiliar with the whole idea of a structured assignment, and may not yet have a coherent sense of number. In such cases, a variety of possible responses can occur; four typical ones are seen in Figure 19.

In the first response, the child has correctly matched the circles and squares, but without apparent concern about the appearance of the marks used in communicating his answer. Such a solution emphasizes conceptualization and deemphasizes execution. In the second response, the child has not conceptualized the problem correctly (that is, the matching of relevant factors—the number of figures—is not correct), but has apparently devoted considerable effort to the creation of an appealing solution in the medium of pencil drawing. The other two responses capture the other logical possibilities. One solution shows evidence of considerable conceptualization and execution, the other reveals neither conceptualization nor execution.

Obviously these characterizations are speculative, and one might make other inferences about the processes involved in a particular solution. Such disagreements are not relevant here. At issue, rather, is the contention that the first three responses can be considered solutions to a problem. In the first and third cases we have a solution to a problem posed by the instructor, in the second case we have a solution to a problem posed by the solver himself. Only in the final case (d) is there no

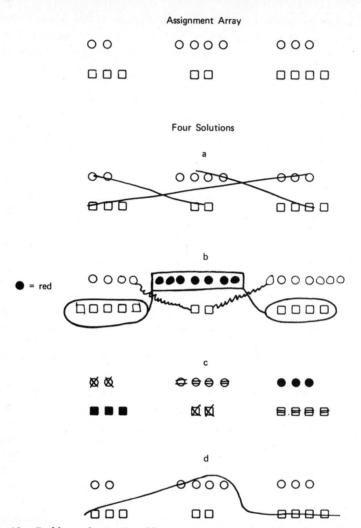

FIGURE 19. Problem-solving. Possible responses to array of circles and squares: a—primarily conceptualization; b—primarily execution; c—execution and conceptualization highlighted; d—neither execution nor conceptualization.

evidence of the problem-solving process; this solution seems better described as casual or even random behavior.

I believe that the kind of problem-solving characteristic of scientists highlights conceptualization. That is, the scientist generally has a specified problem that can be posed in a number of equivalent ways, at least a partial idea of what a solution would look like, and some experience working with the elements involved in the problem. His chief burden is to reanalyze the elements and to find a new configuration or arrangement that answers to the demands or constraints of the problem. As a rule, he can discuss the problem with others and can benefit from their ideas. He can prepare an outline of the final report, lacking only the confirming or contradictory data. Once he has hit upon a conceptualization, the problem is effectively solved. He can either write out the answer himself in some form, or can convey the answer to someone else who can also attend to the final execution or embodiment of his conceptualization. The medium in which the solution is manifest is not crucial—words, symbols, figures, or drawings may each or all be acceptable, so long as the essential factors and insight are retained. This focal idea can be expressed in a number of ways, independently verified by other investigations, and used as the basis for other problems. If the particular realization of the solution is forever lost, this is not crucial, providing someone can remember the general idea. If the solver dies in the process of completing the problem, someone else can probably accomplish its execution adequately. Once a problem has been solved, there is no point in others solving it independently (except as drill); rather, the solution should dictate additional problems which if solved will contribute to the *progress* of the science.

A contrast can readily be drawn with the typical operations of the artist. The artist less frequently borrows his problem from a tradition, generally cannot specify the solution ahead of time, nor can he depend on others to help him or to recognize a solution. Instead he begins with a vague idea and spends the bulk of his time exploring within a given medium. He may also devote considerable effort to conceptualization, but this "thought" is one step removed from his solution, which must eventually appear in the particular artistic medium in which he works. Rembrandt's sketches for a painting and Henry James's notes for a novel are worth little apart from their particular realization. A composer may indeed be able to think out his whole work in his head, but except for the most preliminary phase he will do this in terms of specific notes, rhythms, and harmonies, and not merely in terms of a "slow section," a "crescendo," or a "rondo." He "hears" the work. The artist generally defines his problem as he goes along, discovering new possibilities, and adding new constraints as the materials and his maneuvers dictate. Which problem(s) he has solved is apparent only after he has completed the work. Nor will others necessarily concur on the appropriateness of the solution; since there is no possibility of translation in the arts, since a solution must remain within the particular medium and cannot be converted by logical operations into equivalent forms, individuals may well disagree on the artist's goals and his success at realizing them. The artist's work is, in part, a rhetorical creation, which furnishes its own argument as a valid "solution" or "product." Since the artistic work has only an executionary, and not a conceptualized status, collaboration is only of limited help; the artist cannot readily share his problem with another individual and expect him to produce the same solution. Nor can he expect those who follow after or survive him to build upon his work, or to recreate his destroyed works, unless someone in command of an allographic form can remember them exactly. Problem-solving in the arts is closely tied to the particular execution, and only those factors associated with a given realization in a given medium are relevant to the problem-solving process.

This brief account may seem somewhat removed from our concern— the development and training of the artist. Let me therefore relate it to our guiding themes. We have suggested that the arts are primarily concerned with the capturing within symbolic objects of various kinds of subjective experience, feelings, world views—and we have spoken of these forms of knowledge as entailing and evoking modes, vectors, and related qualities. Let me propose, then, a problem implicitly faced by every artist: How am I to capture within a symbolized medium those properties— modes, vectors, feelings, insights, rhythms, and other forces—which permeate my subjective experience and which I want to convey to others? The artist does not have to think explicitly about these qualities, nor to engage in conceptualizing thought about factors; rather, through a series of experiments and executions within a symbolic medium he attempts to embody a desired mode or quality in an effective way. What is crucial is his sensitivity to the demands of his medium, whatever they may be. Problem-solving in the arts is not primarily conscious; it is the rare artist who would explicitly state a quality and then seek to realize it. On the other hand, the actual activities undertaken by artists at work support the essential reliability of this characterization.

This line of thought converges with a perspective introduced by David Ecker, who argues that problem-solving in the arts is qualitative problem-solving, with qualitative thought being "thinking in the particular qualities of the artistic medium." According to his analysis, artists begin their particular work simply by loosening-up exercises, which slowly reveal an emerging idea. Henry Moore scribbles initially until ideas become conscious and he can exercise more active control; Picasso says "the picture is not thought-out and determined beforehand: rather, while it is being made, it follows the mobility of thought." Once the principal idea of the work has emerged, however, the artist gradually achieves control by solving problems qualitatively related in technique or theme. Problems emerge during the process of creation and, as one is solved, other related ones are likely to emerge. In the course of working, the artist will be manipulating qualities such as "jagged," "open," or "cubist." He may speak of "using a cool green" to get a plane to recede; he may vary his lines in order to make a display less "jagged" and more "open." The problem-solving process naturally takes place within the medium—verbalization of the problem and possible solutions is superfluous. The artist's making and perceiving is directed toward the realization of qualities of the modal-vectoral sort. The artist arranges such means as planes, textures, lines, colors, and rhythms in order to achieve a desired order or quality.

The artist's task then, is to judge or choose among alternative realizations of qualities. There is no need to be conscious of the alternatives: All thought can result from simple experimentation with the medium, from a series of executions. The effective communication of these qualities as a result of his skill at aesthetic problem-solving constitutes the artist's work. The creative artist may strive in his own efforts to recreate his perception and feeling of a mode, and then search for ways of embodying this mode in his medium. His memory of qualities and his capacity to gain access to it became crucial. As Matisse indicated:

> I put down my colors without a preconceived plan. If at the first stop and perhaps without my being conscious of it one tone has particularly pleased me, more often than not when the picture is finished I will note that I have respected this tone while I have progressively altered and transformed the others. . . . To paint an autumn landscape I will not try to remember what colors suit this season, I will only be inspired by the sensation that the season gives me; the icy clearness of the blue sky will express the season just as well as the tonalities of the leaves.

Perhaps, indeed, the accomplished artist is one who can effectively communicate modes and vectors that are perceived universally, while the truly revolutionary artist is one who can communicate his own spectrum or blend of qualities in so effective a way that they become alive for the observer. Only one as gifted as Picasso could justifiably retort, when told that his portrait of Gertrude Stein did not look like its subject, "No matter—it will."

The general problem-solving approach to the arts has proved suggestive to other writers. Elaborating Ecker's discussion, Beardsley speaks of the stages involved in the production of an art work. The artist begins with an *incept*—a line or rhythm, for example—which sets up demands and suggestions as to what may come next and also places limits on it. Here is one writer's description of an incept: "It was there: I had the rhythm, I had the title. . . . I felt the strength of some mysterious force pulling me forward, but I did not yet have the words." Sometimes the incept endures throughout the work, while at other times it may become lost or transfigured. The artist's progress depends on his ability to criticize what he has done, to perceive lacks, to make appropriate revisions, and, above all, to recognize the completed work. In Beardsley's view, work should cease when every possible change is for the worse. This criterion may seem obvious, but is very difficult to realize in practice. Indeed, one salient characteristic of the young artist is his extreme difficulty in determining when the work is complete. He desires to continue making activity until every aspect of a canvas or subject is treated; he hesitates to stop, observe, and resolutely declare his satisfaction.

The role of play in problem-solving has been treated by Klinger. In play, problems can be solved spontaneously as "solutions emerge out of periodic fragmented enactments of salient material." For children, play allows an exploration of elements that have proved difficult to manage, and often points to new maneuvers or options. For adults, fantasy often assumes the problem-solving functions of overt play. Although a direct assault on an artistic problem is sometimes effective, desired qualities may sometimes be better realized as a result of this kind of experimentation with fragments, the undirected making activity characteristic of play. Execution is particularly marked by such undirected but potentially fruitful activity. When this freedom of exploration, this combining of possibilities and schemes is complemented by an ability to discriminate, to perceive when an effect has been realized or a work consummated, the skilled individual will be well equipped for artistic production.

It seems, then, that the artist's procedures may be usefully viewed as a kind of problem-solving, sometimes playful, sometimes intensely serious. Through a variety of executions, the artist succeeds in finding the most appropriate way of presenting the modes, vectors, qualities, or insights he wants to embody in an aesthetic object. Artistic development consists, in large measure, in the individual's increasing ability to communicate to others in a shared symbolic medium the kind of generalized aspects of experience that have been salient in his life. Naturally, the child's feeling life does not remain constant after infancy; his range of experiences and his changing apprehension of interpersonal relations will color both his experience and his evaluations. Nonetheless, for the audience member, as well as for the critic, creator, or performer, continued access to modal-vectoral properties is an essential aspect of participation in the aesthetic process; sharing this experience becomes important during latency and adolescence and seems to be a natural windfall of efforts at solving the artistic problems. Some ways in which the artist masters this form of problem-solving will be reviewed after we consider further the artist's own view of his creating process.

CREATING FROM THE ARTIST'S VIEWPOINT

Although the execution of the art work appears to involve conscious or unconscious problem-solving, from the artist's point of view what he is doing may seem far different from standard notions of scientific problem-solving. The artistic process, even more so than the scientific endeavor, is viewed by practitioners in exceedingly personal and even religious terms. Artists cherish their personal memories and their abilities to recreate emotional states. As Ribot indicated, "artists tend to think that in their work they are expressing a higher order, reflecting the realm of nature." Reflecting this mystical view of artistic creating, Goethe said that "a perfect work of art . . . is a work of the human spirit and in that sense also a work of nature. . . . These high works of art, like the highest works of nature, were produced by men according to true and natural laws. Everything arbitrary, everything fanciful falls together: here is necessity, here is God."

Many artists pay particular heed to the way in which their works unfold. In some cases any stimulus can get the mind working. Mozart was able to perceive a whole piece at once while he was riding about in a coach. Henry James reported that a slight clue, contained in an offhand remark, would be sufficient to stimulate his mind to create a whole story, including latent details: "Most of the stories straining to shape under my hand have sprung from a single small seed, a seed as minute and wind-blown as that casual hint from the spoils of Poynton dropped unwittingly by my neighbor, a mere floating particular in the stream of talk . . . there had been but ten words." And he also indicated the highly developed problem-solving capacity of another artist: "She was blessed with the faculty which, when you give it an inch takes an ell and which for the artist is a much greater source of strength than any accident of residence or of place in the social scale. The power to guess the unseen from the seen, to trace the implications of things, to judge the whole piece by the pattern."

Faulkner reportedly conceived *The Sound and the Fury* after seeing a little girl play in a stream and get her pants wet; Beethoven would listen idly to bird song or let his fingers fall upon the piano until he was struck by something appealing. Valéry and Stravinsky speak of distinctive rhythms that gave rise to works; Schoenberg of a general sense of form and shape. Picasso in working out the sketches for his adaptation of Manet's *Les Déjeuners* used free associations in order to stimulate his thoughts. These free associations were "unmistakably pictorial dissection and analysis which uncovers graphically the hidden psychological sources in Manet's themes." Travel seems to have provided an important impetus for Mozart's creativity. Yet it was the activities and rhythms of life in various places, rather than the sights he observed, which served as a catalyst for Mozart. Like some writers, he paid little attention to his external milieu and was content to work in mundane surroundings.

If most artists let their thoughts wander freely as they launch a new work, some creative individuals require special stimuli. Proust composed only in a cork-lined room. Wagner in his later years relied on fetishes, scarves, perfumes, and other feminine lures to stimulate his mind. Others also report rituals or unusual circumstances accompanying their creative activities: Rossetti needed chloride, DeQuincey opium, Baudelaire hashish, and Churchill alcohol in order to create, while Chopin walked, wept, and broke pens repeatedly, altering a bar of music as many as a hundred times. These stimulants are preconditions for writing rather than sources of ideas, however. Once the artist has got started, by whatever means, he must depend on his craft, which needs to be developed if it is to serve him effectively.

Even though both inspiration and discipline figure in most creative activity, the ratio of these aspects, as well as the ways in which artists combine them, differs widely across talented individuals. One cannot gainsay the difference between Velasquez, who groped, rejected, and revised material, and Goya, who darted to the conclusion of a work with scarcely any exploration; or between Thomas Mann, who composed a given number of lines each day, and Thomas Wolfe, who composed for days at a stretch with scarcely any sleep; or between Mozart, who knew his compositions so well beforehand that he wrote them down like a letter, and Beethoven, who for years worked on passages in his notebook. It seems, in general, that those who have been creative from an early age, like the prodigious Mozart and Picasso, create with less strain and greater stability than those like Van Gogh who have discovered their muse late in life. Characteristically, ideas just come to the prodigy, and he writes them down with little alteration, whereas the craftsman or laborer must seek inspiration, write many drafts, or rework many sketches. Similarly, those who work completely within a medium and who do not engage in much abstraction or alteration in their work, who can rely principally on associations engendered by the sounds of words or tones, or by the feelings of lines, can create more easily than those preoccupied with the underlying formal structure of a work (as a mathematician or a scientifically oriented architect or craftsman might be), or those bent on precision. The ways of the unconscious seem much closer to the fluid associations of a cyclothymic individual (Mozart, Samuel Johnson, G. K. Chesterton, G. F. Handel) than to the analytic proclivities of schizothymic persons (Braque, Dürer or Valéry). Nonetheless, the alteration in tempo between periods of inspiration, discipline, and selection probably affect nearly every artist at some point, in the manner ascribed to the sculptor Lipschitz: "Only after periods of tense and controlled work, he felt a strong urge for 'a kind of free logical expansion' that could not be stopped. He literally exploded."

The various "forces" or "fetishes" in the artist's life are fascinating psychological phenomena, but refractory to generalization and somewhat irrevelant to the nature of artistic skill. We may acknowledge that many artists have "crazy fixations" or require "exotic stimulation," but a greater systematization of the type of stimuli or notions seems less likely to yield insight about the nature of aesthetic productivity than an examination of the kinds of skills common to artists. Thus in analyzing the factors—the making and perceiving skills—that lead to artistry, we will stress those that appear susceptible to training, leaving aside the stimuli and the inspirations which artists often stress.

STUDIES OF CREATIVITY

Psychologists have tried to elucidate the imaginative and creative faculties, either by drawing on clinical intuition or by devising experimental paradigms. Even though these attempts have not been especially notable, some insights about creativity have developed in the last century. The most widely accepted formulation comes from Graham Wallas, who spoke of four stages in the creative process; these levels are scarcely explanatory, but they help to conceptualize the problem. Wallas's stages were designed particularly for the sciences, but students have found them germane to the arts as well: (1) *preparation*, in which the ideas for the work are identified and toyed with; (2) *incubation*, in which the mind may consciously be involved with other things while the unconscious is resolutely playing with and sorting out ideas; (3) *illumination*, in which the creator becomes aware of how all the elements fit together or "gets the picture"; (4) *verification*, in which the final details are checked out and the accuracy assured. A comparison of Wallas's scheme with our own discussion of problem-solving reveals that both stress the importance of preparation and incubation, in which the creator marshals his skill, but that the important aspect for the scientist is the "illumination" or "conceptual breakthrough," while the crucial phase for the artist is the "execution," which is scarcely equivalent to verification. If these qualifications are borne in mind, Wallas's formulation may be applied to the arts, even while acknowledging its primitive nature.

In an experimental investigation of Wallas's formulation, Patrick examined creative thought in poets and nonpoets. He presented both groups with a painting and required them to devise a poem about it. Patrick found the poets deviated more from the stimulus picture in their writing, made more references to the supernatural, employed more literary devices, and spent less time in revision. Another study has contrasted the performances of artists and nonartists as both groups attempted to produce a picture for a Péguy poem. Artists turned out to have more control over their planning and execution, more spontaneity and more practice, a pattern for dealing with the creative situation, and more likelihood for evolving their works gradually. Both these studies support Wallas, but neither is sufficiently meticulous to be revealing.

Perhaps the most comprehensive study of creativity was undertaken several decades ago. Bahle sent a set of poems to a number of eminent European composers and asked them to set one or more to music. He found wide differences in the way the musicians used the poems. Some first chose a text they liked and then invented a melody, others simply used the poems as a pretext to work out a previously determined melody or even ignored the poems altogether. The musicians gravitated toward poems whose emotional tone they thought they understood, rather than toward ones whose words they liked. In selecting a melody, some formed totally new motifs, while others took various patterns and combined them in new ways. Bahle's collected descriptions of the inventions are fascinating, and reveal the manifold ways in which artists create. Indeed it is in part because generalization about artistic creativity at the highest level is so difficult that the developmental approach has been proposed as more productive.

A number of individuals interested in the arts have commented more generally on artistic creativity. For example, the psychologist Bartlett attempted to characterize literary creativity, contrasting the logic of the scientist with that of the artist. He suggested that "artistic thinking is set to achieve a terminus which every person of sensitivity must appreciate even if he will not accept it. . . . It seeks the universality of the mathematical closed system and experimental kinds of thought and at the same time the freedom from demonstration and proof of every day thinking." As the writer or painter proceeds toward the terminus, every occurrence has a greater inevitability. "Something outside him has taken charge and is now settling everything that happens."

In attempting to describe the process of musical composition, the musicologist D. Cooke has found himself drawn to the language of qualities:

It does not seem farcical to suppose that in a tonal composer . . . an unconscious state of affairs exists that can be described metaphorically in the following way: 1) memories of the innumerable expressive uses of each of the tonal tensions must attach themselves together in groups by the association of ideas (or rather by the association of feeling) and each group of this kind must be attached to a kindred group of memories of semi-expressive life experiences and literary and artistic experiences also by the association of feeling; 2) these composite groups must contain within them certain such groups, each attached to a specific use of the tonal tension concerned, i.e., to one of the basic terms of the musical vocabulary, for example, of the vast number of associations connected with the major sixth, many will be attached to the major 6–5 or 8–6, etc.; 3) memories of the expressive uses of certain keys must also attach themselves together by the association of feeling and the groups must also attract memories of life and art experiences, thereby forming the well-known association in the composer's mind between certain keys and certain moods.

Cooke feels that particular effects in the composer's mind have become linked with musical forms or patterns, and that these are drawn upon unconsciously in the composition of music. A desire to capture specific qualities would dictate certain choices in harmony, rhythm, or tonality. According to this view, the artist's task is to transform subjectively-known realities into objective semblances that can be recognized by the audience member. The artist senses various problems in his work-in-progress, and so refers to "tension," "crisis," and "conflict" when discussing the process of creating. The completed work evokes feelings of repose and quietude, and so the artist talks in terms of "balance," "stasis," and "relief" when the work has been realized. Here we encounter support for a problem-solving approach to the arts.

The diversity of views suggests that generalizing about creativity in the arts as a whole is simply too broad a task. My own feeling is that it would be more sensible to study how a few individual works have been created. I am hopeful that a separate study of this problem can be undertaken; this work would doubtless draw heavily upon such excellent sources as Lowes's examination of Coleridge's imagination, Arnheim's study of the sketches for *Guernica,* the notebooks of Gide and Dostoevsky, the successive drafts of compositions such as Stravinsky's *les Noces* or Spender's poems. We would consider how the work fits into the overall corpus of the artist, what ideas led to its inception, which solutions were considered and discarded, and how the final form and details were arrived at. My research so far has indicated only that the process may differ greatly among the arts, and even from one work by an artist to another. Nearly all of Picasso's themes and forms for *Guernica* were contained in earlier works; the major problem was arranging them to achieve the desired terror and stolidness. Stravinsky in writing *Les Noces* was repeatedly confronted with technical problems of performance, and finally had to introduce changes simply so that the work could be performed. Dostoevsky had worked out many of the details of *The Idiot* from the first, but kept searching for the overall theme that would tie the notions together.

> Dostoevsky seems to have started with certain situations, dramatic modes, without having a clear idea of how different situations relate to one another or why his people act as they do. He has no overall conceptions of the action but seems to be trying out various combinations, connections, and relationships. . . . You get the feeling with the numerous endings tried that Dostoevsky is trying to understand the characters. . . . He kept thinking he had the definitive version but he did not.

Dostoevsky's particular experience, where details, characters, and situations are outlined before the overall theme has been worked out, seems exceptional, and may account for the difficulty readers have in assimilating this novel. From such case studies some more generalizations about the nature of the artistic process might be forthcoming, but I have few illusions about the extraordinary difficulty of this task.

More revealing than the experimental literature on creativity is the testimony of those close to the arts. Thomas Mann spoke about the delicate balance between the overall work and the specific aspect being developed:

> I have been struggling and taking thought, have had to grit my teeth and tussle with a single detail, while at the same time holding a more extended and complex content firmly in mind, concentrating my mental powers upon it down to its furthermost ramification.

Maintaining this balance is an extremely delicate aspect of creation, as difficulties persist to the very end:

> In the course of such works one endures to the very last word . . . crucial difficulties still remain to be overcome and what has been done stands in need of being rescued by what remains to be done.

Matisse alluded to the realization that a work is complete:

> Then a moment comes when every part has found its legitimate relationship, and from then on it would be impossible for me to add a stroke to my picture without having to paint it all over again.

And he also described the way in which the work exists as an inimitable whole:

> An artist who wants to transpose a composition on to a larger canvas must conceive it over again in order to preserve its expression. He must alter its character and not just fill in the square into which he had divided his canvas. . . . I cannot copy nature in a servile way. I must interpret nature and submit it to the spirit of the picture.

The different constraints operating on the creativity of various artists are also instructive. Stravinsky, though recognizing the role of inspiration, highlighted the central role of effort and work. He saw composing as a daily routine, and felt that one's creating organ must be kept in order. Creation is not dependent wholly on inspiration, yet he maintained:

> I am far from repudiating inspiration. Quite to the contrary. I consider it to be a moving force that belongs to every human activity and it is by no means a monopoly of the artist, but this power only unfolds when it is set in motion by an effort and this effort is work.

For his part, Schoenberg frequently forgot earlier portions of a piece, but then discovered that the overall work was somehow represented in his unconscious. Writers like Coleridge and Yeats appear to have incorporated in some conscious or unconscious form nearly all they had ever heard or read. Mann pointed out that when he was writing a work he seized upon one of his earlier works as a "guardian angel." Such diverse testimony indicates the risks in generalizing about the artist's attitude toward his work, or the role of experience and the unconscious. While artists may be characterized broadly as capturing qualities in a medium; as communicating their knowledge in aesthetic objects; and as passing through such overall stages as "incubation" and "verification," they approach uniqueness while creating. Regularities may perhaps be found by focusing on the way in which the artist develops, the way in which he acquires skill, comes to know the tradition, and evolves a style. We now turn to findings in this area.

THE DEVELOPMENT OF ARTISTIC SKILLS

Speaking most generally, artistic development involves the education of the making, perceiving, and feeling systems; the individual becomes able to participate in the artistic process, to manipulate, comprehend, and relate to the symbolic media in specifiable ways. Let us focus first on some general characteristics of the skills needed by the artist. Ghiselin has provided a useful summary: "Every genuinely creative worker must attain in one way or another such full understanding of his medium and such skill, ingenuity, and flexibility in handling it, that he can make fresh use of it to construct a device which, when used skillfully by others, will organize their experience in the way that his own experience was organized." How command of a medium can be acquired is perhaps the single most important question in aesthetic education. The preceding discussion of the making system strongly suggests that constant practice with the medium, intensive exercise with the symbol system is the best way to acquire fluency with it, to come to know its uses, potentials, and limitations. Usually this immersion in the medium is self-motivated. Future writers are enamored with words and play with them in every situation. Authors tell of their early fascination for the signs of the zodiac, their pouring over hieroglyphics, their playing with words as other children play with blocks. Musicians stress the importance of early practice, feeling that mastery can be acquired in a relatively effortless way during childhood. The drama teacher Spolin suggests that "skills are developed at the very moment a person is having all the fun and excitement playing a game has to offer; this is the exact time he is truly open to receive them." And the painting teacher, Davie, highlights the importance of an open, unstructured attitude to the medium:

> I work with the idea that art is something basically natural to man. . . . I usually begin with simple exercises in pure idealess activity, direct putting down of black marks, with no end in view, purposeless and aimless. Strangely enough the student finds that to work without thought requires a great deal of mental discipline and it is some time before he achieves an image without the intermediary of reasoning. . . . The next stage entails the introduction of ideas but ideas must also be intuitive without preliminary discrimination or detachments.

Certainly the atmosphere Davie seeks to engender in his older students —that of unfettered making activity—is a spontaneous trait in many children.

Lowenfeld is perhaps the strongest and most articulate proponent of the pedagogical viewpoint introduced here. He cautions against asking the child to comply with verbal specifications, or concentrating explicitly upon a skill. Instead he recommends that problems be set that will enable the child himself, when he is ready, to master a certain technique or principle. In getting a child to represent proportion, for example, it is unproductive to talk in terms of measuring ratios. Instead, the child should be asked to make drawings that involve comparing the "size" of "sitting under a tree," "reaching for an apple on a tree," and "reaching the roof of the Empire State Building." By this means, the child can himself experiment until he arrives at suitable proportions, rather than having to follow an externally imposed regimen. Ideally a task should be suggestive, and should convey a principle, yet should not upset the child if he decides not to execute it. Equipping the child with the appropriate materials and posing questions at the relevant time seem to be the most effective procedures for skill building in the arts. Thus, the writing teacher Mearns cautions against having children rhyme when they write poetry, feeling that this instruction unduly restricts them. But, asking a child to write about a dream, or suggesting a first line, is seen as a liberating rather than as a limiting factor; possibilities are opened even while method of realization is not restricted.

Under ideal circumstances—considerable native talent, enriched environment and contacts, supporting elders—explicit tutelage may be unnecessary, the child will guide himself unerringly toward artistic excellence. Such may have been the case with prodigies like Mozart, Picasso, and Raphael. In most cases, however, skills do not naturally evolve; one is faced with a choice between explicit instruction or the creation of a situation in which that skill is likely to develop. The latter circumstance seems to have been more common in traditional ateliers where the apprentice artist was required to perform gradually more difficult tasks and where, through a combination of emulation and experimentation, he hit upon an appropriate technique. In the absence of such a milieu, artists have often created their own substitute. Thus Stravinsky imitated the styles of others, Mann first followed but later abandoned models, and Keats forced himself to undertake long poems in the knowledge that the exercises would enhance his poetic skills:

> Some of the greatest composers, including Rimsky-Korsakov, Tchaikovsky, Schubert, and Beethoven undertook the most drastic, laborious, and abstract kind of work, going far beyond anything any school of music could conceivably require. They worked out hundreds of exercises in strict counterpoint, copied the music of other composers again and again, and so forth. . . . It extended their flexible command of musical resources.

The sources of great creativity are diverse. Various artists have been able to imitate their peers effortlessly, have broken away from all previous models, or have immersed themselves totally in a tradition. Bach exemplified the latter pattern: "Bach was one of the most conventional composers who ever existed. He accepted forms and formulas ready-made from his predecessors and he was none the worse for it because he succeeded, in spite of those self-imposed blinders to his fancy, in making something greater out of the precedent than it had ever been before."

Bahle proposes a three-stage sequence through which composers have typically passed: a period of imitating the styles of others; a counterpart phase, marked by much experimentation, of rejecting the tradition; and a final period, in which the composer's own style becomes constant, without being rigid, and the composer is free to improvise. These stages suggest that an important part of requisite skill building involves the complete immersion in and familiarity with an existing tradition, after which the artist may define his relation to it. Yet the requirement to reproduce a model may hinder the spontaneous growth of the child's own representational concepts. Children asked to copy adult symbols are retarded in comparison with those who devise their own; college students exposed to the art of their instructor sometimes find it difficult to break away from this model.

We have, then, the paradoxical situation in which imitation is seen as critical in aesthetic development, yet as potentially limiting the child's creativity. To resolve this paradox, what seems needed is a developmental perspective; at first the child should be allowed to explore the medium as freely and completely as possible; next, through careful guidance and posing of problems, he should have the opportunity to build up sufficient skills to capture the qualities and create the effects he desires; finally, having a sense of his own abilities and goals, he should be exposed to the great works of his medium and be encouraged to study and imitate them, so that he can see how effects have been achieved by others working in the same craft. Practically speaking, of course, the child will always see (and perhaps be tempted to imitate) the works of others. Therefore, as a precaution he should be exposed to many kinds of works, and his attention should be called to the varied ways of solving a problem. So long as the young artist does not conclude that the ways to capture a mode or achieve an effect are limited, he should benefit from, rather than be hindered by, exposure to the works of others. But the peak of exposure to models should occur only after the child has had ample opportunities to explore the medium.

Acquiring requisite skill before one comes to reject the tradition is considered essential by most classical masters. Matisse spoke of learning to walk on the ground before one tries the tightrope, and feared the young would see in "the apparent facility and negligence of his drawings" only an excuse for "avoiding the slow and painful preparation which is necessary for the education of any contemporary painter who claims to construct by color alone." Goethe too underscored the importance of total mastery:

For the person who wishes to learn to sing, all the notes which are naturally in his throat come easily to him but the others which are not in his throat are in the beginning extremely difficult for him. Yet he must master them in order to become a singer, for they must all be at his disposal. The same thing holds true for the poet. As long as he merely expresses his few subjective feelings, he does not deserve to be called one, but when he has learned to assimilate the world and to articulate it, he is a poet. And then he is inexhaustible and always has something to say.

Particularly in making realms (like vocalic music) that involve public performance, more formal pedagogic techniques may be advisable.

TRAINING METHODS

Every art form requires certain technical skills. The painter must have the making skills of wielding a brush expertly and of controlling both gross and fine movements, as well as the discrimination skills of noting fine color distinctions and quality of line, subtle features in the physical world, or slight flaws on the canvas. The writer and the composer need not have particular motor skills, but require a keen ear for sounds and an overall sense of form and rhythm, as well as knowledge of harmony, counterpoint, orchestration, syntax, and dialect, and the ability to manipulate tonal and rhythmic sequences fluently. There is a formidable literature on the psychology of skill, but this literature is for the most part restricted to the manner and rate in which simple, discrete tasks are learned (and forgotten) and the degree of correlation between one sort of skill and another. These findings may well be of importance for those involved in teaching a restricted domain of the arts, such as mixing colors, recognizing iambic pentameter, imitating a cadence, or learning a notation; they are less suggestive with regard to the more intricate sorts of skills audience members, critics, performers, and creators must possess if they are to perform their roles effectively.

Training of artists, in particular those whose physical productions are displayed in public (like painters or sculptors), involves a number of considerations. Essential is the acquisition of sufficient motor dexterity, making skill, or control of the body so that the artist need not be self-conscious and can draw on these capacities as required; sufficient practice to ensure mastery and flexibility is crucial here. The principles involved in building up skills and combining them into larger, hierarchically organized units, seem to be those operative in the young child who learns to walk, run, throw, catch, or build a tower. The artist is dependent on such skills and needs to be able to use them effortlessly, when he is in a "fit" of creation (much as the runner calls upon his coordinated movements for another burst of speed at the conclusion of the race, or the accomplished swimmer manages to drag himself ashore though in a half-conscious state). The required background cannot be picked up at the moment of inspiration itself. Thus a history of learning and overlearning of particular rote sequences appears necessary if the skills are to be appropriately and effectively used under pressures of creation. Mozart wrote to his father, "As you know, I can more or less adapt or imitate any kind and any style of composition." Such agility could only have evolved from repeated practice at a wide variety of tasks, which together constitute the important components of the composing skill. Mozart apparently had done so much exploration and imitation that he no longer merely incorporated specific composers—he had incorporated all of Western music.

Training in motor skills is generally indirect, though demonstrations of a developed manual skill are often included. Typically, the individual begins by tackling the skill in a makeshift, awkward way; as he masters subcomponents, the making system (in its wise nature) eliminates excess motion, combines components, and smoothes out the general behavior. Verbal instructions are probably of little help, though certain causative and even impossible instructions—"play this section as if your elbow were attached to your shoulders"—can be facilitative. Despite the generally meager transfer from one motor skill to another, certain individuals do seem to evolve a general coordination, which makes it easier for them to pick up a variety of motor skills.

Most performers and artists need guidance if they are to communicate effectively the modal and qualitative messages characteristic of aesthetic objects. Again direct tutelage may be deceptive, for it may prescribe procedure, instead of fostering the novel ways of achieving effects and qualities that are at a premium in the arts. Certainly, individuals cannot be expected to communicate such aspects unless they have experienced them, but it seems plausible that every mature individual has in some way felt the affects of pain, anger, frenzy, torment, desire, openness, tension and death. Assuming this commonality of experience, coaches often try to get the performer to "feel again" or "relive" the way he felt in a given situation. When an actor complains that he cannot emulate Othello killing Desdemona because he has never slain anyone, the director Boleslavsky may ask him if he's ever been so enraged by flies on a summer's evening that he wants to decimate them. By introducing a situation that embodies the affect, Boleslavsky is able to induce in the actor, without direct tutelage or limiting labeling, the appropriate feeling, which the actor can then convey by his own action, gait, and manner.

The actor must depend not only on his memory of emotions, but also on general keenness of observation. The instructor does not tell the actor to "observe," but rather requires that he enact behaviors that demand careful observation: "show me the way I just poured the tea . . . imitate John lighting a cigarette." Only if the student has previously observed carefully and noticed the relevant behaviors can he execute the task properly. If he makes mistakes or acts grotesquely he will become motivated to take note of the inadequacies in his attentional processes. Indeed it sometimes proves useful to have the actor exaggerate his own actions, so that he can become better acquainted with the proclivities and the potentialities of the instrument on which his livelihood depends.

Effective teaching methods in the arts are rarely publicized, and so when a suggestive piece appears, it immediately engenders much interest. A number of teachers who work with elementary school children, particularly with those in inner-city schools, have reported striking success in the teaching of creative writing. Teachers like Herbert Kohl, George Dennison, and Kenneth Koch have gone into ghetto schools where the children can hardly read and write, and have helped the youngsters to express themselves directly, imaginatively, and often lyrically.

Koch's approach is particularly innovative and fruitful. In his view, a prerequisite for creative writing by youngsters is a permissive, happy, and easy classroom. Being "up-tight" is deadly for all youngsters, and doubly so for ghetto children. The children must understand that spelling and punctuation is unimportant, and no efforts should be made to get them to rhyme or to adopt a rigid poetic form, for that would be too difficult. Rather the child should be encouraged to play, to "be crazy," to experiment. However, it is not enough simply to tell the child to be imaginative; "the best way to help children write freely is by encouragement, by examples, and by various other inspiring means. It can't be done by fiat."

Koch's practice is to propose opening lines for children—not the traditional "A trip I took" or "My summer vacation," but ones that will engender thoughts and images. "One of the main problems children have as writers is not knowing what to write about. Once they have a subject they like, but may have temporarily forgotten, like wishing, they find a great deal to say." Therefore Koch devotes his efforts to thinking of imaginary forms and lines into which the poem can fall. Here are some of his lines and themes: "I dreamed," "I wish," "X is like a ——," "I used to ——, but now," "Write as if you're a snowflake," "Tell a poem with a lie in every line," "I seem to be ——, but really

I am," "How it would feel to be a Christmas tree." Koch feels a "good poetry idea is one that frees a child's imagination and allows him to discover new things about his feelings and thoughts and about language. A bad poetry idea is one that restricts him; anything emphasizing rhythms, meter, syllable count or expression not natural to his speech, such as 'love is.' " Koch appears to have arrived at a method for evoking "good poetry," for the verses collected in his *Wishes, Lies and Dreams* are delightful.

The young artist as well as the novice can benefit from the criticism and suggestions of an accomplished teacher or creator. Master classes or direct criticisms can convey to the young worker certain skills and perceptions he may lack. Some letters written by T. S. Eliot to a young poet, Keith Douglass, are particularly instructive about the sorts of discriminations an accomplished artist communicates to a younger disciple.

Eliot writes to Douglass about one poem:

You have completed one phase which begins with the very accomplished juvenalia and . . . you have started on another which you have not yet mastered. Of the first phase I felt that as might be expected, there is a certain musical monotony in the rhythms. That does not matter in itself because it is a good thing to go on doing one thing until you are sure that its use is exhausted.

Here Eliot is exhibiting a distance from the creative process in poetry that a young novice cannot be expected to have, but which nonetheless may help him to see his works in perspective. In another communication, Eliot comments more specifically on details of the works. One poem is seen as promising, but in need of special attention because of its "ineffective adjectives." On another poem he writes: "I am not sure that its myth is wholly consistent. For instance toward the end you spoke of exorcising the dead lady in the upper room. One does speak of exorcising ghosts from material houses but in this case the lady to be exorcised seems to be very much more substantial than the house in which you have set her. That is what I mean by inconsistent." As for individual verses, Eliot makes short remarks. After Douglass compares himself to a pillar in a glass house, he asks: "Do you mean that you are also glass?" When Douglass compares himself to a mouse, Eliot notes: "I don't think you should be a pillar and like a mouse in the same stanza." When Douglass refers to an impermanent building, the master finds that "this impermanence should have been clearly established earlier in the poem." Eliot encourages the young poet to find "the exact words for specific experiences of the eye." Although Douglass's early death precludes us from determining whether the lessons were of help to him, it seems clear that such technical advice "within the medium" can serve one who is beginning a career in the arts.

Turning now to the training of the perceiving system, the exercising of one's powers of discrimination emerges as particularly crucial for the skilled audience member or critic. Little work has been done on the optimal way to enhance a heightened sensitivity to style, detail, or nuance, but clearly exposure to and study of the tradition is a necessary step. Scattered reports in the literature indicate that an intensive exposure to certain discrete aspects of objects can sharpen one's discerning powers, both in the arts and in general perceptual tasks. For example, several weeks of looking at paintings can result in substantial increases in stylistic and textural sensitivity. Detailed education in the history of the art form is often advisable, since an understanding of the previous way of realizing works may well prove instructive to the future critic. Making certain comparisons are especially instructive, for example, comparing successive drafts of the same work by an artist, or several works of art treating the same subject matter. Indications of differing merit may serve as a means to bring out unnoticed contrasts. Direct questions may be pertinent, since the critic works more commonly in a verbal domain, but even here the peril of imposing blinding categories is manifest. Arnold Schoenberg succinctly describes a regimen for critical minds: "to look for themselves, to observe, compare, define, describe, weigh, test, draw conclusions, and use them . . . skill that is constantly refreshed and enlarged from the depths of the knowledge that is understanding."

Certain technical adjuncts can contribute to an artist's discrimination and understanding. For example, the ability to read and utilize a notation can be of service to musician, actor, or dancer. The issue here is the proper age at which to introduce such aids. Premature instruction may artificially force the child to construe the elements in his art form in a single way; tardy instruction may put him at a disadvantage in comparison with his peers, or may necessitate his "unlearning" various erroneous practices.

Development of a heightened feeling life probably depends on having a range of experience, plus sufficient knowledge of the code and of interpersonal relations so that one can appreciate embodiments of specific affects and modes. Various forms of therapy and sensitivity may conceivably enrich one's feeling life, but it is doubtful that a direct attack on this area is more effective than a general enrichment of one's experience and contacts. As such experiences accumulate, individuals should be able to embody in their own works and discern in works of others subtler aspects of feeling; they should also become sensitive to the relationship among the feelings and modes articulated within given work.

The education of the feeling system depends in large measure on the individual's increasing ability to perceive significances at the variety of levels on which a work of art proceeds. Someone able to appreciate fine features of the code, variations of form, allusions to recondite subject matter should experience a greater variety of feelings than one for whom the work's meaning is univocal. Depth of "felt" affect may be no different but extent will be; in this way, the feeling system follows upon the discrimination system. Strong affective experiences may also sensitize the individual to aspects of art objects he has never noticed before, as when the loss of a loved one heightens sensitivity to tragedy. In this case, feelings have helped to structure perceptions. Correlatively, excessive self-consciousness or intellectualization about work may result in a dulling of the individual's feeling system.

Incorporation of one's feelings into significant art works is by no means a straightforward matter. In trying to account for the failure of some students to realize their literary promise, one writer comments:

> What was missing for many . . . was simply stimulation: something to write about. The best works arose from chance encounters—some starlings nesting near the school led to a particularly rich harvest of writing and painting, and once a boy's clay portrait led to an impressive series of heads and masks. Work of true quality was rare, because so little school work ever captured real experience on the wing.

Skill alone is not enough: Absence of strong feelings and suggestive experiences will thwart the creative spirit, but the providing of the right stimulus can evoke a torrent of creativity. One sixth grade teacher, for example, called the attention of her class to a spider crawling up the wall of the classroom. This apparently insignificant yet suggestive detail inspired several of the students to extremely interesting initial poetic efforts. One of the poems has been reprinted at the close of this chapter.

CONCLUDING REMARKS

This review of aesthetic education has not provided any foolproof methods for producing genius, but it has suggested a number of guidelines. Individuals concerned with training in the arts should become familiar with the nature and developmental course of the principal psychological systems, and should devise tasks that conform to, rather than undercut, these structures. Finding ways that encourage the productive interaction of the systems is a particularly crucial task. The devising of problems can play an important role in art education, but the most valuable problems are those that open up possibilities to the student and that elicit a range of skills and modal-vectoral qualities, rather than those that have only a single, prescribed method for solution. In general, the most critical experience for the participant in the artistic process seems to be intensive experiences of all sorts with the symbolic medium—this procedure appears to lead to the natural growth, development, and integration of the perceiving, feeling, and making systems. This conclusion follows from our view of the arts as a natural developmental path for man. We have also suggested that the skilled pedagogical intervention at appropriate times, the setting of stimulating questions, and requiring students to realize certain kinds of qualities may serve a useful purpose, guiding the course of aesthetic development. Schoenberg describes the chore of the teacher:

training the mind, by bringing the pupil (according to the stage he has reached) face to face with the difficulties, problems, and inherent terms of the given material, by helping him to recognize them, by forcing him to help himself in this respect, which means letting him make his own mistakes and correcting them afterwards, but also being of assistance to him in finding the solution.

In sum, our discussion has led to the following conclusions: the arts may be viewed as a problem-solving process in which execution is emphasized; artistic development involves mastery of a symbolic medium; and aesthetic education involves the guidance of the three developing systems toward a comprehensive mastery of symbolic media. Artistic problem-solving requires the capacity to capture various modes, affects, and subjective insights within a symbolic medium; direct training of this skill is perilous, but a good teacher can devise situations that will draw productively upon the child's various systems.

Once an individual's making, feeling, and perceiving capacity has matured, and his command of a symbolic medium has been demonstrated, he should be able to participate fully in the artistic process. Particularly characteristic of this state is the capacity to perceive and to produce the more subtle aspects of artistic objects. The creator is able to convey aspects of his own thought, personality, or feeling by incorporating them into a medium; the perceiver is able to appreciate not only the manifest content of a work and its relation to its tradition, but also the particular aspects of feeling and perceiving the creator has embodied in the work. These capacities need not involve explicit recognition —the perceiver does not list the emotions felt or devised by the creator, but should be able to sense the life behind the work—but rather those properties of feeling, perceiving, and making he experiences in his own life, and which another individual can also realize. In short, he must be aware of the arts as a communication process, and sensitive to the communication behind the aesthetic objects. The organization of his feeling life into a stable, consistent personality may facilitate these processes.

In selected cultures and in some age or social groups, widely diverse art objects are lumped together. For example, certain primitive groups feature only one style, and individual differences are discouraged. Yet in treating artistic accomplishment as an idealized end state, I maintain that increased individuation is an inevitable concomitant of the developmental process; as the artist continues to create, as the solutions are adapted, as the rhythms and expressions are conveyed, the feelings and percepts embodied become increasingly individualized. So, too, as he studies facets of a work more carefully, the particulars as well as the universals come to stand out. And although an artist may become increasingly distant from the vogues of the present, no artist creates in total isolation. The revolutionary trends associated with Picasso and Stravinsky or with avant-garde artists of today were anticipated elsewhere, by others who had never heard of these particular masters. Villon and Goya may be cited as artists who worked alone, outside the tradition, but Goya visited Italy and Villon wrote in verse forms centuries old. Joyce's language in *Finnegans Wake* is so far removed from that of the nineteenth century English novel that one tends to forget the less dramatic stylistic shifts from the *Dubliners* to *Ulysses* to *Finnegans Wake*. Even as the trend toward individuation continues, the tradition and the code can never be totally subsumed, and serve to affirm the relationship of the work and the artist to society.

An additional component of style change applies to the greatest of artists. Most creative individuals, having evolved a characteristic way of expressing themselves (say Marc Chagall or Aaron Copland), continue to express themselves without pronounced stylistic evolution after their iconoclastic works. As W. H. Auden remarked of the poet Housman, "the range of theme and emotion is narrow . . . and the poems show no development over the years. On the evidence alone, it would be very difficult to say whether a poem appeared in "A Shropshire Lad," published when he was thirty-seven, or in "Last Poems," published when he was sixty-three." Such artists differentiate further without making radically new strides. With the greatest artists, however, the progression seems different.

For these masters, every new work dictates its own style, the appropriate way for the artist at that moment in history to express his particular materials. Understanding of such works may depend on familiarity with the style. of the era, but requires in addition complete immersion in the particular work in order to uncover its unique norms. In his last poems, Keats created a myriad of styles, each suited for the specific character of the work. One may still be able to recognize the artist—Stravinsky à la Pergolesi, Picasso à la Manet are still our contemporaries—but the pervasive way in which an artist immerses himself in these imitative tributes is most remarkable.

I have sought in this chapter to review biographical and psychological characteristics of the young artist and to reveal some of the steps taken by the great, the near great, and the average as they proceed from the art of childhood to that of the master. The emphasis has fallen, perhaps excessively, on the personal and family factors that contribute to development, but I have tried to suggest as well that the surrounding community exerts its influence on the growing child by supplying standards and providing models, by exerting encouragement and criticism, and by insisting on the effective communication of ideas and feelings. We have seen that even the young child, as part of his birthright, has some sense of form, of the overall structure and balance of an art form. The 7-year-old possesses appreciable sensitivity to aesthetic characteristics, and can evince in his behavior a sense of overall rhythm and balance. His works are also pleasing because, uninhibited and devoid of self-consciousness, he is able to manifest his humanness and individuality in his work. Before sophisticated perception and the mastery of an art form can be attained, however, a maturing period is needed. During that interval, the child, with or without tutelage, develops his own individuality, gaining familiarity with the possibilities of the medium and the tradition of the art form. Only then can he perceive stylistic variations, note the differences between works, and respond to the pressures and the opportunities of his era, first in assimilating the styles about him, later in evolving the means of expression peculiarly suited to his personality and his aesthetic aims.

This discussion may conclude, then, with a brief consideration of differences between child and adult participants in the aesthetic process. Certainly the average adult is notoriously lacking in sensitivity—the artistically naive adult and the average 10-year-old perform about the same on aesthetic appreciation tests. Yet, while it might prove difficult to train the typical adult, whose tastes are formed, there are greater hopes of sharpening the artistic capacity of the growing child. We have suggested some approaches in the above discussion. The reasons for greater optimism about the child's potential revolve about his greater innocence and freedom in expression, properties often attributed to adult artists. Several commentators have sought to characterize the child's perceptual, making, and feeling states and to compare them to that of an adult. As Read expressed it, the child has a fresh perceiving system:

an eye uninfluenced by rational or deductive thought, an eye which accepts the correlation of incompatibilities, the self-sufficiency of images which come into the mind uncalled and unchecked by observation. What the child writes or draws might best be described as an act of poetic intuition and a mastery beyond our logical analysis.

Goethe echoes this sentiment:

every child is to a certain extent a genius and every genius to a certain extent a child. The relationship between the two shows itself primarily as the naivete and sublime ingenuousness that are a fundamental characteristic of true genius.

Another striking parallel involves the sensitivity to formal aspects. D'Amico comments:

If the child is like the artist, the similarity is in his awareness of design for its own sake and his ability to subordinate subject matter and story elements to the elements of form, line and color.

Arnheim concurs:

The children are amateurs like the adults. But with their unspoiled sense of form they can still put all aspects of shape and color totally to the service of the intended meaning. In this sense their work is like that of the accomplished artist. In the average adult of our civilization, however, the sense of form fades rather than keeping up with the increasing complexity of the mind.

Finally, Slade points out the continuities between children and adult artists:

After the age of six or so, this gift of rhythm appears naturally in child work, but the adult had to toil hard "for it" and often does not attain it. Those who are most successful in doing so are, for the most part, those who have actually retained it from childhood. We call them great artists.

The problem for students of artistic development is to describe how these traits, at first discernible in all children, become heightened in some, while atrophying in so many more. We have tried to elucidate this problem here, but far more extensive examination will be required before it can be satisfactorily resolved.

We see that the normal child and the accomplished artist have a sense of balance and form, because neither is overly influenced by his critical capacities, his culture's categories, or someone else's patterns of behaving. Yet the attitudes toward art and the ultimate excellence of the age groups are quite dissimilar. Whereas the adult has studied the code and has developed a style, the child merely expresses himself through the most ready means of expression—his calligraphy. Indeed, "the child's gift controls him, whereas the artist controls his gift. A child's will destroys his pictures. The artist does not have an eye at age fifteen. The artist gives reign to his instinct only after he has mastered it." Another crucial difference inheres in the realm of will, control, interest, self-consciousness, and determination. The child plays at his art while the adult artist wrestles with it. "What is for the artist a serious and often very arduous task—training hand and eye to become absolutely obedient and trustworthy servants of the artistic will—is for the child pure pleasure. The child repeats with ceaseless delight every new work, every new grasp, every new stroke." The young child often has the state of mind—relaxation and freshness—which the adult artist seeks. His dominant feeling life and tone are close to that of the artist in his free-flowing periods. Yet only if these tendencies can be supplemented by a sense of control, a powerful technique, and a subtle comprehension of the culture and the code—in short, the developed systems operating within a symbolic medium—can the child become a masterful artist. As Matisse says, "Nothing, I think, is more dangerous for a child painter than to paint a rose because, before he can do so, he has first to forget all the roses that ever were painted. . . . Thus a work of art is the climax of a long work of preparation. The artist takes from his surrounding everything that can nourish his internal vision either directly . . . or by analogy." Such a development takes a lifetime; one lives and works as an artist for many years in order to have the privilege of reexperiencing, if only momentarily and through a symbolic medium, the feeling life of every normal child. This tantalizing connection between the child and the adult artist has fascinated many observers; the ambiguity, nostalgia, and irony surrounding this relationship has been neatly caught in the comic drawing reproduced at the end of the chapter.

In highlighting the developing artist, I have commented little on others who participate in the artistic process: the audience member whose presence and exercised feelings are essential for the creator; the performer who helps to translate conceptions into a palpable form; the critic who discriminates among works and who interprets them for the public. To be sure, much of the above discussion on aesthetic education has applications to those participants as well. Yet there is a sense in which artistic development is most properly concerned with making— and hence with the artist—while other participation in the aesthetic process must, in order.to interact profitably with the artistic work, realize a portion of the artist's experience. Still the trade-off is not wholly one-sided; the artist must depend, as well, on his perceiving and feeling systems. An attempt to repair the imbalance in emphasis is made in the final chapter, as I seek to relate the three developing systems to these different end states. Further comment is also needed on some questions raised in this chapter, and so I have interpolated discussions on the limits of art, quality of art, the relations between art and neurosis, art and psychosis, and art and science. I will try, finally, to suggest the nature of a kind of thinking that has not figured in our discussion— scientific problem-solving; we will consider those cognitive realms where symbol use honors explicit canons of precision and logic. This will require a return to the work of Piaget, which has remained in the background throughout our discussion of development.

THE SPIDER'S WEDDING

I sat on the barn's steps and watched the black spider coming
    towards me.
I felt like screaming
But I moved aside a little, and the dark creature went up a
    beam.
It stopped
And turned back
And stared at me, and stared.
It said
"Move on. My business has nothing to do with you.
I shall stand here until you go."
So I moved on, looking back over my shoulder to see what it
    would do.
As it went on, I ran back silently to see.
After a few minutes, back the spider came
Proud now, with an air of arrogance.
By his side, walked shyly, another spider.
A new bride.
When they came by me, they stood
And stared and stared,
Then they went on.
"Ha. A spider's wedding," I thought.

A SIXTH-GRADE GIRL

FIGURE 20   Drawing by Frascino; © 1972, The New Yorker Magazine, Inc.

SEVEN

THE RELATIONSHIP OF THE ARTS TO SCIENCE, ILLNESS, AND TRUTH

SCIENTIFIC DEVELOPMENT AS DESCRIBED BY PIAGET

The most comprehensive of the systems seeking to elucidate human development is that formulated by Jean Piaget. Concerned mainly with the development of knowledge, Piaget described in detail how conceptions of many scientific and quasi-scientific objects evolve during childhood. His account of these developmental trajectories and the rich assortment of protocols he has collected are invaluable sources about the genesis of reason. What constitutes Piaget's claim to a new psychological paradigm, however, is his demonstration that every child's thought, irrespective of domain, passes through the same stages as it tends towards adult thought.

After a 1- or 2-year sensorimotor period during which the child constructs, on the practical level, a model of time, space, object, and causality, he enters the preoperational period, during which he employs symbols to represent aspects of the world that until then he has known only through action. Piaget's description of the preoperational period, probably the sparest he has written, is a most valuable one, which seems to be generally consistent with the viewpoint adopted here. He suggests that in his initial use of symbols the child abstracts general properties from the world. Initial symbol use involves the principles of the making system; the same landmarks of development that first occur in the sensorimotor period must be reached again on the symbolic level. Piaget emphasizes the making system; he does not have analogies to the perceiving and feeling systems. For him, perceiving is a type of making activity.

Yet Piaget recognizes that the mechanisms operative in perception are different from those operative in "cognition"; and has devoted a number of works to explicating this distinction. Thus a reconciliation between his notions and the model of making and perceiving described here might be possible.

In considering sexual symbolism, affective schemata, and other psychoanalytic concerns, Piaget, despite his disclaimers, comes close to dealing with a separate "feeling" system. If his strong animus against a dualism of thought and feeling precludes his outlining a separate system, still he seems to recognize that the child's feeling life—the particular experiences that arouse powerful affect—may exert strong influence on the percepts and making behavior of the preoperational period. On such occasions Piaget underplays his notion of affect as the "motor" of development, and gives considerable attention to the child's phenomenal reactions to objects and events. Indeed, it might well be possible to reformulate *Play, Dreams, and Imitation* according to the three systems. Play would be the predominance of making over perceiving, imitating would represent the prevalence of perceiving over making, and dreams would represent the esoteric domain in which affective life organizes experience.

Piaget describes play, dreams, and imitation of children up to the age of 5 or so. Nowhere else to my knowledge does Piaget ever pick up the threads he has so tantalizingly introduced in this work. For Piaget, these capacities belong to the figurative realm, that form of cognition dependent upon external configurations; and his own interest lies almost exclusively in the operative realm, wherein active transformation of objects is accentuated. The life of the imagination, which is his primary concern in *Play, Dreams, and Imitation,* ceases to be discussed, and Piaget returns his attention to the questions that have always concerned him—the ways in which the child reasons, uses numbers, and understands causality, geometry, and space. In short, he concentrates on the child as potential scientist. Piaget has won the most adherents and has engendered the greatest controversy by making the claim that every child—certainly every Western child—passes through two further stages of mental evolution.

At about the age of 7, the child becomes capable of a series of mental operations that constitute a structured whole—he constructs a world view through his concrete operations. The operations are actions performed mentally; in our terms, the making system is functioning on the symbolic level. (In addition, mental operations are dependent upon discriminations in the environment; however, such discriminations are not in themselves sufficient to produce operations, which are active transformations, rather than faithful records, of what has been perceived.) The concrete operator, rather than merely arranging material objects in some way, has become cognizant of all kinds of rearrangements, and is able to achieve these rearrangements in his head as well as in his world. Concrete operations involve an understanding that certain dimensions of the manipulable, physical world remain invariant, whatever particular actions may be performed upon them, and that a variety of classifications or seriations are possible so long as one does not shift criteria during the course of an operation. For example, the child realizes that a ball of clay or a container of water does not vary in amount, regardless of the shape of the vessel or wad into which it is converted. The child can master such a conservation because he becomes able mentally to transform the material. In particular, he can realize the central "reversal" operation of pouring the water out or squishing the clay back into its original container or form. A rearrangement of matter, not a creation or annihilation, has taken place. Analogously, the child looks at a series of objects and appreciates that each dimension provides an equally valid way to subdivide them. A set of toys may be grouped according to size, color, or use. He appreciates further that in a multi-colored array there are more objects than there are brown objects, because he is able to perform addition (subtraction and multiplication) of classes. Piaget does not claim that a child at a certain moment suddenly becomes able to solve every concrete problem; while concrete operations are logical procedures, they are (because of the child's piecemeal development) at first tied to particular concrete materials. But Piaget does make the powerful claim that all concrete operational solutions involve schemes isomorphic with a small number of "groupings"; each grouping is a representation in formal language of a large set of problems that require a certain logical operation.

Every normal individual becomes able to handle problems involving concrete operations within a few years of learning to speak. Once he has reached this stage, the child can deal much more surely with the world, because he now has a sophisticated notion of which things change and which remain constant. He can also employ the vocabulary of the sciences with some assuredness. Many individuals never advance beyond concrete operations. A small number lack the potential; for others, the problems and questions that arise in their milieu never require more sophisticated cognitive behavior. Incapacity to progress beyond concrete operations into formal operations prevents the individual from being a scientist, however.

According to Piaget, scientific thought inheres in the ability to create (verbal) propositions that can refer to a specific physical situation, and in the subsequent ability to perform operations (negating and conjoining, as in propositional calculus), exploring on the level of discourse the relations between elements cited in the proposition. The capacity implicitly to perform the operations involved in logical calculus, and to master a Viergruppe that deals with the interrelations between a series of operations, has been termed *formal operations.* In general terms, the formal operator is equipped to solve the sort of problems the scientist tackles in a laboratory. For example, the formal but not the concrete operator can derive the principles governing floating bodies, the oscillation of a pendulum, or the course of a billiard ball. An individual with concrete operations (or even a preoperational subject) can sometimes solve a particular problem through trial-and-error manipulations or guesswork. But the concrete subject is at best able to make a rough statement about the processes involved, and will not be able to make reliable and accurate predictions about variations of the paradigm—one cannot wax hypothetical until one can manipulate propositions. Nor is the correct answer indicative of formal operations; the subject must reveal his reasoning, which must involve *operations on propositions* if he is to be considered a formal operator. The formal operator is both scientifically and verbally sophisticated. He knows what factors contribute to a certain effect, he can alter the effect reliably by manipulating the correct variable, and, most importantly, he can outline a set of governing principles for covering every contingency. He is, by the age of 14, a veritable scientist, a potential collaborator of Piaget's.

Piaget has outlined in compelling fashion the possible nature of exploration and explanation in an important area of human endeavor. He has indicated which characteristics prevent the individual from being a sophisticated scientist until a certain time, and which factors anchor him at a level where he can tinker around and make provocative generalizations but not really follow through consistently on his beliefs. Only the formal operator can partake of that sphere in which, as a consequence of the ability to reason with propositions, the systematic outlining and execution of experiments and the ability to formulate and understand theories become possible. Scientific objects are embedded in propositions, and the propositions are manipulated while the objects remain intact. The distinctions between formal and concrete operations explains why a youngster can be an accomplished chess player at a tender age; he need not consider every alternative, nor convince scientific colleagues of his flawlessness—he need only empirically outsmart an opponent through keener deployment of his perceiving system. The distinction incidentally clarifies why Piaget's first paper (issued at age 11!) was an eyewitness account of observing an albino sparrow—a description rather than a logical demonstration—and why new theorems do not issue from an individual who has yet to attain the formal operations. Far from considering Piaget as refuting my position, it is possible to say that his picture of scientific development complements this description of artistic development. The accounts of sensorimotor and preoperational development feature making and perceiving systems proceeding by assimilation and accommodation of schemes. Piaget does not speak of a feeling system, since he resists speculation about phenomenal experience; yet in his discussions of affective development and the preoperational stage he allows for some of the machinery and the factors we have attributed to the feeling system.

For the early years of development, then, I find no serious disagreement between Piaget and the present outline. Discussion of modal-vectoral properties has suggested, furthermore, that the psychoanalytic, ethological, Wernerian, and Piagetian approaches have striking commonalities which offer promise for a holistic theory of human development. Certain notions of stage and sequence employed here are common to Freud and Piaget. The mechanisms of schematic development and interaction proposed by Piaget, and the hypothesis of special status for certain modes suggested by Lorenz, Freud, and Erikson have also been invoked here. Pursuing this line of argument, we have attempted to demonstrate that modal-vectoral perception, making, and feeling are a basic way of constructing the world, and that this way persists throughout development, enabling the subject to create and appreciate symbolic objects and to experience in a full way interpersonal relations.

It is concerning the years after the age of 6 or so, the height of the symbolic period, that the present position diverges from the Piagetian formulation. The ages 5 to 7 represent an important milestone in aesthetic development, when the child becomes sensitive to and able to incorporate in his own works formal aspects of the arts. While development continues far beyond these years, indeed throughout life, the development is a deepening process involving the same principles, rather than a total reorganization of systems. Piaget's interests, however, lie in the child's progress toward the practice of science. In this realm, additional reorganizations are necessary so that various operations essential to an understanding of the physical world can be performed, first directly with objects, then mentally, and finally on propositions describing the world. This reorganization can and in most cases will affect the developing artist too. My feeling, however, is that the development of operational thought· is not a vital part of artistic development; indeed, it may sometimes be inimical to it. Piaget's waning interest in imagination and in other playful products of the mind suggests that he may also sense the tension between scientific and artistic development. Thus, as indicated in Chapter 1, I have reserved the term *cognition* for the kinds of psychological processes involved in Piagetian operations that cut across particular symbolic media. As these operations do not appear to play a significant role in artistic development, the area we have investigated has been described exclusively in terms of the three developing systems.

FORMAL OPERATIONS AND ART

Vital though formal operations may be for the practicing scientist, they seem of little consequence for participants in the artistic process, with the exception of critics. This is an empirical assertion that should be tested, but the relevant variables are not yet sufficiently well spelled out to make such a test feasible. Perhaps the chief stumbling block is the present status of the term *formal operations*. So far, the principal studies have been done by Piaget and Inhelder. These studies involve posing classical physics problems to a child, and the child's attempt to discover the principles underlying the physical phenomenon. If formal operations should be restricted to this narrow terrain, then it is most likely that artists need not have mastered them. After all, relatively few adults in our society are able to solve such problems, and it is doubtful that anyone in a primitive society could handle them, for the whole emphasis on hypothetic-deductive thought and scientific reasoning seems restricted to certain Western cultures.

One may also think of formal operations in a more general way (as Piaget has sometimes done), as an ability to reflect on one's own thought processes, to weigh arguments, and to deal with hypothetical possibilities. When the definition of formal operations is widened in this way, it becomes more difficult to assert that the capacity is limited to adolescents. After all, younger children certainly talk about possibilities, argue with one another, and entertain alternative courses of action. Preadolescents criticize their own art works incessantly. Still, this type of thinking and reasoning seems most characteristic of adolescents, and indeed the capacity to engage in sustained examination of one's own thought processes and to deal with propositional thought may rest upon certain neurological changes that occur at the onset of puberty (perhaps allied to those that impede language learning).

Caught between an overly wide and a very restrictive notion of formal operations, the assertion that the artist does not need to be able to perform them is difficult to evaluate. Let me therefore confront the question from a different angle: the nature of concrete operations.

According to Piaget, concrete operations (like formal operations) involve the capacity to perform certain kinds of logical operations upon elements. By their nature these operations are related to the particular concrete realm being investigated: thus a child will show ability to conserve, to order, to classify in some realms earlier than in others, because he has had greater experience working with certain materials. This part of the definition of concrete operations seems most relevant to our discussion of artistic development. While one might find it difficult to demonstrate that a practicing artist, performer, or audience member must correctly conserve volume, or multiply classes, any participant in the artistic process clearly will need to achieve competence with at least one concrete area—a particular symbol system. Such a familiarity takes a number of years to develop, as the child discovers the referents for various symbols, the permissible arrangements of these symbols, the way the symbol system is used within a particular culture, the general norms of balance, rhythm, harmony, and form governing its use in the arts. The ability to use a symbol system intelligently, skillfully, and above all, consistently, seems closely related to the possession of concrete operations, to the ability to anticipate arrangement and rearrangement of symbolic elements. It may well be, however, that the formalization of concrete operations will have to be expanded beyond its present series of nine groupings.

Because I find little evidence that an artist need be a formal operator, and am even dubious that the nine groupings of concrete operations are necessary for the artist, I have viewed artistic development as encompassing only two broad stages: a sensorimotor period in which the principles of the making, feeling, and perceiving systems are first manifest; and a symbolic stage in which the three systems recapitulate their development on the symbolic level and in which the child becomes well versed with various symbol systems, preeminently natural language. (The increasing capacity to revise one's own work, which emerges in the preadolescent years, does not require a further cognitive reorganization). The development characteristic of the symbolic stage never ends; one can increase one's mastery of a symbol system indefinitely, and this trend epitomizes the accomplished artist. Nonetheless, we have seen that a child will generally have at least a first-level approximation of competence with that symbol system by the years of middle childhood; and, indeed, development in primitive cultures evaluated according to

Piagetian standards rarely goes beyond the level of logical operations attained by the 10-year-old child in our culture. The outstanding aesthetic and rhetorical products produced by adults in such cultures indicate, however, that increasing mastery of symbolic systems can certainly be expected in the years following latency, even if formal operations are never used.

One might concede that formal operations are not necessary in other cultures, yet maintain that in our culture the artist needs (or is best served by) the possession of formal operations. This question is extremely vexing, because of difficulty in gaining sufficient distance from our culture or sufficient intimacy with another. It is my impression that, while the critic in Western culture definitely needs some type of formal operations, the artist does not need them for his run of skills and functions. He need not deal with his artistic objects in propositional or hypothetical form. Formal operations may even at times serve to hinder artistic development, since the tendency to focus on underlying content, to abstract out meaning, to be sensitive to the explicit demands of a task, to proceed in a systematic and exhaustive manner, and, above all, to translate problems and questions into logical-propositional terms may all militate against the sensitivity to detail and nuance and the faithfulness to the particular properties of object and medium that are so vital for the artist. The stress on critical thought in adolescence is also a mixed blessing for artistic accomplishment. I stress this point because children of adolescent age performed somewhat more poorly in studies of literary and musical skill than those who were still at the concrete level, and the explanation for this poor performance seems plausibly made in terms of the interfering characteristics of formal operations. As further evidence of the incompatibility between scientific development and artistic achievement, we may recall Galton's remarks about the development of abstract thought: "An over-early perception of sharp mental images is antagonistic to the acquirement of habits of highly generalized and abstract thought, especially when these types of reasoning are carried on by words as symbols; if the faculty of seeing the pictures was ever possessed by men who think hard, it is very apt to be lost by disuse." And Herbert Read's conclusion about contemporary artists, though probably too extreme a statement, is worth noting: "My theory is that any decay in art and kind of stylistic decadence, to put it most simply, is due to the artist becoming self-conscious, or, if you like, conscious of elements and styles which are not spontaneous." In contrast, in certain primitive societies all members are regarded as artists, possibly because they are less handicapped by the possession of formal operation.

Still, there may be some forms of art in which formal operations play a facilitating or essential role. Certainly computer art, and other strictly regulated genres such as 12 tone music, call for mathematical sophistication, which may include certain formal operations. Furthermore, self-conscious parodies of others' styles and of one's own style, which have become artistic trademarks during recent centuries, may require an ability to stipulate another person's aesthetic assumptions and to treat them in a systematic way. An argument could be made that such advanced forms as irony, parody, and satire involve formal level mechanisms. The ability to discuss one's own work and that of others, though hardly requiring formal operations, may well be heightened by the acquisition of logical skills.

All the same, one difference between these sorts of practices and those investigated by Piaget seems patent. To solve Piagetian problems one cannot merely manipulate apparatuses. The subject must give reasons for his actions and demonstrate that he has a consistent plan of attack that touches all contingencies. In effect, he must state the physical law with all its ramifications, refute alternative hypotheses, and reconstruct the entire argument on another level of discourse. The artist, however, encounters no need to step outside his particular medium, to comment on what he is doing, to realize his efforts in words, mathematical symbols, or some logical language. All the exploration can be done within the medium itself. In order to perform these high-level practices or achieve high-level effects, much practice with these media is obviously needed. The artist needs to master his chosen symbol system, while at the same time retaining distance from his efforts. Many years may pass before the child is aware of the implications of his work and able to evaluate it realistically. Yet all this can be on the tacit level— there is no need to articulate (or even to be self-conscious) of what one is doing. The effects can all be achieved simply by perceiving what others have done, or what one has done himself, and then by bringing about certain changes in one's making behavior so as to capitalize on those discriminations. I see no reason why the concrete operator cannot achieve all of these tasks, no reason to conclude that propositional reasoning is essential, since these tasks demand only mastery of a medium, not any translation or restatement of the elements into another symbolic tongue. Again, all commenting is done within the medium itself.

The differences between the artist and the scientist reflect two elements on which we have previously dwelled. There is, first of all, the "preformed" nature of artistic symbol systems, the fact that all resources available to the mature artist are in a certain sense present in any use of the medium, ensuring that all works will reflect potentials of the medium. No aspect of literature, of painting, of music is unambiguously absent from all works by children, because the very use of the medium involves resources children cannot suppress. One might be able to demonstrate that children are unaware of the full potential of the medium, but self-consciousness seems beside the point in artistic practice. In sharp contrast, it is simply erroneous to say that the child has all logical reasoning equipment at his disposal from the begnning. Classical and contemporary logic are symbolic systems that depend on some form of instruction by the culture; Piaget's research is full of examples of logical principles that children are clearly unable to appreciate or use correctly. Comprehension of logical principles can be tested by posing problems in a number of different but logically related realms. Such transfer would be an ill-conceived, if not an impossible test of mastery of an aesthetic medium.

The other reason for the different status of the artist's work is that, both for the creator and for the perceiver, the art work inheres in the execution rather the conception. In an art work, there will be a variety of levels and significance, and no one can claim that an observer has totally understood or misunderstood the art work's meaning—much of it inheres in surface aspects that can be appreciated by a young child, other parts may elude even the most skilled critics. In contrast, as a scientific principle has a conceptual status, it can be translated and reformulated by others; it is thus possible to determine whether or not such a tenet had been understood by a child. From the creator's point of view, he is the sole producer of a given art work, and is therefore reflected in it in many ways and levels. No one can presume to complete or to reformulate his work, for the work inheres in its particular form. The kind of translation possible in the realm of science, and reflected in the use of formal operations, is again irrelevant for the creative artist, whose work has no conceptual status apart from its unique realization.

While this discussion cannot pretend to cover all of the aspects involved in determining the operational level of artistic practice, I hope it has suggested that work conducted totally within a symbolic medium, not subject to or requiring recapture in another medium, has a different status from work which, *by its very nature*, is a translation and can be applied in an indefinite number of realms. Precisely because Piaget's theory is so well suited to elucidating the general nature of scientific thought, and because it stresses the importance of abstraction from a concrete area of experience, it is not easily transferred to the artistic realm in which procedures are so different.

THE ARTISTIC AND THE SCIENTIFIC PROCESSES

Consideration of the similarities and distinctions between the scientific process and the artistic process may aid in understanding the limited relevance of Piaget's cognitive theory for the present work. To as great an extent as art, science is a form of communication; the information it conveys is of a different order, however. Whereas the artist is interested in the subjective world, and is intent upon conveying his understanding and feeling for the world of human individuals or the "living" aspects of objects, the scientist more typically investigates the world of objects or treats individuals as objects. The scientist does not create an object in which aspects of himself are embodied so that the beholder can obtain subjective information about the scientist and his ideas. At least, so artistic a view of science is far from the intention of most scientists, who indeed take pains to exorcise traces of themselves from their works. The scientist has set up a series of questions about the world of objects; he seeks to communicate in as simple and unambiguous fashion as possible just what he has discovered about those objects or facets of the world. Further, the scientist does not need to exemplify his message in the object nor to make the form of the message attractive in itself; instead he desires to have the message maximally translatable so it can fit into a variety of contexts, illustrating and elucidating a number of phenomena. The artist, as we have seen, communicates (often wittingly) a part of himself, and is vitally concerned with the *form* of the message. It is perhaps for such reasons that many individuals have questioned the validity of applying the methods and practice of science to the arts. William James cautioned in a letter:

> It strikes me that no good will ever come to Art as such from the analytic study of Aesthetics—harm rather, if the abstraction could in any way be made the basis of practice. The difference between the first and second best things in art absolutely seem to escape verbal definition—it is a matter of a hair, a shade, an inner quiver of some kind—yet what miles away in point of persuasiveness. . . . Absolutely the same verbal formula applies to the supreme success and to the thing that just misses and yet the verbal formulas are all that your aesthetic will give.

And Wolf Kahn speaks of the incompatibility of artist and academe:

> The university cannot provide [future artists] with the proper climate altogether. The academic climate is formed by the prevailing rationalism, verbal modes, and abstract symbols as well as a regard for the intellect and its categories. Artists are dedicated to the irrational, to unconscious processes,

to intuition and to the unique particular. Traditionally artists have been allied with the trades not the scholar. Their audience existed and still exists in the market place rather than the academy.

Whereas the scientist has need of formal operations in order to contribute to and appreciate the work of the scientific community, the artist may pursue his own work without the ability to reason in propositions and without a coherent philosophy, so long as he is able to handle his medium competently. Eliot said of Shakespeare and Dante, "neither did any real thinking—that was not their job," and he said of Henry James that "his mind was so fine, it was never violated by thought." Eliot is here questioning the artist's need to reason like a critic or scientist. Why should the artist describe objects in propositions and then evaluate the propositions with respect to another? Such an exercise is irrelevant to the artist's practice—only his abilities to create objects, to perceive flaws, and to correct them through an alteration in the medium matter. Thus the composer Kirchner contrasts the reconditeness of science with the accessibility of arts:

The riddle of science requires a learned cryptographic methodology not ordinarily available to the non-professional, whereas no amount of abstruse and elegant Gongorism can be used to justify a score's failure to be "understood" by the sensitive non-professional, once an intimacy with the stylistic language is obtained.

And his teacher Schoenberg indicates that too faithful an adherence to principles can be fatal in the arts:

What distinguishes art from science is: that there should not be principles of the kind one has to use on principle; that the one "narrowly" defines what must be left "wide open" in the other: that musical logic does not answer to "if . . . then" but enjoys making use of the possibilities excluded by if–then.

While in the education of scientists efforts are made to provide as many principles as possible and to bring students closely in contact with the work of their teachers, the proximity of a teacher's work and the formalization of artistic principles is thought by many art educators to be damaging. Rules are ultimately there to be imaginatively transformed, deliberately violated, or subtly altered.

Despite these differences, one can discern an approximate isomorphism between the scientific and artistic processes. In each domain there is a message from a creator—in the case of the sciences, the originator of the scientific theorem or the experimenter reporting his result. The audience of the sciences is primarily composed of critics, individuals who share a knowledge of the field and can ascertain whether the creator has made a legitimate contribution to the scientific canons. One could postulate an audience analogous to the audience for *objets d'art,* which reads the scientific journals and scours the newspaper reports chiefly for the pleasurable feeling such reading affords. Although such an audience—composed of readers of *Scientific American* and the *New York Times*—may actually exist, it differs from the aesthetic audience in several ways. First of all, it is limited in size: Despite the magazine's attention to presentation, fewer individuals presumably read the *Scientific American* for its entertainment or arousal value than would read a novel. Then, too, while the art audience must be exposed directly to the aesthetic object—hearing about a performance or painting is scarcely equivalent to seeing them—scientific audiences can be informed second-hand about an interesting discovery. Indeed the original papers might well not be comprehensible to the layman. Furthermore, one may enjoy the audience role simply by hearing a poem (or viewing a painting) which, though not completely understood, can nonetheless elicit pleasant feelings, but comprehension is essential in the select audience of the scientific process. The meaning, rather than the surface features of sound or sight, is of overriding import in the scientific process.

The central dyad of creator-audience seems to be replaced in the scientific process by the tighter network of fellow creators and critics. These roles are often combined and interchangeable—most scientists competent enough to appreciate a scientific investigation are themselves creators. Furthermore, the ability to criticize a piece of science competently is in itself creative, for a penetrating critique of a scientific object may contain within it seeds of a more satisfactory formulation. (In this sense, most academic disciplines—and preeminently, philosophy—involve a merging of creative and critical roles.) In the arts, a critique that surpasses the original object is rare.

The discrepancy between creator and performer does, I think, exist in the sciences, but not in the same way as in the arts. The artistic performer generally examines the plan or score of the creator and seeks to realize it in a way faithful to the creator's intention, while at the same time inducing appropriate response in the audience. Only by an unreasonable stretch of the imagination does a scientific creator of this type exist, though the engineer's role may indeed be viewed in this way. On the other hand, there is certainly a division of labor within the scientific community between those who formulate questions and problems—strictly cognitive and notational steps—and those who go to the laboratory or the world to test such hypotheses. In the one instance, discrimination and conceptualization are primary; in the other instances, careful experimental techniques and, in many cases, a specific manual and making skills are required. That different temperaments and personalities characterize the researcher and the theoretician in the sciences is clear; in fact, the qualities of the researcher—the less pensive, more dogged, outgoing, rugged, extroverted scientist—may well approach the traits of the artistic performer, who is also, in a sense, realizing someone else's notions. Still the role of performer and creator are far more frequently united in the sciences than in the arts, because the lack of audience and the relatively straightforward procedures of most experimental tasks enables a relatively larger proportion of scientists to "perform" in their field.

Some remarks have already been made about problem-solving in the sciences and the arts. The scientist generally takes his problem from a commonly recognized area on which other scientists may well be working, and he draws on a variety of acceptable methods to solve it. He has some notion of his goal, and some checks along the way as to his success. In most cases he and his fellow scientists will agree when the problem has been solved, the formula derived, the model constructed. Conceptualization is vital, execution often delegable. The artist, on the other hand, only rarely tries to solve a particular problem that the tradition has handed him and that others are also tackling (except some highly general problems as "imitating nature"; more specific tasks are assigned chiefly as drill). The artist's problem is more likely to be the representation or articulation of a modal/vectoral quality. He will rely on his own rather than on "established" methods or techniques to accomplish the problem, he will encounter a variety of unanticipated problems along the way, and will have only intuitive notions of his success in execution. While the solution of scientific problem will usually be apparent, there may be disputes about the artist's accomplishment. The tensions of problem-solving, followed by a release at the resolution, nevertheless characterize both processes.

Interestingly enough, while the problem-solving behavior of the average scientist and artist are not strikingly similar, there are stronger affinities at the poles of scientific and artistic creation. The purely commercial artist may follow formulas to such an extent that he is akin to the scientist performing routine calculations. At the other extreme, the most original scientist, such as Darwin or Freud, who is charting out a wholly new area of investigation, shares characteristics with the revolutionary artist. He too must "convince others" of his orientation, devise fresh language and novel procedures, conceptualize a field anew, and rely heavily on subjective intuitions. And, like good works of art, pioneering works in a new scientific area often defy translation. Probably the chief difference between science and art at this level is that the scientist is still intent upon objectifying what he is studying and retains as his goal the eventual translation of his findings into some more general conceptual coin. He seeks agreement with his formulation rather than approval of its form or evocation of pleasurable affect. Even the most scientifically oriented artists, such as Leonardo, the Impressionists, or the Cubists, would not consider replacing their works by some kind of more conclusive and inclusive formula, and remain relatively uninterested in the audience's "agreement" with their views.

Although the scientist who wants to propagandize his views or launch a new field requires the creative, communicative qualities of his aesthetic counterparts, his relation to the scientific tradition is more stringently dictated. The scientist works within a paradigm that has been fairly well established in his field, and tries to answer questions raised by that paradigm. His problems are dictated by recent research in the field, permissible operations are legislated, and only the foolhardy researcher remains ignorant of what his colleagues have accomplished. To be sure, the artist belongs to a tradition as well; few artists create objects that, when viewed from sufficient perspective, appear radically different from those of their contemporaries or immediate predecessors.

Unless he chooses to do so, the artist need not strive to answer problems that others about him are seeking to solve, immerse himself in the most recent work of the field, nor choose a genre with strong constraints. The arts are not cumulative, at least not in the same way as the sciences. An artist can master the medium and get a feeling for what is possible by studying the literature, painting, or music of the sixteenth century, as readily as by immersing himself in contemporary productions. Some might think him peculiar, but ultimately he will be judged on how well he deploys aesthetic materials, and not on the contemporaneousness of his achievement. And if his tastes happen to attach more to the sixteenth than to the twentieth century, this factor will not deter others from considering his works. But the prospect of a scientist familiar only with past centuries or especially attached to the sixteenth century is patently ludicrous, and would rightly be rejected by those colleagues interested in a systematic cumulation rather than in a hodgepodge of scientific knowledge. Should a scientist die while in the midst of a work, it is likely that others could finish it; if all his works were destroyed, they could be reconstructed by those privy to his conceptualization. But who can finish a dead artist's work? The work inheres in his execution, and an approximate recreation of a burnt painting or fragmentary score is unacceptable.

CREATIVITY IN ART AND SCIENCE

In the recent spate of literature on creativity spurred by fears of Russian technological superiority, American psychology has made much of the faculty of divergent thinking—for example, the ability to think of a variety of uses for an implement, word, or picture. This capacity is considered important to creators in all realms, though it is used more frequently as an index for scientific potential. Thomas Kuhn has rightly pointed out a confusion inherent in this formulation of the scientific process:

> Most of you are really in search of the inventive personality, a sort of person who does emphasize divergent thinking but whom the United States has already produced in abundance. In the process you may be ignoring certain of the essential requisites of the basic scientist, a rather different sort of person to whose ranks America's contribution have as yet been notoriously sparse.

Kuhn suggests that the scientist, as opposed to the inventor, has rather strong convergent tendencies: far from looking for new uses for something extant, he has a sense of specific problems that must be solved if certain discrepancies in the scientific corpus are to be comprehended. This unifying aim motivates a scientist; even if he should eventually come to reject the whole paradigm and initiate a novel approach, this result will grow out of his attempts to work within a tradition, rather than out of any desire on his part to be revolutionary.

If the "divergent model" is not particularly applicable to the enterprise of science, it is scarcely appropriate for the arts. That artist is rare indeed who is interested in thinking of new uses for an item or in combining items in a new way, for their own sake; the items he works with are the ones that spontaneously occur to him or that arise out of his work. The artist may search for new means as he strives to complete an object, but these will grow out of his knowledge of technique, not out of verbal associations of the type honored in science.

For a scientist, as for an artist, the medium in which one works is important. The crucial medium for most scientists is a logical language, which they bring to bear on data and questions from a particular discipline. Scientists have mastered this medium when they are able to solve problems in the manner of logician—to conceptualize the variables and relate them in an appropriate way. The artist has mastered his medium —words, paints, colors—when he has the capacity to express and execute a desired feeling or theme in an effective manner. Inventiveness may be helpful for the artist or scientist, but it is only a byproduct, hardly a goal. An analysis of the skills involved in artistic creativity suggests that attempts to train divergent thought may be as paltry or misplaced in the arts as they appear to be in the sciences.

Among the mechanisms that aid creative thinkers in the sciences and the arts is a developed sense of gestalt perception that enables the individual to bring numerous perspectives to bear on the same process. We have already noted the pervasiveness of gestalt perception in the arts, and should now acknowledge its centrality in the sciences as well. Lorenz has attempted to describe this aspect of the perceiving system:

> When the scientist confronted with a multitude of irregular and apparently irreconcilable facts, suddenly "sees" the general regularity ruling them all, when the explanation of the hitherto inexplicable all at once "jumps out" at him with the suddenness of a revelation, the experience of this happening is fundamentally similar to that other when the hidden Gestalt in a puzzle picture surprisingly stares out from the confusing background of irrelevant details.

Lorenz claims that this form of perception is more suggestive and central to scientific practice than the sort of logical operations needed to execute formal proofs.

> Without intuition the world would present to us nothing but an impenetrable and chaotic tangle of unconnected facts. It would be quite impossible for us to find the laws and regularities prevailing in this apparent chaos if the mathematical and statistical operations of our conscious mind were all that we had at our disposal. It is here that the unconsciously working computer of our Gestalt perception is distinctly superior to all conscious performed computations. This superiority is due to the fact that intuition, like other highly differentiated types of Gestalt perception, is able to draw into simultaneous consideration a far greater number of premises than any of our conscious conclusions. It is the practically unlimited capacity for taking in relevant details and leaving out the irrelevant ones which makes the computer of this highest form of Gestalt perception so immensely sensitive an organ. The most important advantage of intuition is that it is "seeing" in the deepest sense of the word.

Once the scientist has determined what problem he wishes to solve, the large reservoir of information that he has accumulated in the past is drawn upon in a variety of ways as he searches for a solution. The inventor Edwin Land has described this process, highlighting the importance of the atmosphere in which a solution is most likely to emerge.

> I find it very important to work autonomously for long hours when I am beginning to see solutions to a problem. At such times atavistic competences seem to come welling up. You are handling so many variables at a barely conscious level that you can't afford to be interrupted. If you are it may take a year to cover the same ground you could cover otherwise in sixty hours.

The story of Einstein repairing to his room for two weeks and coming downstairs with the theory of relativity in hand illustrates the same phenomenon (as does Moses' receipt of the Ten Commandments!). Yet it is patent that such discoveries only befall Pasteur's "prepared man," and that among the atavistic competences unmistakably lies the ability to perform operations and handle variables in the manner described by Piaget. In matters of invention and creation, the ability to think visually, to perceive connections, is insufficient without the capacity to carry one's findings through to their final form. This is the aspect of discovery insufficiently stressed by the Gestalt psychologists.

In the final analysis, human creativity has numerous parallels across realms, with inspiration, intuition, and gestalt perception playing an indispensable role in the activities of both scientists and artists. Many individuals have experienced those moments when the materials over which they have been struggling suddenly fit together, and the execution of the work follows of itself. (Of course this is only because they have previously mastered a medium or language.) It is not, then, in the phenomenal experience of creativity that artist and scientist can be differentiated, but rather in the kind of subject matter and symbolic systems with which they work, the kind of competences that are relevant (for example, keen discriminatory powers vs operational sophistication), the questions they deem interesting, the nature of their respective fields, and the kinds of individuals or personalities that gravitate to them. Having examined the differences in mode of procedure, a brief consideration of the kind of personalities found among artists and scientists seems appropriate.

PERSONALITY TRAITS OF ARTISTS AND SCIENTISTS

The psychologist Roe has uncovered certain characteristics that differentiate scientists from one another and from the nonscientific community. By and large, the scientist did not have a particularly happy childhood; he was withdrawn, generally preferring to be alone or with one or two close friends who shared his interests. Except for theoretical physicists, who seem to be the most brilliant individuals as well as the most voracious readers, future scientists tended to read chiefly in mathematics and science, where they were notably precocious. Social scientists were more often interested in the humanities and literature, not infrequently turning to the study of man after determining that they could not succeed in a literary career.

Physical scientists decide to enter the sciences at a very early age, and in many cases do competent work while in their late teens or early twenties, and highly original work before they are 30. Unlike writers, there is no range of personal experiences they must have undergone before they can make significant contributions. Their minds are very receptive, they have easily mastered the knowledge of the past, and their lack of blinders, preconceptions, or fixed categories render the most gifted peculiarly susceptible to new patterns and to solutions for important problems in their field.

Major research scientists devote themselves wholly to the laboratory and their work, thus having little or no social life. They generally do not like gatherings, except among close colleagues, and their hobbies, if any, involve natural materials or animals. A surprising percentage have lost one or another parent before the age of 10, thereby making them lonely and also exceptionally independent. Unlike artists, they tend to handle whatever emotional problems they have by rendering them less personal, or through the defense of sublimation. A history of dating is rare, and if they marry it is usually to individuals who shared their interest, and often with the understanding that their work comes first. As Ellis once noted:

A passionate devotion to intellectual pursuits seems often to be associated with a lack of passion in the ordinary relationships of life, while excessive shyness really betrays also feebleness of the emotional impulse. . . . Even in many cases in which marriage occurs, it is easy to see that the relationship was rooted in the man's intellectual passion.

A fascinating case of this early involvement in science is J. D. Watson, whose scientific career leading up to the discovery of a model for DNA at the age of 23 is compellingly described in *The Double Helix*.

Some interesting differences obtain between the kinds of individuals who are found in certain of the sciences and certain of the arts. Biologists tend to think in pictures, have a morphological view of things, and translate words into images, while the faculty for seeing images is meager among physical scientists, particularly those oriented toward theoretical questions. The main interests of different kinds of scientists are clearly reflected in their responses to an inkblot test; social scientists locate human beings, biologists discern animals, and physicists perceive objects. Experimental scientists are doers who like to engage in making activity, whereas theoretical scientists are perceivers who discern patterns in what they observe and communicate these gestalten to others. The extent which these gifts sometimes fall to different individuals is illustrated by the example of Freud. A very poor experimentalist, clumsy in the laboratory, and impatient for results, he was nevertheless an excellent observer, with brilliant intuitions about structure and functions.

In examining the results of a number of factorial tests, McFarlane Smith has uncovered a factor that he labels *spatial ability*. According to Smith, this ability to think in terms of abstract spatial factors is highly correlated with scientific aptitude, especially in the more theoretical areas of science. It is typically found in schizothymic persons, individuals like Sherlock Holmes who are lean and drawn in appearance, tense and nervous, susceptible to the emergence of split personality or delusions. The possessor of spatial ability is gifted at playing with abstract notions or configurations in his mind, shifting them about, discerning underlying patterns. He scores well in tests of inverse drawing, pattern completion and perception, spatial analogies, embedded figures, angle recognition, and shape dissection and copying. The expert in spatial thought is contrasted with another ideal type, the cyclothyme, who has extreme swings of affect and may be susceptible to manic-depressive fits. The cyclothymic tends, like Dr. Watson, to be fat, lazy, and relaxed, with a tendency to let words, sounds, or other symbolic sorts of material flow endlessly. He is not much given to problem solving (stating a problem and pursuing its solution), but is skilled at collecting a variety of details and fitting them together in an interesting manner.

In contrast to traditional investigators who have drawn a line between scientific and artistic talent, Smith suggests that the forms of ability he discerns cut across that dichotomy. One finds within the sciences individuals who excel in abstract sorts of problem-solving (Newton), and within the arts painters and architects (Leonardo) who share this ability as well as its concomitant temperament. Conversely, other scientists are much more interested in data collecting, in the details of the sciences, in spurning the deductive method, in spinning elaborate webs about what they find. These individuals tend to be glib verbally and of an extrovert nature; they are epitomized by such ebullient writers as Samuel Johnson and G. K. Chesterton, and such fluent composers as Haydn, Bach, Gluck, and Mozart. If introspective reports have validity, the latter group does its thinking primarily in the material of words and sounds themselves, while the former creates in a more abstract, less linguistic medium. If one regards the typical scientist as the abstract physicist, the typical artist as the fluent writer, it may be legitimate to generalize about artists and scientists. But if the net is too widely cast, the generalizations will lose power. Failure to be prudent in this matter accounts, I think, for the sometimes contradictory generalizations one finds in the literature concerning artists and scientists. I find it most helpful, therefore, to think of the art/science dichotomy as intersecting the schizoid/cyclothyme dichotomy in the following manner:

	Artists	Scientists
schizothymic	Giacometti	Newton
cyclothymic	Samuel Johnson	Darwin

Our earlier remarks about kinds of problem-solving should be tempered by the recognition that artists and scientists may differ greatly in aptitudes, personality, procedures, and amount and range of talents. The interaction between feeling life and area of interest is instructive, and studies like Smith's will be helpful in elucidating the kinds of skills developed by a range of practitioners in the arts and sciences.

The interests of an individual as a child may be symptomatic for his later career choice. One might, for instance, differentiate between the young scientist who prefers to examine the inside of apparatuses and to unravel their mechanisms, and the artist who makes himself a splendid doll out of a chip of wood. In one case, an analytic interest dominates; in the other, a constructive impulse. Furthermore, in the artistic individual, the impulse to create is attached to a self-conscious ego, while in the scientific type there tends to be dissociation between the personality of the individual (which in many cases is less prominent) and his work. I would speculate that the young artist typically strives to restore idyllic personal relations he believes were once dominant by communicating his feelings to others. One encounters many letters by artists in which they berate themselves for undermining personal relationships, while insisting that their motives were unsullied. Multiple identification with other individuals and a rich life of the imagination are also common features of future artists.

In contrast, the scientist, perhaps because of his more repressive and puritanical background, shows little interest in relations with other individuals, greater independence, and less interest in feeling per se. While the young scientist may not have rejected the possibility of a more perfect world, he is likely to seek it through an understanding of or relationship with nature. Communication with others about oneself takes on far less importance here. Two conditions may mediate the choice of a scientific career. Without experiencing any deficiency in interpersonal relations, one may turn to a science because of a driving curiosity about some area; or a perceived deficiency in interpersonal relations may seem so great that one rejects other persons altogether and turns to science for impersonal solace. Perhaps an individual characterized by an alteration in understanding and frustration, and a pervading interest in and concern with people, might become intrigued with the social sciences and strive to understand personality or people. It is not surprising that many social scientists were first attracted to the arts, in which aspects of the subjective world can be more directly exploited and explored.

Given the different backgrounds and orientations of the typical artist and scientist, the capacity to retain an interest in both domains is of some interest. I would imagine that schizothymic as well as cyclothymic individuals should prove able to maintain an interest in an art and a science, though the particular ones that interest them would depend on personality type. Thus Strindberg was both an effulgent writer and a tireless collector of data about the sciences; Leonardo used abstract faculties to illuminate painting and architecture, anatomy, and mechanics; Goethe made contributions both to the arts and to the sciences. More often, however, a strong interest in objects seems to conflict with an interest in persons, and the kinds of creativity leading to substantive contributions in one area militate against, if they do not preclude, contributions in other areas. It is not that artists are uninterested in sciences; the two cultures are not completely isolated. Nonetheless, in most cases, the individual's creative potential is directed toward an art or a science, while the interest in the other branch is more purely receptive or leisurely. Simple limitation of resources and time would alone favor such a dissociation. Some individuals, furthermore, are strongly oriented toward a single area, having little or no aptitude for any other; consider, for example, the lightning calculators, the chess prodigies who are able to do little else, the master mnemonist who is unable to comprehend metaphoric or poetic language.

A less appealing possibility is that increasing interest in a single domain renders one less sensitive to other areas. In a famous passage, Darwin describes the waning of his aesthetic sensitivities as his mind became increasingly interested in objects, his curious and lamentable loss of the higher aesthetic taste:

> Up to the ages of thirty or beyond, poetry of many kinds, such as the works of Milton, Gray, Byron, Wordsworth, Coleridge and Shelley, gave me great pleasure and even as a schoolboy I took tremendous delight in Shakespeare, especially the historical plays. I have also said that formerly pictures gave me considerable and music very great delight. But now for many years I cannot endure to read a line of poetry, I have tried lately to read Shakespeare and found it so intolerably dull that it nauseated me. I have also lost my taste for pictures and music. . . . My mind seems to have become a kind of machine for grinding general laws out of large collections of facts, but why this should have caused the atrophy of that part of the brain alone, on which

the higher states depend, I cannot conceive. A man with a mind more highly organized or better constituted than mine, would not, I suppose, thus have suffered: and if I had to live my life again, I would have made a rule to read some poetry and listen to some music at least once every week; for perhaps the parts of my brain not atrophied would thus have been kept active through use.

Such a tendency toward exclusive concentration on scientific quandaries may become sufficiently dominating that, as a precaution, one should perhaps deliberately set aside time for involving faculties that would normally fall into disuse. Particularly in view of the assumed trend toward increasing rigidity in later years, the active pursuit of an interest in areas other than one's own seems crucial. Inasmuch as learning of entirely new fields, be they arts or sciences, is quite arduous later in life, individuals are advised to remain "prepared."

Darwin also commented that "the loss of these tastes is a loss of happiness and may possibly be injurious to the intellect, and more probably to the moral character, by enfeebling the emotions." Here he appears to be suggesting that a concentration on making and perceiving in his own discipline has weakened the feeling aspect of his life. Ever on the alert for patterns, generalizations, laws, he is no longer simply able to enjoy the role of audience member, allowing the artist to communicate his feelings or knowledge to him. In short, he has become the full-fledged critic, so intent on discrimination that he is no longer able to experience pleasurable feelings as he beholds an aesthetic work. The press of the formal operation, the primacy of propositional reasoning has impeded the naive spontaneous and complete immersion into concrete matter. As Housman once pointed out, "Perfect understanding will sometimes almost destroy pleasure."

THE AUDIENCE MEMBER

Earlier, I dealt at length with the notion of three *developing systems*, which exist in relatively autonomous form at first, yet come increasingly to interact with and to feed into another, finally recapitulating their development on the level of symbol use. While interaction of systems is the rule in every normal person, in certain individuals one or another of these systems may come to predominate. According to my formulation, the member of the audience is one who evaluates objects he has perceived or made primarily in terms of his phenomenal affective reactions. The member of the audience views an art work or performance and is content merely to feel pleasure, tension, or resolution. "The business of the consumer is to consume, that is, to enlighten and enrich his life through seeing and hearing, not to dissect the formal means by which such enlightenment and enrichment is accomplished." Naturally his ability to understand the work of art, to decipher symbols, can enhance his appreciation: there is a variety of levels on which the, work might operate, and these levels can only influence one's feeling life to the extent that they are appropriately apprehended. Furthermore, as he matures the audience member gains familiarity with a larger number of experiences and develops finer emotions, which should place him increasingly in tune with the interests and meanings of the creator. (To the extent that the artist's feelings are very idiosyncratic, the audience member may or may not be in sympathy with a particular presentation.) Yet such comprehension is not an end in itself, but only a means to a fuller enjoyment of the role of audience members.

The cultivation of one's feelings and impressions remains the central concern of the individual who participates in the aesthetic process, as a contemplator of *objets d'art,* a member of the audience. For such individuals, whose attraction to art stems from its effect on their feelings, the particular feelings treated within a work are often crucial:

What do the majority of the people call aesthetic pleasure? what happens when they like a work of art, for instance a theatrical production? The answer is beyond doubt; the people like a drama when they have succeeded in becoming interested in the human destinies which are proposed to them. The loves, hatreds, sorrow and joys of their characters move their hearts.

In a sense, then, because they may concentrate on the content rather than on the formal aspects of the work members of an audience may retain a somewhat primitive relationship to an art work. Yet, heightened interest in the formal properties is certainly consistent with audience membership and characterizes its most developed realization.

Even as the artist is placing himself and his emotions into the work, the member of the audience must renounce a part of himself so that he can enter into the world of the aesthetic object and appreciate the feeling and ideas contained therein. The typical audience member probably has a more modest sense of self, a less powerful and assertive ego, and a greater susceptibility to suggestion than the creator; there may be an asymmetry between the artist's effort over a long period of time and the audience's response over a short interval. Fry refers to the state of mind of the typical audience member when he declares that "There is something in the common phraseology by which we talk of seeing a point or an argument whereas we feel the harmony of a work of art and, for some reason, we attach a more constant emotional quality to feeling than to seeing."

The course by which the audience's feelings should be aroused does not lend itself to easy generalization. However, some appreciation of the notion of style and some realization that the creating individual communicates aspects of himself in an object do seem necessary if the audience member is to fully appreciate the work. If he believes that what is upon the stage is a genuine incident rather than a representation or a comment, he is an audience member of a most primitive sort. If he merely regards the object as an aspect of the real world, rather than as a human creation, he is merely orienting, rather than exhibiting the sense of distance inherent in the aesthetic process. The developed member of the audience must realize that the work is an embodiment of another individual's life, not merely a pretty object or a representation of something he likes. Of course he may be unable to appreciate the many nuances and surface features that differentiate a work of art from other slices of reality. Yet all these discriminations are, in a sense, secondary; only if and insofar as his affective life is altered is he participating as an audience member in the artistic process.

Several artists have indicated their belief that only other competent artists working within the same medium can make judgments about works of art. Eliot declared, "I consider that the only jury of judgment is that of the ablest poetic practitioners of my time." Speaking of Samuel Johnson, he said, "Because he was a poet himself and a good poet, what he wrote about poetry must be read with respect." Goethe claimed that "one can only grasp what one can produce oneself," and Virgil Thomson has argued that only musicians can tell quality in music, and that all the audience receives from a work is a subjective impression. Thomson's remarks may be relevant for the typical audience member, but the most developed connoisseur who can see much and feel deeply about a work may well have a keen appreciation of the medium. This appreciation need not be a conscious one—many artists may be as deficient in the terminology and the technical underpinnings of the medium as they are versed in the tools of their trade. The kind of familiarity that is essential is merely sufficient immersion so that one can intuit how the medium is employed and discriminate between better and poorer exploitation of it. The artist need not be able to evaluate critically the works of others, only his own: "Every true poet is necessarily a first-rate critic; not necessarily of others' work, but of his own."

In many cases, individual audience members will experience the same modes as their peers while contemplating a work. If this occurs naturally, such reactions are quite legitimate. But a line must be drawn between art and ritual, for in the latter case the feeling to be experienced is prescribed, the possibility of a flexible reaction precluded. In addition, an unchanging reaction on the part of an audience member to a work or a set of works is somewhat suspect, for this uniformity implies a shallowness of feeling or inadequate discriminating powers. As he becomes further acquainted with a significant work of art, the audience member should undergo increased differentiation of feelings. It is the province of lasting art that every fresh viewing or hearing can yield deeper understanding and satisfaction. In sum, then, any individual who experiences feelings in relationship to his perception of an art object may be thought of as an audience member. Audience members may differ widely, however, in the extent to which they are affected by subtler aspects of the work. The modal-vectoral sensitivity of the audience member, as well as his appreciation of interpersonal relations and his capacity for discrimination, are all relevant to his becoming a mature audience member, to whom the multifarious facets of an aesthetic work are accessible. The difference between the skilled critic and the developed audience member seems to lie in the way in which the critic can characterize his reactions to an art work: "The difference, I say, between the criticisms of professionals and laymen is essentially that the former are able to trace the aesthetic pleasure or displeasure which they feel to certain features of the objects while the latter are not able to do it."

THE CRITIC

In I. A. Richard's succinct formulation, criticism is the endeavor to discriminate between experiences and to evaluate them. The critic is an individual who goes beyond the audience member; he studies works, compares them with one another, and describes his conclusions to others. Minds of this sort operate by noting "the provenance and the surface manner of whatever is being examined, person, place, or thing, and then rapidly, clearly, without any sparring or hesitating, or qualifications, the underlying structure is exposed and articulated and its significance studied." This ability assumes intimate familiarity both with the particular work and with the medium and its tradition; the capacity is long in coming and seems dependent on the ability to use formal operations, to engage in hypothetical thought, and to reason about propositions. Criticism is thereby discriminable from other aspects of the artistic process, which do not, in any comparable sense, appear to rely on operational intelligence. The critical act goes well beyond simple perceiving, or making of an aesthetic symbolic object; it involves an ability to operate on a verbal characterization of the object. Thus criticism can count on a reality beyond itself, a reality to which it refers, which it may order and clarify, but which remains "out there." The critic can operate on the work of art since, in so doing, he does not transform it; instead he creates propositions about the work and applies a variety of formal operations to these propositions. The critic "must translate his experience of literature into intellectual terms, assimilate it to a coherent scheme which must be rational if it is to be knowledge." In contrast, the artist's operations upon the work—his making activity—ineffably change the work.

The claim that formal operations are unnecessary for participants in the arts is sufficiently controversial to require review. While the 7- or 8-year-old is scarcely a full-fledged participant in the artistic process, he does, in my view, have the ability to work with raw materials and the intellectual capacity to become an artist, performer, or audience member. Lacking are quantitative aspects: additional experiences, more intimate knowledge of the media, ability to concentrate long enough or hold enough details in mind. These capacities will take time to evolve, but do not appear qualitatively different from the thought or functioning of the school-age child. They require only continued accumulation of experience and knowledge by the same means of skill development and integration of increasingly fine discriminatory and feeling responses. There is no point after the acquisition of the ability to work with a concrete symbolic medium at which one can justifiably claim that a certain youngster has entered into a new stage and is for the first time, a bonafide artist. But until the child is able to reason logically about verbal propositions, during the stage of formal operations, he will be unable to undertake critical activity of the type described here.

The work of an artist seems well described by Piaget's phrase, *concrete operations*. Indeed the artist undertakes a wide variety of operations, whatever his medium, but in all cases he is operating with a concrete medium. Myriad problems arise for the composer, painter, or writer, but these emerge in words, notes, color, shapes, and lines, not in an abstract propositional formulation of the same. (So, too, the audience can come to appreciate the medium intuitively, being aware of its components, even though unable to characterize them in a technical language.) The worker must have sufficient distance from his object to evaluate or alter it, but explicit, orderly comparison with other objects is not essential. His knowledge of the media and his cognizance of his own goal suffice. By continuing to make and to perceive what he has made, the child can become an accomplished craftsman and artist, even though he may never be able to solve the kinds of scientific-logic questions posed by Piaget. The latter kinds of problems involve a capacity to neglect the concrete properties of a given situation, to step outside

of the material, to objectify the variables and manipulate them imper-
sonally. These capacities are essential to the critic as well as to any
scientist who must remain aware of all the factors, conduct hypothetical
experiments, and manipulate verbal propositions.

In contrast to the scientist, the artist (or performer) is never called
upon to provide a unique logical solution that others could, by manipulation of equivalent variables, arrive at independently; any results that
effectively capture a quality will suffice. The concrete procedures employed by the 8-year-old may be adequate. The art, but not the science,
of a young child may be notable, lacking though it may the polish or
niche within a tradition seen in the works of mature individuals. This
distinction between the prerequisites of scientist and artist explains
why, both in primitive cultures and in our own, many who would be
baffled by Piaget's formal problems and who cannot realize the logical
calculus in their thought processes can nonetheless make and appreciate
meaningful artistic objects.

Whereas feeling plays a constitutive role in the presenting and discerning of affect in aesthetic objects, the feeling system may be to some
extent antagonistic to the scientific process. The scientist must be wary
of his unsupported feelings and of the convincing but erroneous explanation, and must apply a cold and clinical eye to whatever properties
or ideas he produces. He must spurn personal involvement, while the
artist must retain the ability to treat this personal involvement. The
critic is thus placed in a delicate intermediary position. He must be
detached from aesthetic objects while remaining sensitive to the variegated components of the aesthetic communication. To the extent that
the scientist-critic overemphasizes this detachment from objects, he may
cease to be a relevant commentator in the arts.

I have suggested in earlier chapters that every child passes through
two principal stages—in the first, like other organisms he merely perceives, makes, and feels in regard to material objects; in the second,
unlike any nonhuman organism he becomes able to realize and express
in symbols what he perceives, makes, or feels. The third level or stage,
the ability to manipulate verbal propositions that express knowledge
about the world as if they were objects, is germane to the realm of the
scientist, and hence to Piagetian research. Some such capacity would
seem required for artistic critics, but I do not see a necessary role for
such formal operations in the workaday life of the artist. Thus we see
that this area, which differs sufficiently from the manipulation of elements within a symbol system to warrant a separate term, (*scientific*)
cognition, plays an insubstantial role in artistic development.

Two groups of individuals are particularly attracted to criticism.

The first is composed of creative artists, for example poets, who in early middle age become dissatisfied with their work, and are curious to discover their relationship to the literary tradition. Criticism here provides a fresh distance from one's work, and hence follows upon it; the critic has made (and made it) before he criticizes. Members of the other group also frequently began as creators but determine, either through their own observation or through feedback from others, that their work will be of only mediocre quality. Such creators, while competent, may lack total exposure of self, complete immersion in the medium, the overriding desire to embody and to place oneself into an aesthetic object, or a sufficiently compelling set of experiences on which to draw. Like St. Beuve or Renan, they often come from learned households, where they read carefully and widely from an early age, and excelled in school. The relationship with the father tends to be positive or neutral, and often the father himself has educated the future critic. Such individuals typically grew up in rather rigid, puritanical homes, where a great deal of sublimation has gone into learning and there is a strong sense of tradition and the past. In their distance from objects and in their desire to concentrate on work itself, rather than on their own personality, these individuals are often closer to the scientist than to the artist. The critic sees himself as belonging to a line of workers carrying on a tradition, not as someone who embodies in himself some postulate or principle. This self-picture comes through frequently in his writings. If he differs from the scientist, it is in his distaste for purely logical thinking and laboratory work, and his greater interest in subjective aspects of experience, historical tradition, and erudition for its own sake.

THE PERFORMER

Performers have generally engaged in and enjoyed public activities from an early age. Often these individuals come from stage families and appeared in public during childhood. The ability to put on public displays, however, is scarcely equivalent to developed performance, as Sartre's account demonstrates. An enormous difference exists between acting so as to entertain, and conforming to the dimensions of a specific role. Only when they become aware of their role, of their distance from others, only when they become able to realize and convey the subtleties of a notated piece or an artist's conception can such individuals be considered established performers.

To be sure, the desire to please others through one's own behavior and speech is characteristic of most youths, but seems particularly "in the blood" of those who, as legend has it, were "born in a stage trunk." Youngsters who, either because of their family's calling or their own unusual gifts, have performed early in their lives become enamored of the sound of enthusiastic applause and may well seek to perpetuate it. As the actor William Redfield has suggested, "the actor's psyche responds reflexively to praise, even when he fears it's undeserved." Eventually, however, youthful performers come to realize that mere presence on the stage will no longer ensure applause. They must now develop a skill of some sort, acquire a genuine relationship with the audience, comprehend what pleases or engages the feeling system of those on the other side of the lights. This capacity requires a sufficient decline of egocentrism and development of interpersonal relations so that the child no longer performs in a completely spontaneous manner, but rather in a way sensitive to the audience's taste.

Until the school years the ability to comprehend the requirements of a role and to adapt an appropriate stance *vis à vis* the audience is beyond most individuals. By 7 or 8, however, the demands of performing seem understood by children, who can distinguish between "real" and "pretend." Relating to the audience poses a somewhat more difficult problem for an actor or a circus entertainer than for a performing musician. The latter can attract plaudits merely for technical virtuosity on an instrument, while the actor tends to be judged in terms of his whole person. He puts himself, his body, his present existence on the line in an all-consuming way.

Actors may make their bodies into objects and immerse themselves fully in work. Because their behavior, gait, and expressive repertoire is so prominent a feature of their performance, however, total suppression of their own personality is at best an elusive ideal. While performing on an instrument is, at least in some ways, a technical skill that can be acquired through training (though ability to express oneself as a musician probably must be preceded by development of a personality and the experience of a meaningful life), the practice of portraying other persons seems to demand a certain kind of temperament. Like the artist, the actor must have a strong sense of self (a developed ego), but unlike the artist he is constantly called upon to submerge it totally and to enter the skin of another, perhaps entirely different person. Though Littlewood quips, "any man who has courage on the stage and is willing to make a fool of himself can, in fact, become a good actor," such a demand places him in a tenuous public position. It is not surprising that many performers have been somewhat unhappy individuals who welcomed the opportunity to simulate other sorts of people. Yet having to act as someone else may exact a toll, unless the actor can realize that most challenging of goals—being himself through superlative realization of other characters.

While there have been, to my knowledge, no detailed studies of the personalities of critics or audience members, Taft has done a careful and thorough inventory of the typical personalities and experiences of actors. He found that most actors tend to come from a stage family, and participated in the theater at an early age. The modal theatrical individual was asocial, neurotic, and unstable, coming from a family that lacked parental harmony. Actors themselves had difficulty establishing normal family ties, and were characterized by a large proportion of divorces, homosexual ties, or isolation from others. Actors are, as a rule, little interested in money; they are above average in verbal intelligence, and high in originality, emotionality, idealism, and self-centeredness. Despite their sensitivity to the behavior of others and their ability to portray a variety of characters, actors tend to be insensitive to each other's feelings. While they may engage in elaborate relationships with people and may even have exhibitionist tendencies, they often do not enjoy being with other people, treating them merely as objects to be amused, teased, or manipulated. Taft points out that his negative picture of actors by no means applies to all individuals in the theater; several of those studied were very attractive personalities, gifted and stable. It is worth remarking that the tremendous, often inconsistent demands made on the functioning actor, particularly in contemporary society, probably contribute to his difficulties in adjustment and intersubjective relations. And it must be stressed that the sometime association of neurosis and performing implies no causal connection; indeed performing skill is evidence that the individual has not been dominated by whatever neurotic traits he may have.

Little is known about the natural and acquired skills of actors, though many seem to possess an uncanny ability to observe the manner in which an individual behaves and then to mimic it. Often they will have paid relatively little attention to what has been said, as a little child ignores utterances that are too complex, but still will be able to capture the style and the nuances of the imitated individual. Actor Nicol Williamson has said: "Some people can remember rational processes of argument. I can't. What I do remember, after ten or fifteen years, is exactly how a man fiddled with matchbox while he was talking. Nervously. Tensely. I slot it with lots of other details I pick up about him. Ten years later I take them out and mix in some of myself: and then I've got something separate that I've made."

A strong dislike of school often emerges in an actor's biography. This antipathy may be a natural consequences, as the emphasis in school falls increasingly on what is said, rather than on how it is said. Future actors are engrossed in the style, setting, or atmosphere of a situation at the very time they are expected to be attending to the substance or the underlying meaning. Formal operations can pose problems for the developing actor.

While it would be absurd to maintain that performers do not understand artistic works, there may be something to the theory that, like others, they have begun by imitating what they incompletely understood, but have continued to employ this faculty for mimetic purposes even after achieving understanding. Various reports cite performers whose understanding was inadequate: Groucho Marx traces the origin of his public humor to his inability to comprehend highbrow discussions. Stravinsky indicates that the Russian ballet master Nijinsky comprehended nothing about music and was an atrocious creator and choreographer, yet his ability to interpret familiar music was incomparable. The director Peter Hall indicates that an actor need not understand a concept intellectually, but he must believe it; for the director, however, comprehension is the point of departure.

Because of difficulty in understanding avant-garde movements, many performers have had trouble interpreting innovative works. This task requires considerable creative capacity as well as an ability to master new uses of media. In order that the original dancers might learn Stravinsky's *Petrouchka,* they had to remember everything by ear, as their knowledge of the musical score was unsatisfactory. Rehearsals had to be stopped continually, and excursions into mathematics were necessary. Once the particular rhythm and emotion to be conveyed has been made clear to an actor, however, a performance can be superlative. The performer then depends on his memory of emotions and modal-vectoral properties and his developed technique. Consider, for example, this account of the premier of *Petrouchka*: "I have seen no one approach Nijinsky's rendering of Petrouchka, for . . . he suggested a puppet that sometimes aped a human being whereas all the other interpreters conveyed a dancer imitating a puppet." The way in which this mastery is achieved becomes irrelevant for the performer, as long as he has a formula for reenacting the role. Yet to protect his performance from chance factors, the performer must develop an arsenal of skills. In this, he is a creator, and is subject to the same developmental principles as anyone involved in highly intricate making activity.

The ability to read notations is a helpful, but not essential, adjunct for most performing artists. Strict constructionists, like Stravinsky, feel that all necessary information is in the score and severely criticizes those "free way" conductors who do not strictly adhere to the notation. Yet rarely, if ever, can the notation be realized literally, and most notations leave the performer considerable leeway in any case. For example, a close analysis of two gifted pianists' performances of Chopin revealed that the accented notes were not played with greater intensity than the unaccented notes, that duration accounted for measure accents, and that tempo rubato was used to define phrases. Both pianists played the melody note before other notes of the chord, and played it more intensively. Instructors in the performing arts would not be surprised at this finding, for they generally reject a strict, metrical realization of a script; performers are encouraged to achieve desired effects, even at the cost of violating the letter of a notation.

Historically, performing was exclusively a making activity, inseparable from creating. With the development of printing and notations, however, a separate role dependent on a specified relation to a created object has evolved. While most performers in the artistic process are clearly distinct from the creators, greater flexibility is found in the musical realm. Although in theory the composer's work ends as the conductor's work begins, it is not uncommon for the composer to conduct. This shift of roles involves an appreciable dislocation, for the composer's life is a private, sedentary one, ordinarily quite removed from the world. Nonetheless, many composers have been excellent conductors, notably of their own music, because they bring to the podium comprehensive knowledge, together with a consistent, authoritative notion of how their music should sound. Part of the conductor's mission is to inspire the orchestra, and the presence of the composer as conductor may make the performers especially alert, and may thus evoke their best efforts. Particularly revealing are differences between the public and private persons of the musicians, which sometimes emerge in the performance of works. Strauss underplayed the romantic tendencies of his work while conducting, and Schoenberg suppressed the latent hysteria of *Pierrot Lunaire*. In such instances an allographic art becomes more clearly specified through an autographic participation on the part of the creator. Aspects of feeling and perception of importance to the creator can be conveyed, and technology can preserve them for posterity. If one can receive insight into the basic character of music by hearing its composer conduct it, a reintegration of two cardinal roles in the artistic process becomes possible.

Whether the performer is the creator of a work or only its realizer, he may find himself subjected to extremely demanding pressures, particularly if he is considered outstanding and is expected to exhibit his excellence at all times. Actor Nicol Williamson provided an example of this dimension of the performer's life, when he stalked off the stage, announcing he would never act again. He relented, of course, but talked candidly about the tensions of consistently maintaining peak excellence. The actor wants to be perfect in the role, and yet he constantly criticizes his own mistakes. "How can you perform the same thing night after night," wonders Williamson. He compares himself to a race horse—"I have to win and I know when I run well and when I run badly." More than all the others in the artistic process, performers are directly on display, and so must develop strong internal controls and the capacity to regulate their own feelings. Their life is characterized by conflict between their own, often powerful personalities, and the necessity of suspending their egos in order to realize someone else's. Consquently, the appearance of a creator in his own play can be a fascinating phenomena, particularly when the role of the character is antithetical to the personality of the creator.

Even the creative artist, whatever his disclaimers, is ineluctably bound up with the reactions of his audience. The desire for triumph and fame haunts many involved in the arts, and success cannot come unless one's works are esteemed. Here is the public dimension in an artist's life —He may disdain and scorn the audience, but he is, in a very real sense, as dependent upon it as the performer is. Cézanne wanted to shock the public while also seducing it: "With an apple I want to astonish Paris," he once declared. Tolstoy noted, "I felt the need to be known and loved of all the world . . . so that they would troop around me and thank me for something." Goethe conceded: "The world does all it can to make us indifferent praise or blame but it never quite succeeds, for when its verdict agrees somewhat with our own convictions we gladly resign out of our resignation and return to them." The artist may, with reason, berate the audience's incapacity to appreciate him, but he must continue seeking to communicate, because the collaboration of audience and artist is essential in all art.

The artistic circle, then, is a closed one, in which a member cannot thrive, nor even exist, without the tacit or active cooperation of the other participants. There is an intrinsic unity and completeness to the arts so viewed, just as there is a similar sort of organization of the processes politicians, entrepreneurs, or scientists participate in. A disruption of one of the factors—lack of good performers, excessive powers for critics, an audience that does not enjoy, creators who destroy their work or who are not allowed to create freely—can disrupt the aesthetic enterprise. Anxiety that the aesthetic circle is threatening to disintegrate appears periodically and is, indeed, a preoccupation of current critics. Fortunately the centrality of symbols and communication in human life renders it likely that such unstable conditions will be transitory. The interdependence of the four roles in the artistic process is ensured by their common existence in a cultural setting in which continued, effective communication is at a premium.

In a similar way, the three systems in the individual cannot exist alone. If the making system, perceiving system, or feeling system proceeds too far ahead of, behind, or in disjunction with the other systems, an unproductive imbalance sets in. Equally undesirable are the maker who overdoes idle activity or who compulsively engages in some sort of function, without regard to what he perceives or feels; the hedonist who indulges his feelings totally and lets his discriminatory powers fall into disuse; and the critic who is so alert to differences and discrepancies that he can neither appreciate the integrity of experience, nor achieve a satisfactory product of his own. The consummate artist must include in his making activity aspects of his feelings and of his discriminations. The audience member who is to feel in the fullest sense must be able to discriminate and to participate, at least vicariously, in the making process as well. The performer and critic, too, are enriched to the extent that they have a comprehensive view of the creative process, to the extent that their feelings and discriminations are mobilized throughout the aesthetic process. Making may culminate in skill or in routine, feeling may become differentiated and fine or one dimensional and rigid, perception leads to discrimination, blindness, or carping. Whether the fruitful or the worthless end state is attained seems to depend on the extent to which the three systems interact with and are strengthened by one another.

Despite their dependence on the other participants in the aesthetic process, artists are most intimately tied to the center of the aesthetic circle—their own work of art. For all, the work of art is tremendously important; for many, their works of art are their life. A few of the possible relations that may obtain between the mature artist and his work, between creating subject and symbolic object, should now be mentioned.

THE ARTIST AND HIS WORK

The most commonly held, romantic notion of the artist postulates that his work means all to him. "No man can earn for himself the right to be called an artist unless, in need of paint and brushes, he is willing to sell his mother," according to one anonymous source. One reads of Messerschmidt, who killed his model to that he could capture the details of dying, and of artists who committed suicide when they discovered details, such as the horseshoes on the feet of an equestrian statue, missing. Picasso is reportedly so anxious about the completion of the work, equating the final act with death, that he insists on viewing his productions as a series of experiments, and speaks of all his work as "in process."

The central position occupied by work in a composer's life is revealed in Mozart's biography. In his first letter to his father following his mother's death, Mozart dwelled on his own work. While his child was born, he composed quartets in the adjoining room. Indeed, Mozart freely admitted that composing was his only pleasure; similarly, Beethoven said that his art alone kept him alive. Stravinsky, Van Gogh, and Goethe voiced similar sentiments. Even Picasso indicates that "an artist works of necessity: he himself is only a trifling bit of the world . . . no more importance should be attached to him than to plenty of other things which please us in the world though we cannot explain them." And Arnold Schoenberg, initially neglected by most of his contemporaries, refers wittily to the close identification between artist and work:

> But Beethoven, when Grillparzer called the Ninth a jumble, or Wagner, when one found him trivial—how could they go on writing? I know only one answer: they had things to be said. Once, in the army, I was asked if I was really the composer A[rnold] S[choenberg], 'Somebody had to be,' I said, 'and nobody else wanted to, so I took it on, myself'. Perhaps I too had to say things—unpopular things, it seems—that had to be said.

In all these cases, the artist's identity and self-esteem is so closely tied to his work that he links his fate to its course.

Closely allied to the artist whose works are all important is the artist who, for whatever reason, has a compulsive need to work. He may work because he loves it, because he can do nothing else, because he thrives on fame and public recognition, because he has a message that must be communicated. Playwright John Whiting comments: "I suppose there have been people who have actually given up the theater and not written any more plays, because the critics have said they couldn't do it. . . . I can't probably. But I do—that's the point—it is sort of a compulsive thing." Wagner indicated that he had to compose but titilated himself by putting it off—note his reference to "the voluptuous pleasures of resistance"; while Simenon, author of hundreds of novels, speaks the interplay between the artist's need to work and his particular character disorder: "I don't think an artist can ever be happy because I think that if a man has the urge to be an artist, it is because he needs to find himself. Every writer tries to find himself through his characters, through all his writing." As in the cases where artists feel dependent on their works, these compulsive practitioners have made their output central. Whether they differ from the first group more in rhetoric or substance is difficult to determine.

Of a somewhat different and rarer type is the artist capable of a clearcut break between his artistic work and his other life—in a productive way he is a dual person. Some artists write just a certain number of lines per day and then proceed to live a normal life. They may hold another job, be a responsible family person, pursue totally unrelated interests. These artists can succeed either because they have other interests that are equally powerful, have unusual will power, or have found themselves unable to function when their art has become all-consuming. Thomas Mann, for example, was both creator and citizen; he made a clear division between his role as a stolid, reliable member of the bourgeoisie and his role as an artist who explored the depths of experience.

Even those occasional artists who are able to separate themselves from their work devote themselves fully and mercilessly to it during times of creative activity. Close identification between the artist and his work is an important and perhaps necessary component of the artistic process. If the arts involve the communication of deeply felt affects and truths on the part of a skilled individual, it is important that the communicator be completely involved in his activity, and feel it is of crucial importance. Any hesitancy, doubt, or inconstancy on his part will be detected by audiences that have learned to differentiate genuine from feigned communications.

The identification with and mastery of a tradition is an important aspect of the artist's relationship to his work. Perhaps, as Rank thought, the great artist must, at least potentially, recapitulate in himself the whole evolution of art, collective as well as individual; he must assimilate typical conflicts of humanity in order to produce works that are collective yet individual. Certainly, a drive to absorb the tradition is characteristic of many of the most renowned artists. Shakespeare read everything: Stravinsky and Picasso exhausted the work of past masters. It is paradoxically the most assiduous student of artistic history who goes on to set contemporary fashions.

In addition to a mastery of great works of the past, the greatest artists are said to have had the rare but invaluable faculty of "negative capability." Their works exemplify a complete submergence of the creator's personality into that of the other subject. In a famous letter, Keats refers to this capacity:

As to the poetical character, itself, it is not itself—it has no self—it is everything and nothing—it has no character—it enjoys light and shadow—it lives in gusto, be it foul or fair, high or low, rich or poor, mean or elevated. . . . A poet is the most unpoetical thing in existence because he has no identity—he is continually in form—and filling some other body. . . . When I am in a room with people if I ever am free from speculating on creations of my own brain, then not myself goes home to myself, but the identity of everyone in the room begins to press upon me [so] that I am in a very little time annihilated—not only among men: it would be same in a Nursery of children.

Hazlitt wrote similarly of Shakespeare:

He was the least of an egotist that it was possible to be. He was nothing in himself, but he was all that others were, or that they could become. He had not only had in himself the germs of every faculty and feeling but he could follow them by anticipation, intuitively, into all their conceivable ramifications, through every change of fortune, or conflict or passion, or turn of thought. . . . He had only to think of anything in order to become that thing, with all the circumstances belonging to it.

Although this capacity to identify with all things may seem at odds with the forthright communication of self characteristic of creative individuals, the contradiction is only apparent. Artists with negative capability are individuals who identify in a profound way with a myriad of creations and experiences. In communicating these identifications they are actually seizing upon and conveying aspects of their subjective experience and protean personalities.

Even if the greatest artists can capture all they envisage within the work, the artist's output should not be equated with his public works. In the artist's own mind, he often creates a world he is only partially able to convey in the art object:

The artist lives not only with his performances (which he tends to forget) but with his own private view of what he thinks he has done, and, more important, what he still plans to do. For the writer, what exists in print is only a small, perhaps misleading fraction of the great thing to be accomplished. For the critic, however, it is the entire thing.

And when the work itself does not achieve success, artists may undergo varied reactions. Some can acknowledge their failures, but frequently denial or restructuring results. Many young artists will hide or destroy their works, and some will even deny their creative efforts. When his dramas were poorly received, even a great artist like Henry James simply created a privileged play in which he was performer and producer. Unable to tolerate a setback in his chosen field, he took over the whole aesthetic process himself. Hawthorne was so embarrassed by the failure of his novel *Fanshawe* that he burnt all the copies of this youthful work he could retrieve.

Many artists have a feeling of present or imminent greatness; indeed, such a self-evaluation may even anticipate the completion of their first art works. Van Gogh was a teacher and a missionary before he became a painter—he knew he had important visions to communicate, but had not yet found the medium with which to communicate. Keats, intoxicated by the idea of greatness, reverentially visited the Elgin marbles and reread the works of Milton and Shakespeare. Sartre identified with the individuals in a book about prodigies, and Schoenberg foretold his greatness in the history of music. Such feelings, along with the tremendous identification and involvement in one's own work, suggest that the gifted artist may differ in his personality and self-evaluation from most other individuals. He is not of a different species, but his energy, drive, and single-mindedness do distinguish him. These traits, which may also characterize some critics and performers, seem particularly characteristic of those individuals who inject themselves and their feelings into a separate object, an object they have created. This kind of total experience may be difficult for nonartists to appreciate.

ART AND NEUROSIS

The belief in one's greatness, the **capacity** for negative capability, the need to create one's own world, all unusual features, certainly need not designate neurosis or abnormality. Yet an obstinate tradition argues that madness and genius are near allies, that the artist is a neurotic—that neurosis is indeed essential to his creative powers. Hazlitt suggested that "poets live in an ideal world where they make everything out according to their wishes and fantasies." According to his analysis, Byron's "misshapen feet" compelled him to write verses and wreak revenge: "There is no knowing the effect of such sort of things, of defects we wish to balance. Do you suppose we owe nothing to Pope's deformity? He said to himself, 'If my person be crooked, my verses shall be strait.'" Toulouse-Lautrec claimed, "If my legs had been a little longer, I should never have painted." Edmund Wilson's piquant phrase, "The Wound and the Bow," is a modern version of this position. Wilson's reference is to the saga of Philoctetes: "the victim of a malodorous disease which renders him abhorrent to society and periodically degrades him is also a master of superhuman art which everybody has to respect and which the normal man finds he needs."

In a masterly essay, Lionel Trilling has reviewed the arguments regarding poetic madness and has concluded that, while it may be in the interests of the artist and of the audience to perpetuate the myth, there is no necessity for it. Trilling argues that it is the task of the artist to display his unconscious, and that the artist is no doubt more aware than most of what happens to him and feels more bound to present it. This trait is, however, a sign of candor, not neurosis. Trilling concedes that, as a group, scientists are less concerned than artists with questions or details of personality, but that if one is seeking signs of abnormality, such widespread traints of scientists as compulsiveness and indifference to persons could be suspect. In other words, if one clings to a theory of "poetic madness," one might just as well attribute neurosis to prominent scientists as to prominent artists.

Trilling's position strikes me as eminently intelligent. Certainly, individuals who achieve great success, possess unusual talents, and work single-mindedly in creative activity will manifest these traits: One's personality always illuminates numerous aspects of an individual. A relationship between personality and career is hardly restricted to the artist, however. Commentators may have been misled because the artist is in the habit of exposing his particular problems—indeed, to the extent that he suppresses them, he would be unfaithful to his craft, his audience, and himself. But to suggest that madness and artistry are necessarily connected seems no more plausible than to insist on an intrinsic relationship between neurosis and any other occupation. If we are all mad—scientists, artists, professionals—we cannot use madness to account for genius. If we all have problems, why single out those who reflect them in their works? And, most important, if many involved in a particular craft are quite normal, it is illegitimate to trace that craft to neurosis. Perhaps the neuroses of artists are more interesting than others; but it is not these traits or personalities or neuroses as such that characterize artists, but rather the way in which the artist employs them.

In his neurosis the artist resembles others. In his ability to objectify it or achieve distant from it he differs. The artist's genius should be defined in terms of his faculties of perception, representation, realization, making, and feeling. The one part of the artist that is indubitably healthy, whatever may be sick, is that which gives him the power to conceive, plan, and bring his work to fruition. Indeed his talent is sufficient indication that mental derangement is not dominant. He still has motivation, a sense of form, and the power to guide, control, and execute acceptable art works. As Plokker comments:

Although Vincent Van Gogh was a schizophrenic, Verlaine a drunkard, Wilde a homosexual, Dostoevsky probably an epileptic, their morbid structure does not disturb us when we turn to their work, to the form they succeeded in giving to what they wanted to express, even if its content were often morbid. A detailed study of the life of an artist provides us with practically nothing as far as his real artistic nature is concerned.

It may be that in some kinds of neuroses the subject matter and themes endure, while the ability to execute the work carefully, to iron out errors, and to remain critical disappears. Here the technical skill has atrophied, while leaving untouched the intriguing subject matter. In other forms of illness, the artist may retain his sense of form but use it to present an increasingly bizarre series of topics. Disputes as to the merits of an artist may be tied to these peculiar forms of impairment. Thus, some individuals are tremendously attracted to the works of Kafka, while others find them unreadable; perhaps only certain individuals can accept or find meaningful this writer's "aberrant" view of the world. Far fewer would question his technical mastery of the short story or the *Zettel*.

The dissociation between neurosis and art has been captured by Rank, who maintains that the artist makes aesthetic capital out of his personality. Thomas Mann is said to have displaced his conflict onto the protagonist of *Death in Venice,* thereby safeguarding his own artistic life. The neurotic differs, in that he unwilling to accept his own personality, and accordingly invests his energy into denying his own characteristics. Van Gogh was tremendously unhappy and socially maladapted because his appearance and his manner were equally abhorrent to others. He had a tremendous unfulfilled need for friendship and was frightfully lonely. Yet Van Gogh threw himself into his work like a man possessed in order that he might not lose completely his sanity. When this solution failed he could only go mad or kill himself.

Some artists clearly experience psychological difficulties, but it would be a fatal error to confound unusualness with insanity. To one psychologist, Amy Lowell's responses to a word association test were the most unusual of anyone outside a mental institution, but obviously no conclusion about insanity need follow from this finding. Indeed it seems more probable that the artistic genius must be essentially sane, if one wants to use such terms. "He must retain the crucial faculty directed toward his own literary productions. No great literary work can possibly be produced if this endowment is lacking."

The relationship between artist and work involves reciprocal effects. Thomas Mann suggests that the artist survives by treating his conflicts in his work. "The truth is that every piece of work is a realization, fragmentary but complete in itself, of our individuality and this kind of realization is the sole and painful way of getting the particular experience." Jung says somewhere that an art may seize a person and, for better or worse, make him its instrument. Thus Goethe did not create Faust, Faust created Goethe. The relationship between artist and work, far from being destructive, may have a soothing, rehabilitating effect. Mann and Stravinsky stressed the salubrious role played by their work during times of illness, while Kafka insisted that his writing preserved his sanity. The writing of *Dichtung und Wahrheit* was cathartic for Goethe. He felt thereafter like a new man: "I felt as if after a general confession, once more happy and free and justified in beginning a new life."

The relationship between artist and work is of particular interest in the case of the "one-work artist," the individual who pens one exemplary piece and then is no longer able to produce anything of significance. This phenomenon, virtually unheard of in other art forms, seems fairly common in literature. Perhaps details of one's life are less important in nonliterary art, but a highly interesting life may allow even an unskilled writer to produce one compelling novel. Yet it is not possible to produce a first-rate poem, painting, or musical composition unless one has mastered a medium, for the distance from one's own experience to finished skill in these arts is so great. Once such fluency with a symbolic medium has been obtained, however, many works on a variety of themes can be produced.

All individuals may indeed have potential literary material in them, the expression of their own lives; many have sufficient technical skill to express this work, but perhaps insufficient skill to produce others. Thereafter they can only repeat the same work, or try unsuccessfully to write about something less familiar to them. For a while Norman Mailer seemed a victim of this tendency, but eventually he evolved a new genre in which he was able to realize his promise. Other individuals may find that the work they have written has achieved its intended therapeutic purposes, and they no longer have any thing to "get off their chest"; or the success may go to their heads and they may attempt works that are too ambitious. Here the successful work gives the artist an inflated notion of his talents, paradoxically jeopardizing his future productivity. Chukovsky suggests that this was the case with the writer Ershov, who wrote a very successful children's book:

> Throughout his long life, Ershov never again returned to the simple style of his masterpiece—to the peasant vernacular—but strived to cultivate the high-flown poetic style of his times. . . . A master of the Russian folk idiom, he rejected this idiom over which he had complete control, scorned it, and never again made any attempt to return to it in his creative work.

In another sense, of course, every artist, even those who write numerous masterworks, may be said to have one book. Mann questioned whether his first novel, *Buddenbrooks*, was not also his only one. In this case, however, either the work has many different aspects that can be amplified anew, or the man is sufficiently skilled to find additional latent forms and sets of themes in his single work.

ART AND PSYCHOSIS

The works of the more seriously mentally ill have rarely been regarded as serious artistic productions, because they are not successful communications, being in general too rigid and stereotyped to permit interesting readings. Although aesthetically barren, these works are of considerable diagnostic value. They reveal some of the problems or difficulties of the patient, and are also suggestive of the factors that thwart artistic development and accomplishment. Kris has reviewed the lives of a number of such artists. He indicates that psychotic art is typically mysterious and that one encounters difficulty entering the world of the patient. Pictures are often ambiguous, allowing several interpretations. Rarely are situations represented so that they exemplify human experiences: Expressions are frozen, stereotyped, unnatural. Furthermore, "though these productions of the psychotic tend to be prolific, the level of his skill remains essentially unchanged." Apparently, evolution of style presupposes a certain intactness of ego function, and in the absence of such cohesiveness, behavior becomes inflexible and unchanging. Obviously, then, changes in the work of the psychotic are of great significance, as they may herald a renaissance, a reassertion of a living, changing aspect of the person.

An instructive view of psychotic art, accompanied by several hundred examples, has been offered by J. R. Plokker. This author concentrates on the art of schizophrenics, noting that the content and style of their art differs across phases of their diseases. The schizophrenic who paints does so naturally, without regard to aesthetic or cultural criteria. In the absence of artistic skill prior to the onset of the disease, no artistic works of quality will be produced once the disease has revealed itself. Yet at least 5 percent of nonpainters do start to paint spontaneously after the onset of schizophrenia.

While Plokker is skeptical about the results of painting therapy, he does indicate that "by allowing the patient to draw or paint regularly, it is often possible to follow the course of the illness. Improvement and deterioration are often clearly reflected in such work." Such works may be cathartic and may hang together for the patient, but for the observer "who naturally has not been able to follow the associative series, there is merely a chaotic, senseless, whole." Patients can work for years on the same, small, insignificant picture without acquiring any new skill; their development appears to have been frozen at a certain level. "The artist who is mentally healthy—to whatever movement he wishes to belong— shows intellectual expansion; the schizophrenic knows no development in the positive sense; he retraces his own steps, is regressive." Indeed the psychotic is able neither to copy a drawing correctly, nor to copy facial expressions, nor to interpret their significance. The interpersonal aspect crucial to art as a communicative process is absent.

Yet, in spite of this impairment, schizophrenics are able to communicate certain aspects of their condition. Symbols of rejection abound, and imagery of cutting off is frequent. Signs like flowers can signal an improvement. In particular, the art of schizophrenic patients is permeated by certain kinds of modal and vectoral properties, specifically those of a bleak or depressive taint like closedness, isolation, or emptiness. When on rare occasions a nonartist suffering a psychotic breakdown does produce an impressive picture, it is because he has successfully captured in a picture a strong feeling of emptiness or loneliness. Success in such a communication may even aid in a return to health.

Because of the possibility that one's participation in the artistic process may facilitate or signal an improvement in one's psychological state, the art work of individuals who appear to be benefiting therapeutically from their work with a medium has engendered considerable interest. Just as neurotic children can often communicate their difficulties and feelings more effectively through play than through verbal encounters, individuals with various maladies may better be able to gain access to others and themselves through their artistic endeavors. If, as I have argued, the arts provide natural means of making and expressing for all individuals, those who are markedly disturbed may find aesthetic forms more accessible than other symbolic communicative systems. Some patients, indeed, seem to reject all symbolic media, yet prove able to communicate via physical movement in dance. The organizing power of rhythm and music seems helpful here. The possibility for psychic balance seems dependent on the preservation of areas accessible to spontaneous emotional expression. Therapists would seem well advised to consider which symbolic medium might potentially help disturbed individuals.

Guardedly optimistic about the role of artistic endeavors in treating the emotionally disturbed is the therapist M. Naumburg. Naumburg views the arts as an instrument with which certain patients are able to work out their difficulties, come to grips with their feelings, and chart their passage back to health. She argues that

When inner experiences of a patient are projected into plastic form, art often becomes a more immediate mode of expression than words. Thus the use of spontaneous art as a chief means of therapy has tended to increase rather than retard verbalization. This happens whenever the patient, eager to make the meaning of his symbolic designs more understandable to the therapist, elaborates their significance in words. . . . Those who began their spontaneous creations with fragmented or divided forms, eventually succeeded in producing, as their condition improved, satisfying nonschizophrenic types of art.

Naumburg also stresses the informative role the patient's art can play for the therapist, pointing out that patients are often able to picture childhood memories and long-suppressed traumatic experiences before they can verbalize them. "When unconscious art projections are accepted by the therapist as symbolic speech, verbal interpretation of their meaning to the patient becomes unnecessary."

It is extraordinarily difficult to judge whether the arts serve merely as a vehicle to occupy the patient and provide information to the therapist, or whether they can play a constructive role in a patient's return to health. Studies using different aesthetic media have demonstrated that a regular program of music or art therapy does frequently correlate with improvement in the patient's condition. The difficulty with these studies is in the choice of a control group; a surprising number of studies use no control group at all, and those that do use controls often give the members no treatment at all. But a clear demonstration of the efficacy of the arts can only come about if controls include equally effective and committed therapists who also present an interesting activity, though one outside the arts.

Occasional claims have been made that the arts aid children who suffer from severe neurosis or psychosis. For example, Wolff reports that children suffering from stereotypical behaviors have sometimes been helped by involvement in the arts: "In each instance it seems to the outsider that the therapist has entered into the apparently aimless, self-sufficient stereotype with the patient and has then conveyed the mannerism into a behavior that can be entrained on external synchronizers (for example, music) or related to concrete events and persons in the environment." Other investigators describe young patients whose involvement with music, painting, or poetry has signaled a return to health. It should be pointed out, however, that the arts need not necessarily aid the ailing child; at least one student of autism proposes that music therapy simply serves to reinforce the bizarre features of the child's ailment and that the child would be far better off exposed to no music at all.

The precise role played by the arts in rehabilitation or therapy is also open to dispute. It would be comforting to aestheticians, and in conformity with the theory of this book, if exposure to the formal aspects of the arts were the decisive factor in bringing about an improved condition. There is at least as much evidence to suggest, however, that patients are aided by the sentimental messages found on mawkish greeting cards as by the formal elegance of a Shakespearean sonnet or a Bach fugue. Even if it is the message rather than the structure of the art work that helps certain patients, however, it still appears probable that active involvement with artistic production—as a writer, painter, actor, sculptor, or musician—can serve as an effective therapeutic agent. Such involvement necessarily involves formal as well as content aspects of the art work. And, in certain cases, one finds noted artists suffering from mental disorders who deliberately and effectively portray their bizarre experiences in their works. A more fruitful step toward the realization and reintegration of the three developing systems is difficult to envisage.

While it would be most promising to find that the arts can aid in the cure of psychological diseases, evidence on this question is most limited. Certainly the causal connection is in doubt: There is no way of determining whether an aesthetic breakthrough is a symptom or a cause of psychological improvement. What is crucial for our purposes is the way in which the individual's psychological health and well being seems to be so closely correlated with his capacity to participate spontaneously and fully in the artistic process. Severe impairments destroy one's ability to function as a creator, audience member, performer, or critic, because one is no longer able to communicate with other persons. One might still be able to perform difficult calculations or earn great sums of money, but the fact of being cut off from other persons, and from one's own humanness, seems to cripple an individual in the artistic realm. Art is so closely tied to the developmental process that any impairment in development, due to psychosis, regression, or senility, has immediate ramifications in one's aesthetic activities. The fact that the arts deal with those qualities, modes and vectors that are basic and universal to mankind— and that psychosis impairs the artistic process—suggests that the most fundamental processes and content of human communication are in jeopardy. Reestablishing the human aspects of communication and symbol use appears a prerequisite before normal development and participation in the artistic process can be resumed.

ART AND TRUTH

Insight into the therapeutic qualities of arts can be gained by a consideration of what makes for bad or false art. Edmund Wilson has focused on the relevant aspect in his contention that the worst quality for an artist is an inability to be truthful to his own thoughts and feelings. Such inauthenticity or falseness is immediately apparent in the person's work. In speaking of the genuineness or legitimacy of works, one alludes to the truthfulness of the voice behind the words in a poem, or to the integrity of activity behind a painting. Art depends upon truth "to him who can recognize it," says Schoenberg; "one must tell the ice cold truth to be great," Mann has his literary Goethe declare.

While beauty and truth have often been equated, it has also been claimed that "art is not truth . . . the artist must know the manner whereby to convince the others of the truthfulness of his lies." But a more careful formulation suggests that art is not truth, as construed by some scientists. Far from consisting of a list of facts or a conceptualization that can be reliably agreed upon by a team of investigators, art is the execution and communication of the subjective insights of an individual. The feelings and beliefs of the artist are so communicated that others may share these intuitions about the quality and the forms of life. Artistic truth is, simply, an artist's effort to communicate his thoughts and feelings as directly or completely as he can. The effect on the writer when his voice is stilled or threatened can be seen dramatically in this account by a writer who later escaped from Soviet Russia:

That most normal, most fundamental and natural of desires—to speak the truth, or at least to say what you think—is a forgotten unrealizable dream. Throughout his conscious life a man lives in fear of saying something he should not say. And I can no longer be like this. Every word that I put down here is a cry of pain, of truth, of sincerity, and of suffering, because I am hardly ever to know whether my words are published, but I shall go on writing because that is the only way I have a few minutes when I can breath freely.

When so characterized, art is reminiscent of basic trust, that sense of genuineness and spontaneity communicated by the mother at the beginning weeks of life and intuitively grasped by the child. Although there is no intermediary object in this early form of mutuality, it may well be that such primordial interaction provides the model for all subsequent communication, and that the qualities important at each stage of the life cycle become embodied in art works. Communications among individuals must be direct at first, but eventually the developmental process also enables the child to appreciate and to communicate his genuine feelings and thoughts through symbolic objects. The means used for communication will differ over the years, but the essential requirements for an effective and deeply felt communication can be discerned in the initial contacts between mother and child.

The vision and the truth of the artist are different from those of the scientist; in no respect are they inferior. Men like Leonardo and Goethe who contributed both to the arts and to the sciences were driven by equal passions to capture truths about the physical world and about human life in whatever medium or discipline they chose. The truths of science tend to involve the structure of the world; those of art, the forms and intuitions of individuals. But both are esteemed equally by those engaged with them. The search for truth is a dominant theme in the works describing these individuals. Ernest Jones talks about Freud's tremendous desire to attain the truth; Goethe said, "I flee from what is impure . . . may the idea of purity which extends to this bite of food . . . grow even more shining within me. . . . The first and last thing required of genius is truth." And in speaking to Eckermann about his own art, he declared "I have never tried to pretend in my poetry. I have never put on verse or expressed otherwise things I do not live, things that did not make me feel hot under the collar or that did not keep me awake nights. I wrote love poems only when I was in love." When truth is sought by the most gifted investigators and creators, any gap between art and science disappears. Havelock Ellis indicates that "we have to recognize that the true man of science is an artist. . . . It was by his wonderful imagination that Newton was constantly discovering new tracks and new processes in the region of the unknown." Coleridge declared: "Poetry [has] a logic of its own as severe as that of science; and more difficult, because more subtle, more complex, and dependent on more and more fugitive causes."

In spite of important differences in the personality, attitudes, training, and skills of those involved in the arts and sciences, this fundamental drive—to discover and preserve aspects of truth about life—will be found among all creative individuals of ability. Characterized by a zealous pursuit of the truths about life, the world, and their own feelings, these outstanding individuals are able to communicate only because they have mastered a technical skill or a medium, and because they are powerfully motivated to share their discoveries with others. Of course, in an ultimate sense, none of these men will ever attain Truth, even if such an entity should happen to exist. What is crucial and characteristic is that the most superlative practitioners of art and science feel compelled to express as directly, completely, and honestly as possible all that they have been able to find out about their world and about themselves.

Even though their goals converge with one another, scientist and artist continue to work in distinctive ways. The scientist attempts to communicate his truths in as generalized, abstract, and explicit a form as possible, optimally in logical expressions, whereas the artist embodies his truths in objects or media, which, in their bright colors, rough surfaces, or muted tones, exemplify aspects of what is perceived and felt. In their exploitation of the concrete, the sensuous, the immediate, the available, in their frequent avoidance of formalism and abstraction, the arts seem to draw more directly on the untutored proclivities of human beings. At least, the artistic process engages the perceiving, feeling, and making systems in a way close to their operation in the developing child, and thus in a more intimate manner than do the sciences. Free of dependence on verbalization and hypothetic-deductive thinking, the arts refer more specifically to aspects of the individual's own life, and cause profound changes in his own feelings, percepts, and actions. Indeed, even formal reasoning seems easier to understand when it is embedded in a concrete form, such as a story or poem. Art has the singular potential for bringing man closer to other men, by highlighting their common traits, and so its use as a therapeutic mechanism can readily be appreciated. This aspect appears to be sensed by children who, in Read's formulation, "use their drawings not as expression of their perceptual images, not of their pent-up feelings but rather as a feeler, a spontaneous reaching out to the external world, at first tentative but capable of becoming the main factor in the adjustment of the individual to society." As a result, the arts may be drawn on to help children express themselves. And indeed one of the most persistent findings in the recent outpouring of literature about educational innovation is that hitherto awkward and unexpressive children when given the needed medium for expression, can communicate their thoughts, desires, and percepts freely and passionately.

Because the arts provide a natural means for men to act and to communicate, they can reveal vital and elusive information about the experiences and subjective life of others. Insight into the thoughts and feelings of those who live in primitive or preliterate societies has been difficult to obtain, because tasks adopted from Western society are so differently structured, and the native languages may contain many deceptive facets. Our own view of the arts and the artistic process, rooted in modern Western culture, is necessarily parochial, and yet it is plausible that research on other cultures and other eras will provide some support for the ideas put forth. The manifold difficulties involved in understanding another civilization can to some extent be obviated by an examination of the aesthetic products of a culture—its drawings, its music, above all its myths. Such examination may yield rich insight into the structure and the content of the savage mind, the mind of every human. And just as the arts may provide a better key to appreciate the nature of the human primitive mind, they can provide critical clues for the understanding of the minds of children. Because children see, feel, and make from the first, all their experiences enrich the systems on which their eventual participation in the aesthetic process will be based. As they acquire various symbol systems, master the communicative potential of these systems, and gain an increasing sense of themselves and of others and a feeling for artistic media, the insights they have acquired can be communicated to other persons. While they are still too young for formal schooling, some intuition for the formal aspects of various art forms will already be evident in their productions. Those who are especially gifted can already participate in the musical arts. Their increased commerce with the world of other individuals, their refined knowledge of the tradition and codes, and their increasing skills with various making activities soon enable them to participate more fully in a range of symbolic forms.

Some individuals who have particularly strong wills, organizing ideas, dominant personalities, drive, motivation, and talent will go on to create new aesthetic objects. Others, with strong discriminatory and logical powers, will likely become critics or enter the scientific realm. Still others will draw on deep capacities for feeling or keen sensitivities to the details of experience and the subtleties of interpersonal interactions, entering the aesthetic process as performers or audience members. The three developing systems will continue to serve these individuals as they become adults, but the possibility of a derailment, accentuation, or interaction of the systems will give rise to wide individual differences. These alternative paths are important—for the differences as well as the similarities among men, the identifying features that constitute an individual's thought, feeling, and style, are of great moment and interest in the arts. Nonetheless, the ultimate impact and import of the arts depends on certain universal qualities and forms, readily acquired or present from the first, which can impel and affect all men, because these men belong to the same species and have grown together. These universals, most readily and most profoundly captured in art objects, help define the human condition. They make the arts central to our understanding of human development.

BIBLIOGRAPHICAL NOTES

CHAPTER 1

Page 1. Examples of the earliest studies of children are found in W. Dennis (ed.), *Historical Readings in Developmental Psychology* (New York: Appleton-Century-Crofts, 1972). Perhaps the best known observations of infants during that era were those of Charles Darwin, "A Biographical Sketch of an Infant," *Mind*, 1877, **2**, 286–294. For a collection of early observations on children, see W. Kessen (ed.), *The Child* (New York: Wiley, 1965).

Page 1. Among Gesell's writings are A. Gesell et al., *The Child from Five to Ten* (New York: Harper, 1946); *The First Five Years of Life* (New York: Harper, 1940).

Page 2. S. Bijou and D. Baer present their views of child development in *Child Development: Universal Stage of Infancy* (New York: Appleton-Century-Crofts, 1965), Vol. 2, 83. G. Terrell's point of view is expressed in "The Need for Simplicity in Research," *Child Development*, 1958, **29**, 308.

Page 2. Critical discussions of the behaviorist point of view can be found in N. Chomsky, "Review of B. F. Skinner's *Verbal Behavior*," *Language*, 1959, **35**, 26–58; W. Köhler, *Gestalt Psychology* (New York: Liveright, 1929); J. Fodor, *Psychological Explanation* (New York: Random House, 1968); and many other philosophical and psychological writings.

Page 3. Examples of eclectic theorizing in developmental psychology include D. Berlyne, *Structure and Direction in Thinking* (New York: Wiley, 1965); J. Langer, *Theories of Development* (New York: Holt, Rinehart and Winston, 1969); P. H. Wolff, "The Developmental Psychologies of Jean Piaget and Psychoanalysis," *Psychological Issues*, 1960, **2**; P. H. Wolff, "Cognitive Considerations for a Psychoanalytic Theory of Language Acquisition," in R. Holt (ed.), *Motives and Thought* (New York: International Universities Press, 1967), pp. 299–343.

Page 3. Freud's comments on children and women are found in "Three Contributions to the Theory of Sex," in A. A. Brill (ed.), *The Basic Writings of Sigmund Freud* (New York: Random House, 1938), pp. 592–593.

Page 4. Freud's further views on children are found in the volume edited by Brill, for example on page 596. See also "Sexual Theories of Children," *Standard Edition* (London: Hogarth, 1959), Vol. 9, pp. 209–226; and "Sexual Enlightenment of Children," *ibid.*, Vol. 9, pp. 129–141.

Page 4. Critiques of Freud's views of the newborn are found in J. Piaget, *Play, Dreams, and Imitation* (New York: Norton, 1962); and T. Gouin-Décarie, *Intelligence and Affectivity in Early Childhood* (New York: International Universities Press, 1965).

Page 4. Modifications within the psychoanalytic school have come from E. Erikson, *Childhood and Society* (New York: Norton, 1963); R. Spitz, *The First Year of Life* (New York: International Universities Press, 1965); and A. Freud, *Normality and Pathology in Children* (New York: International Universities Press, 1965).

Page 4. Freud's characterization of his own work "as a psychoanalyst" is quoted in the essay by Thomas Mann, "Freud's Position in the History of Modern Thought," in *Past Masters and Other Essays* (New York: Knopf, 1933), p. 191.

Page 4. Freud on child as little adult: "Sexual Lives of Human Beings," *Standard Edition* (London: Hogarth, 1963), Vol. 16, pp. 303–319.

Page 5. Limitations of psychoanalysis: S. Freud, "Infantile Sexuality," in A. A. Brill (ed.), *Basic Writings of Sigmund Freud* (New York: Random House, 1938), p. 599.

Page 6. Piaget's statements about what is neglected in his own work are quoted in P. H. Wolff, "La théorie sensori-motrice de l'intelligence et la psychologie du développement générale," in *Psychologie et epistémologie génétique: Thèmes Piagetiens* (Paris: Dunod, 1966), p. 246; and in J. Piaget and B. Inhelder, *L'image mentale chez l'enfant* (Paris: Presses Universitaires de Paris, 1966), p. vii. An introduction to Piaget's theory can be found in J. Flavell, *The Developmental Psychology of Jean Piaget* (Princeton: Van Nostrand, 1963); H. Furth, *Piaget and Knowledge* (Englewood Cliffs, N.J.: Prentice-Hall, 1968); H. Gardner, *The Quest for Mind* (New York: Knopf, 1973), Chapter 3.

Page 6. Piaget's contrast of figurativity and operativity is found in J. Piaget and B. Inhelder, *L'image mentale chez l'enfant* (Paris: Presses Universitaires de Paris, 1966).

Page 6. For Piaget's views on affect, see his lectures, "Les relations entre l'affectivité et l'intelligence dans le développement mental de l'enfant" (Paris: Centre de documentation universitaire, 1954); and J. Piaget and B. Inhelder, *The Psychology of the Child* (New York: Basic Books, 1968).

Page 6. Ordinarily a master at assimilating the ideas of others to his own framework, Piaget has never satisfactorily related his ideas to those of Freud. Strongly attracted to psychoanalytic thought, favorably received by Freud in the early 1920s, a contributor to the study of dream life who was himself analyzed, Piaget obviously has a high regard for Freud's contribution and accepts many of the psychoanalytic insights. Nevertheless, Piaget continues to feel that some aspects are difficult to incorporate into general psychology and into his own developmental theory.

In a tortuous chapter in *Play, Dreams, and Imitation* (New York: Norton, 1962), Piaget attempts to integrate the Freudian view of symbolism with his own notions about the "semiotic" (symbolic) realm in the child. The discussion oscillates between an acceptance and a critique of Freud's findings. For example, Piaget asserts at one point that certain symbols seem more potent to the child because "the content of these symbols is more directly related to the child's ego and involves relatively permanent affective schemas" (pp. 174-5).

While Piaget seems to be begging the crucial question of what confers a special value upon certain symbols, he does suggest further on that, in the case of such "secondary symbols . . . it is a matter of intimate, permanent concerns, of secret and often inexpressible desires" (p. 175). In this latter passage, Piaget appears to have accepted the Freudian approach to the content of the child's mind, but he never elaborates this line of thought, thereby avoiding a discussion of the nature of these intimate and inexpressible desires. In other passages as well, Piaget seems on the verge of embracing the psychoanalytic position, only to retreat when its implications appear to challenge his own carefully constructed position. Genuine integration is never achieved.

Piaget would like to assimilate Freud to the general findings of experimental psychology and into his own model of cognitive development. He shrewdly points to the weaknesses and contradictions in Freud's formulations—the homuncular censor, the unwarranted assumptions about infantile memory and consciousness, the outmoded associationism. He also makes a persuasive demonstration of the continuity between conscious and unconscious thought in the child. Yet, rather than modifying his own formulations in order to retain what is valid in the Freudian picture, Piaget is content merely to *praise* the method and the facts, and to *state* that certain symbols are secondary (unconscious, not comprehended by the child) because they have "more intense affectivity" (p. 171), pertain to particular kinds of content, and have closer connection between the ego and the desires involved. Furthermore, the dynamics of the child's affective life are explicitly skirted when Piaget allows "there is probably something to be said for the idea" (p. 175) that the breast occupies a special place in the child's mental life and in his definition of repression as "an automatic or spontaneous regulation resulting from the interaction of affective schemas whose roots elude consciousness" (p. 204).

Piaget might have been more successful in coordinating his views with those of Freud if he had not suspected weaknesses in his own formulation, and if he had been acquainted at the time of his writing with the works of the ethologists. Such careful observers of animal behavior as Konrad Lorenz (cf. his *Studies in Animal and Human Behavior* [Cambridge: Harvard University Press, 1970]) have offered a plausible account of how certain experiences may acquire special status because of the time of their occurrence and the role they assume in the development of the child. Reconciling these approaches to affect is a task that cannot be accomplished here; but the direction in which such a synthesis might proceed will be limned in the following chapters.

Page 7. T. Gouin-Décarie, *Intelligence and Affectivity in Early Childhood* (New York: International Universities Press, 1965). For P. H. Wolff, see references cited in note to chapter 1, p. 3. D. Carmichael, "Irony, A Developmental and Cognitive Study," Unpublished doctoral dissertation, University of California at Berkeley, 1965.

Page 8. Abrams's formulation is found in *The Mirror and the Lamp: Romantic Theory and the Critical Tradition* (New York: Norton, 1968).

Page 8. G. Birkhoff, *Aesthetic Measure* (Cambridge: Harvard University Press, 1933).

Page 8. Tests of Birkhoff's theory have been made by J. H. Beebe-Center and C. C. Pratt, "A Test of Birkhoff's Aesthetic Measure," *Journal of General Psychology*, 1937, **17**, 335–350; R. C. Davis, "An Evaluation and Test of

Birkhoff's Aesthetic Measure Formula," *Journal of General Psychology*, 1936, **15**, 231–240; and H. Eysenck and M. Castle, "Training in Art as a Factor in the Determination of Preference Judgments for Polygons," *British Journal of Psychology*, 1970, **61**, 65–81. See also D. Berlyne, *Conflict, Arousal and Curiosity* (New York: McGraw-Hill, 1960), pp. 238–240.

Page 9. On the imitative view of aesthetic creation, see J. Biederman, *Art as the Evolution of Visual Knowledge* (Red Wing, Minn.: Author, 1948); Leonardo da Vinci, *Treatise on Painting*, trans. A. P. McMahon (Princeton: Princeton University Press, 1956), Vol. 1, p. 212; and E. H. Gombrich, *Art and Illusion* (New York; Pantheon, 1960), p. 90.

Page 9. See N. Frye, *An Anatomy of Criticism* (New York: Atheneum, 1967).

Page 10. On the relationship between perceiving, imitating, and reproducing, see J. S. Bruner, "On Perceptual Readiness," *Psychological Review*, 1957, **64**, 123–152; E. H. Gombrich, *Art and Illusion* (New York: Pantheon, 1960); and J. Piaget, *The Mechanism of Perception* (New York: Basic Books, 1969).

Page 10. Berlyne's position is described in his book *Conflict, Arousal and Curiosity* (New York: McGraw-Hill, 1960). His more recent *Aesthetics and Psychobiology* (New York: Appleton-Century-Crofts, 1971) was not available for study during the writing of this book.

Page 11. The application of information theory to art is found in L. Meyer, *Emotion and Meaning in Music* (Chicago: University of Chicago Press, 1956); L. Meyer, "Some Remarks on Value and Greatness in Music," *Journal of Aesthetics and Art Criticism*, 1959, **17**, 486–500; and A. Moles, *Information Theory and Esthetic Perception* (Urbana, Ill.: University of Illinois Press, 1966). The quotation comes from page 105 of the latter work.

Page 12. The view that creative geniuses are qualitatively no different from other persons is expressed by J. P. Guilford, "A Psychometric Approach to Creativity," in H. H. Anderson (ed.), *Creativity in Childhood and Adolescence: A Diversity of Approaches* (Palo Alto, Calif.: Science and Behavior Books, 1965). See pages 7 and 10.

Page 13. Ability to provide novel ideas: Guilford, *Ibid.*, p. 10.

Page 14. The school of semiotic aesthetics includes E. Cassirer, *The Philosophy of Symbolic Forms* (New Haven: Yale University Press, 1953–1957); and S. K. Langer, *Philosophy in a New Key* (New York: Mentor, 1958).

Pages 14–15. Langer's remarks on feeling are found in *Mind: An Essay on Human Feeling* (Baltimore: Johns Hopkins University Press, 1967), p. 112. Langer's argument that art forms are "virtual experience" is propounded in *Feeling and Form* (New York: Scribner's, 1953). Her most recent and most complete statement is in *Mind: An Essay on Human Feeling*.

Page 16. The Gestalt position, including remarks about the arts, can be found in K. Koffka, *Principles of Gestalt Psychology* (New York: Harcourt, Brace, 1935); W. Köhler, *Gestalt Psychology* (New York: Liveright, 1929); and R. Arnheim (Berkeley: University of California Press, 1954). Arnheim's more recent writings include *Picasso's* Guernica (Berkeley: University of California Press, 1962); *Toward a Psychology of Art* (Berkeley: University of California Press, 1966); and *Visual Thinking* (Berkeley: University of California Press, 1969).

Page 17. For Freud's views on art see his papers collected in *On Creativity and the Unconscious*, ed. B. Nelson (New York: Harper, 1958). L. Trilling discusses these views in an insightful essay "Freud and Literature," in *The Liberal Imagination* (Garden City, N.Y.: Doubleday, 1954), pp. 44–64. Freud's lament on the relative difficulty of scientific thinking is quoted in E. Jones, *The Life and Work of Sigmund Freud* (New York: Basic Books, 1957), Vol. 3, p. 449.

Page 17. Freud's pessimistic conclusion about the possibility of explaining the arts is found in his essay on *Leonardo: A Study in Psychosexuality* (New York: Vintage Books, 1967), p. 119.

Page 17. O. Rank, *Art and Artist* (New York: Knopf, 1932).

Page 18. Freud on play: "Creative Writers and Daydreaming," in *Standard Edition of the Complete Psychological Works of Sigmund Freud,* Vol. 9 (London: Hogarth, 1959), pp. 143–144. Piaget on the child as artist: in E. Ziegfeld, (ed.), *Education and Art* (Paris: UNESCO, 1953), p. 22. Werner and Kaplan put forth their theory in *Symbol Formation* (New York: Wiley, 1963).

Page 20. On Piaget as a new paradigm in psychology see H. Furth, *Piaget and Knowledge* (Englewood Cliffs, N.J.: Prentice-Hall, 1968); and H. Gardner, *The Quest for Mind* (New York: Knopf, 1973).

Page 20. Remarks on the child and the artist: R. Arnheim, *Art and Visual Perception* (Berkeley: University of California Press, 1954). p. 164. E. Jaensch, quoted in H. Read, *Education through Art* (New York: Pantheon, n.d.), p. 58.

Page 20. R. Spitz, *The First Year of Life* (New York: International Universities Press, 1965), p. 136; T. Mann, *Essays* (New York: Vintage Books, 1957), p. 322; H. Matisse, in E. Ziegfeld (ed.), *Education and Art* (Paris: UNESCO, 1953), p. 21; L. Tolstoy, quoted in K. Chukovsky, *From Two to Five* (Berkeley: University of California Press, 1968), p. 140; Goethe, quoted in D. Katz and R. Katz, *Conversations with Children* (London: Kegan Paul, 1936), p. 7; W. Pfleiderer, the psychologist, quoted in H. Eng, *The Psychology of Child and Youth Drawing* (New York: Humanities Press, 1957), p. 190.

Page 21. Real task of psychology: D. Katz and R. Katz, cited in the previous reference, p. 302.

Page 22. On the leading role that can be played by affect, see P. Wolff, "Developmental and Motivational Concepts in Piaget's Sensori-Motor Theory of Intelligence," *Journal of the American Academy of Child Psychiatry,* 1963, **2**, 241; and J. Bowlby, quoted in J. Tanner and B. Inhelder (eds.), *Discussions on Child Development* (New York: International Universities Press, 1960), Vol. 4, pp. 42–43.

Page 23. W. James, *Principles of Psychology* (New York: Dover, 1950), Vol. 1, pp. 309–310.

Page 28. Arnheim on the critic and the audience member: *Toward a Psychology of Art* (Berkeley: University of California Press, 1966), p. 15.

Page 30. Analytic philosophers on definition of art: See M. Weitz, "The Role of Theory in Esthetics," in M. Rader (ed.), *A Modern Book of Esthetics* (New York: Holt, Rinehart and Winston, 1960), pp. 199–208; and M. Cohen, "Aesthetic Essence," in M. Black (ed.), *Philosophy in America* (Ithaca, N.Y.: Cornell University Press, 1965), pp. 115–133.

Page 31. Communication by artist and scientist: E. Schachtel, *Metamorphosis* (New York: Basic Books, 1959), p. 168.

Page 31. On nontranslatability in the arts, see S. K. Langer, *Philosophy in a New Key* (New York: Mentor, 1961), Chapter 4.

Page 32. The verses are of course by Pope, from his *Essay on Criticism.*

Pages 32–33. Sapir writes about translation in *Language* (New York: Harcourt, Brace, 1921), p. 239.

Page 33. Conrad on the sensuousness of art: Preface to *The Nigger of Narcissus* (Garden City, N.Y.: Doubleday, 1925), p. xii.

Page 34. The auditory imagination: T. S. Eliot, *The Uses of Poetry and the Uses of Criticism* (London: Faber & Faber, 1933), p. 111.

Pages 34–35. Tolstoy's definition of art: *What Is Art?* (London: Walter Scott, n.d.), p. 48.

Page 35. On notation of dance, see N. Goodman, *Languages of Art* (Indianapolis, Ind.: Bobbs-Merrill, 1968), pp. 214–218.

Page 36. N. Wiener, *The Human Use of Human Beings* (Garden City, N.Y.: Doubleday, n.d.).

Page 36. All that is felt: Goethe, quoted in T. Mann, *Essays* (New York: Vintage Books, 1957), p. 57.

Page 37. For Langer's definition of feeling, see references cited in note to Chapter 1, p. 14.

Pages 38–39. On starting point of aesthetics, see C. Bell, quoted in R. Arnheim, *Toward a Psychology of Art* (Berkeley: University of California Press, 1966), p. 200. The poetess Marianne Moore spoke of ecstasy in the creation of arts, quoted in J. Ashbury, "Straight Lines over Rough Terrains: Review of Marianne Moore's Collected Poems," *New York Times Book Review*, November 26, 1967, p. 42.

Page 41. Support for the three systems: J. Dewey, quoted in M. Rader (ed.), *A Modern Book of Esthetics* (New York: Holt, Rinehart and Winston, 1960), p. 70; H. Janson, in S. Hook (ed.), *Art and Philosophy* (New York: New York University Press, 1966), p. 27; Thomas Mann, *Essays* (New York: Vintage Books, 1957), p. 303.

Page 43. N. Rorem, quoted in *The New York Times*, July 6, 1969, Section 2, 1–3.

Page 43. The distinction between autographic and allographic arts is developed in N. Goodman, *Languages of Art* (Indianapolis, Ind.: Bobbs-Merrill, 1968), pp. 113–122. The discussion of symbols also relies heavily on Goodman's treatment.

Page 43. On style in the autographic and allographic arts, see H. Gardner, "The Development of Sensitivity to Artistic Styles," *Journal of Aesthetics and Art Criticism,* 1971, 29, 515–527.

Page 45. Piaget on groupings, groups and operations: J. Piaget, *Traité de logique* (Paris: Colin, 1949).

CHAPTER 2

Pages 53–54. D. Morris, *The Biology of Art* (Chicago: Aldine•Atherton, 1967). The first quotation comes from p. 22, the second from p. 109. For further studies of chimpanzee art, see P. Schiller, "Figural Preferences in the Drawings of a Chimpanzee," *Journal of Comparative Psychology,* 1951, 44, 101–111; V. Bukin, "Investigation of the Capabilities of the Chimpanzee for the Reproduction of Graphical Movements of Man," *Voprosy Psikhologii,* 1961, 2, 107–108 (abstract).

Page 55. The classic study of bird song is W. H. Thorpe, *Bird Song* (Cambridge: Cambridge University Press, 1961). See also P. Marler, "A Comparative Approach to Vocal Learning: Song Development in White Crowned Sparrows," *Journal of Comparative and Physiological Psychology,* 1970, **71**, 2, 1–25; M. Konishi, "The Role of Auditory Feedback in the Control of Vocalization in the White-crowned Sparrow," Z. *Tierpsychologie,* 1965, **22**, 770–783; F. Nottebohm, "Ontogeny of Bird Song," *Science,* 1970, **167**, 950–956; and P. Marler and W. Hamilton, *Mechanisms of Animal Behavior* (New York: Wiley, 1966). The parallel between bird song and language has been developed by P. Marler in his 1970 article.

Page 55. Deafening of birds: Konishi, 1965.

Page 56. Templates: Marler, 1970.

Page 57. The most gifted antiphonal singers are described in W. H. Thorpe, *Learning and Instinct in Animals* (London: Methuen, 1956), p. 356; and in A. Koestler, *The Act of Creation* (London: Hutchinson, 1964), p. 492.

Page 57. On asymmetrical neural organization in birds, see F. Nottebohm, "Neural lateralization of vocal control in a passerine bird," *Journal of Experimental Zoology* 1971, **177**, 229–261.

Page 58. On figure in aesthetic perception, see H. Gardner, "On Figure and Texture in Aesthetic Perception," *British Journal of Aesthetics,* 1972, **12**, 40–59.

Page 59. On skill mastery, see J. S. Bruner, "Origins of Problem-Solving Strategies in Skill Acquisition," in R. Rudner and I. Scheffler (eds.), *Logic and Art: Essays in Honor of Nelson Goodman* (Indianapolis, Ind.: Bobbs-Merrill, 1972), pp. 100–121. The quotation comes from V. Denenberg (ed.), *Education of the Infant and the Young Child* (New York: Academic Press, 1970), p. 113.

Pages 59–60. Four stages of learning: K. Fischer, "The Structure and Development of Sensory-Motor Actions," Unpublished doctoral dissertation, Harvard University, 1970.

Page 60. Autonomy of motor organs: E. von Holst and U. von St. Paul, "On the Functional Organization of Drives," *Animal Behavior,* 1963, **11**, 1–20; P. Weiss, "Autonomous versus Reflexogenous Activity of the Central Nervous System," *Proceedings of the American Philosophical Society,* 1941, **84**, 53–64.

Page 60. P. H. Wolff, "The Role of Biological Rhythms in Early Psychological Development," *Bulletin of the Menninger Clinic,* 1967, **31**, 197–218. K. Lashley, "The Problem of Serial Order in Behavior," in L. Jeffress (ed.), *Cerebral Mechanisms in Behavior: The Hixon Symposium* (New York: Wiley, 1951), pp. 112–136.

Page 61. Piaget on infant development: J. Piaget, *The Origins of Intelligence in Children* (New York: Norton, 1952).

Page 61. Köhler's studies of chimpanzees are found in *The Mentality of Apes* (New York: Harcourt, Brace, 1925).

Page 61. On human sucking, see P. H. Wolff, "Sucking Patterns of Infant Mammals," *Brain Behavior and Evolution,* 1968, **1**, 354–367; P. H. Wolff, "The Role of Biological Rhythms in Early Psychological Development," *Bulletin of the Menninger Clinic,* 1967, **31**, 197–218; W. Kessen, "Sucking and Looking: Two Organized Congenital Patterns of Behavior in the Human New Born," in H. Stevenson (ed.), *Early Behavior: Comparative and Developmental Approaches*

(New York: Wiley, 1967), pp. 147–180. J. S. Bruner, *Processes of Cognitive Growth in Infancy* (Barre, Mass.: Clark University Press, 1968).

Page 63. Object concept: J. Piaget, *The Construction of Reality in the Child* (New York: Basic Books, 1954).

Page 63. On the keen perceiving systems of animals, see S. Barnett, *Instinct and Intelligence* (Englewood Cliffs, N.J.: Prentice-Hall, 1967); J. P. Scott, *Animal Behavior* (Garden City, N.Y.: Doubleday, 1965); W. Schleidt, *Signals in the Animal World* (New York: McGraw-Hill, 1968).

Page 64. Imprinting: See I. Eibl-Eibesfeldt, *Ethology* (New York: Holt, Rinehart and Winston, 1970), pp. 225 ff.

Page 64. The notion of tropistic perception draws on the ethologists: K. Lorenz, *Studies in Animal and Human Behavior* (Cambridge: Harvard University Press, 1970); and on the research of D. Hubel and T. Wiesel, e.g., "Receptive fields, binocular interaction and functional architecture in the cat's visual cortex," *Journal of Physiology*, 1962, **160**, 106–154; and D. Hubel, "The Visual Cortex of the Cat," *Scientific American*, 1963, **209**, 54–62. Properties of the infant's perceptual system are discussed in W. Kessen, article cited in note to Chapter 2, p. 61.

Page 65. Preferential perception has been studied experimentally by A. Taylor et al., "Changing Color Preferences of Chickens," *Animal Behavior*, 1969, **17**, 3–8; E. Hess, "Imprinting and the Critical Period Concept," in L. Bliss (ed.), *Roots of Behavior* (New York: Harper, 1962); R. Hinde, *Animal Behavior* (New York: McGraw-Hill, 1966), p. 269; F. Buytendijk, *Mind of the Dog* (Boston: Houghton Mifflin, 1935); V. Vaidya, "Form Perception in *Papilio Demoleus L.*," *Behavior*, 1969, **33**, 212–221; and many other investigators.

Page 65. On infant's visual preferences, see R. Fantz, "The Origin of Form Perception," *Scientific American*, 1961, **204**, 66–72; and J. Kagan, *Change and Continuity in Infancy* (New York: Wiley, 1971).

Page 66. Konrad Lorenz has developed the notion of gestalt perception. See his seminal essay, "The Role of Gestalt Perception in Animal and Human Behavior," in L. L. Whyte (ed.), *Aspects of Form* (Bloomington, Ind.: Midland Books, 1966), pp. 157–178. The quotation comes from p. 160.

Page 66. Face perception: R. Ahrens, "Beiträge zur Entwicklung des Physiognomie und Mimikerkennens," *Z. für Experimentelle und Angenwadte Psychologie*, 1954, **2**, 412–494, 599–633.

Page 66. Three-month-old's perception: T. G. Bower, "Perceptual Functioning in Early Infancy," in R. Robinson (ed.) *Brain and Early Behavior* (New York: Academic Press, 1969), p. 219.

Page 66. Development of the perceptual system in infants: E. J. Gibson, *Principles of Perceptual Learning and Development* (New York: Appleton-Century-Crofts, 1969).

Page 67. Increasingly fine discrimination in perceptual system: J. J. Gibson and E. J. Gibson, "Perceptual Learning: Differentiation or Enrichment?" *Psychological Review*, 1955, **62**, 32–41.

Page 67. Pigeon's concept of a human: R. Herrnstein and D. Loveland, "Complex Visual Concept in the Pigeon," *Science*, 1964, **146**, 549–551.

Page 67. Lorenz on the scientist: see essay cited in note to Chapter 2, p. 66.

Page 67. On limitations of the perceptual capacities of animals, see D. Hebb, *The Organization of Behavior* (New York: Wiley, 1964); and E. J. Gibson, "The Development of Perception as an Adaptive Process," *American Scientist*, 1970, **58**, 98–107.

Page 68. Discriminations made by toddlers: see H. Gardner, "The Development of Sensitivity to Artistic Styles," *Journal of Aesthetics and Art Criticism*, 1971, **29**, 515–527.

Page 68. Gestalt-free perception: A. Ehrenzweig, *The Psychoanalysis of Artistic Vision and Hearing* (New York: Braziller, 1965).

Page 68. Autocentric and allocentric perception: E. Schachtel, *Metamorphosis* (New York: Basic Books, 1959), p. 96.

Page 69. Perceptual texture: H. Gardner, "On Figure and Texture in Aesthetic Perception," *British Journal of Aesthetics*, 1972, **12**, 40–59.

Page 70. On the feelings of animals, see F. Buytendijk, *The Mind of the Dog* (Boston: Houghton Mifflin, 1935), p. 62; and T. H. Huxley, quoted in G. Romanes, *Mental Evolution in Man* (New York: Appleton, 1889), p. 6.

Page 71. On pleasure and punishment centers, see J. Olds and P. Milner, "Positive Reinforcement Produced by Electrical Stimulation of Septal Area and Other Regions of the Brain," *Journal of Comparative and Physiological Psychology*, 1954, **47**, 554–604; J. M. Delgado, W. W. Roberts, and N. E. Miller, "Learning by Electrical Stimulation of the Brain," *American Journal of Physiology*, 1954, **179**, 587-593.

Page 71. On expressive gestures and behaviors in animals, see C. Darwin, *The Expression of Emotions in Man and Animals* (Chicago: University of Chicago Press, 1967); I. Eibl-Eibesfeldt, *Ethology* (New York: Holt, Rinehart and Winston, 1970); D. Hamburg, "Observations of Mother-Infant Interaction in Primate Field Studies," in B. Foss (ed.), *Determinants of Infant Behavior* (London: Methuen, 1969), Vol. 4, pp. 3–15.

Page 71. Lorenz describes the courting goose in *On Aggression* (New York: Bantam, 1967), p. 202.

Page 72. Conceptions of feeling: J. B. Watson, *Behavior* (New York: People's Institute Publishing Company, 1925); K. Bridges, "A Genetic Theory of the Emotions," *Journal of Genetic Psychology*, 1930, **37**, 514–527.

Page 73. Wolff on organismic states: P. H. Wolff, "The Causes, Organization, and Control of Behavior in the Neonate," *Psychological Issues*, 1966, **5**, 1.

Page 74. Meaning of infant smiling: J. Kagan, *Change and Continuity in Infancy* (New York: Wiley, 1971); J. Ambrose, "The Development of the Smiling Response in Early Infancy," in B. Foss (ed.), *op. cit.*, 1969, Vol. 4, pp. 81–110.

Page 75. Bifurcation of the world into good and bad: R. Spitz, *No and Yes* (New York: International Universities Press, 1957). M. Klein, *The Psychoanalysis of Children* (London: Hogarth, 1932). H. Wallon, *Les origines de la pensée chez l'enfant* (Paris: Boivin, 1945), Vol. 1.

Page 76. Immediacy of signaling behavior in animals: N. Tinbergen, *Social Behavior* (New York: Wiley, 1953), p. 74.

Page 78. Development of prehension: J. Piaget, *The Origins of Intelligence in Children* (New York: Norton, 1952); B. White, P. Castle, and R. Held, "Ob-

360 BIBLIOGRAPHICAL NOTES

servations on the Development of Visually-Directed Reaching," *Child Development,* 1964, **35**, 349–364.

Page 79. On problem-solving, see H. Gardner, "Problem-Solving in the Arts," *Journal of Aesthetic Education,* 1971, **5**, 93–114.

Page 80. On problem-solving limitations in different species, see R. Hinde, *Animal Behavior* (New York: McGraw-Hill, 1966); W. Köhler, *The Mentality of Apes* (New York: Harcourt, Brace, 1925); E. J. Gibson, "The Development of Perception as an Adaptive Process," *American Scientist,* 1970, **58**, 98–107.

Page 80. On aspects of animal imitation, see J. Aronfreed, "The Problem of Imitation," in L. Lipsitt and H. Reese (eds.), *Advances in Child Behavior and Development* (New York: Academic Press, 1969), Vol. 4, pp. 210–320; P. Klopfer, "Social Interaction in Discrimination Learning with Special Reference to Feeding Behavior," *Behavior,* 1959, **14**, 282–299; P. Chesler, "Maternal Influences in Learning by Observation in Kittens," *Science,* 1969, **166**, 901–903.

Page 81. Accounts of the social behavior of primates, including descriptions of dominance hierarchies, are found in Eibl-Eibesfeldt, *Ethology* (New York: Holt, Rinehart and Winston, 1970); and I. DeVore and K. Hall in "Baboon Social Behavior" in I. DeVore (ed.), *Primate Behavior* (New York: Holt, Rinehart and Winston, 1965) pp. 53–111.

Page 81. Animal communication: T. Sebeok (ed.), *Animal Communication* (Bloomington, Ind.: Indiana University Press, 1968). Discussion of chimpanzee sign language use can be found in R. A. Gardner and B. Gardner, "Teaching Sign Language to a Chimpanzee," *Science,* 1969, **165**, 664–670.

Page 82. Bee dance: K. von Frisch, *The Dance Language and the Orientation of Bees* (Cambridge: Harvard University Press, 1967).

Page 82. Expression and nominal forms of animal communication are discussed in D. McNeill, *The Acquisition of Language* (New York: Harper and Row, 1970).

Page 83. On rituals in animal life see K. Lorenz, *King Solomon's Ring* (New York: Crowell-Apollo, 1961); J. Huxley (ed.), *Philosophical Transactions of the Royal Society of London,* Series B, Vol. 251, 1966.

Page 84. The quotations about incipient symbol use come from S. Langer, *Philosophy in a New Key* (Cambridge: Harvard University Press, 1971), pp. 110, 111.

Page 84. The great interest in chimpanzee language results from the work of the Gardners (see reference to Chapter 2, p. 81) and the work of D. Premack "A Functional Analysis of Language," *Journal of the Experimental Analysis of Behavior,* 1970, **14**, 107–125. For a thoughtful discussion of the issues raised by this work, see D. Ploog and T. Melnechuk, (eds.), "Are Apes Capable of Language?" *Neurosciences Research Program Bulletin,* 1971, **9**, No. 5.

Page 84. On animals' reading of pictures, see R. K. Davenport and C. M. Rogers, "Perceptions of Photographs by Apes," *Behavior,* 1971, **39**, 318–320.

CHAPTER 3

Page 89. Object permanence: See J. Piaget, *The Construction of Reality in the Child* (New York: Basic Books, 1958), Chapter 1. Cats' performances on these tasks are described in H. Gruber, et al., "The Development of Object Permanence in the Cat," *Developmental Psychology,* 1971, **4**, 9–15.

Page 90. Geschwind's theory is expounded in "The Development of the Brain and the Evolution of Language," *Monograph Series on Language and Linguistics*, 1964, **17**, 155–169, and "Neurological Foundations in Language," in H. Myklebust (ed.), *Progress in Learning Disabilities* (New York: Grune and Stratton, 1967), pp. 182–197. Evidence on cross-modal associations in chimpanzees appears in R. Davenport and C. Rogers, "Intermodal Equivalence of Stimuli in Apes," *Science*, 1970, **168**, 279–281.

Page 91. On elaboration of sensory experience, see G. Murphy, *Human Potentialities* (New York: Basic Books, 1958), p. 34.

Page 91. Infant bifurcation of the sound spectrum: P. Eimas et al., "Speech Perception in Infants," *Science*, 1971, **171**, 303–306.

Page 92. A detailed consideration of the emotional tie between child and mother is found in J. Bowlby, *Attachment and Loss* (New York: Basic Books, 1969).

Page 92. The development of the object concept in relation to persons is described by S. Bell, "The Development of the Concept of Object as Related to Infant-Mother Attachment," *Child Development*, 1970, **41**, 291–312.

Page 92. Developmental trends in the mother-child relation is the subject of L. W. Sander, "The Longitudinal Course of Early Mother-Child Interaction: Cross-Case Comparison in a Sample of Mother-Child Pairs," in B. Foss (ed.), *Determinants of Infant Behavior* (London: Methuen, 1969), Vol. 4, 189–227. This relationship has also been studied by M. Ainsworth, *Infancy in Uganda* (Baltimore: Johns Hopkins University Press, 1967).

Page 93. Animals and mirrors: G. Gallup "Chimpanzees: Self-recognition," *Science*, 1970, **167**, 86–87.

Page 93. Baldwin's theory of the self: J. Baldwin, *Mental Development in the Child and the Race* (New York: Macmillan, 1897).

Page 94. The quotations from Baldwin are found on p. 124 of the above-cited book.

Page 96. Erikson discusses basic trust in *Childhood and Society* (New York: Norton, 1963), pp. 247–251.

Page 96. Piaget's views on basic trust as informational uncertainty are found in J. Tanner and B. Inhelder, *Discussions on Child Development* (New York: International Universities Press, 1960), Vol. 4, pp. 6–7.

Page 97. For discussion of eye-to-eye contact, see T. Bergman, M. M. Haith, and L. Mann, "Development of Eye Contact and Facial Scanning in Infants," paper presented at the Society for Research in Child Development Meetings, April, 1971; also D. Freedman, "A Biological View of Man's Social Behavior," in W. Etkin (ed.), *Social Behavior from Fish to Man* (Chicago: University of Chicago Press, 1967), pp. 152–189.

Page 97. For an exposition of the ethologist's position, see I. Eibl-Eibesfeldt, *Ethology* (New York: Holt, Rinehart and Winston, 1970).

Page 98. I have developed my ideas about modes and vectors in "From Mode to Symbol: Thoughts on the Genesis of the Arts," *British Journal of Aesthetics*, 1970, **10**, 359–375, and *The Quest for Mind* (New York: Knopf, 1973), Chapter 5.

Page 98. Erikson's description of the organ modes is found in *Childhood and Society* (New York: Norton, 1963), pp. 72–97.

Page 99. All mouth and thumb: E. Erikson, reference cited above, p. 32.

Page 99. Physiological "modes" (like taking in or letting go) should not be confused with "sensory modes" or "modalities" (like visual and auditory).

Page 101. Erikson's writings contain numerous examples of the psychological reality of modes and vectors. P. H. Wolff also treats this issue in his essay "Cognitive Considerations for a Psychoanalytic Theory of Language Acquisition," in R. Holt (ed.), *Motives and Thought* (New York: International Universities Press, 1967), pp. 299–343.

Page 101. On the sequence of the erogenous zones, see S. Freud, "Three Contributions to the Theory of Sex," in A. A. Brill (ed.), *The Basic Writings of Sigmund Freud* (New York: Random House, 1938), pp. 553–632.

Page 102. Piaget's observations are reported in *Play, Dreams and Imitation* (New York: Norton, 1962), pp. 38–39; *The Origins of Intelligence in Children* (New York: Norton, 1963), pp. 337–338, 241. The other examples of modal behaviors come from D. Slobin and C. Welsh, "Elicited Imitation as a Research Tool in Developmental Psycholinguistics," unpublished manuscript, University of California, 1968; K. Koffka, *The Growth of the Mind* (Patterson, N.J.: Littlefield Adams, 1959); H. Werner and B. Kaplan, *Symbol Formation* (New York: Wiley, 1963); J. Gardner and H. Gardner, "A Note on Selective Imitation in a Six-Week-Old Infant," *Child Development*, 1970, **41**, 911–916.

Page 103. The quotations come from H. Werner and B. Kaplan (see above reference), p. 86; L. Kubie, "Body Symbolization and the Development of Language," *Psychoanalytic Quarterly*, 1934, **3**, 430–437; P. H. Wolff, see pp. 331–332 of article cited in note to Chapter 3, p. 101.

Page 105. On the Gestalt position: See W. Köhler, *Gestalt Psychology* (New York: Liveright, 1929).

Page 107. Artistic metaphor: E. H. Gombrich, *Meditations on a Hobby-Horse* (London: Phaidon, 1963), p. 48.

Pages 108–109. On initial symbol use see R. Spitz, *No and Yes* (New York: International Universities Press, 1957); R. Jakobson, "Why Mama and Papa?" in *Selected Writings* (Hague: Mouton, 1962), Vol. 1, pp. 538–545.

Page 110. The points of view that are seen as converging may be found in such works as H. Werner and B. Kaplan, *Symbol Formation* (New York: Wiley, 1963); K. Koffka, *The Growth of Mind* (Paterson, N.J.: Littlefield Adams, 1959); E. Erikson, *Childhood and Society* (New York: Norton, 1963); J. Piaget, *Play, Dreams and Imitation* (New York: Norton, 1962).

Page 111. Evidence for the psychological reality of these general properties can be found in the above-cited books. For a review of the empirical literature, see C. Pratt, "Aesthetics," in *Annual Review of Psychology*, 1961, **12**, 71–91. For introspective accounts by practicing artists, see B. Ghiselin, *The Creative Process* (New York: Mentor, 1959).

Page 113. Neurological, linguistic, and physiological evidence in support of the modal hypothesis can be found in C. Trevarthen, "Two Mechanisms of Vision in Primates," *Psychologische Forschung*, 1968, **31**, 299–337; P. Eimas et al., "Speech Perception in Infants," *Science*, 1971, **171**, 303–306.

Page 115. On treating objects in a personal (subjective) way, see F. Helder and M. Simmel, "A Study of Apparent Behavior," *American Journal of Psychology*, 1944, **57**, 243–259.

Page 117. On prodigious children, see K. Koffka, *The Growth of the Mind* (Paterson, N.J.: Littlefield, Adams, 1959), p. 330.

Page 117. Piaget's examples of youthful creativity are found in *The Origins of Intelligence in Children* (New York: Norton, 1952), pp. 274, 332–333.

Page 119. Hypersensitivity in young children: P. Bergmann and S. Escalona, "Unusual Sensitivities in the Very Young Child," in *Psychoanalytic Study of the Child* (New York: International Universities Press, 1949), Vols. 3–4, 333–362.

CHAPTER 4

Page 127. On interaction of systems: B. White, P. Castle, and R. Held, "Observations on the Development of Visually-Directed Reaching," *Child Development,* 1964, **35**, 349–364.

Page 127. The treatment of symbols owes much to the work of N. Goodman, *Languages of Art* (Indianapolis, Ind.: Bobbs-Merrill, 1968). See also H. Gardner, V. Howard, and D. Perkins, "Symbol Systems: A Philosophical, Psychological, and Educational Investigation," to appear in D. Olson (ed.), 1973 *Yearbook of the National Society for the Study of Education,* in press.

Page 130. On meaning of music, see L. Meyer, *Emotion and Meaning in Music* (Chicago: Phoenix Books, 1961); S. Langer, *Philosophy in a New Key* (New York: Mentor, 1961), Chapter 8.

Page 132. References on the Piagetian and Freudian points of view can be found in the notes to Chapter 1, pages 3–7.

Page 133. The embryonic nature of language development: U. Bellugi and R. Brown, "The Acquisition of Language," *Monograph of the Society for Research in Child Development,* 1964, **29**, 1.

Page 133. Piaget on equilibration: "The Role of the Concept of Equilibrium in Psychological Explanation," in D. Elkind (ed.), *Six Psychological Studies* (New York: Vintage Books, 1968). Bruner's critique: "A Review of Inhelder and Piaget's *The Growth of Logical Thinking from Childhood to Adolescence,*" *British Journal of Psychology,* 1959, **50**, 363–370.

Page 133. Levels of perceptual organization: P. Schilder, quoted in A. Ehrenzweig, *The Psychoanalysis of Artistic Vision and Hearing* (New York: Braziller, 1965); J. Flavell and J. Draguns, "A Microgenetic Approach to Perception and Thought," *Psychological Bulletin,* 1957, **54**, 197–217; M. Parish et al., "Hypnotice Age-Regression and Magnitude of the Ponzo and Poggendorff Illusions," *Science,* 1968, **159**, 1375–1376.

Page 134. E. Kris, *Psychoanalytic Explorations in Art* (New York: Shocken, 1964), pp. 25, 253.

Page 135. For summaries of trends in cognitive development, see J. S. Bruner, et al., *Studies in Cognitive Growth* (New York: Wiley, 1966); H. Pick and A. Pick, "Sensory and Perceptual Development," in P. Mussen (ed.), *Carmichael's Manual of Child Psychology* (New York: Wiley, 1971) Vol. 1; H. Stevenson, "Learning in Children," also in P. Mussen (ed.), Vol. 1.

Page 135. On regression, see J. Mehler and T. Bever, "The Study of Competence in Cognitive Psychology," *International Journal of Psychology,* 1968, 3, 273–280.

Page 135. Werner's developmental trajectory is described in his classic *Comparative Psychology of Mental Development* (New York: Wiley, 1961).

Page 136. Tolstoy is quoted in K. Chukovsky, *From Two to Five* (Berkeley: University of California Press, 1968), p. 4.

Page 137. A review of the burgeoning literature on language development can be found in D. Slobin, *Psycholinguistics* (Glenview, Ill.: Scott, Foresman, 1971); D. McNeill, *The Acquisition of Language* (New York: Harper and Row, 1971); R. Brown, *A First Language* (Cambridge: Harvard University Press, 1972); F. Smith and G. Miller (eds.), *The Genesis of Language* (Cambridge: MIT Press, 1966).

Page 137. E. Lenneberg, *The Biological Foundations of Language* (New York: Wiley, 1967), p. 279.

Page 138. Mama: M. Lewis, *How Children Learn to Speak* (London: Harrap, 1957).

Page 139. Private language: G. Révész, *The Origin and Prehistory of Language* (New York: Philosophical Library, 1956), p. 62. O. Jesperson, *Die Sprache* (Heidelberg: C. Winter, 1925).

Page 139. W. Stern, *The Psychology of Early Childhood* (New York: Holt, 1929), p. 160.

Page 139. On language environment and interpersonal communication see L. Vygotsky, *Thought and Language* (Cambridge: MIT Press, 1962).

Page 140. Language and behavioral control: A. R. Luria, *Speech and the Development of Mental Processes in the Child* (London: Penguin, 1971).

Page 141. Nighttime monologues come from R. Weir, *Language in the Crib* (Hague: Mouton, 1962), p. 130, p. 131; and pp. 138–139. Weir's summary of the latter paragraph appears on p. 141.

Page 144. Semantic deviation: P. Carlson and M. Anisfeld, "Some Observations on the Linguistic Competence of a Two Year Old Child," *Child Development*, 1969, **40**, 569–575. P. Menyuk, *Sentences Children Use* (Cambridge: MIT Press, 1969).

Page 144. Little Hans: S. Freud, "Analysis of a Phobia in a Five Year Old Boy," in *The Complete Psychological Works of Sigmund Freud* (Standard Edition) (London: Hogarth, 1962), Vol. 10.

Page 145. On the intrinsic aspects of language, see K. Burke, *Language as Symbolic Action* (Berkeley: University of California Press, 1966); *The Rhetoric of Religion* (Boston: Beacon Press, 1961).

Page 145. Figures of speech in Adam's conversation come from protocols collected by Professor Roger Brown, Harvard University. These protocols were analyzed by Judith Gardner in an unpublished paper, "Metaphoric Use of Language by Children," 1967.

Page 145. Other sources of children's literary usage are J. Piaget, *Play, Dreams, and Imitation* (New York: Norton, 1962); R. Weir, *Language in the Crib* (Hague: Mouton, 1962).

Page 146. Poetry as prototypical art form: See N. Chomsky, *Cartesian Linguistics* (New York: Harper and Row, 1966).

Page 146. Synesthesia in nursery school children: G. Lawlor and E. Lawlor, "Color-Mood Associations in Young Children," *Journal of Genetic Psychology*, 1965, **107**, 29–32; G. S. Hall, "The Contents of Children's Minds," *Princeton Review* New Series, 1883; H. Gardner, "Metaphors and Modalities," paper presented at the meetings of the Society for Research in Child Development, Philadelphia, 1973.

Page 147. The symbolic quality of modes: E. Erikson in J. Tanner and B. Inhelder (eds.), *Discussions on Child Development* (New York: International Universities Press, 1960), Vol. 4, p. 152.

Page 147. For explication of the relation between the psychology of symbol use and Freudian theory, see D. Rapaport, *Organization and Pathology of Thought* (New York: Columbia University Press, 1951), *passim.*

Page 148. Kubie's examples of modal play: L. Kubie, "Body Symbolization and the Development of Language," *Psychoanalytic Quarterly,* 1934, 3, 430–444; Adam's illustration, see note to p. 145 above.

Pages 148–149. The examples collected by Piaget appear in *Play, Dreams, and Imitation* (New York: Norton, 1962), Chapter 9.

Page 149. Art in a concentration camp (Terezin): *I Never Saw Another Butterfly* (New York: McGraw-Hill, n.d.).

Page 149. Literature occasioned by the death of Dr. Martin Luther King was reported in J. Mathews and E. Holsendolph, "The Children Write Their Own Postscript," *New York Times Sunday Magazine,* June 2, 1968, 63–77.

Page 151. Consistencies within the corpus of young children: See H. Read, *Education through Art* (New York: Pantheon, n.d.).

Page 152. On children's fears, see A. Jersild et al., *Children's Fears, Dreams, Wishes* (New York: Teacher's College Press, 1933).

Page 153. Feelings inspiring children: D. Katz and R. Katz, *Conversations with Children* (London: Kegan Paul, 1936), p. 89. I. A. Richards, *Principles of Literary Criticism* (New York: Harcourt, Brace, 1929), pp. 205–206.

Page 153. Physical involvement with art objects: E. Jaques-Dalcroze, *Rhythm, Music, and Education* (London: Dalcroze Society, 1967).

Page 154. Evidence on the potential of symbols to capture modal-vectoral properties: H. Werner and B. Kaplan, *Symbol Formation* (New York: Wiley, 1963); S. Honkavaara, "The Psychology of Expression," *British Journal of Psychology Monograph Supplements* (Cambridge: Cambridge University Press, 1961). G. Pratt, "Aesthetics," in *Annual Review of Psychology,* 1961, 12, 71–91.

Page 154. On the perceptual sensitivities of young children, see H. Gardner, "The Development of Sensitivity to Artistic Styles," *Journal of Aesthetics and Art Criticism,* 1971, 29, 515–527; "On Figure and Texture in Aesthetic Perception," *British Journal of Aesthetics,* 1972, 12, 40–59; "Style Sensitivity in Children," *Human Development,* 1972, 15, 325–338.

Page 155. W. Stern and K. Bühler have studied the development of the capacity to read pictures. W. Stern, *The Psychology of Early Childhood up to the Sixth Year of Age* (New York: Holt, 1926); K. Bühler, *The Mental Development of the Child* (London: Routledge and Kegan Paul, 1949). Hochberg and Brooks demonstrated that a 2-year-old child without prior exposure to pictures was able to identfy their referents: J. Hochberg and V. Brooks, "Pictorial Recognition as an Unlearned Ability: A Study of One Child's Performance," *American Journal of Psychology,* 1962, 75, 634–638.

Page 156. A. Ehrenzweig, *The Hidden Order of Art* (Berkeley: University of California Press, 1967), p. 18.

Page 157. Effect of training on textural sensitivity: H. Gardner, "The Development of Sensitivity to Figural and Stylistic Aspects of Paintings," *Harvard Project Zero Technical Report,* 1971, 3.

Page 157. Incidental learning: See, for example, G. A. Hale, L. K. Miller, and H. Stevenson, "Incidental Learning of Film Content: A Developmental Study," *Child Development,* 1968, **39,** 69–77; A. Siegel and H. Stevenson, "Incidental Learning: A Developmental Study," *Child Development,* 1966, **37,** 811–817.

Page 158. Experimental studies of skill learning include J. Hicks, "Study of the Acquisition of Motor Skill in Young Children," *University of Iowa Studies in Child Welfare,* 1931, **4,** 5; T. Jones, *The Development of Certain Motor Skills and Play Activities in Young Children* (New York: Teacher's College Bureau of Publications, 1959); B. Wellman, "The Development of Motor Coordination in Young Children: An Experimental Study in Hand and Arm Movements," *University of Iowa Studies in Child Welfare,* 1926, **3,** 4. The quotation comes from Hicks, 1937.

Page 159. On schemes in drawing, see R. Arnheim, *Art and Visual Perception* (Berkeley: University of California Press, 1954), Chapter 4.

Page 159. On the neurological mechanisms of skilled behavior: A. R. Luria, *The Higher Cortical Functions in Man* (New York: Basic Books, 1966).

Page 160. On the neurological foundations of language, see N. Geschwind, "The Organization of Language and the Brain," *Science,* 1970, **170,** 440–444.

Page 160. On linguistic and nonlinguistic mechanisms, see H. Gardner, V. Howard, and D. Perkins, "Symbol Systems: A Philosophical, Psychological, and Educational Investigation," to appear in D. Olson (ed.), 1973 *Yearbook of the National Society for the Study of Education,* in press.

Page 161. Valéry's thoughts are found in his *Collected Works* (New York: Pantheon, 1958), Vol. 7, p. 69.

Page 164. Views of play: J. Piaget, *Play, Dreams, and Imitation* (New York: Norton, 1962); L. Bender and P. Schilder, "Form as a Principle in the Play of Children," *Journal of Genetic Psychology,* 1936, **49,** 254–261; K. Lorenz, in J. Tanner and B. Inhelder (eds.), *Discussions on Child Development* (New York: International Universities Press, 1957), Vol. 2, p. 78; E. Klinger, "The Development of Imaginative Behavior," *Psychological Bulletin,* 1969, **72,** 277–298; L. Vygotsky, "Play and its Role in the Mental Development of the Child," *Soviet Psychology,* 1967, **5,** 3, 6–18.

Page 166. Play as antecedent for the arts: J. Sully, *Studies of Childhood* (New York: Appleton, 1896), p. 116.

Page 169. On the child's expression of his personality in his works: H. Read, *Education through Art* (New York: Pantheon, n.d.); R. Alschuler and L. Hattwick, *Painting and Personality* (Chicago: University of Chicago Press, 1947).

Page 169. Children's stories are collected in E. Pitcher and E. Prelinger, *Children Tell Stories* (New York: International Universities Press, 1963) and L. Ames, "Children's Stories," *Genetic Psychology Monographs,* 1966, **23,** 337–396. I have analyzed their stylistic properties in an unpublished paper, "The Child's Creation of Literature," 1967.

Page 169. Leveling and sharpening: R. Gardner, P. Holzman, G. Klein, H. Linton, and D. Spence, "Cognitive Control: A Study of Individual Consistencies in Cognitive Behavior," *Psychological Issues,* 1959, **1,** 4.

Page 170. A review of studies of style sensitivity can be found in H. Gardner, "Style Sensitivity in Children," *Human Development,* 1972, **15,** 325–338.

Page 170. Research on children's rhythmic capacity: M. Stambak, "Trois épreuves de rythme," in R. Zazzo (ed.), *Manuel pour l'examen psychologique de l'enfant* (Paris: Delachaux et Niestlé, 1960). H. Gardner, "Children's Duplication of Rhythmic Patterns," *Journal of Research in Music Education,* 1971, **19,** 355–360. F. Präger, "Untersuchung über Rhythmische Leistungsfähikgeit von Kindern," *Z. Angew. Psych.,* 1925, **26,** 1–42; M. Wight, "The Effect of Training upon Rhythmic Ability and Other Problems Related to Rhythm," *Child Development,* 1937, **8,** 2, 159–172. On children's notation, see J. Bamberger, research reported in Harvard Project Zero Final Summary Report, 1972, available at Harvard Graduate School of Education. Children's sensitivity to spontaneous rhythms: K. Chukovsky, *From Two to Five* (Berkeley: University of California Press, 1968).

Pages 170–171. Modal matching in children: B. Bond and S. S. Stevens, "Cross-modality Matching of Brightness to Loudness by Five-Year Olds," *Perception and Psychophysics,* 1969, **6,** 337–339.

Page 171. S. Honkavaara, "The Psychology of Expression," *British Journal of Psychology Monograph Supplement* (Cambridge: Cambridge University Press, 1961).

Page 171. N. Frijda, "Recognition of Emotion," in L. Berkowitz (ed.), *Advances in Experimental Social Psychology* (New York: Academic Press, 1969), Vol. 4, pp. 167–224.

Pages 176–177. Stern's trajectory of artistic development is found in W. Stern, *The Psychology of Early Childhood up to the Sixth Year of Age* (New York: Holt, 1926).

Page 177. Goethe's remark quoted in J. P. Eckermann, *Conversations with Goethe* (New York: Ungar, 1964), p. 112.

CHAPTER 5

Page 178. H. Werner, *The Comparative Psychology of Mental Development* (New York: Wiley, 1961); R. Shuter, *The Psychology of Musical Ability* (London: Methuen, 1968). H. Read, *Education through Art* (New York: Pantheon, n.d.); I. Child, "Esthetics," in G. Lindzey and E. Aronson, *Handbook of Social Psychology* (Reading, Mass.: Addison-Wesley, 1969), Vol. 3, pp. 853–916.

Page 179. On agreements across cultures, see R. Francès, *Psychologie de l'esthétique* (Paris: Presses Universitaires de France, 1968).

Page 180. For a critique of the value of consensual judgments of perceived affect and qualities, see S. Langer, *Mind: An Essay on Human Feeling* (Baltimore: Johns Hopkins University Press, 1967), pp. 181–182.

Page 182. For a discussion of structural methods see H. Gardner, *The Quest for Mind* (New York: Knopf, 1973).

Page 184. On the analysis of literary works, see H. Gardner and J. Gardner, "Children's Literary Skills," *Journal of Experimental Education,* 1971, **39,** 42–46.

Page 187. Intensive studies of individual artists: R. Arnheim, *Picasso's Guernica* (Berkeley: University of California Press, 1962); J. L. Lowes, *The Road to Xanadu* (Boston: Houghton Mifflin, 1964); Erikson's studies of great men: *Young Man Luther* (New York: Norton, 1968), *Gandhi's Truth* (New York: Norton, 1969).

Page 187. Music as the most formal art: W. Pater, *The Renaissance* (London: Collins, 1961), p. 135.

Page 188. The genetic character of musical ability: R. Gerard, "The Biological Basis of Imagination," in B. Ghiselin (ed.), *The Creative Process* (New York: Mentor, 1959), p. 234. See also A. Giordina, "Contributions to the Study of Hereditarian Factors in Musical Aptitude," *Arc. Psicol. Neurol. Psych.* (abstract), 1960.

Page 188. Artistic capacities at an early age (or not at all): A. Gesell et al., *The Child From Five to Ten* (New York: Harper, 1946), p. 258.

Page 188. "Mechanical process in the brain": M. Grozmann, "The Exceptionally Bright Child," in *Proceedings of the National Association for the Study and Education of Exceptional Children*, April 1910, p. 2. The recent newspaper article appeared in *The New York Times*, 1971. I do not have the exact reference.

Page 188. Musical ability and autism: B. Rimland, *Infantile Autism* (New York: Appleton-Century-Crofts, 1964). Jo Ann Euper, in T. Gaston (ed.), *Music Therapy* (New York: Macmillan, 1968), pp. 181–190.

Page 189. C. Lévi-Strauss, "Overture to the Raw and the Cooked," in "Structuralism," *Yale French Studies*, 1966, 36–37, p. 15.

Page 189. Révész study of a prodigy: G. Révész, *The Psychology of a Musical Prodigy* (New York: Harcourt, Brace, 1925).

Page 190. On the general dimensions of musical development, see R. Shuter, *The Psychology of Musical Ability* (London: Methuen, 1968); J. Mursell, *Education for Musical Growth* (Boston: Ginn, 1948).

Page 190. Music as kinesthetic: see E. Jaques-Dalcroze, *Rhythm, Music and Education* (London: Dalcroze Society, 1967).

Page 190. Youthful musical accomplishment: The Suzuki method has produced thousands of preschoolers who can perform selections on a violin—cf. R. Lundin, *An Objective Psychology of Music* (New York: Ronald, 1967); and Boris Lang, who claims success in the teaching of a musical notation at this age. See his *Silent Pianos*, unpublished book available from the author.

Page 191. Study of singing capacity: M. S. Hattwick and H. M. Williams, *Measurement of Musical Development II* in *University of Iowa Studies in Child Welfare*, 1935, 11, **2**, 63–66.

Pages 191–192. On the training of musical capacity, see E. N. Drexler, "A Study of the Development of the Ability to Carry a Melody at the Pre-School Level," *Child Development*, 1938, 9, 319–332; W. Graves, "Factors Associated with Children Taking Music Lessons," *Journal of Genetic Psychology*, 1947, 65–80. More optimistic is R. W. Lundin, (see reference cited in note for Chapter 5, p. 190). Testimony on the trainability of absolute pitch is found in W. Sullivan, "Absolute Pitch Can Be Learned, Canadian Study Indicates," *New York Times*, June 12, 1968.

Page 192. Werner on the microgenesis of children's melodies: *Die Melodische Erfindung im Früher Kindesalter* (Vienna: A. Holder, 1917). The table is found in H. Werner, *Comparative Psychology of Mental Development* (New York: Science Editions, 1961), p. 123.

Pages 192, 194. Pflederer-Zimmerman's studies: "Conservation and the Development of Musical Intelligence," *Journal of Research in Music Education,* 1967, 15, 215–223; "The Responses of Children to Musical Tasks Embodying Piaget's Principle of Conservation," *Journal of Research in Music Education,* 1964, 12, 251–268.

Page 194. Bamberger's studies have not yet been published. Some of her findings are presented in the *Harvard Project Zero Summary Report,* 1972 (available at the Harvard Graduate School of Education).

Page 195. H. Gardner, "Children's Sensitivity to Musical Styles," *Merrill-Palmer Quarterly,* 1973, in press.

Page 196. Studies of musical preference: R. Getz, "The Effect of Repetition on Listening Responses," *Journal of Research in Music Education,* 1966, 14, 78–92. R. Hornyak, "An Analysis of Student Attitudes Toward Contemporary American Music," *Council for Research in Music,* 1966, 8, 1–14. V. Baumann, "Teen-Age Music Preferences," *Journal of Research in Music Education,* 1960, 8, 75–84; C. P. Archibeque, "Developing a Taste for Contemporary Music," *Journal of Research in Music Education,* 1966, 14, 2, 142–147.

Page 196. On the flowering of musical ability at ages 5 to 7: G. Révész, *Introduction to the Psychology of Music* (Norman, Okla: University of Oklahoma Press, 1954), p. 175; S. Belaiew-Exemplarsky, quoted in J. Mursell, *Education for Musical Growth* (Boston: Ginn, 1948).

Page 197. Balinese music: C. McPhee, "Children and Music in Bali," in M. Mead and M. Wolfenstein (eds.), *Childhood in Contemporary Cultures* (Chicago: University of Chicago Press, 1963).

Page 198. Greater precociousness in music: J. Berger, *The Success and Failure of Picasso* (London: Penguin, 1965).

Page 198. On the child's appreciation of difference properties of language, see U. Aurnhammer-Firth, "Emphasis and Meaning in Recall in Normal and Autistic Children," *Language and Speech,* 1969, 12, 29–38. R. Jakobson, *Child Language, Aphasia, and Phonological Universals* (Hague: Mouton, 1968). See also the references cited in the notes to Chapter 4, pp. 136–146.

Page 199. K. Chukovsky's ideas are put forth in *From Two to Five* (Berkeley: University of California Press, 1968). The various quotations come from pp. 1, 2, 3, 11, 89, 93, 149.

Page 201. Support for Chukovsky's claims: P. Carlson and M. Anisfeld, "Some Observations on the Linguistic Competence of a Two Year Old Child," *Child Development,* 1969, 40, 569–575. R. Burling, "The Metrics of Children's Verse," *American Anthropologist,* 1966, 68, 1418–1441; W. Stern, *The Psychology of Early Childhood Up to the Sixth Year of Age* (New York: Holt, 1926), p. 229.

Page 202. Literary taste in children: K. Bühler, *The Mental Development of the Child* (London: Routledge and Kegan Paul, 1949). D. White, *Books Before Five* (New York: Oxford University Press, 1956). The Jones story is found on page 76 of the latter book.

Page 203. The collections of children's stories that I have used are L. Ames, "Children's Stories," *Genetic Psychology Monographs*, 1966, **23**, 337–396; and E. Pitcher and E. Prelinger, *Children Tell Stories* (New York: International Universities Press, 1963). My epigenetic analysis has been more fully worked out in an unpublished paper, "The Child's Creation of Literature," 1967. The stories cited come from Pitcher and Prelinger, pp. 30, 32, 44, 73, 81, 104, 39–40, 82, 113, 135, 124, 101, 126.

Page 211. "Children's Literary Skills" are reviewed in a study of the same name by H. Gardner and J. Gardner, which appears in the *Journal of Experimental Education*, 1971, **39**, 42–46.

Page 212. Empirical studies of children's literary capacities and preferences include: W. R. Wees and W. Line, "The Influence of the Form of a Representation upon Reproduction: The Principle of Determination," *British Journal of Psychology*, 1937, **28**, 167–189; C. Weisgerber, "Accuracy in Judging Emotional Expressions as Related to Understanding of Literature," *Journal of Social Psychology*, 1957, **36**, 253–258; M. L. Northway, "The Nature of 'Difficulty' with Reference to a Study of Whole-Part Learning," *British Journal of Psychology*, 1936, **27**, 399–413; L. Rhozina, "Some Conditions that Arouse Interest in the Subjective Experiences and Thought of Literary Heroes," *Voprosy Psikhologii*, 1966, · **2**, 139–146 (abstract).

Page 212. Damon's study reported in W. Damon, "The Child's Conception of Literary Emotion," Unpublished honors thesis, Harvard College, 1967. Carmichael's study: D. Carmichael, "Irony: A Cognitive and Developmental Study," Unpublished doctoral dissertation, University of California at Berkeley, 1966.

Page 213. Children's poems in classic forms: the limerick, p. 96; the parody of Sandburg, p. 99; in S. Lane and M. Kemp, *An Approach to Creative Writing in the Primary School* (London: Blackie, 1967).

Page 214. Anyone can write poems: C. Lévi-Strauss, *The Raw and the Cooked* (New York: Harper and Row, 1969), p. 18.

Page 214. Under the influence: K. Chukovsky, *From Two to Five* (Berkeley: University of California Press, 1968), p. 87.

Page 215. Animal art: see references in Chapter 2, pp. 53–57.

Page 216. Kellogg's work is reviewed in R. Kellogg, *Analyzing Children's Art* (Palo Alto, Calif.: National Press Books, 1969). Research by E. Gibson supports her claim. See "The Ontogeny of Reading: Analysis and Experiment," invited address at the American Psychological Association, 1970.

Page 217. Students of children's paintings include the following: V. Lowenfeld, *Creative and Mental Growth* (New York: Macmillan, 1957); G. Britsch, *Theorie der Bildenden Kunst* (Ratingen: Henn, 1966); G. Luquet, *Le dessin enfantin* (Paris: Alcan, 1927); H. Eng, *The Psychology of Child and Youth Drawing* (New York: Humanities Press, 1957); H. Eng, *The Psychology of Children's Drawings from the First Stroke to the Colored Drawing* (New York: Harcourt, Brace, 1931); R. Griffith, *Imagination in Early Childhood* (London: Kegan Paul, 1935); E. Cooke, "Our Art Teaching and Child Nature," *Journal of Education* (London) 1896, 8, 12–15. See also the writings of K. Lansing, J. Bell, B. Lark-Horovitz, A. Douglass, C. Burt, H. Read, G. Hildreth, and H. Schaefer-Simmern.

Page 217. H. Schaefer-Simmern's ideas are propounded in *The Unfolding of Artistic Activity* (Berkeley: University of California Press, 1948).

Page 219. Paintings as projective devices: R. Alschuler and L. Hattwick, *Painting and Personality* (Chicago: University of Chicago Press, 1947); T. Waehner, "Interpretation of Spontaneous Drawings and Paintings," *Genetic Psychology Monographs*, 1946, **33**, 1–70. R. Windsor, "An Experimental Study of Easel Painting as a Projective Technique with Nursery School Children," *Journal of Genetic Psychology*, 1949, **75**, 75–83.

Page 219. Children's copies: A. Mundy-Castle, "Gestalt Continuation and Design Copying in Ghanaian Children," unpublished manuscript, Harvard University, 1969; F. Graham, et al., "Development in Pre-School Children of the Ability to Copy Forms," *Child Development*, 1960, **31**, 339–359.

Page 219. Children's affects and their drawings: F. Baumgarten, "Die Politische Karikaturzeichnung des Kindes als Massenpsychologisches Phänomen," Z. *Kinderpsychiatrie*, 1948, **15**, 92–100. W. Reichenberg-Hackett, "Changes in Goodenough Drawings after a Gratifying Experience," *American Journal of Orthopsychiatry*, 1953, **25**, 501–516.

Page 219. Sequences in children's drawings: J. Jirasek, "Some Qualitative Changes in the Development of Children's Figure Drawings," *Ceskosliovenska Psychologie*, 1965, **9**, 403–406 (abstract); E. Barnhart, "Developmental Stages in Compositional Construction in Children's Drawings," *Journal of Experimental Education*, 1942, **11**, 158–184. H. Lewis, "The Relation of Picture Preference to Developmental Status in Drawing," *Journal of Educational Research*, 1963, **57**, 443–446; F. Goodenough and D. Harris, "Studies in the Psychology of Children's Drawings, II: 1928–1949," *Psychological Bulletin*, 1950, **47**, 363–443.

Page 220. Emergence of perspective and spatial representation: A. Leroy, "Représentations de la perspective dans les dessins d'enfants," *Enfance*, 1951, **4**, 286–307. S. Lester, "Children's Drawings: A Study of the Pictorial Representation of Three-Dimensional Spatial Relations," unpublished honors thesis, Radcliffe College, 1970.

Page 220. Decline in the quality of reproductions: M. Kerr, "Children's Drawings of Houses," *British Journal of Medical Psychology*, 1937, **16**, 206–218. V. Lowenfeld and W. L. Brittain, *Creative and Mental Growth* (New York: Macmillan, 1970); M. Richards et al., "Developmental Changes in Children's Drawings," *British Journal of Educational Psychology*, 1967, **37**, 73–80; H. Read, *Education through Art* (New York: Pantheon, n.d.). The quote comes from R. Alschuler and L. Hattwick, *Painting and Personality* (Chicago: University of Chicago Press, 1969), p. 9.

Page 220. Individual differences in drawings: H. Read (see previous reference); V. Lowenfeld and W. L. Brittain (see previous reference); R. O'Grady, "A Study of Selected Aspects of Finger Painting by Special Class Children," *Journal of Genetic Psychology*, 1954, **84**, 27–38; M. Dow, "Playground Behavior Differentiating Artistic from Non-Artistic Children," *Psychological Monographs*, 1933, **45**, 83–94. The description of movie-making can be found in Chapter 4, pp. 175–176.

Page 221. Relationship between drawings and handwriting: G. Hildreth, "Developmental Sequences in Name Writing," *Child Development*, 1936, **7**, 291–303.

Page 222. Spencer's remark appears in *Education: Intellectual, Moral, and Physical* (London: G. Manwaring, 1861).

Page 222. N. Meier's studies appear in a series of monographs "Iowa Studies in Psychology: Studies in the Psychology of Art," *Psychological Monographs*, Vols. **45, 48, 51**, 1933, 1936, 1939.

Page 223. Child's studies are summarized in I. Child, "Esthetics," in G. Lindzey and E. Aronson, *Handbook of Social Psychology* (Reading, Mass.: Addison-Wesley, 1969), Vol. 3, pp. 853–916.

Page 223. P. Machotka's work appears in "Le développement des critères esthétiques chez l'enfant," *Enfance*, 1963, 4–5, 357–379; and "Aesthetic Criteria in Childhood," *Child Development*, 1966, 37, 877–885.

Page 224. Social influences on aesthetic judgments: R. Birney and J. Houston, "The Effects of Creativity, Norm Distance, and Instructions on Social Influence," *Journal of Personality*, 1961, 29, 294–302; D. Ausubel et al., "Prestige Suggestions in Children's Art Preferences," *Journal of General Psychology*, 1929, 2, 362–366.

Page 224. Rationales for children's perceptions: J. MacLeish, "Sex Differences in Children's Art Judgments," *Leeds Int. Educ. Res. and Stud.*, 1951, 3, 70–83; L. Barbey, "Le sens esthétique des images de l'enfant," *Nouvelle Revue Pédadogique*, 1949, 4, 450–454; N. M. Zubareva, "Esthetic Perception of Still Life by Pre-School Children," *Voprosy Psikhologii*, 1965, 5, 50–58 (abstract); A. Corcoran, "Color Usage in Nursery School Painting," *Child Development*, 1954, 25, 107–113; J. Subes, "L'appréciation esthétique d'œuvres d'enfants par les enfants," *Enfance*, 1958, 2, 115–130; H. Lewis, "The Relation of Picture Preference to Developmental Status in Drawing," *Journal of Educational Research*, 1963, 57, 443–446. H. Voillaume, "Les activités picturales des enfants et les réactions comparées des enfants et des adultes devant les œuvres d'enfants," *Psychologie Française*, 1965, 10, 170–187.

Page 224. Studies of style sensitivity are reviewed in H. Gardner, "Style Sensitivity in Children," *Human Development*, 1972, 15, 325–338; H. Gardner, "The Development of Sensitivity to Artistic Styles," *Journal of Aesthetics and Art Criticism*, 1971, 29, 515–527.

Page 224. Art training: See J. McFee, *Preparation for Art* (San Francisco: Wadsworth, 1961); H. J. McWhinnie, "Perceptual Learning: Possible or Impossible," Unpublished paper, Ohio State University, 1970; K. Beittel, "Teaching of Drawing," Cooperative Research Project No. 3149, December 1966, Pennsylvania State University.

Page 225. Communication in art: D. Korzenik, "Children's Drawings: Changes in Representation between the Ages of Five and Seven," Unpublished doctoral dissertation, Harvard University, 1972.

Page 225. K. Lansing's claims appear in his book, *Art, Artists, and Art Education* (New York: McGraw-Hill, 1969); H. Schaefer-Simmern's remarks in his book *The Unfolding of Artistic Activity* (Berkeley: University of California Press, 1948); P. Duquet, "Creative Communication," in E. Ziegfeld, *Education and Art* (Paris: UNESCO, 1953), p. 45.

Page 226. The young child as natural poet: H. Taylor, "Music as a Source of Knowledge," *Music Educator's Journal*, 1964, 51, 36.

Page 230. Children without aesthetic sensitivity: J. Sully, *Studies of Childhood* (New York: Appleton, 1896), p. 299.

Page 231. W. Preyer's prodigy: *The Mind of the Child* (New York: Appleton, 1889).

CHAPTER 6

Page 242. Sartre tells the story of his life in *The Words* (New York: Braziller, 1964). Quotes: "I'm a promising poodle," p. 31; "I keep creating myself," p. 32; "I had given the wrong role," p. 108; "I was not yet working," p. 52.

Page 246. Rank on the artist: O. Rank, *Art and Artist* (New York: Knopf, 1932).

Page 247. Thomas Wolfe on the novelist: quoted in introduction to *Look Homeward Angel* (New York: Modern Library, 1929), p. xi; Gant speaking, p. 193.

Page 248. Experimental evidence on multiple models: H. Biller et al., "Sex Role Development and Creative Potential in Kindergarten Age Boys," *Developmental Psychology*, 1969, 1, 747–749. The quotation about architects comes from D. MacKinnon, "The Nature and Nurture of Creative Talent," in D. Wolfele (ed.), *The Discovery of Talent* (Cambridge: Harvard University Press, 1969), p. 203.

Page 248. Socialization and artistic quality: H. Barry, "The Relationship between Child Training and the Pictorial Arts," *Journal of Abnormal and Social Psychology*, 1957, 54, 380–383.

Page 248. Stravinsky's earliest recollections are reported in I. Stravinsky, *Autobiography* (New York: Norton, 1962).

Page 249. Chateaubriand: See T. Ribot, *Essay on the Creative Imagination* (Chicago: Open Court Publishing Company, 1906), p. 76.

Page 250. Working in the Kris condition: P. Greenacre, "Play in Relation to the Creative Imagination," *Psychoanalytic Study of the Child* (New York: International Universities Press, 1959), Vol. 14, 61–80.

Page 250. For psychoanalytic views of the artist, see H. Ruitenbeck (ed.), *The Creative Imagination* (Chicago: Quadrangle, 1965); *The Literary Imagination* (Chicago: Quadrangle, 1965); *Psychoanalysis and Literature* (New York: Dutton, 1964).

Page 251. On the Brontës: L. Dooley, "Psychoanalysis of the Character and Genius of Emily Brontë," in H. Ruitenbeck (ed.), *The Literary Imagination, supra,* p. 58.

Page 252. The artist's special sensitivity: U. Neisser, quoted in J. S. Bruner et al., *Studies in Cognitive Growth* (New York: Wiley, 1966), p. 66.

Page 252. W. H. Hudson, quoted in J. Dewey, *Art as Experience* (New York: Capricorn, 1958), p. 125.

Page 253. Freud's view of the firstborn: Quoted in E. Jones, *The Life and Work of Sigmund Freud* (New York: Basic Books, 1953), Vol. 1, p. 5.

Page 253. Harold Schonberg on Camille Saint-Saens: "It All Came Too Easily for Camille Saint-Saens," *New York Times*, January 12, 1969, Section 2, p. 17.

Page 254. N. Podhoretz on writing: *Making It* (New York: Random House, 1967), pp. 248–249.

Page 254. The theme of the artist's warp is developed in Edmund Wilson's *The Wound and the Bow* (London: Methuen-University Paperbacks, 1961).

Page 255. Charles Chaplin, *My Autobiography* (New York: Simon and Schuster, 1964). John Lennon, quoted in the *Harvard Crimson*, October 1, 1968, p. 3.

Page 255. Lewis Carroll: Cf. J. Skinner, "Lewis Carroll's Adventures in Wonderland," in H. Ruitenbeck, *Psychoanalysis and Literature* (New York: Dutton, 1964).

Page 257. Testimony on the latency period: V. Lowenfeld, *Creative and Mental Growth* (New York: Macmillan, 1947), p. 233; V. S. Pritchett, *The Cab at the Door* (London: Chatto and Windus, 1968), p. 102.

Page 257. On second language learning, see E. Lenneberg, *Biological Foundations of Language* (New York: Wiley, 1967).

Page 258. Running the gamut of experience, Thomas Wolfe, quoted in H. Muller, *Thomas Wolfe* (Norfolk, Conn.: New Directions, 1947), pp. 24–25.

Page 258. Adolescence "universal change": I. Kaufman, *Art and Education in Contemporary Culture* (New York: Macmillan, 1966), p. 140; the regression of creativity, H. Read, *Education through Art* (New York: Pantheon, n.d.), pp. 165–166.

Page 259. Adolescent declines in certain tasks, see E. Lenneberg, cited in reference to p. 257; M. Richards et al., "Developmental Changes in Children's Drawings," *British Journal of Educational Psychology*, 1967, **37**, 73–80; R. Wolman, "A Developmental Study of the Perception of People," *Genetic Psychology Monograph*, 1967, **76**, 95–140; H. Gardner, "Children's Sensitivity to Musical Style," *Merrill-Palmer Quarterly*, in press; H. Gardner and J. Gardner, "Children's Literary Skills," *Journal of Experimental Education*, 1971, **39**, 42–46. See also the literature on incidental learning, cited in the note to Chapter 4, p. 157.

Page 259. I. Stravinsky, *Autobiography* (New York: Norton, 1962). For a brilliant discussion of the characteristics of adolescence, see E. Erikson, *Identity: Youth and Crisis* (New York: Norton, 1968).

Pages 259–260. On dislike of school: W. Kahn, "Uses of Painting Today," *Daedalus*, 1969, **98**, 3, 747–754. Hogarth, quoted in H. Read, *Education through Art* (New York: Pantheon, n.d.), p. 43.

Page 261. Children's relationships to objects: V. Rosen, "Some Effects of Artistic Talent on Character Style," *Psychoanalytic Quarterly*, 1964, 33, 1–24.

Page 261. Early self-consciousness: An unnamed artist, quoted in S. Langer, *Feeling and Form* (New York: Scribner's, 1953), p. 390.

Page 262. On development of style sensitivity, see H. Gardner, "The Development of Sensitivity to Artistic Styles," *Journal of Aesthetics and Art Criticism*, 1971, **39**, 515–527; also "Style Sensitivity in Children," *Human Development op. cit.*

Pages 262–263. Günther Schuller in *Encounter with the Performing Arts* (New York State Education Department, 1968), p. 58.

Page 263. G. B. Shaw on style: quoted in the *New York Times Book Review*, August 17, 1969, p. 1.

Page 263. A. Malraux, *The Voices of Silence* (Garden City, N.Y.: Doubleday, 1963), p. 281.

Page 264. Keats: Reported in W. J. Bate, *John Keats* (New York: Galaxy, 1966), p. 73. Goethe, quoted in the same book, p. 193. On qualities of artistic genius: A. Germant, *Nature of the Genius* (Springfield, Ill.: Charles Thomas, 1961).

Page 264. A. Schoenberg, *Letters* (E. Stein, ed.) (New York: St. Martin's Press, 1965), p. 26. W. Kahn, "Uses of Painting Today," *Daedalus*, 1969, 98, 752.

Page 265. G. Révész, *Introduction to the Psychology of Music* (Norman, Okla.: Oklahoma University Press, 1954), p. 180; H. Moore quoted by Grace Glueck,

"Henry Moore Gives Views on Sculpture," *New York Times,* April 10, 1970, p. 23.

Page 265. Universals and modes: C. Jung, *Psyche and Symbol* (Garden City, N.Y.: Doubleday Anchor, 1958), *passim;*

Pages 265–266. Gestalt psychologists: See references cited in note to Chapter 1, p. 16.

Page 266. Other scholars who speak to the issue of universals and modes include H. Read, *Education through Art* (New York: Pantheon, n.d.); N. Frye, *Anatomy of Criticism* (New York: Atheneum, 1967); P. Fraisse, *Les structures rythmiques* (Louvain: Publ. Univ. de Louvain, 1956); K. Chukovsky, *From Two to Five* (Berkeley: University of California Press, 1968); R. Burling, "The Metrics of Children's Verse," *American Anthropologist,* 1966, **68,** 1418–1441; J. Borges, Charles Eliot Norton Lectures, Harvard University, 1967.

Page 266. Lévi-Strauss, *The Savage Mind* (Chicago: University of Chicago Press, 1966). See also H. Gardner, *The Quest for Mind* (New York: Knopf, 1973).

Page 267. For support of the modal-vectoral hypothesis, see Chapter 3, and the references cited in the notes to pp. 110-111.

Page 268. Prototype of the inspired artist: J. G. Sulzer, quoted in M. H. Abrams, *The Mirror and the Lamp* (New York: Norton, 1958), p. 88; Goethe: See J. P. Eckermann, *Conversations with Goethe* (London: G. Bell and Sons, 1874), p. 260. Mozart: Quoted in S. Sitwell, *Mozart* (New York: Appleton-Century-Crofts, 1932).

Page 269. Coleridge: Cf. J. L. Lowes, *The Road to Xanadu* (Boston: Houghton Mifflin, 1964); Mozart, quoted in G. Révész, *Introduction to the Psychology of Music* (Norman, Okla.: University of Oklahoma Press, 1954), p. 200. Picasso, quoted in R. Arnheim, *Picasso's Guernica* (Berkeley: University of California Press, 1962), p. 13.

Page 269. F. Nietzsche, quoted in G. Révész (see note to Chapter 6), p. 202.

Page 270. My thoughts on problem-solving are more fully developed in "Problem-Solving in the Arts," *Journal of Aesthetic Education,* 1971, **5,** 93–114.

Page 274. D. Ecker, "The Artistic Process as Qualitative Problem-Solving," *Journal of Aesthetics and Art Criticism,* 1963, **21,** 283–290. The Picasso quote is found on p. 285.

Page 275. H. Matisse, "Notes of a Painter," in E. Vivas and M. Krieger (eds.), *The Problems of Aesthetics* (New York: Rinehart, 1953), p. 259.

Pages 275–276. M. Beardsley, "On the Creation of Art," *Journal of Aesthetics and Art Criticism,* 1965, **23,** 291–304. The writer describing an incept is the poet Howard Nemerov; see his edited book *Poets on Poetry* (New York: Basic Books, 1966), p. 188.

Page 277. E. Klinger, "The Development of Imaginative Behavior," *Psychological Bulletin,* 1969, **72,** 295.

Page 277. T. Ribot, *Essay on the Creative Imagination* (Chicago: Open Court Publishing Company, 1906).

Page 277. Goethe, quoted in M. Abrams, *The Mirror and the Lamp* (New York: Norton, 1958), p. 206.

Page 277. H. James: First quote, in R. P. Blackmur (ed.), *The Art of the Novel*

(New York: Scribner's, 1934), p. 11; second quote, in *Partial Portrait* (London: Macmillan, 1888), p. 390.

Pages 277–278. On strange conditions surrounding creative activity, see A. Schoenberg, *Letters*, (E. Stein, ed.) (New York: St. Martin's Press, 1965), p. 51. Picasso: J. Barchelon, "Development of Artistic Stylization," *Psychoanalytic Study of the Child* (New York: International Universities Press, 1964), Vol. 19, 256–274. A. Einstein, *Mozart: His Character and His Work* (London: Cass, 1959); B. Ghiselin, in C. W. Taylor and F. Barron (eds.), *Scientific Creativity* (New York: Wiley, 1964), p. 358.

Page 278. Anthony Storr described the various stimulants used by artists in "Problems of Creativity," unpublished paper, Harvard University, 1969.

Page 278. Different styles of creation: F. Bartlett, *Thinking* (New York: Basic Books, 1958), p. 194; A. Einstein (see reference cited in note to Chapter 6, p. 277); S. Spender, "The Making of a Poem," in B. Ghiselin (ed.), *The Creative Process* (New York: Mentor, 1959), 112–124.

Page 279. On cyclothymes and schizothymes, see note to Chapter 7, p. 320. Description of Lipschitz: R. Arnheim, *Toward a Psychology of Art* (Berkeley: Univ. of California Press, 1966), p. 290.

Page 279. Wallas's formulation is found in *The Art of Thought* (New York: Harcourt, Brace, 1931). Patrick's study: "Creative Thought in Artists," *Journal of Psychology*, 1937, **4**, 35–73; "Creative Thought in Poets," *Archives of Psychology*, 1935, no. 178. See also J. Eindhoven and W. Vinacke, "Creative Process in Painting," *Journal of Genetic Psychology*, 1952, **47**, 139–164.

Page 280. J. Bahle, *Der Musikalische Schaffensprozess* (Leipzig: Herzel, 1936); *Eingebung und Tat in Musikalischen Schaffen* (Leipzig: Herzel, 1939).

Page 280. General comments on artistic creativity: F. Bartlett, *Thinking* (New York: Basic Books, 1958), p. 192; D. Cooke, *The Language of Music* (Oxford: Oxford University Press, 1959), p. 174.

Page 281. Sources for careful examinations of individual works: J. L. Lowes, *The Road to Xanadu* (Boston: Houghton Mifflin, 1964); R. Arnheim, *Picasso's Guernica* (Berkeley: University of California Press, 1962).

Page 282. Dostoevsky's creation of *The Idiot*: F. Dostoevsky, *The Notebooks for The Idiot* (E. Wasiolek, ed.) (Chicago: University of Chicago Press, 1967), p. 23.

Page 282. The testimony of artists: Thomas Mann, "A Man and a Dog," in *Death in Venice and Seven Other Stories* (New York: Vintage, 1936), p. 264; *Story of a Novel* (New York: Knopf, 1961), p. 229.

Page 282. H. Matisse, "Notes of a Painter," quoted in E. Vivas and M. Krieger (eds.), *The Problems of Esthetics* (Holt, Rinehart and Winston, 1963), p. 256.

Page 283. Stravinsky on composing: In G. Révész, *Introduction to the Psychology of Music* (Norman, Okla.: University of Oklahoma Press, 1954), p. 201.

Page 283. A. Schoenberg, *Letters* (E. Stein, ed.) (New York: St. Martin's Press, 1965), p. 152; T. Mann, quoted in C. Neider (ed.), *The Stature of Thomas Mann* (Norfolk, Conn.: New Directions, 1947), p. 226.

Pages 283–284. Ghiselin on artists' skills, B. Ghiselin, *The Creative Process* (New York: Mentor, 1961), p. 29.

Page 284. Testimony of teachers: V. Spolin, *Improvisation for the Theater* (Evanston, Ill.: Northwestern University Press, 1963), pp. 4–5; A. Davie, "The Developing Process," manuscript quoted in D. Morris, *The Biology of Art* (Chicago: Aldine·Atherton, 1967), p. 198.

Page 284. V. Lowenfeld, *Creative and Mental Growth* (New York: Macmillan, 1947); H. Mearns, *Creative Power: The Education of Youth in the Creative Arts* (New York: Dover, 1958).

Page 285. Keats's self-education: In W. J. Bate, *John Keats* (New York: Galaxy, 1966), p. 604. Composers' experiences: J. Mursell, *Education for Musical Growth* (Boston: Ginn, 1948).

Page 285. Regarding Bach: E. Blom, *The Limitations of Music* (London: Macmillan, 1928), p. 114. J. Bahle, *Eingebung und Tat in Musikalischen Schaffen* (Leipzig: Herzel, 1936). On children's imitation of adult works, see R. Arnheim, *Toward a Psychology of Art* (Berkeley: University of California Press, 1966); M. R. Gaitskell, "Art in the Kindergarten," in E. Ziegfeld (ed.), *Education and Art* (Paris: UNESCO, 1953), 39–40; J. Doerter, "Influences of College Art Instruction Upon Student Painting Styles," *Studies in Art Education*, 1966, 7, 2, 46–53. R. Kellogg, *Analyzing Children's Art* (Palo Alto, Calif.: National Press Books, 1969).

Page 286. Matisse, quoted in *New York Times*, December 28, 1969, Section 6, p. 16; Goethe, in J. P. Eckermann, *Conversations with Goethe* (New York: Ungar, 1964), p. 71.

Page 287. Reviews of the literature on the psychology of skill are found in R. Seashore, "Work and Motor Performance," in S. S. Stevens (ed.), *Handbook of Experimental Psychology* (New York: Wiley, 1951), 1341–1362; D. Wolfele, "Training," in *Ibid.*, 1267–1286; A. Welford, *Fundamentals of Skill* (London: Methuen, 1968); E. Bilodeau (ed.), *Acquisition of Skill* (New York: Academic Press, 1966).

Page 288. Mozart, quoted in A. Einstein, *Mozart: His Character and His Work* (London: Cass, 1959), p. 103.

Page 288. General coordination: Cf. N. Bernstein, *The Coordination and Regulation of Movements* (London: Pergamon, 1967).

Page 288. Boleslavsky's teaching techniques: R. Boleslavsky, *Acting: The First Six Lessons* (New York: Theater Arts, 1943). H. Kohl, *Thirty-Six Children* (New York: New American Library, 1967); G. Dennison, *The Lives of Children* (New York: Random House, 1969); K. Koch, *Wishes, Lies, and Dreams* (New York: Chelsea House, 1970). The quotation is from Koch, p. 7.

Page 290. T. S. Eliot's letters to Douglass are printed in Antony Coleman, "T. S. Eliot and Keith Douglass," *Times Literary Supplement*, February 7, 1970, p. 731.

Page 291. A. Schoenberg on a regimen for critical minds: *Letters* (E. Stein, ed.) (New York: St. Martin's Press, 1965), p. 135.

Page 291. N. Goodman, on the role of merit judgments in the arts: "Merit as Means," *Art and Philosophy* (S. Hook, ed.) (New York: New York University Press, 1966), pp. 56–57.

Page 291. On the teaching of notations: H. Gardner, V. Howard, and D. Perkins, "Symbol Systems: A Philosophical, Psychological, and Educational Investigation," in D. Olson (ed.), *1973 Yearbook of the National Society for the Study of Education,* in press.

Page 292. Lack of stimulation for young writers: E. Richardson, characterized by J. Feathersone, "Teaching Teacher," *New Republic,* December 7, 1968, p. 23.

Page 292. The exercise in writing poetry about spiders is reported in M. Langdon, *Let the Children Write* (London: Longmans, Green and Co., 1961), June Robinson's poem reprinted at the close of this chapter is found on page 15 of that book.

Page 293. Schoenberg on the chore of the teacher: *Letters* (E. Stein, ed.) (New York: St. Martin's Press, 1965), p. 196.

Page 294. Auden on Housman: "Books," *New Yorker,* February 19, 1972, p. 114.

Page 296. The child and the adult seen as artists: H. Read, *Education through Art* (New York: Pantheon, n.d.), pp. 202, 209; Goethe, quoted in A. Schopenauer, *The World as Will and Representation* (Indian Hills, Colo.: Falcon's Wing Press, 1958), Vol. 2, p. 392; V. D'Amico, *Creative Teaching in Art* (Scranton, Pa.: International Textbook, 1953); R. Arnheim, *Visual Thinking* (Berkeley: University of California Press, 1969), p. 262; P. Slade, *Child Drama* (London: University of London Press, 1954), p. 26.

Page 297. The child's gift controls him: A. Malraux, *The Voices of Silence* (Garden City, N.Y.: Doubleday, 1963), p. 280; The child plays at his art: W. Pfleiderer, quoted in H. Eng, *The Psychology of Child and Youth Drawing* (New York: Humanities Press, 1957), p. 190.

Page 297. Matisse: "The Nature of Creative Activity," in E. Ziegfeld (ed.), *Education and Art* (Paris: UNESCO, 1953), pp. 21–22.

CHAPTER 7

Page 301. Piaget's views on operational thought are presented at length in B. Inhelder and J. Piaget, *The Growth of Logical Thinking from Childhood to Adolescence* (New York: Basic Books, 1958). See also H. Gardner, *The Quest for Mind* (New York: Knopf, 1973), Chapter 3.

Pages 301–302. Piaget on relationship between perception and cognition: J. Piaget, *The Psychology of Intelligence* (Paterson, N.J.: Littlefield Adams, 1963); *The Mechanisms of Perception* (New York: Basic Books, 1969).

Page 302. Piaget's discussion of figurativity and operativity can be found in many of his recent writings. For a useful introduction to this duality, see H. Furth, *Piaget and Knowledge* (Englewood Cliffs, N.J.: Prentice-Hall, 1969), Part 4.

Page 308. Galton, quoted in R. Arnheim, *Visual Thinking* (Berkeley: University of California Press, 1969).

Page 308. H. Read, quoted in M. Smith (ed.), *The Artist in Tribal Society* (New York: Glencoe, 1961), p. 112.

Page 311. William James: H. James (ed.), *The Letters of William James* (Boston: Atlantic Monthly Press, 1920), Vol. 2, pp. 86–87. Wolf Kahn, "Uses of Painting Today," *Daedalus,* 1969, 98, 751.

Page 312. Eliot's comments on thought: "Shakespeare and the Stoicism of Seneca," *Selected Essays, 1917–1932* (New York: Harcourt, Brace, 1964) L. Kirchner, "Notes on Understanding," *Daedalus,* 1969, 98, 739–745. A. Schoenberg, *Letters* (E. Stein, ed.), (New York: St. Martin's Press, 1965), p. 210.

Pages 313–314. On contrast between researcher and theorist, see A. Roe, cited in note to Chapter 7, p. 318.

Page 316. Kuhn on the scientific process: "The Essential Tension," in C. Taylor and F. Barron (eds.), *Scientific Creativity: Its Recognition and Development* (New York: Wiley, 1964), p. 354.

Page 317. K. Lorenz, "The Role of Gestalt Perception in Animal and Human Behavior," in L. L. Whyte, *Aspects of Form* (Bloomington, Ind.: Midland Books, 1966), p. 176; the second quotation is also from p. 176.

Page 317. Edwin Land quoted in C. Taylor and F. Barron (eds.) (see note to Chapter 7, p. 316) p. 69.

Page 318. A. Roe has studied the differences between artists and scientists: *The Making of a Scientist* (New York: Dodd Mead, 1952); *The Psychology of Occupations* (New York: Wiley, 1964). On the earlier literary interests of social scientists, see R. Brown, "The Secret Drawer: Review of a *History of Psychology in Autobiography*," *Contemporary Psychology*, 1969, 14, 51–53.

Page 319. H. Ellis, quoted in W. Bowerman, *Studies in Genius* (New York: Philosophical Library, 1947), p. 94.

Page 319. J. D. Watson, *The Double Helix* (New York: Atheneum, 1967).

Page 320. Freud is described in this manner by E. Jones, *The Life and Work of Sigmund Freud* (New York: Basic Books, 1953), pp. 53–55.

Page 320. McFarlane Smith, *Spatial Ability* (San Francisco: Knapp, 1964).

Pages 322–323. C. Darwin, quoted in H. Read, *Education through Art* (New York: Pantheon, n.d.), p. 253. The second quote appears on page 253 of the same book.

Page 323. Housman is quoted on p. 256 of E. Kris, *Psychoanalytic Explorations in Art* (New York: Schocken, 1964).

Pages 323–324. The business of the consumer: R. Arnheim, *Toward a Psychology of Art* (Berkeley: University of California Press, 1966), p. 15.

Page 324. The majority of people call aesthetic pleasure: Ortega y Gasset, "The Dehumanization of Art," in M. Rader (ed.), *A Modern Book of Esthetics* (New York: Holt, Rinehart and Winston, 1960), p. 343.

Page 324. Seeing and feeling: R. Fry, *Vision and Design* (New York: Meridian. 1956), p. 92.

Page 325. Eliot on criticism: T. S. Eliot, *Milton* (London: British Academy, 1947), p. 2. V. Thomson, "What is Quality in Music?" *New York Review of Books,* June 19, 1969, p. 312.

Page 325. "Every true poet": P. Valéry, *Collected Works* (New York: Pantheon, 1958), Vol. 7, p. 76.

Page 326. Difference between critic and audience: C. Ducasse, quoted in M. Rader (ed.), *A Modern Book of Esthetics* (New York: Holt, Rinehart and Winston, 1960), p. 494.

Page 326. I. A. Richards, *Principles of Literary Criticism* (New York: Harcourt, Brace, 1924), p. 2.

Page 326. They note the provenance: J. Thompson, "Early Wilson," *New York Review of Books,* September 28, 1967, p. 8.

Page 327. Critic must translate: R. Wellek and A. Warren, *Theory of Literature* (London: Peregrine, 1963).

Page 329. On characteristics of critics: G. Watson, *The Literary Critics* (London: Penguin, 1964), and *The Critical Moment* (London: Faber and Faber, 1963).

Page 330. W. Redfield, *Letters from an Actor* (London: Cassell, 1967), p. 33.

Page 330. J. Littlewood, quoted in C. Marowitz and S. Trussler, *Theater at Work* (New York: Hill and Wang, 1967), p. 144.

Page 331. R. Taft, "A Psychological Assessment of Professional Actors and Related Professions," *Genetic Psychology Monographs*, 1961, **64**, 309–383.

Page 331. N. Williamson quoted in K. Tynan, "Profile of Nicol Williamson," *New Yorker*, January 15, 1972, p. 56.

Page 332. Stravinsky on Nijinsky: *Stravinsky in Conversations with Robert Craft* (London: Penguin, 1968), pp. 170–171.

Page 332. Peter Hall, quoted in C. Marowitz and S. Trussler, *Theater at Work* (New York: Hill and Wang, 1967), p. 150.

Page 332. On the premiere of *Petrouchka*: C. Beaumont, quoted in C. Hann (ed.), *Stravinsky's Petrouchka: An Authoritative Score* (New York: Norton, 1967).

Page 333. Performances of Chopin: M. T. Henderson, "Rhythmic Organization in Artistic Piano Performance," *University of Iowa Studies in the Psychology of Music*, 1936, **4**, 281–305 (abstract).

Page 333. N. Williamson, reported in the *Boston Globe*, June 18, 1969, p. 32.

Page 334. Cézanne; I am unable to locate this quotation. Tolstoy, quoted in "Goethe and Tolstoy," by Thomas Mann, *Essays* (New York: Vintage, 1957), p. 86. Goethe, quoted in Mann, *Ibid.*, p. 63.

Page 335. Messerschmidt: described in E. Kris, *Psychoanalytic Explorations in Art* (New York: Schocken, 1964), Chapter 4. Picasso: Quoted in R. Arnheim, *Picasso's Guernica* (Berkeley: University of California Press, 1962).

Page 336. Mozart: quoted in J. Bahle, *Eingebung und Tat in Musikalischen Schaffen* (Leipzig: Herzel, 1939). Beethoven, quoted in T. Ribot, *Essay on the Creative Imagination* (Chicago: Open Court Publishing Company, 1906), p. 148.

Page 336. Picasso: J. Berger, *The Success and Failure of Picasso* (London: Penguin, 1965), p. 29.

Page 336. A. Schoenberg, *Letters* (E. Stein, ed.) (New York, St. Martin's Press, 1965), p. 290.

Page 336. John Whiting, quoted in Marowitz and Trussler, *Theater at Work* (New York: Hill and Wang, 1967), p. 29; Wagner, quoted in Thomas Mann, *Essays* (New York: Vintage, 1957), p. 220. Simenon, quoted in A. Storr, "Problems of Creativity," Unpublished paper, Harvard University, 1969, p. 24.

Page 337. On Thomas Mann, see H. Gardner, "Mann's Portrayals of the Artists," Unpublished paper, Harvard University, 1970.

Page 337. O. Rank, *Art and Artist* (New York: Knopf, 1932).

Page 337. Keats: quoted in W. J. Bate, *John Keats* (New York: Galaxy Books, 1966), pp. 260–261.

Page 338. W. Hazlitt, quoted in W. J. Bate, *Ibid.*, pp. 259–260.

Page 338. The artist lives not with his performance: G. Vidal, "The Subject Doesn't Object," *New York Times Book Review*, October 1, 1968, p. 1.

Page 338. H. James, see L. Edel, *Henry James: The Treacherous Years* (London: Hart-Davis, 1969). Hawthorne: G. Oberndorf, "Psychoanalysis in Literature and its Therapeutic Value," in H. Ruitenbeek (ed.), *Psychoanalysis and Literature* (New York: Dutton, 1964).

Page 339. W. Hazlitt, quoted in M. H. Abrams, *The Mirror and the Lamp* (New York: Norton, 1958), p. 142.

Page 339. Toulouse-Lautrec, quoted in J. R. Plokker, *Art from the Mentally Disturbed* (Boston: Little, Brown, 1965). E. Wilson, *The Wound and the Bow* (London: Methuen–University Paperbacks, 1961), p. 263.

Page 339. L. Trilling, "Art and Neurosis," *The Liberal Imagination* (Garden City, N.Y.: Anchor Books, 1954).

Page 340. J. R. Plokker (cited in note to Chapter 7, p. 339), p. 133.

Page 341. M. Foucault, *Madness in Civilization* (New York: Pantheon, 1965).

Page 341. O. Rank, *Art and Artist* (New York: Knopf, 1932).

Page 341. Amy Lowell: Cf. M. T. Bingham, "Beyond Psychology," in *Homo Sapiens Auduboniensis: A Tribute to W. Bingham* (New York: National Audubon Society, 1953), 5–29.

Page 341. What artist must retain: A. Jacobson, "Genius and Manic-Depressive Insanity: Dean Swift," in H. Ruitenbeek, *The Literary Imagination* (Chicago: Quadrangle, 1965), 433–443.

Page 341. Thomas Mann, quoted by Tessman in H. H. Anderson (ed.), *Creativity in Childhood and Adolescence: A Diversity of Approaches* (Palo Alto, Calif.: Science and Behavior Books, 1965), p. 25.

Page 342. Goethe: I am unable to locate this quotation.

Page 342. K. Chukovsky, *From Two to Five* (Berkeley: University of California Press, 1968), p. 141.

Page 343. Unchanged level of skill: E. Kris, *Psychoanalytic Explorations in Art* (New York: Schocken, 1964), p. 92.

Page 343. J. R. Plokker, *Art from the Mentally Disturbed* (Boston: Little, Brown, 1965), pp. 110, 73.

Page 344. Dance and therapy: E. Rosen, *Dance in Psychotherapy* (New York: Teacher's College–Columbia University Press, 1957).

Pages 344–345. Naumburg on art therapy: *Schizophrenic Art* (New York: Grune & Stratton, 1950), p. 26.

Page 345. P. H. Wolff, "The Role of Biological Rhythms in Early Psychological Development," *Bulletin of the Menninger Clinic,* 1967, **31**, p. 217.

Page 345. Different views on music therapy: T. Gaston (ed.), *Music Therapy* (New York: Macmillan, 1968).

Page 346. Edmund Wilson on truth in art: *The Wound and the Bow* (London: Methuen–University Paperbacks, 1961).

Page 346. Schoenberg: *Letters* (E. Stein, ed.) (New York, St. Martin's Press, 1965), p. 97.

Page 346. T. Mann, *The Beloved Returns* (New York: Knopf, 1940), p. 328.

Page 347. J. Berger on art and truth: *The Success and Failure of Picasso* (London: Penguin, 1965), p. 34.

Page 347. V. Kuznetsev is the writer who escaped from Russia. He is quoted in *New York Times,* August 7, 1969, p. 14.

Page 348. On Freud and truth, see E. Jones, *The Life and Work of Sigmund Freud* (New York: Basic Books, 1963), Vol. 1, p. 321, *passim.* Goethe: "I flee from what is impure": Quoted in E. Hitschmann, "Psychoanalytic Comments about the Personality of Goethe," in H. Ruitenbeek (ed.), *The Literary Imagination* (Chicago: Quadrangle, 1965), p. 129. Goethe: "I have never tried to pretend in my poetry": See J. P. Eckermann, *Conversations with Goethe* (New York: Ungar, 1964), p. 188.

Page 348. H. Ellis, *The Dance of Life* (Boston: Houghton Mifflin, 1923), p. 72.

Page 348. Coleridge, quoted in G. Watson, *The Literary Critics* (London: Penguin, 1964), p. 120.

Page 349. H. Read, *Education through Art* (New York: Pantheon, n.d.), p. 167.

Page 349. On the arts as an approach to the savage mind: H. Gardner, "Piaget and Lévi-Strauss: The Quest for Mind," *Social Research,* 1970, 37, 348–365.

AUTHOR INDEX

Abrams, M., 8, 20
  quoted, 20
Alschuler, R., 219
Anisfeld, M., 201
  quoted, 144
Anthony (Weir), 141
  quoted, 141, 142, 143
Arnheim, R., 16, 28, 187, 281, 296
  quoted, 28, 296, 324
Auden, W. H., 247, 294
  quoted, 294

Bach, J. S., 14, 285, 320, 345
Baer, D., 2
Bahle, 280, 286
Baldwin, J. M., 93, 94, 95
  quoted, 94
Balzac, H. de, 247
Bamberger, J., xvii, 194, 195
Bartlett, F., 280
  quoted, 280
Beardsley, M., 275
Beaumont, C., quoted, 332
Beauvoir, S. de, 245, 247
Beethoven, L. v., 43, 189, 252, 253, 285, 336
Belaiew-Exemplarsky, S., quoted, 196
Bell, C., quoted, 38–39
Bellugi, U., 133
  quoted, 133
Bender, L., 164
  quoted, 164
Berger, J., quoted, 347
Bergmann, P., quoted, 119

Berlioz, H., 254
  quoted, 254
Berlyne, D., 10
Bernstein, L., 253
Biederman, J., 9
  quoted, 9
Bijou, S., 2
  quoted, 2
Birkhoff, G., 8
Blake, W., 253
Boleslavsky, R., 288
  quoted, 289
Bowlby, J., 22
  quoted, 22
Brahms, J., 131
Braque, G., 274
Bridgeman, D., 195
Bridges, K., 72
Brontë, C., 251
Brontë, E., 248, 251
Brown, R., xviii, 133
  quoted, 133
Bruner, J., 176
  quoted, 59
Bühler, K., 202
Burling, R., 201
Buytendijk, F., quoted, 70
Byron, G., 339
  quoted, 339

Carlson., P., quoted, 144
Carmichael, D., 7
Carroll, L., 255

383

SUBJECT INDEX